100 GREAT BOOKS

SYNOPSES, QUIZZES, AND TESTS FOR INDEPENDENT READING

BONNIE A. HELMS

J. WESTON WALCH PUBLISHER

PORTLAND, MAINE

Users' Guide
to
Walch Reproducible Books

As part of our general effort to provide educational materials which are as practical and economical as possible, we have designated this publication a "reproducible book." The designation means that purchase of the book includes purchase of the right to limited reproduction of all pages on which this symbol appears:

Here is the basic Walch policy: We grant to individual purchasers of this book the right to make sufficient copies of reproducible pages for use by all students of a single teacher. This permission is limited to a single teacher, and does not apply to entire schools or school systems, so institutions purchasing the book should pass the permission on to a single teacher. Copying of the book or its parts for resale is prohibited.

Any questions regarding this policy or requests to purchase further reproduction rights should be addressed to:

Permissions Editor
J. Weston Walch, Publisher
P.O. Box 658
Portland, ME 04104-0658

—*J. Weston Walch, Publisher*

1   2   3   4   5   6   7   8   9   10

ISBN 0-8251-1899-9

Copyright © 1991
J. Weston Walch, Publisher
P.O. Box 658 • Portland, Maine 04104-0658

Printed in the United States of America

Author's Note of Appreciation

To Mary Jane Stone, whose mind, hands, and loving heart have assisted in the preparation of this book.

To Maurice Stone, whose gentle strength and sense of humor gave much needed moral support.

To Jane Carter, whose editorial guidance and words of encouragement made completion of this manuscript possible.

To the students of Westbrook High School, whom I have been privileged to teach.

Contents

The letter before each author's name indicates the book's approximate reading level: Easy, Medium, or Difficult. Answer keys for the tests in each section appear at the end of that section.

Unit 3: History in Fiction   115

Synopses   117

Quizzes and Tests

Unit 4: *Science Fiction, Fantasy, and the Supernatural* 171

Unit 5: *Social Issues and Moral Challenge* 215

To the Teacher

In his essay "Of Studies," discussing the education of a Renaissance gentleman, Sir Francis Bacon gave reading top priority. "Reading maketh a full man, conference a ready man, and writing an exact man." A learning experience which advances the student's personal growth should include reading, discussion, and writing.

Jessica Fletcher, popular detective-author character on the CBS television series "Murder, She Wrote," was asked in one episode, "How do I become a writer?" Jessica replied, "Read! Read! Read!" Reading and writing are Siamese twins. An author with a perfectly polished style who has no ideas has nothing to communicate to the audience. Reading good literature is one of the writer's chief resources because books open new windows on the world.

Reading great books helps students realize that literature's significant themes are universal problems, questions that people from the cave to the computer have needed to answer. "Why am I here? Where am I headed? How can I relate to the world around me? What ideals do I dare to believe in?"

No author should be allowed to waste the reader's time. A book worth reading addresses themes that matter. Plot, setting, and characterization are vehicles for expressing these ideas. Although different authors may not agree on the answers, a student matures by considering various answers to these universal questions.

Great books are also passports to adventure. Many titles in *100 More Great Books* take readers to spheres they will never visit: Australia in Colleen McCullough's *The Thornbirds*, India in *The Jewel in the Crown*, Dickens's England in *David Copperfield*, the battlefields of World War II in Leon Uris's *Battle Cry*.

Designed for students of all ability levels from grades seven through twelve, *100 More Great Books*, a sequel to *150 Great Books*, is divided into seven topical units, each containing both fiction and nonfiction titles. As an aid in selecting titles appropriate for the students' varied reading levels, the titles have been graded with three different designations. (E) indicates easy reading for reluctant or problem readers. Although the vocabulary and sentence structure of these (E) selections may be simple, the contents of each title will help students learn to think. (M) indicates medium or average vocabulary and concepts. Students reading on grade level can handle these titles easily. (D) indicates longer or more difficult titles. Providing a challenge for the mature reader, these books take the student far from his or her daily experience to an adult level of psychological or emotional complexity. Books guaranteed to stretch the student's mind include Tolstoy's *Anna Karenina* and Henry James's *The Portrait of a Lady*. Both novels portray the struggle of a sensitive individual against the rigid demands of society. Having more complex sentence structure and more difficult vocabulary, titles designated (D) take longer to read. Although the student may complete fewer titles, each (D) selection is well worth the capable student's effort.

Material for each title includes a bibliographical entry to help locate the book and a plot summary to assist the teacher in discussing the book with the students. Next, each test in the volume has three forms of evaluation: (1) Twenty objective questions which test the basics of plot, character, setting, and theme. Does the student understand the story line? (2) Five short-answer questions which require reading for inference. What larger ideas, perhaps indirectly stated, does the author wish the reader to grasp? Answering these questions will help the student's writing skills, since the directions require that the questions be answered in complete sentences. (3) The challenge essay requires a more mature level of thinking. How do the characters develop? What contrasts does the author present? How is this book related to other books on the same subject? The challenge question asks for the student's opinions supported by information gained from the reading. These challenge questions could be used to teach paragraph development by examples, facts, or comparison and contrast.

Answer keys follow the test sections. Brief suggested answers are provided for the short-answer questions and the challenge essays. Teachers should allow students some latitude in their short-answer and essay responses, since several possible answers may be equally correct. If the teacher questions a student's response, the student may be required to prove his or her answer by reference to the book.

The tests provided in *100 More Great Books* may be used in a variety of ways. If an entire class has read a particular title, the test in this collection would provide a closed-book evaluation. In using a test for an entire class, however, not all questions may be suitable for all students. For example, in a heterogeneous classroom, slower students might answer only the objective questions discussing plot, characterization, and setting. More advanced students could work with inference and theme by responding to the short-answer questions. The challenge essays deal primarily with ideas or comparisons.

Material in *100 More Great Books* is designed to provide a creative alternative to more traditional book reports. Most of these tests are designed for open-book evaluations as part of an independent reading program. Various methods of point evaluation can be developed for using these tests. At the beginning of each quarter or semester, a point system can be established for keeping track of outside reading. The student receives points for the number of books he or she reads and the number of test questions answered correctly. More difficult books should have greater point value. For example, each (E) easy title could be worth 1 point, each (M) medium title 2 points, and each (D) difficult title 3 points. The students should know from

the beginning what percentage of their total grades will come from their outside reading.

During the quarter, as a student completes the reading of a title, he or she will be given a copy of the test. The student will take the test outside of class. Next, using the answer key, the student can check his or her own objective work. Students may place finished work in a folder, which the teacher will evaluate every two or three weeks. Each student should have a conference time, perhaps once every two or three weeks, when he or she can discuss the readings with the teacher. The importance of this independent reading program will also be emphasized if class time is set aside for both teacher and students to read. This sustained silent reading might take place for about half an hour every other week.

Included in this volume is a brief glossary of the literary terms which occur in many of the test questions. Class discussion of these terms will give students a basic literary vocabulary. The teacher should make copies of this glossary so that each student will have this list for reference as he or she reads and writes.

Establish a minimum requirement for the outside reading assignment; for example, require two books per ranking period. Encourage your students to exceed the minimum. This is the point where real learning begins.

Students generally do not know a great deal about what titles are available. The teacher should use the summaries provided in this volume to become familiar with the various titles. To help students make reading selections, post on your classroom bulletin board a copy of the *100 More Great Books* table of contents. Point out the various topics. Then turn the students loose in the library. Provide the librarian with a copy of the table of contents also. He or she will be the students' greatest ally as the independent reading program progresses.

100 More Great Books is designed to be as flexible as possible. Many titles in this volume fit into more than one unit. For example, Alice Walker's *The Color Purple* reflects family life, but also deals with the social issue of racial discrimination.

Literature is not just for the English or language arts class. Many titles in this collection could be used as parallel readings in history or social studies classes. Leon Uris's *Battle Cry* is a vivid presentation of combat in World War II. Woodward and Bernstein's *All the President's Men* reviews the history of the Watergate scandal. Any classroom study will be deepened by an independent reading program.

Each student brings to the classroom his or her aptitudes and experiences. Life has already taught the teenager a variety of lessons, some positive and others negative. The teacher's job is to help the individual build on the positive experiences and cope with the fall-out from the negative ones. Experiences may produce different reactions to different books. For one student, a novel about child abuse may be someone else's story; for another, a book like Margaret Dickson's *Maddy's Song* may be a horrible personal reality. The teacher needs to be sensitive to these individual differences, especially in conference discussions and essay evaluations. Some title summaries contain cautions which will help teachers and students determine subject matter appropriateness.

Students are badly short-changed if the only books they ever read are the ones assigned in class and if the only ideas the student gains come from the teacher's lecture notes. One college advertisement says, "A mind is a terrible thing to waste." Reading books which contain differing philosophies should help students begin to ask questions on several levels. "Do I understand what this book is about? What is this author trying to prove? Is this author right in his or her view of human nature? Does my experience prove this book true?" Caution: Discuss with your students the important difference between understanding what a book is about and agreeing with its message. Although not all students will agree, a different answer is not necessarily a wrong one.

Personal maturity should be the goal of all education. Considering universal truths through literature helps students grow. This mental growth produced by evaluation and analysis begins to free the student from the tunnel vision of bigotry and prejudice. The most valuable product of any reading experience is the understanding that others, though very different, may be equally and wonderfully human.

Glossary of Literary Terms

This glossary provides a basic vocabulary for your study of literature. Terms defined here frequently appear in the short-answer or essay questions that you will be asked to answer as part of your reading evaluations.

Plot—a sequence of events; what happens in the story. In a standard work of fiction, the plot is divided into four sections.

1. Exposition—the introduction which establishes the setting and introduces the characters.

2. Rising action—a complication or problem develops.

3. Climax—the turning point in the action which determines the outcome.

4. Denouement—the events following the climax. In these concluding scenes, mysteries are unraveled and confusions are set straight.

Protagonist—the most important character in a work of fiction.

Antagonist—the major character or force opposing the main character.

Conflict—the tension or struggle between the protagonist and the antagonist. Without conflict, there would be no plot.

Three basic kinds of conflict are most common in works of fiction:

1. Person against person—two characters are locked in a conflict of wills or purpose.

2. Person against environment—conflict between the character and physical nature or the forces of society.

3. Person against self—internal or psychological conflict in which the character must choose:
   a. Between good and evil
   b. Between two good outcomes or two evil outcomes—the "frying pan to the fire" type of choice.

Note: A novel of any length usually contains several kinds of conflict. One type, however, will provide the focus for the action.

Foreshadowing—significant hints given by the author which help the reader predict the outcome of the action.

Flashback—a scene or scenes inserted to show events that happened before the action of the main plot; knowledge of such events is essential to the reader's understanding of the story line.

Epiphany—the turning point, a moment of insight or awareness that changes a character's outlook significantly.

Characterization—methods by which an author makes his creations live for the reader. Common methods of character presentation include characterization:

1. By what the character says
2. By what the character does
3. By what the other characters say about him or her
4. By what the character thinks
5. By the author's physical description of looks, gestures, or habits.

Developing character—one who undergoes an important change or learns a significant lesson as a result of his or her experiences. This character behaves differently at the end of the story than at the beginning.

Static character—one whom experience has not changed.

Stock character—a type familiar to the reader. This character has occurred so often in fiction that the reader can predict behavior.

Flat character—one who has only one or two significant traits, who is presented as being either all good or all bad. Note: flat characters are often very important to the action.

Round character—one who is "human." He or she is a complex mixture of strength and weakness, good and bad. In a well-developed novel, the protagonist is usually round.

Foils—characters in fiction who serve as contrasts in both personality and motivation, for example, the hero and the villain.

Setting—the time and place of the action.

Mood—the emotion, feeling, atmosphere or tone that a fictional work presents, for example, romance or terror. The mood in fiction is how the reader feels as he or she reads.

Theme—the central ideas or truths that a plot illustrates. Usually a novel will have one main theme and several lesser themes. The idea may be presented in two ways:

a. Explicit—the author states the theme or themes for the reader.
b. Implicit—the reader must infer the theme from the action and characterization.

© 1991 J. Weston Walch, Publisher

100 More Great Books: Synopses, Quizzes, and Tests

Slant—the approach that an author takes toward human experience, the way that he or she sees life. Slant will play a large part in determining both characterization and theme.

Point of view—who is telling the story.

There are two basic types:

1. First-person point of view—the story is told by one of the characters involved.

    a) First-person major—the protagonist tells the story.

    b) One of the minor characters tells the story.

2. Third-person point of view—the story is told by the author or an outside narrator.

    a) Third-person objective—the "newspaper" approach. Only objective action may be narrated: who, what, when, where, how.

    b) Third-person omniscient—the author enters the minds of one or more characters. Thought patterns become an important part of the action.

Multiple point of view—the author changes narrators and uses different "voices" in different parts of the story.

Viewpoint character—the character through whose eyes we see the action. An author must limit the viewpoint to what that character would experience or understand.

Irony—a situation with a twist in meaning.

1. Verbal irony—saying one thing, but meaning another.

2. Situational irony—one thing is expected to happen, but something else occurs.

3. Dramatic irony—when the reader has information which the characters do not, and that knowledge significantly affects the outcome of the plot.

Historical novel—a plot presenting imaginary characters involved in actual historical events.

Sociological novel—a plot focusing on human relationships or social problems. These novels are frequently used as teaching vehicles to advocate social change.

Psychological novel—plot focuses on character development, usually of the protagonist. In these novels, the "inner landscape" of the character's mind frequently becomes the most important sphere of action.

© 1991 J. Weston Walch, Publisher   *100 More Great Books: Synopses, Quizzes, and Tests*

Note: A multi-purpose novel may fit into more than one of these categories. For example, Margaret Mitchell's *Gone With the Wind* is a historical novel of the Civil War and also a psychological study of Scarlett O'Hara.

Biography—a life story written by an author other than the subject.

Autobiography—a life story written by the subject.

© 1991 J. Weston Walch, Publisher

Unit 1
Adventure and Survival

Synopses

Run Silent, Run Deep

by Edward L. Beach

Henry Holt and Company, New York, 1955.

Run Silent, Run Deep, although a work of fiction, is based on the author's experiences as a submarine commander in the Pacific during World War II. The narrator, Edward Richardson, begins as a training commander just before the war breaks out. After Pearl Harbor, the commander's new submarine, the *Walrus*, goes on patrol off the coast of Japan. The reader can almost feel the tension as the submariners seek to destroy Japanese ships. Jim Bledsoe, Richardson's executive officer, matures to assume a command of his own. Richardson must constantly control his personal feelings so that he can function well as a commander.

After Jim is killed, submarine warfare for Richardson becomes almost an act of personal revenge. Each ship must fight for its life against Bungo Pete, the clever Japanese opponent who knows the names and locations of American subs. The crewmen must also deal with their feelings of frustration and loneliness for the wives left at home. Richardson's story ends in heroism as he helps to save three lives.

Run Silent, Run Deep views warfare as the day-by-day experience of sailors who struggle to serve their country. The book would interest students who are learning about World War II. It is also another special portrait in courage.

Lorna Doone

by R. D. Blackmore

Penguin Books, Inc., New York, 1984.

Lorna Doone, the seventeenth-century love story of yeoman farmer John Ridd and the beautiful, aristocratic Lorna Doone, is set in the wilds of southwestern England. As an old man, John narrates his story.

John and Lorna met as children. As he matures, John faces the conflict of loving a woman whose family killed his father. The tale of John and Lorna's love is paralleled with John's sister Annie's romance with Tom Faggus, the local highwayman.

Although Lorna's grandfather approves of their love, John must rescue Lorna from the evil Carver Doone. John also moves into the world beyond Plover Farm as he travels to London. He later becomes involved in the civil feud between King Charles II and the Duke of Monmouth.

After Lorna is robbed by the cunning Counselor Doone, John learns that she is really a countess, and has no Doone blood. By helping catch some thieves, John earns the king's gratitude and a knighthood. The Doones are driven from the valley in one great battle. Finally, on John's wedding day, he must confront Carver in a personal showdown to avenge his father's death.

Lorna Doone has an exciting plot and a great deal of good description. Although the language is sometimes archaic, the story will still appeal to the modern reader.

The Pilgrim's Progress

by John Bunyan

Dodd, Mead and Company, New York, 1979.

Bunyan's religious allegory explains Christian theology in terms of a journey. The narrator sees in a dream the experience of the man Christian as he travels from the City of Destruction to the Celestial City. The hero of Bunyan's tale represents the "Everyman" of sixteenth- and seventeenth-century morality tales.

Christian has been warned by Evangelist to escape from his home before the town is destroyed. Since he cannot persuade anyone else to go with him, Christian sets out on his journey alone. Soon becoming discouraged, he falls into the Slough of Despond. After entering on the way through a wicker gate, Christian is terribly burdened. He is instructed to go to a cross, where his load falls off.

As his journey progresses, Christian meets many people whose names are symbolic of life's experiences. Faithful is Christian's companion until they reach the evil town of Vanity Fair. Imprisoned and killed for his belief, Faithful becomes an example to Hopeful, who joins Christian on the pilgrimage. Both Christian and Hopeful nearly perish when they wander from the way and are imprisoned by Giant Despair in Doubting Castle. Along the way Christian meets other travelers who reject his path: Ignorance, Talkative, By-ends, and Atheist. He and Hopeful attempt to convert these men, but fail. After finally passing through the River of Death, Christian and Hopeful are ushered into the presence of the King.

Bunyan's religious classic pictures life as a journey beginning with a decision to change one's way of life. The book's theme is that a traveler must keep to the right road, in spite of difficulties, to reach the goal. Despite the book's heavy theological tone, Bunyan's story is valuable reading. His images have been adopted by succeeding generations of authors. The story is therefore a basic reference work for understanding the symbols in other literary works.

The Inn of the Sixth Happiness

by Alan Burgess

E. P. Dutton and Company, New York, 1957.

The Inn of the Sixth Happiness is the remarkable biography of Gladys Aylward, English missionary in northern rural China from 1930 until 1940. Having been rejected for Chinese missionary service, Gladys was determined to get to China. Surviving a difficult trip through a battleground between the Russians and the Chinese, she finally joined Jeanne Lawson, an elderly missionary who needed a companion.

Gladys and Jeanne worked with the mountain people, established an inn for trailworn mule drivers, and preached Christianity. After Jeanne's death, Gladys carried on alone. Her remarkable career included civil service for the Mandarin who ruled the city. After she stopped a prison riot single-handed, Gladys received the Chinese name Ai-weh-deh, the virtuous one.

The Japanese invasion in 1938 destroyed the peaceful life of Chinese rural society. Gladys, by this time a naturalized Chinese citizen, traveled unnoticed through the battle lines, carrying information on Japanese troop maneuvers to the area's Chinese defenders. When the Japanese army threatened total devastation, Gladys guided almost one hundred children through the mountains to the safety of the land beyond the Yellow River.

A story as fascinating as any fiction, *The Inn of the Sixth Happiness* celebrates faith which shines as a light in the darkness of evil and despair. Gladys Aylward personifies Hemingway's definition of courage as "grace under pressure."

The Heart of Darkness

by Joseph Conrad

in Joseph Conrad: Three Short Novels, Bantam Books, New York, 1960.

The Heart of Darkness tells of one man's journey into darkest Africa and into the depth of his own soul. Marlowe tells his story to a group of businessmen on a boating trip down the Thames. Marlowe was hired by a European trading company to pilot a steamer deep into the jungle and bring out a cargo of ivory. When Marlowe arrives in Africa, he first hears of Kurtz, a man with powerful charisma who lives deep in the jungle.

As Marlowe journeys to the interior, he begins to be hypnotized by the jungle's dark spell. Surviving storms and cannibal attacks, Marlowe finally arrives at Kurtz's station. He finds that the great man who has written about improving life for the natives now wants to exterminate them. Conrad's talent for dramatic narrative peaks as he ironically contrasts the real Kurtz with the Kurtz of people's opinions and imaginations. The dying man has no hope, but sees instead the horrible darkness of death.

Returning to Europe, Marlowe cannot tell Kurtz's fiancée the truth about her beloved's death. Because the darkness is so great, only a lie will allow any hope to remain.

Two Years Before the Mast

by Richard Henry Dana

P. F. Collier and Sons, New York, 1937.

Two Years Before the Mast recounts Dana's experiences as a common sailor aboard an American merchant ship between 1834 and 1836. The author describes the thrills, hardships, and monotony of a seaman's life. He also sympathizes with the hardships that the average sailor faces.

After the brig *Pilgrim* survived the dangerous weather of Cape Horn, the crew spent two years sailing the California coast. Before the ship could return to Boston, the hold had to be filled with hides, which were exchanged for the goods the commercial ships carried. Interested in everything he sees, Dana describes each port and the people he met. Spanish California comes to life through his vivid description. Dana's return trip on the vessel *Alert* was made through the dangerous Straits of Magellan.

The author narrates from first-hand experience the daily hardships of the seaman's life. A brutal captain abuses and overworks his men. Weather makes life difficult as the men are forced to furl the sails to prevent the vessel's destruction. Collecting hides for cargo means long hours of hard work.

Two Years Before the Mast was written by an intellectual who, by choice, became a sailor. His descriptive skills make Dana's story an adventure well worth reading.

The Three Musketeers

by Alexandre Dumas

Washington Square Press, New York, 1961.

The Three Musketeers, a tale of swashbuckling adventure in seventeenth-century France, tells the exploits of four friends: Athos, Porthos, Aramis, and D'Artagnan. Arriving in Paris fresh from the province of Gascony, D'Artagnan becomes quickly entangled in the conflict between the Musketeers of Louis XIII and the forces of Cardinal Richelieu. Through his love for Constance Bonacieux, D'Artagnan becomes a messenger for the Queen of France in her romantic intrigue with the English enemy, the Duke of Buckingham. The young man helps rescue the Queen's diamonds and prevents her dishonor before the King and his court.

The Musketeers' enemies are the Cardinal's spies, the Count de Rochefort and Milady Clare de Winter, a destructive genius and mistress of a thousand disguises. Harboring a personal grudge against D'Artagnan for his rejection of her, Milady manages to seduce men everywhere and to escape from the strongest prison.

The Musketeers are able to help raise the siege of La Rochelle, but are unable to prevent Buckingham's assassination. Exhibiting extraordinary daring, the four friends hold off an entire regiment while they casually have breakfast. The adventure moves to its climax as the Musketeers combine forces to bring Milady to justice.

One of the great adventure yarns in world literature, *The Three Musketeers* will hold the attention of any student fascinated by fast swordplay and court intrigue.

Lord of the Flies

by William Golding

Coward-McCann, Inc., New York, 1962.

Lord of the Flies is a story of survival after an atomic war. Thrown from a destroyed plane, a group of British schoolboys attempt to establish civilization on a deserted island. The dark side of human nature dominates as the children become a tribe of savages.

Ralph, the chosen leader, attempts to keep social order, represented by the conch shell used to call assemblies. Piggy the thinker and Simon the mystic help Ralph build shelters and make a signal fire to get the boys rescued. However, Jack the hunter soon dominates. The boys become savages, hunting first wild pigs and finally each other.

Fear of the "beast," the evil which dominates the island, kills any hope of survival. Simon and Piggy are both murdered as each tries to speak with the voice of common sense. Finally only the arrival of a ship saves Ralph from death at the hands of the tribe.

William Golding believes that our coating of civilization is very thin. If outside authority is removed, man will quickly become an animal. *Lord of the Flies* is a completely realistic novel.

Dove

by Robin Lee Graham

Harper and Row, New York, 1972.

Dove is the thrilling account of Robin Graham's five-year solo odyssey, encircling the globe in a sailboat. Leaving California at the age of sixteen, Robin met adventure in every port of call: American Samoa, Australia, South Africa, and the Galapagos Islands. Robin also found love. He and Patti met in the romantic setting of the Polynesian Islands. Traveling by boat and train, Patti followed Robin on his solo journey and met him in various ports. They were married in South Africa. Sharing a sense of adventure and a love of the sea, Robin and Patti loved to observe the wildlife in each area.

Robin's greatest enemy on his journey was loneliness. Several different cats kept him company. He kept a record of his travels by speaking into a tape recorder. Robin became a celebrity as *National Geographic* followed his journey and did a series of stories about his travels. Recounting both the lone sailor's adventures and his feelings, *Dove* shows Robin as a very sensitive person.

Robin also tells of the adjustment difficulties that he had when he returned to civilization. Being a celebrity was a real problem. He also could not adjust to being closed in, either in a career or in a college classroom. He and Patti grew in their love for each other, especially through the birth of their daughter, Quimby.

Dove would be of special interest to students who enjoy sailing. Robin Graham's story would appeal to the young person who must experience life on his or her own terms.

Kon-Tiki

by Thor Heyerdahl ════════════════════════════

Rand McNally and Company, New York, 1950.

Kon-Tiki recounts the exciting voyage of six men who set out to prove that the Polynesian Islands were settled by ancient voyagers from South America. Using a balsa raft as the Incas did, the crew of the *Kon-Tiki* followed the westward route of those who worshipped Tiki, the sun god. By radio, their only concession to civilization, the crew kept in contact with the outside world.

Sharks, whales, and dolphins became their traveling companions. Heyerdahl and his crew also saw marine creatures that no one knew existed. The *Kon-Tiki* followed the winds, rolled over the waves, and survived storms.

After one hundred days at sea, the men landed on a deserted island. The raft was wrecked on a reef, but the log base survived. The voyagers were welcomed by the Polynesians, whose folk tales contained memories of the original Tiki voyagers.

Kon-Tiki appeals to the spirit of adventure in everyone. Students interested in marine biology will find Heyerdahl's accounts of the behavior of the sea creatures fascinating. Readers will admire the strength of men who dared to risk their lives for an idea.

A Walk Across America

by Peter Jenkins ════════════════════════════

Fawcett Crest, New York, 1979.

A Walk Across America is the account of Peter Jenkins's personal quest to understand what America is all about. Brought up in Greenwich, Connecticut, Peter accepted the standards of urban American culture. Personal difficulties prompted him to seek for deeper meanings.

After training to get himself into condition for his walk, Peter left Alfred, New York, with his dog Cooper on October 15, 1973. He met many ordinary people who helped drastically change his view of life: Homer Davenport, an old mountain man; the Olivers, who became his second family; M. C. Jenkins, a southern rancher; Governor George Wallace of Alabama. Peter's greatest joy came, however, as he and Cooper lived close to nature.

Peter experienced many hardships during his travels. He became seriously ill. His life was threatened by "rednecks" who resented his hippie appearance. Most difficult of all was Cooper's death. On the road to finding his own faith,

Jenkins rejected the communal philosophy of mystic Stephen Gaskin. He found God in a revival in New Orleans. The first portion of Peter's trip ended in New Orleans on April 15, 1975.

Peter Jenkins's first-hand narrative makes *A Walk Across America* a wonderful book. The author's clarification of his own values will help students engaged in the "walk" for identity which each person must make.

Coming Into the Country
by John McPhee

Farrar and Straus, New York, 1977.

Coming Into the Country recounts the author's adventures with Alaska and her people. "The Country," or Yukon Territory, attracts many kinds of people: trappers, miners, those who have come north to escape from civilization. McPhee met some of these fascinating characters during his travels. John Borg established his own empire in Eagle, near the Arctic Circle. Sarge Waller came to Alaska when he felt that the Marine Corps had gone soft. Joe Vogler wants Alaska to be an independent nation.

McPhee believes that Alaska is the last frontier, a way of life which must be saved from the government executives and the oil companies. Championing individuality, the author opposes government land regulations that would prohibit free use of natural resources.

McPhee writes with color and enthusiasm gained from personal experiences. The men and women he met in Alaska were survivors, strong enough to meet nature's challenge. This book would interest students who like hunting, fishing, or exciting accounts of life in the wild.

Kidnapped
by Robert Louis Stevenson

Harper and Row, New York, 1965.

Kidnapped is the adventure of David Balfour. In 1751, David, the disinherited heir of the Scottish House of Shaws, journeys to find his Uncle Ebeneezer, who lives in the run-down family mansion. Because he fears David's claim to the estate, Ebeneezer arranges with Captain Hoseason to kidnap the boy and sell him as a white slave in the Carolinas.

Hoseason's ship, the *Covenant*, runs over a small boat. The rescued passenger, Alan Breck Stewart, a fugitive from the soldiers of King George, is a champion fighter for the clans of Scotland. When Hoseason's men plan to turn Alan over to the English, Alan and David join forces and defeat the sailors.

After the ship runs aground, David and Alan become wanted men when they are implicated in the murder of Colin Roy, the king's agent. Living off the land for several weeks, David finally returns to Mr. Rankeillor, the lawyer who can verify David's claim to his inheritance. Forced to admit the kidnapping plot, Ebeneezer gives David the income of the estates. Alan returns to France to continue fighting for the cause of Scotland.

Name_____   Date_____

Run Silent, Run Deep by Edward L. Beach

Select the letter of the word or phrase which correctly completes each sentence.

_____   1. Commander Richardson served during most of World War II in (A) the North Atlantic (B) Italy (C) the Pacific (D) Australia.

_____   2. Jim did not qualify on his first command trials because (A) he lost control in an emergency (B) he did not understand the workings of a submarine (C) he could not lead men (D) Richardson refused to recommend him.

_____   3. The *Walrus*'s first encounter at sea was with (A) a German sub (B) a Japanese sub (C) a Japanese destroyer (D) Bungo Pete.

_____   4. Before he left for the Pacific, Jim (A) decided to resign from the submarine service (B) refused to serve on Richardson's ship (C) apologized to Richardson for his attitude (D) married Laura.

_____   5. When they arrived at Pearl Harbor, Richardson was surprised by (A) the extent of the damage (B) the number of ships that were there (C) the poor weather (D) getting orders from the Admiral to return to Panama.

_____   6. Bungo Pete was (A) a nickname for Richardson's commander (B) a small dog that was the ship's mascot (C) a Japanese submarine expert (D) the owner of a small store on Midway Island.

_____   7. The greatest danger to the *Walrus* during her patrols came from (A) Japanese planes (B) torpedoes (C) depth charges.(D) bad weather.

_____   8. Russo was (A) Richardson's second in command (B) the captain of another sub (C) the navigator (D) the ship's cook.

_____   9. Jim's attitude toward combat could best be described as (A) uncertain and cowardly (B) excited and reckless (C) careful and thorough (D) cold and indifferent.

_____ 10. The Japanese learned the names and locations of American submarines (A) from special radio signals (B) from reports sent by traitors in the American Navy (C) from the trash thrown overboard (D) by intercepting the letters sent home by sailors.

(continued)

© 1991 J. Weston Walch, Publisher

Name _____   Date_____

Run Silent, Run Deep by Edward L. Beach

_____ 11. Jim assumed command of the *Walrus* when (A) Richardson was injured (B) he was recommended by the admiral (C) Richardson had to return to the United States (D) the war was over.

_____ 12. One of the other officers on the *Walrus* was (A) Blunt (B) Keith (C) Gibbs (D) Falcon.

_____ 13. While in Pearl Harbor, Richardson helped to (A) train other submariners (B) put out a fire (C) design a better firing mechanism for torpedoes (D) all of the above.

_____ 14. The *Eel* was (A) Jim's new command (B) one of the Navy's most modern ships (C) a captured Japanese vessel (D) an old ship left over from World War I.

_____ 15. Richardson wanted most to destroy Bungo Pete to (A) help the U.S. win the war (B) drive the Japanese out of Midway Island (C) avenge the destruction of the *Walrus* (D) get even for the destruction of Pearl Harbor.

_____ 16. Richardson hated himself for (A) not marrying Laura (B) deliberately killing men in lifeboats (C) sinking so many Japanese ships (D) getting his ship trapped in a combat zone.

_____ 17. The men of the *Eel* went on their last mission to (A) rescue injured pilots (B) bomb a Japanese city (C) take supplies to other subs (D) protect the coast of Australia.

_____ 18. Richardson was almost drowned because (A) he was shot in the leg (B) someone forgot to untie a rope (C) he couldn't swim well (D) he fell overboard.

_____ 19. In rescuing the pilots, Richardson had help from (A) the U.S. Air Force (B) a radio contact on shore (C) Keith at the helm of the *Eel* (D) Jim and the *Walrus*.

_____ 20. For his heroism, Richardson received (A) a bronze battle star (B) The Congressional Medal of Honor (C) a promotion (D) an increase in pay.

Name_____ Date_____

Run Silent, Run Deep by Edward L. Beach

Answer the following questions in two or three complete sentences.

1. How did Richardson and Jim differ in their actions in time of combat?

_____

_____

_____

2. How was life difficult for the wives of the men in the submarine service?

_____

_____

_____

3. What special equipment did the *Walrus* have for going on patrol in the Pacific?

_____

_____

_____

4. What special security precautions had to be taken as the submarines entered the war zone?

_____

_____

_____

5. How does Richardson get revenge for Jim's death?

_____

_____

_____

Challenge Question

Discuss Richardson's internal conflict in *Run Silent, Run Deep*. What personal battles did he have to fight which helped him mature as an officer and as a man?

Name_____ Date_____

Lorna Doone by R. D. Blackmore

Select the letter of the word or phrase which correctly completes each sentence.

_____ 1. The story is told (A) by Annie (B) by a third-person narrator (C) by John (D) by one of John's sons.

_____ 2. John had to leave school because (A) his father could not afford to pay his school bills (B) his mother died (C) he flunked out (D) the Doones killed his father.

_____ 3. The area where the Doones lived was called (A) Bagworthy (B) Tiverton (C) London (D) Oare.

_____ 4. John first met Lorna when (A) he rescued her from Carver (B) he climbed a waterfall (C) he saw her at the king's reception (D) she came to Plover Farm.

_____ 5. The family member that John was closest to was (A) Lizzie (B) Annie (C) Uncle Reuben (D) his mother.

_____ 6. Jeremy Stickles (A) took John to London for the first time (B) was an agent of the king (C) saved John's life (D) all of the above.

_____ 7. The person most loyal to Lorna was (A) Sir Ensor (B) Gwenny (C) Charleworth (D) Counselor.

_____ 8. Annie and Tom were able to marry when (A) Tom was pardoned by the king (B) Tom saved enough money (C) the crops were good (D) the local clergyman gave his approval.

_____ 9. The extreme weather described in the novel was (A) snow (B) rain (C) wind (D) thunder.

_____ 10. Reuben Huckabuck and his men were involved in (A) smuggling (B) political rebellion (C) mining (D) cattle rustling.

_____ 11. Lorna's most valuable possession proved to be (A) her ring (B) her necklace (C) a herd of horses (D) her houses and lands.

(continued)

© 1991 J. Weston Walch, Publisher   *100 More Great Books: Synopses, Quizzes, and Tests*

Name_____   Date_____

Lorna Doone by R. D. Blackmore

_____ 12. Counselor Doone was able to steal Lorna's necklace by (A) raiding the house at night (B) knocking John unconscious (C) putting Lorna in prison (D) tricking Annie.

_____ 13. The one person in the story whose feelings John Ridd injured was (A) his mother (B) Ruth (C) Lizzie (D) Lorna.

_____ 14. Lorna's real identity is verified by (A) Betty (B) Benita (C) Counselor (D) Ruth.

_____ 15. Lorna's guardian was (A) Counselor Doone (B) Judge Jeffreys (C) Lord Brandir (D) King Charles.

_____ 16. To repay John for his courage in catching the robbers, King Charles gave John (A) a knighthood and coat of arms (B) Lorna's necklace (C) the land that belonged to the Doones (D) a commission in the royal navy.

_____ 17. When Doone Glen was attacked, all of the following events happened *except* (A) Counselor was shot (B) the houses were burned (C) Charleworth was killed (D) John led the attack.

_____ 18. Lorna almost died when (A) a horse threw her (B) Carver shot her on her wedding day (C) John carried her home in the snow (D) Gwenny gave her poison.

_____ 19. Both John and Lorna were saved from death by (A) Ruth (B) Annie (C) John's mother (D) Gwenny Carfax.   .

_____ 20. All of the following are true of John Ridd *except* (A) he was strong and tall (B) he became a nobleman (C) he shot Carver Doone (D) he saved the life of Tom Faggus.

© 1991 J. Weston Walch, Publisher

100 More Great Books: Synopses, Quizzes, and Tests

Name_____ Date_____

Lorna Doone by R. D. Blackmore

Answer the following questions in two or three complete sentences.

1. Why were the Doones hated and feared by the people in the valley?

_____

_____

_____

2. Describe how John and Lorna met and fell in love.

_____

_____

_____

3. How did John rescue Lorna from death by starvation in Carver's home?

_____

_____

_____

4. What part does Jeremy Stickles play in bringing John and Lorna together?

_____

_____

_____

5. How does John finally get revenge for the death of his father?

_____

_____

_____

Challenge Question

Even though the title of this novel is *Lorna Doone*, John Ridd is the hero of the narrative. Write an essay describing some strengths of character that John shows as he battles to win Lorna and to drive the Doones from Exmoor.

© 1991 J. Weston Walch, Publisher   *100 More Great Books: Synopses, Quizzes, and Tests*

Name _____ Date_____

The Pilgrim's Progress by John Bunyan

Complete each sentence with the name of the correct person or place.

1. _____ first warns Christian to leave his home.

2. _____ starts out with Christian, but becomes discouraged and turns back.

3. Christian is equipped with armor for his journey at the house of

   _____ .

4. Christian is severely wounded in his battle against _____ .

5. _____ is the city which represents the forces of evil.

6. _____ dies for his faith.

7. _____ is the only true entrance by which one may begin the journey to the Celestial City.

8. Christian is joined on the second part of his pilgrimage by _____ .

9. _____ has only words, but no true deeds to match them.

10. _____ suggests that they leave the path because the meadow looks easier.

11. The pilgrims are imprisoned by _____ .

12. The key of Promise opens every lock in _____ .

13. Christian and Hopeful are nourished by fruit and water from the

    _____ .

14. Christian and Hopeful are both trapped in the net of _____ .

15. The pilgrims get their first sight of the Celestial City from the tops of

    _____ .

16. _____ gets to the city, but is robbed of everything except his precious jewel.

17. In order to approach the city gate, Christian must cross the _____ .

18. _____ is refused admission to the city because his name is not written in the Book.

19. The angels of the Celestial City are called _____ .

20. Any person admitted to the city must possess the _____ .

© 1991 J. Weston Walch, Publisher

Name _____ Date_____

The Pilgrim's Progress by John Bunyan

Answer the following questions in two or three complete sentences.

1. Describe some of the people who try to discourage Christian as he prepares to begin his journey.

   _____

   _____

   _____

2. How is Christian freed of his burden?

   _____

   _____

   _____

3. Why is the companionship of Faithful and Hopeful important to Christian?

   _____

   _____

   _____

4. List three different encounters which almost defeat Christian.

   _____

   _____

   _____

5. What symbolism does Bunyan use to describe death?

   _____

   _____

   _____

Challenge Question

Define allegory. Discuss some of the important symbols which make *The Pilgrim's Progress* an allegory of Christian theology.

Name_____ Date_____

The Inn of the Sixth Happiness by Alan Burgess

Match each description in Column A with the correct name in Column B.

Column A	Column B
_____ 1. Rejected Gladys for missionary service	A. Yang
_____ 2. Explorer of China in whose home Gladys worked as a maid	B. Ai-weh-deh
_____ 3. Russian city where Gladys was rescued by an unknown woman	C. Vladivostok
_____ 4. Elderly missionary with whom Gladys worked during her first years in China	D. Linnan
_____ 5. Chinese cook at the inn	E. Yamen
_____ 6. Girl Gladys bought from a child seller	F. Ninepence
_____ 7. Nationalist Chinese officer with whom Gladys fell in love	G. Yangcheng
_____ 8. Walled mountain city where Gladys worked during her first peaceful years in China	H. General Ley
_____ 9. Small mountain village where Gladys established a hospital for refugees fleeing Japanese brutality in the valley below	I. China Inland Mission
_____ 10. Welsh missionary who refused to renounce his faith, even when tortured by the Japanese	J. Sian
_____ 11. Ruler who accepted Christianity because of the example he saw in Gladys Aylward's life	K. Mandarin
_____ 12. Gladys's Chinese name, which means "Virtuous One"	L. Jeanne Lawson
_____ 13. City to which Gladys led the refugee children who came with her from the mountains	M. Yellow River
_____ 14. Guerrilla priest who forced Gladys to examine the conflict between fighting evil and living one's Christian faith	N. Francis Younghusband
_____ 15. Center of civil government in a Chinese city	O. Madame Chiang Kai-shek
_____ 16. Agency that sold Gladys her ticket to China	P. Bei Chai Chuang
_____ 17. Christian mule driver whose family was brutally murdered by the Japanese soldiers	Q. Mullers'
_____ 18. Children crossed here miraculously when God provided a boat	R. Lao-yang-kwei
_____ 19. Chinese word for white man, which means "foreign devil"	S. Hsi Lein
_____ 20. Had charge of the New Life Movement, which helped refugees who fled the Japanese occupation	T. David Davis

© 1991 J. Weston Walch, Publisher   *100 More Great Books: Synopses, Quizzes, and Tests*

Name_____   Date_____

The Inn of the Sixth Happiness by Alan Burgess

Answer the following questions in two or three complete sentences.

1. Describe the difficulties Gladys Aylward had getting to China.

   _____

   _____

   _____

2. Why did Jeanne and Gladys decide to start The Inn of the Sixth Happiness?

   _____

   _____

   _____

3. How did Gladys help her people survive when the Japanese invaded the area?

   _____

   _____

   _____

4. What problem did Gladys and General Ley have in common?

   _____

   _____

   _____

5. What "miracles" helped Gladys get her group of children across the mountains to safety?

   _____

   _____

   _____

Challenge Question

Author Alan Burgess states that, "In all his wild adventures, man had not as yet discovered a substitute for faith." Write an essay discussing how the life of Gladys Aylward illustrates faith that attempts the impossible.

© 1991 J. Weston Walch, Publisher

100 More Great Books: Synopses, Quizzes, and Tests

Name _____ Date _____

The Heart of Darkness by Joseph Conrad

Place a T before each true statement, and an F before each false statement.

_____   1. Marlowe's narrative takes place in the bar of an English gentleman's club.

_____   2. Marlowe's aunt helped him make contact with the company that later employed him.

_____   3. When Marlowe landed at the coast station, Kurtz met his ship.

_____   4. The most valuable cargo that Marlowe's company was bringing out of Africa was diamonds.

_____   5. Kurtz had been sending out more ivory than any of the other agents employed by the company.

_____   6. The other agency employees liked Kurtz because he had many progressive ideas for the improvement of life in Africa.

_____   7. Kurtz's painting, which Marlowe saw in the agency office, portrayed the woman Kurtz intended to marry.

_____   8. The silence bothered Marlowe more than any other feature of the jungle.

_____   9. The Congo River was easy to navigate because the water was of uniform depth.

_____ 10. Fog made river navigation difficult.

_____ 11. When the steersman died, Marlowe allowed the cannibals in his crew to divide and consume the corpse.

_____ 12. When he arrived at Kurtz's station, Marlowe found the buildings old but well cared for.

_____ 13. As he journeyed down river, Marlowe found a book that Kurtz had left behind.

_____ 14. Kurtz's most remarkable feature was his voice.

_____ 15. The young Russian hated Kurtz and wanted Marlowe to kill him.

_____ 16. Kurtz had obtained his ivory by raiding native villages and killing their people.

_____ 17. The fence around Kurtz's compound was decorated with native shields and war spears.

_____ 18. As he was dying, Kurtz had a vision of a world of light and peace beyond the grave.

_____ 19. Kurtz's fiancée thought that Kurtz was a great and loving man.

_____ 20. Marlowe tells the woman the truth about Kurtz's dying words.

© 1991 J. Weston Walch, Publisher

Name_____ Date_____

The Heart of Darkness by Joseph Conrad

Answer the following questions in two or three complete sentences.

1. What was Marlowe's job with the trading company? How did he get his job?

_____

_____

_____

2. What does Marlowe learn about Kurtz before he meets the man?

_____

_____

_____

3. How does the spell of the jungle capture Marlowe?

_____

_____

_____

4. How is Kurtz's manuscript a symbol of the contradictions in the man's personality?

_____

_____

_____

5. What effect does Marlowe's story have on the men who listen to him?

_____

_____

_____

Challenge Question

Write an essay explaining Joseph Conrad's use of foreshadowing and irony in *The Heart of Darkness.*

© 1991 J. Weston Walch, Publisher

Name _____ Date_____

Two Years Before the Mast
by Richard Henry Dana

Select the letter of the word or phrase which correctly completes each sentence.

_____ 1. The ship on which Dana sailed was (A) a naval vessel (B) a merchant ship (C) a whaler (D) registered to a British company.

_____ 2. The worst weather the *Pilgrim* encountered was (A) around the tip of South America (B) near the Equator (C) off the coast of California (D) in San Francisco Bay.

_____ 3. Which of the following did Dana and his fellow sailors *not* load onto their ship? (A) hides (B) water (C) whale oil (D) wood

_____ 4. The man most directly in charge of the crew during any voyage was (A) the first mate (B) the captain (C) the second mate (D) the company agent.

_____ 5. The Kanakas were natives of (A) Kansas (B) Mexico (C) the South Sea islands (D) Canada.

_____ 6. John was flogged when he (A) questioned injustice to another sailor (B) planned a mutiny (C) was caught stealing (D) refused to stand watch.

_____ 7. Dana remembered Tom Harris as a (A) natural leader (B) troublemaker (C) man with a remarkable memory (D) loafer.

_____ 8. Dana spent his spare time doing all of the following *except* (A) gambling (B) reading (C) telling stories (D) mending his clothing.

_____ 9. The most difficult harbor for the ships to get into and out of was (A) Los Angeles (B) San Diego (C) San Pedro (D) Santa Barbara.

_____ 10. The sailors carried the hides to the boats (A) in large sacks (B) one at a time (C) on their heads (D) on the backs of pack mules.

_____ 11. Dana was able to get passage back to Boston only after he (A) bribed the first mate (B) paid another man to exchange places with him (C) contacted the American consul (D) received permission from the ship's owners.

(continued)

© 1991 J. Weston Walch, Publisher

100 More Great Books: Synopses, Quizzes, and Tests

Name_____ Date_____

Two Years Before the Mast
by Richard Henry Dana

_____ 12. Dana decided to leave college and go to sea because he was (A) bored with school (B) having problems with his eyes (C) offered a chance to write a book (D) failing his courses.

_____ 13. "Steeving" was the process of (A) cleaning the decks (B) trimming the sails (C) polishing the brass (D) packing the hides into the hold.

_____ 14. The main difference between the _Pilgrim_ and the _Alert_ was (A) the intelligence of the crew (B) the kind of cargo (C) the way the men were treated (D) the route the vessel took.

_____ 15. "Reefing the sails" was (A) furling the sails in preparation for bad weather (B) mending sails that had been torn (C) opening the sails wide to catch the wind (D) replacing tattered sails with ones that looked better.

_____ 16. The passenger on Dana's homeward voyage was (A) the company agent (B) the captain's brother (C) one of Dana's college professors (D) a Spanish nobleman.

_____ 17. The most important information that ships gave each other was (A) weather reports (B) news from home (C) word of political events in the United States (D) accounts of meetings with the Indians.

_____ 18. The "presidio" was (A) the leader of an Indian tribe (B) the mayor of San Diego (C) the military and administrative center of each California town (D) a nickname for the captain of the ship.

_____ 19. Dana believed that the most important port for the future of California would be (A) San Diego (B) San Francisco (C) Monterey (D) Santa Barbara.

_____ 20. After his first visit to California, Richard Henry Dana (A) became a professional sailor (B) never left New England again (C) became a ship owner (D) went back to California twenty years later.

Name_____ Date_____

Two Years Before the Mast
by Richard Henry Dana

Answer the following questions in two or three complete sentences.

1. Describe some of the hardships that Dana experienced during his two years at sea.

2. How did Dana fit in with his less educated shipmates?

3. What examples of injustice did Dana observe during his time at sea?

4. Under what circumstances did the weather become the sailors' enemy?

5. What unusual aspects of life in California does Dana describe for his readers?

Challenge Question

Write an essay describing the character traits shown by Richard Henry Dana that helped him survive as a seaman.

Name_____ Date_____

The Three Musketeers by Alexandre Dumas

Match each description in Column A with the correct name in Column B.

Column A	Column B
_____ 1. Had power in France that even the King feared	A. Athos
_____ 2. Most jolly and sociable of the Musketeers	B. Aramis
_____ 3. Faithful servant to D'Artagnan	C. Planchet
_____ 4. English lover of the Queen of France	D. Bazin
_____ 5. Landlord whose wife became D'Artagnan's mistress	E. Richelieu
_____ 6. Arrived in Paris riding an ugly yellow horse	F. Anne of Austria
_____ 7. Musketeer who had once been married to Milady	G. La Rochelle
_____ 8. Last English outpost on French soil	H. Bonacieux
_____ 9. Escaped from an English prison by pretending to be a Puritan	I. Rochefort
	J. Milady
_____ 10. Maid who helped D'Artagnan escape from Milady's bedroom	K. Lord de Winter
_____ 11. Escorted the Duke of Buckingham to his secret meeting with the Queen	L. Porthos
	M. Kitty
_____ 12. Musketeer who had once been a priest	N. D'Artagnan
_____ 13. Cardinal's agent who had a scar on his face	O. Constance Bonacieux
_____ 14. Servant who hoped to get promotion in the church through his master	P. Mme Coquenard
_____ 15. Gave D'Artagnan a diamond ring as a reward for faithful service	Q. Bethune
_____ 16. Intended to deport Milady to the prison colonies of America	R. Buckingham
_____ 17. Faithful soldier who became an assassin	S. Armentiers
_____ 18. Convent in which Mme Bonacieux found refuge	T. Felton
_____ 19. Mistress of Porthos	
_____ 20. Town where Milady was finally captured and brought to justice	

© 1991 J. Weston Walch, Publisher

Name _____ Date_____

The Three Musketeers by Alexandre Dumas

Answer the following questions in two or three complete sentences.

1. Under what circumstances did D'Artagnan meet the three Musketeers?

   _____

   _____

   _____

2. How did D'Artagnan help to save the Queen from disgrace?

   _____

   _____

   _____

3. In what ways is Milady the personification of evil?

   _____

   _____

   _____

4. Describe the conflict between the forces of the King and the forces of the Cardinal.

   _____

   _____

   _____

5. How is Milady finally brought to justice?

   _____

   _____

   _____

Challenge Question

Discuss the ways in which the triumph of justice in *The Three Musketeers* comes through the bravery of the protagonists. Then describe events in which the outcome is determined by fate or chance.

© 1991 J. Weston Walch, Publisher

100 More Great Books: Synopses, Quizzes, and Tests

Name_____ Date_____

Lord of the Flies by William Golding

Select the letter of the word or phrase which correctly completes each sentence.

_____ 1. The first physical aspect of the island that Ralph is aware of is (A) the beach (B) the rock (C) the intense heat (D) the jungle.

_____ 2. The easiest available food supply on the island is (A) fish (B) fruit (C) plants and vegetables (D) fresh crab found on the beach.

_____ 3. Ralph feels that the group's greatest need is (A) rest (B) shelter (C) a strict leader (D) organization.

_____ 4. The boy who holds the conch shell (A) is the leader for the day (B) may speak to the group (C) has to keep the fire going (D) may lead the hunt.

_____ 5. The greatest division among the boys is by (A) size (B) class in school (C) age (D) hair color.

_____ 6. As a schoolboy, Jack led (A) the football team (B) the literary society (C) a street gang (D) the choir.

_____ 7. The first death on the island is (A) Simon (B) one of the little boys (C) Piggy (D) Roger.

_____ 8. Piggy (A) was popular at school (B) was in good health (C) lived with his aunt (D) had a father in the navy.

_____ 9. The first real division between Ralph and Jack comes (A) when the fire goes out (B) after Simon dies (C) when the shell is broken (D) when Jack refuses to give Ralph any meat.

_____ 10. The evil lord of the island spoke only to (A) Roger (B) Simon (C) Ralph (D) Piggy.

_____ 11. The "beast from the air" is (A) imaginary (B) a wild eagle that lands on the island (C) a dead airman (D) a strangely shaped rock formation.

_____ 12. The symbol of man's creative powers on the island is (A) Piggy's glasses (B) the shell (C) the fire (D) Jack's knife.

(continued)

© 1991 J. Weston Walch, Publisher

Name_____ Date_____

Lord of the Flies by William Golding

_____ 13. Jack and his tribe occupy a natural fort (A) in the heart of the jungle (B) at Castle Rock (C) inside the wreckage of the plane (D) on the mountaintop where the signal fire had been built.

_____ 14. Jack wins most of the boys to his side by promising them (A) food (B) rescue (C) fun (D) shelter.

_____ 15. The most vicious boy in Jack's tribe is (A) Maurice (B) Roger (C) Percival (D) Henry.

_____ 16. Last to leave Ralph and join Jack's tribe is (A) Piggy (B) Simon (C) Sam-neric (D) Maurice.

_____ 17. Piggy is killed when (A) he and Ralph go to Castle Rock (B) he tries to get his spectacles back (C) Roger pushes a rock down on him (D) all of the above.

_____ 18. The action which contributes most to Jack's triumph is (A) stealing Piggy's glasses (B) killing the wild pig (C) giving meat to his troops (D) killing Ralph.

_____ 19. A powerful symbol of the evil force on the island is (A) the motion of the tides (B) the pig's head on a stick (C) the forest fire (D) Castle Rock.

_____ 20. Jack fails to kill Ralph (A) because Ralph is able to hide in the jungle (B) when a rescue ship arrives (C) since Ralph can run faster (D) because Maurice and Percival help Ralph.

Name_____ Date_____

Lord of the Flies by William Golding

Answer the following questions in two or three complete sentences.

1. What steps do Ralph and Piggy take toward helping the boys survive?

   _____

   _____

   _____

2. In *Lord of the Flies*, how does fire have both positive and negative power?

   _____

   _____

   _____

3. What truth does Simon try to bring to the others? Why does he fail?

   _____

   _____

   _____

4. How does Jack convince the other boys to join his tribe?

   _____

   _____

   _____

5. How does Ralph fight for survival?

   _____

   _____

   _____

Challenge Question

Write an essay describing how the evil in the boys themselves destroys attempts at civilization and order. How does this evil relate to the larger world from which the boys have come?

© 1991 J. Weston Walch, Publisher

Name _____   Date_____

Dove by Robin Lee Graham

Supply the correct word or phrase to complete each sentence.

1. Robin began his voyage from the port of _____ .

2. The family member who most approved of Robin's plans was _____ .

3. The type of weather which proved the greatest danger to the *Dove* was

   _____ .

4. Robin's only companions on his voyage across the Pacific were _____ .

5. Robin and Patti first met on the island of _____ .

6. Robin's greatest difficulty on his voyage was in dealing with _____ .

7. Robin kept a record of his experiences by _____ .

8. Robin loved the people and the food most in _____ .

9. Robin's adventures were recounted and photographed by _____ .

10. In Africa, Patti and Robin traveled on a _____ , which they

    nicknamed _____ .

11. Robin found most evidence of World War II on the island of _____ .

12. Patti and Robin were married in _____ .

13. Before Robin began the last leg of his journey, he and his wife spent a wonderful

    vacation in _____ .   .

14. Robin had to abandon his original boat because _____ .

15. Robin feared most for the destruction of the fish and wildlife in

    _____ .

16. Robin learned to sail well, but he never learned to _____ properly.

17. Robin rejected a scholarship offer to _____ .

18. Robin and Patti's daughter _____ was born on the island of

    _____ .

19. Robin's voyage lasted a total of _____ .

20. Robin and Patti finally decided to settle in _____ .

© 1991 J. Weston Walch, Publisher

Name_____ Date_____

Dove by Robin Lee Graham

Answer the following questions in two or three complete sentences.

1. What experiences prepared Robin for his solo voyage?

   _____

   _____

   _____

2. Why did Robin like the people of Fiji so much?

   _____

   _____

   _____

3. In what ways did Patti give Robin support for his journey?

   _____

   _____

   _____

4. At what point was Robin tempted to quit?

   _____

   _____

   _____

5. How did the permanent lifestyle that Robin and Patti adopted reflect Robin's experiences at sea?

   _____

   _____

   _____

Challenge Question

How does Robin Graham's account of his adventures prove the statement that his father made about him: "Robin is more concerned with living than with longevity"?

© 1991 J. Weston Walch, Publisher   *100 More Great Books: Synopses, Quizzes, and Tests*

Name_____   Date_____

Kon-Tiki by Thor Heyerdahl

Place a T before each true statement, and an F before each false statement.

_____   1. All scientists and archaeologists that Heyerdahl explained his proposal to were enthusiastic about helping to sponsor the *Kon-Tiki's* voyage.

_____   2. The *Kon-Tiki's* radio operators were experienced veterans of World War II.

_____   3. Heyerdahl and his men encountered strong opposition from Peruvian government officials as they gathered the materials for building their raft.

_____   4. Most of the equipment on the *Kon-Tiki* was supplied by the Norwegian government for testing purposes.

_____   5. Heyerdahl had visited the Polynesian Islands several times before he made the voyage on the *Kon-Tiki*.

_____   6. The *Kon-Tiki* resembled the ancient Inca craft, except that Heyerdahl's raft carried an engine and a radio.

_____   7. The decks and the cabin of the *Kon-Tiki* were made of bamboo.

_____   8. A tugboat towed the *Kon-Tiki* far enough from land to get the raft out of the major shipping channels.

_____   9. Easter Island was the first destination of the *Kon-Tiki* and her crew.

_____   10. All six men took turns steering and standing watch.

_____   11. The most serious accident that occurred was when one of the crew was bitten by a shark.

_____   12. Dolphins were frequently used as bait to trap larger sea creatures.

_____   13. Both vegetable and animal plankton were an excellent food source for the *Kon-Tiki's* crew.

_____   14. The parrot, their pet on the voyage, successfully completed the journey to the Polynesian Islands.

(continued)

© 1991 J. Weston Walch, Publisher

Name_____   Date_____

Kon-Tiki by Thor Heyerdahl

_____ 15. Heyerdahl believes that the ancient Indian voyagers were driven out of South America by a natural disaster such as an earthquake or a volcanic eruption.

_____ 16. The men were able to land on the first Polynesian island they sighted.

_____ 17. Although the *Kon-Tiki* was wrecked on a reef, the log base of the raft survived.

_____ 18. The Polynesian natives who greeted the *Kon-Tiki*'s crew were gentle, hospitable people.

_____ 19. The radio contact who monitored most of the *Kon-Tiki*'s voyage was an amateur operator in Cuba.

_____ 20. Heyerdahl believes that the voyage proved absolutely that the Polynesian Islands were settled by those who traveled west by raft.

Name _____   Date _____

Kon-Tiki by Thor Heyerdahl

Answer the following questions in two or three complete sentences.

1. What was Heyerdahl attempting to prove by sailing west on the *Kon-Tiki*?

   _____

   _____

   _____

2. How did the *Kon-Tiki*'s construction help her to be a very seaworthy boat?

   _____

   _____

   _____

3. What close calls did the crew of the *Kon-Tiki* experience during their voyage?

   _____

   _____

   _____

4. What kind of a welcome did the men receive at the end of the trip?

   _____

   _____

   _____

5. Why was the voyage of the *Kon-Tiki* important to the world's scientific community?

   _____

   _____

   _____

Challenge Question

   Write an essay describing the personality traits that enabled Thor Heyerdahl and the members of his crew to complete the *Kon-Tiki* adventure.

Name_____   Date_____

A Walk Across America by Peter Jenkins

Match each description in Column A with the correct name in Column B.

Column A   **Column B**

_____ 1. Peter's brother who traveled with him for part of his walk

_____ 2. Peter's black "mother"

_____ 3. Small town where Peter's life was threatened

_____ 4. Peter's faithful canine companion

_____ 5. Old man who had built his cavelike house in the side of a mountain

_____ 6. University from which Peter graduated

_____ 7. The Oliver brothers' nickname for Peter

_____ 8. Camera given to Peter by *National Geographic*

_____ 9. Leader of "The Farm," a hippie commune

_____ 10. Peter's work partner at the lumber mill

_____ 11. City that had achieved harmony with nature

_____ 12. Southern rancher who thought Peter was a distant relative

_____ 13. Southern evangelist who helped Peter find a real experience with God .

_____ 14. Was pleased because Peter called him "grandfather"

_____ 15. Urged Peter to continue walking to meet the real people of America

_____ 16. Girl Peter met and married in New Orleans

_____ 17. Black community where Peter lived for several months

_____ 18. Place where Peter trained to get his body ready for the journey

_____ 19. Where Peter was attacked and accused of being a drug pusher

_____ 20. Loaned Peter a suit and some shoes so that Peter could attend church

Column B

A. Cooper

B. Stephen Gaskin

C. Mary Elizabeth

D. Zack

E. Pau Pau

F. Barbara

G. Homer Davenport

H. George Wallace

I. Nikon

J. Robbinsville

K. Alfred

L. James Robison

M. Shelby County

N. Scott

O. Al

P. Mount California

Q. Mobile

R. M. C. Jenkins

S. Smokey Hollow

T. Lemm

© 1991 J. Weston Walch, Publisher

Name _____ Date_____

A Walk Across America by Peter Jenkins

Answer the following questions in two or three complete sentences.

1. What did Peter Jenkins hope to learn as he walked across America?

   _____

   _____

   _____

2. How did Peter get ready for his trip?

   _____

   _____

   _____

3. Why was Cooper important to Peter?

   _____

   _____

   _____

4. Why did Peter decide not to stay on "The Farm"?

   _____

   _____

   _____

5. List four times during the journey when Peter's life was in danger.

   _____

   _____

   _____

Challenge Question

Discuss the character development of Peter Jenkins. How did he change during his walk from New York State to New Orleans? What were some of the most significant lessons that he learned?

© 1991 J. Weston Walch, Publisher

Name_____ Date_____

Coming Into the Country by John McPhee

Match each description in Column A with the correct name in Column B.

Column A

_____ 1. Mayor and postmaster of Eagle, Alaska

_____ 2. Designed a kayak suitable for navigating Alaska's rivers

_____ 3. Eskimo member of the committee that worked to select a new capital

_____ 4. First capital of Alaska

_____ 5. Chief of Eagle's Indian community

_____ 6. Wild land with ice beneath its surface

_____ 7. Airman whose life was saved when he found a well-stocked cabin

_____ 8. Advocate of Alaskan independence

_____ 9. Came to Alaska because he thought the Marines had become too soft

_____ 10. Mining which uses a steady flow of water from a hose or pipe

_____ 11. Passed out after trying to pull his own tooth with pliers

_____ 12. Husband and wife who own and fix almost any machine in existence

_____ 13. In the opinion of the river people, the "crime capital" of Alaska

_____ 14. Mining done by washing soil through a pan or wooden frame

_____ 15. Alaska's southernmost city

_____ 16. Federal official who was exploring land to find places suitable for national parks

_____ 17. Proposed a referendum to find a new location for Alaska's capital

_____ 18. Left her first husband to become a wilderness pioneer wife

_____ 19. Held the first religious services in Eagle in 1899

_____ 20. Northern Alaskan river which goes around in a circle

Column B

A. Leon Crane

B. Ed and Ginny Gelvin

C. Anchorage

D. Kaufmann

E. Willie Hensley

F. Tundra

G. Sarge Waller

H. Hydraulic

I. James Kirk

J. John Borge

K. Donna Kneeland

L. Joe Vogler

M. Placer

N. Klepper

O. Juneau

P. Sitka

Q. Richard Cook

R. Harris

S. Michael David

T. Kobuk

© 1991 J. Weston Walch, Publisher

Name_____ Date_____

Coming Into the Country by John McPhee

Answer the following questions in two or three complete sentences.

1. What natural features make Alaska a very special place?

_____

_____

_____

2. Why does the author believe that government regulation of land will spoil the Alaskan wilderness?

_____

_____

_____

3. What are some of the greatest difficulties one faces when traveling in the Alaskan wilderness?

_____

_____

_____

4. What special problems are faced by Alaska's natives, the Indians and the Eskimos?

_____

_____

_____

5. Why did the committee sent to select the site for a new Alaskan capital city have a difficult task?

_____

_____

_____

Challenge Question

John McPhee met many people who found a new way of life in Alaska. Write an essay describing the rugged people of these wildernesses. Consider in your answer why these people came, why they stayed, and how they survived.

© 1991 J. Weston Walch, Publisher

Name_____ Date_____

Kidnapped by Robert Louis Stevenson

Fill in the blanks with the word or phrase needed to complete each sentence.

1. David's boyhood friend and teacher was _____ .

2. David journeys to the House of Shaws after _____ .

3. _____ calls down a curse on the owners of the House of Shaws.

4. Uncle Ebeneezer tries to kill David by _____ .

5. Hoseason kidnaps David by _____ .

6. A victim of brutality on board the ship *Covenant* is _____ .

7. David is freed from being a prisoner in the hold of the ship by _____ .

8. David saves Alan's life when he overhears _____ .

9. Alan and David successfully defend the _____ .

10. As a sign that David is his friend, Alan gives David _____ .

11. David almost dies when he believes that he is _____ .

12. Alan's greatest enemy in Scotland is_____ , whose nickname is

    _____ .

13. David and Alan have to avoid the king's troops because the two of them are

    _____ .

14. Alan is wanted by the English troops because he _____ .

15. David and Alan are almost captured by the English soldiers when David _____

    _____ .

16. The two fugitives are hidden by _____ in his hideout called

    _____ .

17. David becomes very angry when Alan _____ .

18. _____ is the lawyer who helps David prove his claim to his
    inheritance.

19. David learns that his father had given up the House of Shaws to his uncle because

    _____ .

20. At the end of the novel, Alan _____ .

© 1991 J. Weston Walch, Publisher   *100 More Great Books: Synopses, Quizzes, and Tests*

Name _____ Date_____

Kidnapped by Robert Louis Stevenson

Answer the following questions in two or three complete sentences.

1. What advice does Mr. Campbell give David as the boy leaves home for the first time?

   _____

   _____

   _____

2. Why is Ebeneezer Balfour afraid of David?

   _____

   _____

   _____

3. Under what circumstances does David become the cabin boy on the *Covenant*?

   _____

   _____

   _____

4. In their flight across the heather, how do David and Alan avoid the English soldiers?

   _____

   _____

   _____

5. How does Alan help David gain his rightful inheritance?

   _____

   _____

   _____

Challenge Question

Discuss Stevenson's portrait of Alan Breck. In what ways is he a "Robin Hood" type of romantic hero?

Answer Keys

Run Silent, Run Deep by Edward L. Beach

Multiple Choice:

1. C	6. C	11. A	16. B
2. A	7. C	12. B	17. A
3. A	8. D	13. D	18. B
4. D	9. B	14. B	19. C
5. A	10. C	15. C	20. B

Short Answers:

1. Richardson was more level-headed. He tended to be less impulsive in dangerous situations. Jim wanted to rush in quickly. He enjoyed the excitement of combat. Richardson fought a war to win the objective. Jim seemed to fight because he enjoyed the thrill.

2. Their husbands were gone for long periods of time. Letters were infrequent. Some men never came home. The greatest difficulties would be loneliness, waiting, and fear of death.

3. The *Walrus* had special radar so that it could more easily detect Japanese ships, guns to shoot small boats that might be armed by the enemy. Extra metal was removed so that it could move more quickly and quietly.

4. Total blackout, letters censored, long periods of travel submerged so that they would not be seen. Even the trash had to be disguised to conceal their identity.

5. He ruthlessly hunts down and destroys Bungo Pete. He even kills all of the ship's survivors. This is the one point when Richardson comes close to losing his control as a commander.

Challenge Question:

His first battle is his love for Laura, who belongs to Jim. He also battles to control his own fears so that he can lead his men. His crew must come before his personal wishes. After Jim's death, Richardson must control his hatred or at least channel it in a constructive direction to destroy the enemy. The first-person point of view in *Run Silent, Run Deep* is very important because the reader gets inside the commander's mind as well as reading about his actions. The resolution of his struggle after Jim's death comes as he saves other injured men from dying.

Lorna Doone by R. D. Blackmore

Multiple Choice:

1. C	6. D	11. B	16. A
2. D	7. B	12. D	17. A
3. A	8. A	13. B	18. B
4. B	9. A	14. B	19. A
5. B	10. C	15. C	20. C

Short Answers:

1. The Doones were outlaws banished by the king. They robbed and killed travelers. They raided people's farms and stole their crops. The Doones seemed to have little sense of right and wrong. They broke every law and never seemed to be punished for their evil actions.

2. John met her first when he climbed the waterfall. Lorna showed him a secret path into Doone Glen. They continued to meet in her secret bower. John watched for her signal in the rooks' nests.

3. During the heavy snow, John came in on snowshoes and found Lorna a prisoner. Bringing back a sled, he carried Lorna and Gwenny to safety.

4. Jeremy stays at the house of Benita Odom. She tells Jeremy the story of Lorna's true birth. Benita had been Lorna's nurse. She saw Lorna's mother and brother die. Benita later recognizes Lorna. John then knows that Lorna is not a Doone, one of the clan who killed his father.

   Jeremy saved John from being shot during the rebellion. Jeremy also takes John to London, where John and Lorna are reunited.

5. John chases Carver onto the moors. Although wounded himself, John battles with Carver until the evil man finally sinks into the quicksand.

Challenge Question:

   John Ridd is physically strong, but nonviolent. He will not carry a gun, but prefers to use the strength of his arms and body in a battle. He does not draw a pistol, even after Carver has shot him. In the attack on Doone Glen, John carefully spares the women and children. John is loyal to his family. He goes into battle looking for Tom when his sister Annie asks him to do so. He is honest, never giving in to the schemes of others. He will not become a spy, even for the king, among his own people. John is faithful. He continues to love none but Lorna, even when it seems that she has gone from him forever.

The Pilgrim's Progress by John Bunyan

Fill-ins:

1. Evangelist
2. Pliable
3. Interpreter
4. Apollyon
5. Vanity Fair
6. Faithful
7. The Wicker Gate
8. Hopeful
9. Talkative
10. Christian
11. Giant Despair
12. Doubting Castle
13. River of Life
14. Flattery
15. Delectable Mountains
16. Little-Faith
17. River of Death
18. Ignorance
19. The Shining Ones
20. Scroll of Admission

Short Answers:

1. Obstinate tells Christian that he is quite wrong. Pliable deserts him when things become hard. Mr. Worldly-Wise tries to convince Christian that he can save himself by his own actions.

2. He follows the way from the Wicker Gate and goes up the hill to the Cross. When Christian kneels at the Cross, the burden falls off and rolls down into a tomb.

3. Christian is encouraged by his companions as they discuss ideas and keep each other on the right road.

4. The Slough of Despond discourages him. Vanity Fair places all of the world's pleasures in the center of his way. Doubting Castle imprisons him and almost drives him to suicide.

5. Christian goes under the water of a deep river. When he reaches the other shore, his old garments are replaced with bright and shining new ones.

Challenge Question:

An allegory is a story in which all characters and situations represent abstractions. Leaving the City of Destruction represents a quest for salvation. Each obstacle that Christian encounters represents a life experience. Each person symbolizes an attitude. Vanity Fair is all the pleasures of the world. Apollyon is the evil that must be fought. The Slough of Despond and Doubting Castle are experiences of depression. Faith and Hope, represented by Christian's companions, are the attitudes which make life's progress possible. Crossing the River and entering the Celestial City represent Death and Immortality.

The Inn of the Sixth Happiness by Alan Burgess

Matching:

1. I	4. L	7. D	10. T	13. J	16. Q	19. R
2. N	5. A	8. G	11. K	14. H	17. S	20. O
3. C	6. F	9. P	12. B	15. E	18. M	

Short Answers:

1. The China Mission refused to accept her. She had no money. When she did make the trip, she came into the war zone between the Russians and the Chinese. She was almost raped by a Russian agent. She had to detour by way of Japan and then travel a long distance into the heart of China. Sheer determination and refusal to quit kept her going on this impossible journey.

2. They believed that the inn would provide them with an income. Giving hospitality also gave the missionaries an opportunity to preach Christianity to the travelers whom they served.

3. Gladys led her group out of the city and away from the Japanese invaders. She helped them to survive in the mountains and to avoid the Japanese who were searching for them. She was able to lead the groups because she knew the mountain paths so thoroughly. Gladys also established hospitals for nursing the wounded.

4. Both Gladys and General Ley followed the Christian gospel which taught people to love their enemies. Conflict arose when an individual had to decide to use force against evil. Both Gladys and the General were against killing. Both realized, however, that men had to die if the Japanese threat was to be driven back and the Chinese nation preserved.

5. Survival through the rough mountain trek was by itself a miracle. When they got to the Yellow River, no boats were to be seen. An officer who heard the children singing provided a way across. They made the last part of the trip on a coal train. The children were blackened by the coal and hidden from the Japanese bullets. The children were finally put on a train to Fufeng, where they could safely continue their lives.

Challenge Question:

Gladys Aylward refused to accept defeat. When the circumstances seemed completely hopeless, she kept going. Her trip to China illustrates this perseverance, as does her final trek across the mountains. Acting on an inner spiritual intuition, Gladys frequently got her group to safety just before the enemy arrived.

She acted fearlessly with no regard for her personal health or safety. Alone she entered a prison compound to stop a riot. She challenged established authority to fight for the rights of women and abused children. Gladys continued even when she was sick and wounded.

Her actions spoke more of Gladys Aylward's Christian faith than her words did. From the simple peasants to the Mandarin, people believed what she said because they saw the way she lived.

The Heart of Darkness by Joseph Conrad

True or False:

1. F	5. T	9. F	13. F	17. F
2. T	6. F	10. T	14. T	18. F
3. F	7. F	11. F	15. F	19. T
4. F	8. T	12. F	16. T	20. F

Short Answers:

1. Marlowe had to repair a battered river steamer and take the boat into the interior of Africa to bring out a cargo of ivory. He got the job because his aunt recommended him to the management of the company.

2. The accountant tells him that Kurtz sends out more ivory than anyone else. He sees Kurtz's strange drawing of the blindfolded woman. Marlowe hears the other men talk about Kurtz and his plans for improving the natives. He learns about the change in Kurtz from the Russian.

3. Marlowe is drawn to the jungle as he sails down the coast. Later, going into the interior, Marlowe feels the spell of its evil influence. This evil is symbolized by the fog. Kurtz has been destroyed by Africa's dark evil. Marlowe is able to leave, but he is marked forever by his encounter with Africa's darkness. The man who listens to Marlowe also comes under Africa's spell.

4. The manuscript dealt with ways to bring civilization to Africa's people. Kurtz had written on the bottom as a postscript, "Exterminate the brutes!" We learn that the great white trader obtained his ivory by violence.

5. Although most of the men are not affected, the young man who framed Marlowe's narrative has been drawn toward Africa's evil heart. He feels the great darkness closing in around him.

Challenge Question:

Foreshadowing comes in the hints of danger and evil that Marlowe gets from the company doctor. The trip down the coast begins his journey toward the darkness. The fog foreshadows the mystery. The human heads on the poles around Kurtz's home foreshadow the reader's learning the truth about Kurtz's destructive nature. We are prepared for the final horror which Kurtz faces in death because the mood has been growing more intense as Marlowe tells the various stages of his journey into the interior of the dark continent.

The greatest irony is Kurtz himself. The man who writes a manuscript about progress really lives by violence and extermination. The story line centers on the ironic contrast between the Kurtz that other people describe and the Kurtz that Marlowe finally sees. The final irony occurs when Marlowe returns to Europe with Kurtz's letters and manuscripts. Marlowe can't tell the woman who loves Kurtz the truth. To give her any hope, he must allow her to live with her fantasy.

Two Years Before the Mast by Richard Henry Dana

Multiple Choice:

1. B	6. A	11. B	16. C
2. A	7. C	12. B	17. B
3. C	8. A	13. D	18. C
4. A	9. D	14. C	19. B
5. C	10. C	15. A	20. D

Short Answers:

1. He survived rain, snow and ice storms. Conditions were crowded in the ship's quarters. He frequently had to work long hours with very little rest. He became ill with a bad tooth and a swollen jaw. Once the captain "hazed" or drove the men simply because he enjoyed abusing them.

2. Dana struggled to do all of a sailor's tasks and to make no difference between himself and the other men. When he had the chance to read, he did this in private and did not flaunt his education before the others. In dress and manner, the college man became one of the crew.

3. Two men were flogged without reason. The crewmen had no means of expressing their opinions or of getting injustice corrected. Men who could pay were able to get home sooner. Those who could not spent months more in California. Men were driven without necessary rest. Dana saw more of these injustices on the *Pilgrim*. When he made the return trip on the *Alert*, conditions for the crew were much better.

4. Off the California coast, ships sometimes had no wind and could not sail. On other occasions, strong southwest winds drove ships far off course. Coming around Cape Horn, the sailors battled snow and ice. As they approached Boston, the fog was so heavy that the ship had to wait several days before docking.

5. Herds of wild horses could be caught and ridden. Music and dancing accompanied festivals, such as weddings. The priests at the mission entertained the men and gave them the best meals they had on the trip. Basically, Dana saw most of those who lived in California as men who either wanted to get rich quick or had come to the west coast because they had failed elsewhere.

Challenge Question:

Dana was determined to experience the whole life of a sailor. He learned quickly to climb the rigging and to respond to commands. Even though he had eye problems, he was otherwise physically strong enough to do the work. He fitted in well and got along with everyone. Even when he was ill, he fought his way back to work as soon as possible. He never complained, even when food was poor or conditions were rough. The intellectual quickly became tough. At the end of the two years, Dana was a highly competent sailor.

The Three Musketeers by Alexandre Dumas

Matching:

1. E	6. N	11. O	16. K
2. L	7. A	12. B	17. T
3. C	8. G	13. I	18. Q
4. R	9. J	14. D	19. P
5. H	10. M	15. F	20. S

Short Answers:

1. Entering the palace of M. Treville, the commander of the Musketeers, D'Artagnan saw Rochefort, whom he had encountered on the road. As D'Artagnan pursued his enemy, he bumped into all three of the Musketeers. Each of them challenged D'Artagnan to a duel. When the time came to fight, the Musketeers were attacked by the Cardinal's men. D'Artagnan joined in their defense and the Musketeers became his staunch friends.

2. The King commanded the Queen to wear his diamonds, which she had given to the Duke of Buckingham. Milady had stolen two of these diamonds. D'Artagnan went to England to tell the Duke of the Queen's plight. Buckingham had the stolen diamonds replaced. D'Artagnan returned the entire set to Paris in time to save the Queen's honor.

3. Milady is a spy and clever killer, who can corrupt even the most faithful servants. Her beauty is dangerous. She can inspire trust in anyone, as she does with Felton and Constance. Her physical attraction is so great that she even traps D'Artagnan for a time. She had also deceived Athos when he was her husband. Milady fools everyone who trusts her. She is a fiend with the beauty of an angel.

4. Richelieu desires to be the power in the Kingdom. Even King Louis XIII is afraid of him. Only the forces of M. Treville and the Musketeers oppose the Cardinal's forces. One of the Cardinal's main objectives is to disgrace the Queen by exposing her affair with Buckingham. D'Artagnan repeatedly refuses Richelieu's offer of position to stay loyal to his friends. In the end, the Cardinal is forced to pardon D'Artagnan because of a letter of authority written by the Cardinal himself.

5. After Milady is captured in Armentiers, each of the men accuses her of one murder that she committed. The spy is then executed by the same man who had branded her. Her body is dumped into the river as a sign of evil which has been destroyed.

Challenge Question:

Luck frequently combines with daring in the adventures of The Three Musketeers. The Musketeers bravely take risks to carry messages to England and to rescue Constance. They also show unusual courage as they eat breakfast within range of the guns at La Rochelle. They ride faster and handle swords better than any other men in the kingdom.

Chance and fate play a large part in this novel. Porthos and Athos happen to overhear Milady's discussion with the Cardinal and are able to warn de Winter about the evil spy's intentions. D'Artagnan chances to follow Constance and to find out that she is involved in helping Buckingham meet with the Queen. The host at the inn happens to give them the sheet of paper so that they know in what town Milady plans to meet Rochefort.

Lord of the Flies by William Golding

Multiple Choice:

1. C	6. D	11. C	16. C
2. B	7. B	12. A	17. D
3. D	8. C	13. B	18. A
4. B	9. A	14. C	19. B
5. A	10. B	15. B	20. B

Short Answers:

1. Ralph, the doer, and Piggy, the thinker, try to establish a society. Ralph organizes the boys to build shelters on the beach. He calls meetings to give them instructions and to allow each person to express an opinion. Using Piggy's glasses, they light a signal fire. The boys keep the fire going in shifts so that they may be rescued.

2. Fire used positively could be a signal for their salvation. Fire can also be a killer. When the first fire gets out of control, the small scar-faced boy is killed. At the end of the novel, Jack uses fire to burn the island and kill Ralph. Ironically, this destructive smoke attracts the ship that rescues them.

3. Simon carries the message that the "beast" is really a dead man. He also knows that the evil the boys fear is inside themselves. His message would have set them free. Simon falls when the hunters turn on him, as the beast, and murder the messenger who would have freed them from terror.

4. Ralph has insisted that the boys must work, organize, and survive. Jack lures them with a promise of food and fun. The pig dances and chant of the tribe hypnotize everyone. Even Ralph and Piggy are temporarily drawn into the circle.

5. First Ralph goes to the depths of the jungle so that Jack's men cannot see him. Next he tries to run ahead of the hunters back to the open end of the island. His escape plan fails when Jack tries to burn him out. Ralph would have been Jack's last victim if the ship had not arrived.

Challenge Question:

The British schoolboys represent the inborn evil tendencies in all men. Beelzebub, the Lord of the Flies, rules the island. Represented by the pig's head, evil tells Simon, "I'm part of you." As the artificial social restraints, represented effectively by clothing, fall away, natural evil emerges. Hunting and killing come more naturally than organizing and preparing for rescue.

Jack is the natural man. Freed from all social restrictions, he becomes a painted savage. Jack's negative leadership is stronger than Ralph's positive influence. After the ritual killing of the pig, the next step becomes Simon's murder. Even Ralph and Piggy, who represent good, witness the killing and pretend not to notice. Natural evil is the absolute victor when Roger kills Piggy.

William Golding does not carry evil to its final conclusion because Ralph is rescued by the outside world. Those very adults, however, are no different from the boys on the island. The grownups use bombs, rather than rocks and sticks, to destroy each other.

Dove by Robin Lee Graham

Fill-ins:

1. Long Beach, California
2. his father
3. hurricanes
4. two kittens, Suzette and Joliette
5. Fiji
6. loneliness
7. talking into a tape recorder
8. Polynesia
9. *National Geographic* magazine
10. motorcycle, Elsa
11. Guadalcanal
12. South Africa
13. the Bahamas
14. she was no longer seaworthy
15. Galapagos Islands
16. cook
17. Stanford University
18. Quimby, Catalina
19. five years
20. Montana

Short Answers:

1. A trip with his family to the South Pacific, a trip with his friends on the HIC out of Hawaii. Almost drowning taught Robin a lot of things not to do.

2. They were open and trusting, with no locks on their houses. He also liked their customs and their food.

3. Her letters, radio calls to him from various ships, sharing of his feelings, helping him when he was most discouraged.

4. He was tempted to scuttle the boat in the Bahamas and not to finish the voyage through the Panama Canal and back to California.

5. They settled far away from others and built their home in their own way. They used natural childbirth for their daughter. They wanted to live close to nature and teach their child themselves.

Challenge Question:

Robin was not content to follow the lifestyle of others. He took great physical risks in his small boat. The exciting quality of his experiences made the dangers worthwhile. Being close to nature mattered more than making money. He liked primitive lifestyles, even though they offered little in terms of material possessions. He hated being a celebrity

because he felt that his and Patti's experiences were very private. His experiences gave him more "life" in five years than most people have in sixty or seventy years.

Kon-Tiki by Thor Heyerdahl

True or False:

1. F	5. T	9. F	13. F	17. T
2. T	6. F	10. T	14. F	18. T
3. F	7. T	11. F	15. F	19. F
4. F	8. T	12. T	16. F	20. F

Short Answers:

1. Heyerdahl believed that the Polynesian Islands were settled by Indians sailing west from Peru. These ancient peoples, according to the author's thesis, left South America after their countries were invaded. Similar plant growth in Polynesia and Peru, as well as common words and concepts in language, convinced Heyerdahl that these two ancient peoples were one.

2. The balsa wood logs would float like a cork over any wave. The spaces between the logs allowed waves to simply wash through the raft. If the raft were tipped or swamped, it immediately resumed an upright position.

3. One man was in swimming and was chased by a shark. Two were in the small rubber boat and were almost unable to get back to the raft. Another was bitten by a dolphin. The most dangerous moment of all came when the raft was wrecked on the reef. The men made it to shore and also saved all their equipment.

4. The Polynesians welcomed their white visitors with music and feasting. The natives believed that the raft was similar to the craft that their ancestors had used. These island people thought that Heyerdahl and his crew had come west with the sun, just as their ancestors had.

5. The weather information the *Kon-Tiki* reported was valuable because no ships usually reported from that part of the world. The equipment the *Kon-Tiki* tested for the U.S. government would be used later by the American armed forces. The voyage was important to archaeologists in proving that a balsa raft such as the Indians had could indeed make such a voyage.

Challenge Question:

The men of the *Kon-Tiki* were not afraid to take chances, to go where people had never been before. The explorers were not afraid of physical hardship. Each was strong and in good health. Fear seemed to be unknown among the crew members. The men on the *Kon-Tiki* worked together as a unit. Each man thought of the others before himself. The project goal and the completion of the voyage became most important. This is the key element in any successful exploration.

A Walk Across America by Peter Jenkins

Matching:

1. N	5. G	9. B	13. L	17. S
2. C	6. K	10. T	14. E	18. P
3. J	7. O	11. Q	15. H	19. M
4. A	8. I	12. R	16. F	20. D

Short Answers:

1. Peter wanted to see America for himself. He needed to look beyond the stereotypes he had been taught so that he could know for himself whether America was good or bad.

2. He prepared his own body and Cooper's by working out to build his stamina. He learned to keep going even when he hurt. Peter and Cooper ran greater distances each day until they could both make it to the top of a mountain. Peter also selected his gear carefully so that he would be able to carry everything he needed to survive.

3. Cooper was Peter's "forever friend," the companion spirit who saved Peter from loneliness. Cooper's enthusiasm kept Peter going. He also saved Peter by being aware of dangers that Peter could not see. After Cooper was killed, Peter had difficulty going on alone.

4. Although he agreed with their philosophy of living with nature, he could not accept their spiritual philosophy. Peter realized that, if he remained, he would have to give up his identity. He could not surrender his individuality to anyone.

5. While on the trail, Peter became ill with influenza. When he was attacked by a German shepherd, Cooper saved his life. The men in the small town threatened to lynch Peter. He was attacked by four drunks who thought Peter was a drug pusher.

Challenge Question:

After graduating from college, Peter rejected the lifestyle he had grown up with. He was coming to hate America because he thought it was commercial and shallow. However, he decided before he left to seek the country's soul—to learn for himself what America was all about.

As Peter traveled, he grew to understand nature. He admired men like Homer Davenport, who lived entirely off the land. Surviving in bad weather helped Peter experience physical reality. From the Olivers, his adopted black family, he learned goodness and the joy of living. He admired their strength and faith, even in the poverty of their surroundings.

Peter learned to deal with grief as he went on alone after Cooper died. He was able to stand up to the roughnecks in Mississippi. He found love when he met and married Barbara in New Orleans.

Because of his wealthy background, Peter Jenkins had a very protected adolescence. During his journey across America, Peter became a man as his experience taught him to form his own value system.

Coming Into the Country by John McPhee

Matching:

1. J	6. F	11. Q	16. D
2. N	7. A	12. B	17. R
3. E	8. L	13. C	18. K
4. P	9. G	14. M	19. I
5. S	10. H	15. O	20. T

Short Answers:

1. Answers might include: open space, clean air and water, abundant fish and wildlife, room for people to be free without being intruded on by their neighbors.

2. People won't be free to settle where they wish if the government controls large areas of land. Independent people view federal regulation as interference.

3. Large spaces without roads or maps bring a sense of disorientation, even for those in airplanes. Unpredictable changes in wind or climate can make nature the enemy. Intense cold brings danger from exposure in winter. Cabins built and left stocked can be critical in saving the lives of those lost or stranded. Animals enraged when attacked by man can be a danger.

4. Natives are destroyed when they have to become "white." Alaskans do not understand the white man's passion to own land. When Indians become wealthy through gold or oil, the natives' uniqueness is destroyed. Illegal liquor is also a great danger to the natives.

5. Juneau and Anchorage both wanted the capital there. Many wilderness sites were rejected because the river people and the hunters did not want the land destroyed by the building of a city.

Challenge Question:

Wilderness people came because they were dissatisfied with life in the "Lower Forty-Eight." Those who felt trapped by regulations or people came for a free life. They had to learn to adapt, to cope with nature and to survive in difficult circumstances. They stayed because life in Alaska gave them more satisfaction than life anywhere else.

Kidnapped by Robert Louis Stevenson

Fill-ins:

1. Mr. Campbell, the minister
2. his father dies
3. Jennet Clouston
4. getting David to walk off the end of an unfinished staircase
5. luring David on board his ship and having the boat sail back to shore
6. Ransome, the cabin boy
7. Riach, the second mate
8. Hoseason's men planning to turn Alan over to the English
9. round-house
10. a silver button
11. marooned on an island
12. Colin Roy, the Red Fox
13. wanted for Colin Roy's murder
14. deserted from the English army
15. falls asleep on watch
16. Cluny MacPherson, the Cage
17. loses David's money playing cards
18. Mr. Rankeillor
19. David's father fell in love with his mother
20. returns to France

Short Answers:

1. He advises David to take his father's letter to the House of Shaws and to be a credit to the family name of Balfour.

2. Ebeneezer knows that David is the rightful heir to the House of Shaws. He is afraid that David will take the money and the estate. For this reason, Ebeneezer first tries to kill David and then plots to have him kidnapped.

3. After David is freed from the brig, Ransome, the cabin boy, is killed by Shuan, the first mate, in a drunken rage. David takes Ransome's place and serves the ship's officers.

4. Alan has clansmen all over Scotland who protect the two. Alan also knows the land well enough to find good hiding places.

5. While the lawyer and his clerk hide near the house, Alan knocks loudly. He tells David's uncle that he has David and wants to know how much the old man will pay for the lad. He tricks Ebeneezer into admitting how much he paid Hoseason. With this evidence of Ebeneezer's attempt to get rid of David, Mr. Rankeillor forces Ebeneezer to give the boy his rightful inheritance.

Challenge Question:

Alan Breck, like Robin Hood, is a man outside the law who champions the right. Scotland has been taken over by the English. Alan's chief, Ardshiel, has been forced into exile in France. Alan seeks to restore the rights of Scotland.

This noble bandit dresses colorfully. A master swordsman, Alan, with David, defeats a shipload of sailors. Alan is clever in solving impossible dilemmas. He always seems to know the right place to hide. Alan is also very charming. He persuades the tavern girl to steal a boat for them. David can't really stay angry with him. Although David would have been safer if he had left Alan, the bandit has a charismatic character that makes David want to follow him.

Unit 2

The Maturing Self

Synopses

Winesburg, Ohio   No

by Sherwood Anderson ════════════════════

Viking Press, New York, 1958.

Winesburg, Ohio studies life under a microscope in a small midwestern town. George Willard, reporter for the local newspaper, witnesses the sufferings of the "grotesques," characters whose frustrated desires have warped their personalities. Each character fails to communicate his feelings. Wing Biddlebaum is driven from the students he desires to help. Jesse Bentley's search for God terrifies his grandson David. Women are also trapped by Winesburg. Kate Swift, Alice Hindeman, and George's own mother Elizabeth all experience unfulfilled desires. In this town, all efforts at expression are misunderstood. George's own romance with Helen White leads only to the young reporter's leaving Winesburg to find his way in a wider world.

Anderson's novel reads more like a collection of short stories. The theme of frustration and the character of George Willard give the narrative a common thread. *Winesburg, Ohio* presents in-depth characterization. In a limited space, Anderson's people feel deeply.

Midnight Hour Encores   ok

by Bruce Brooks ════════════════════

Harper and Row, New York, 1986.

Sibilance T. Spooner, an exceptionally talented cellist, lives with her father, Cabot, whom she has nicknamed Taxi. Sib's mother abandoned her child in the hippie days of the sixties because the mother wanted to "do her own thing." Father and daughter live a comfortable life in which each understands the other's needs.

When she is sixteen, Sib asks her father to take her to California to meet her mother, now a successful interior decorator. Sib has an ulterior motive: She wishes to meet a Russian cellist who has defected to the West and is teaching in San Francisco.

By introducing Sib to the music and the people who were involved in the culture of the sixties, Taxi tries to help Sib understand why her mother abandoned her. As they travel across the country, Taxi explains the feelings he and Connie had.

When Taxi and Sib arrive in California, Sib meets her mother and the cellist Dzyga. She wins the audition. She must then choose between her father's world and her mother's.

The story is told from Sib's point of view. The novel is a significant study in growing up as Sib comes to understand her father, her mother, and herself.

The Stranger
by Albert Camus

Random House, New York, 1942.

The Stranger is the story of Meursault, an office worker in French Algiers. Watching the world rather than being involved with life, this man is a stranger to feelings. The world in which he lives is "benignly indifferent."

No relationships have any real significance. When his mother dies, Meursault feels no grief or loss. Instead he lives for momentary pleasure with his mistress, Marie. When his friend Raymond abuses an Arab woman, her relatives follow Meursault and Raymond to the beach. Using Raymond's gun, Meursault kills a man he does not even know.

At his trial, the state accuses Meursault of premeditated homicide. Even as he is sentenced to death, the prisoner experiences no remorse. He thinks only of life in the sensual "now." Meursault is a completely amoral character, one for whom right and wrong do not exist.

A very significant twentieth-century French novelist, Camus was an existentialist, believing that simply being is all that matters. Essences, or ideas, such as faith and love do not exist in his world.

David Copperfield
by Charles Dickens

Random House, New York, 1950.

David Copperfield, Dickens's great autobiographical novel, reflects the experiences of the author's life. Born several months after his father's death, David develops a strong attachment to his mother and his nurse Peggotty. After David's mother marries the cruel Mr. Murdstone, David is sent to Salem House, a brutal school run by Mr. Creakle. At school David makes two friends who greatly influence his later life: James Steerforth and Thomas Traddles.

After his mother's death, David is sent by his stepfather to work in a London factory. He lives with the family of the eccentric Mr. Micawber, who is always in debt and waiting for something to "turn up." David runs away from London and journeys on foot to Dover. There the lad is befriended by his aunt, Betsey Trotwood, who rejected David earlier because he was born a boy instead of a girl.

Going to school in Canterbury, David lives with Mr. Wickfield and his daughter Agnes, who becomes one of the lasting loves of David's life. Passing through London after finishing school, he meets his old friend Steerforth, who leads David into trouble. Steerforth eventually runs away with Emily Peggotty. His selfish actions ruin several lives. The sacrificing love of Emily's uncle, who never stops seeking his lost niece, is contrasted with the selfishness of Mrs. Steerforth and her companion, Rosa Dartle.

David works toward becoming a lawyer and falls in love with Dora Spenlow, his employer's daughter. David also watches the evil genius, Uriah Heep, who is plotting to destroy Mr. Wickfield by preying on the old lawyer's weaknesses.

David and Dora are married; they play house for a time like two children. After Dora sickens and dies, David is forced to deal with his own grief and move toward becoming a man.

By the story's end, Dickens brings together the strands of his complicated plot. Uriah Heep is exposed by Mr. Micawber, who has become his clerk. Mr. Peggotty reclaims his fallen niece. David finally marries Agnes.

A long book, but well worth reading, *David Copperfield* is a fine example of Dickens's writing style. The novel contains characters that have become common names in literature.

Oliver Twist oK

by Charles Dickens

Bantam Classics Edition, New York, 1982.

Oliver Twist is Dickens's classic tale of the abused child who, through a series of fantastic coincidences, finds his way to family and fortune. When Oliver's mother dies in childbirth, the child experiences the brutality of the workhouse personified by the beadle, Mr. Bumble. After being apprenticed to an undertaker and subjected to further cruelty, Oliver runs away to London. He falls into the custody of Fagin, who exploits children by training them as pickpockets and thieves. When Oliver is arrested for a theft committed by the other boys, he is aided by Mr. Brownlow, who seeks to rescue the child from a life of crime.

Oliver is recaptured by Nancy, the girlfriend of criminal Bill Sikes. Bill uses Oliver to help with a burglary. Oliver is injured in the holdup and found by the kindly Mrs. Maylie and her niece Rose. In their care, Oliver finds the love he has never known.

The mysterious Monks confers with Fagin to recapture Oliver. Although Nancy wants to help Oliver, she will not accept sanctuary for herself or compromise Bill. Believing that Nancy has betrayed him, Bill brutally murders the girl who loves him.

Rose Maylie and Mr. Brownlow unravel the mystery of Oliver's parentage. The evil Monks, Oliver's half-brother, is forced to acknowledge Oliver. The former orphan receives his inheritance. Rose is Oliver's mother's sister. At the novel's end, the criminals are brought to justice. Sikes dies attempting to escape; Fagin is hanged.

Oliver Twist has a complicated plot. The reader must carefully follow the plot line until all mysteries are solved. The novel is one of Dickens's most powerful depictions of the underworld of nineteenth-century London.

Maddy's Song

No

by Margaret Dickson

Houghton Mifflin Company, Boston, 1985.

Maddy's Song is the story of Maddy Dow, a young musical prodigy who struggles to protect her brothers and sisters from their abusive father. In the small town of Freedom, Maine, Jack Dow appears to be the perfect employee, church deacon, and father. In reality, he is an emotionally sick man who beats and humiliates his wife and children, but never allows the bruises to show. Eleanor Hebert, wife of Jack Dow's employer, and her daughter, Elaine, become indirect victims of Jack Dow's violence.

Hired to direct the Freedom Community Chorus, Professor Jonah Sears discovers Maddy's talent when she auditions to be accompanist. Maddy's great-aunts Bea and Ann give Maddy the affection she has never known at home.

As the novel moves to its startling climax, the town of Freedom is shaken to its foundations. Exploring the hidden world of the Dow family, *Maddy's Song* is a deeply moving story of innocence in a life-and-death struggle against evil and the need for love in every human soul.

Silas Marner

No

by George Eliot

New American Library, New York, 1960.

Silas Marner is a story of redemption through love. Betrayed by his friend and exiled from his religious fellowship, Silas Marner comes to live in the village of Raveloe. Because he earns a good living as a weaver, Silas accumulates a hoard of gold, which becomes the focus of his life. The weaver cuts himself off from all human contact and lives in isolation.

Godfrey and Dunstan Cass, sons of the squire of Raveloe, indirectly influence Silas's life. Godfrey loves the beautiful Nancy Lammeter, but he is secretly married to Molly, who has borne his child. Dunstan knows his brother's secret and blackmails Godfrey. Wandering into Silas's cottage after killing Godfrey's horse, Dunstan steals Silas's gold. The distraught weaver tries to get help from the local people, but the thief is never caught.

Meanwhile, after Godfrey's wife dies in the snow, Silas finds the child Eppie on his hearth. She becomes the center of Silas's life. With the help of Dolly Winthrop, Silas becomes both mother and father to the child. Influenced by Eppie's love, Silas joins the town life of Raveloe and becomes a whole man again.

Fifteen years later, Dunstan's body and Silas's money bags are found in the stone quarry. After confessing the secrets of his past to his wife, Godfrey wants to acknowledge Eppie as his daughter. Eppie refuses, however, because Silas is the only father that she has ever known. The novel ends positively with Eppie's marriage to Aaron, her childhood playmate.

Them That Glitter and Them That Don't ~No~

by Bette Greene

Alfred A. Knopf, New York, 1983.

Them That Glitter introduces Carol Ann Delaney, a gypsy girl from the wrong side of the tracks who dreams of becoming Carlotta Dell, famous singer and composer. Carol Ann's parents are both irresponsible. Her mother is indifferent to the children's needs; her father is a weak drunkard. Carol Ann is forced to be mother to her younger brother and sister. Getting out of Bainesville and becoming a star will give her family food to eat and give Carol Ann a sense of identity.

The dream moves closer to fulfillment when Carol Ann's special musical talent is discovered by Jean McCaffrey, who offers to teach the young gypsy to read music. The dream is hurt by Amber Huntington, the rich snob who pretends to be Carol Ann's friend. At her high school graduation, Carol Ann must deal with the fact that her family has abandoned her. She must find her own road to identity.

Greene's protagonist is an outcast who is special. This young musician grows up in a hostile world. The novel's plot and characters recount a real struggle for maturity against overwhelming odds.

A Portrait of the Artist as a Young Man ~No~

by James Joyce

Viking Press, New York, 1916.

A Portrait of the Artist as a Young Man charts the growth of Stephen Dedalus from childhood to young manhood. Several major events influence Stephen's development: his education at a private Catholic school, his father's bankruptcy, an awakening sexual consciousness, and Stephen's increasing fascination with language.

The novel is a thinly veiled account of James Joyce's own boyhood. As a child, Stephen is aware of the tension between his Aunt Dante and his father. The small boy does not understand that the quarrel is really between the ideals of Irish nationalism and the Catholic Church. As Stephen grows, the conflict becomes more personal. The young man's sensitivity causes Stephen to feel deeply the effects of his surroundings. On a religious retreat, Stephen intensely feels his sinfulness and determines to find absolution. However, the temptations of the world become more compelling than religious mysticism. He rejects the priesthood to become a writer.

The story is told using the narrative device of stream of consciousness; the reader moves in the time line of Stephen's memories. Each sensory image becomes an open door to a whole new train of thought. The reader understands Stephen's actions by entering the young writer's mind. The beautifully crafted prose of the novel provides inspiration for students who themselves wish to become writers.

Carrie

by Stephen King

Doubleday and Company, New York, 1974.

Carrie White is a victim. She is abused by her mother, a religious fanatic. Since she is the object of every student prank, school for Carrie is a place of torment. This very shy girl, however, possesses an extraordinary power: telekinesis, the ability to move objects with her mind.

When Carrie is under stress, her power begins to work. As a child, in the extremity of her torment, Carrie pelted the house with stones.

After Carrie is cruelly humiliated in the girls' locker room, Sue Snell, one of Chamberlain High School's kinder students, wants to make amends to Carrie. She asks her boyfriend Tommy to invite Carrie to the school prom. What begins as a beautiful evening for Carrie ends in a deluge of horror for the entire town. Christine Hargensen, a vindictive student, destroys Carrie's triumph by dumping buckets of pigs' blood over her. Carrie then uses her powers to create a holocaust in which she destroys her mother, Chris, and all her other tormentors.

The narrative of this book is in three parts: the story told through Carrie's consciousness, both in the present and with flashbacks to her childhood; the report of the commission that investigated the disaster; and Sue Snell's memories of the night's ghastly events. The novel's ending presents telekinesis as a frightening possibility.

The characters and events in this novel are presented very graphically. Descriptions and language might not be suitable for all students.

I Will Call It Georgie's Blues

by Suzanne Newton

Viking Press, New York, 1983.

Neal Sloan, a Baptist minister's son, fights to find his identity. His overbearing, insecure father dominates the lives of Neal, his sister Aileen, and his little brother Georgie. Each member of Neal's family struggles against the perfection demanded of the minister's children. Aileen rebels; Neal takes refuge in his music. Only Georgie is left without defense. The frail little boy finally suffers a nervous breakdown.

At first Neal keeps his musical gifts a secret. His teacher, Mrs. Talbot, allows the gifted boy the use of her piano and introduces him to the world of jazz. Georgie's crisis finally forces Neal to be honest. He learns the relief of playing for the world. The author has created a very moving story of a talented boy's reach toward manhood.

Jacob Have I Loved   No

by Katherine Paterson

Avon Books, New York, 1980.

Jacob Have I Loved, set on Rass, an island in Chesapeake Bay in the 1940's, is the story of Louise Bradshaw, the unloved elder twin, the "Esau" of her family. Louise's sister Caroline, born younger and weaker, has all the family charm and gets all the attention. Also a trial to Louise is her Bible-quoting grandmother who constantly spouts verses of doom and gloom. Louise is closest to her father since she shares his love of the sea.

Jealous of the attention that Caroline receives, Louise wishes she were a man so that she could join her father in his crabbing and oystering business. The author of this novel shows us the watermen of the Chesapeake and their world through Louise's loving eyes. The descriptions of the island and its life-style form a beautiful part of the novel.

Louise and her friend Cal befriend Hiram Wallace, a returned islander who left years before under mysterious circumstances. As Louise grows up, she experiences the first stirrings of physical love. Louise and her family survive a hurricane. Louise experiences feelings she cannot understand when she reaches out to touch the Captain as they view his demolished home.

As World War II interrupts island life, Cal goes off to join the navy and Caroline leaves for music school in New York. Louise matures to find her own way. When Cal returns from the service, Louise learns that it is Caroline that he intends to marry. Again Louise must deal with her feelings of anger toward the sister who gets everything.

Louise also finally leaves Rass. Becoming a nurse-midwife, Louise helps the birthing of twins. Only when she too must save the weaker baby can Louise forgive Caroline for being "Jacob" who received more love.

Although this novel is easy reading, the author profoundly explores the inner world of a maturing adolescent.

Davita's Harp   ok

by Chaim Potok

Ballantine Books, New York, 1985.

Students who have read Potok's other books will enjoy *Davita's Harp*. The language is beautiful as reality is presented through the eyes of a sensitive girl.

Ilana Davita Chandal has a Gentile father and a Jewish mother. Both parents have abandoned religion for a new belief, Communism. Davita overhears meetings of her parents' political friends. The family moves frequently because the neighbors disapprove of the Chandals' opinions. Two symbols of continuity dominate Davita's childhood: a painting of running horses that hangs in her parents' bedroom, and the singing harp on their front door.

Great changes invade the child's world. Jakob Daw, a writer friend of her mother's, comes from Europe to stay with the family. He tells the child strangely symbolic stories which make her aware of the world's suffering. Aunt Sarah, a Christian nurse, arrives when Davita's mother is ill. Her prayers awaken the child's spiritual sensitivities.

Davita's father and mother both turned to Communism as a replacement for their lost faith. Davita in her turn finds her way back to her Jewish heritage. After her father is killed in the Spanish Civil War, Davita begins to study Hebrew. She alone wants to say Kaddish, the Jewish ritual of atonement, in her father's honor. She excels in her Hebrew studies and becomes a scholar her father would have been proud of.

Davita's mother becomes disillusioned with Communism. She marries Ezra Dinn and is healed of her pain by returning to the faith of her childhood. Davita too finds the strength of faith which, at the novel's end, she can pass on to her new baby sister.

The author does a brilliant job of presenting the adult world through the eyes of the child. Davita is a sensitive child whose harp becomes tuned to the music of faith and individuality.

Words by Heart
by Ouida Sebestyen

Little, Brown and Company, Boston, 1979.

Lena, a black girl with a "Magic Mind," wins a Bible-quoting contest. She then finds how deep racial hatred can be. Lena's father had brought his family to Kansas, hoping to find a better way of life than that in the all-black communities of the South. Her stepmother Claudie is afraid for Lena because she understands fear and prejudice. Mrs. Chism, the white woman that Lena works for, shows Lena another kind of loneliness. Lena herself must learn to forgive when her father is attacked by the Haneys, a poor white family whose job Lena's father has taken. In the book's powerful climax, Lena learns that the Bible verses which she has memorized must be practiced if life is to have true value.

Homecoming
by Cynthia Voigt

Atheneum, New York, 1982.

Homecoming recounts the journey of the four Tillerman children (Dicey, James, Maybeth, and Sammy) from Cape Cod to Maryland. The kids are abandoned by their troubled mother in a supermarket parking lot. Led by Dicey, the oldest at thirteen, they begin the journey to the only relative they have ever heard about, Aunt Cilla in Bridgeport, Connecticut. They camp in a state park and carry grocery bags to earn money for food. Help comes from Windy and Stewart, two college students, who take the children by car on the last leg of the journey.

The group finally arrives in Bridgeport, only to find that Aunt Cilla has died. Aunt Cilla's daughter, Cousin Eunice, agrees to take the children in. However, life there proves too oppressive; the group again hits the road. The goal this time is their grandmother's home in Maryland. On this leg of the trip, help comes from two weekend sailors and the members of a circus troupe. Gram is reluctant to take the children in. Under Dicey's leadership, however, the children and the elderly lady soon become a family.

Each child develops a personality. Dicey is the leader, the survivor. James craves books more than food. Maybeth is shy to the point of appearing mentally handicapped. Sammy needs the security of being loved.

Homecoming contains excellent descriptions of characters and landscape. As the children travel across several states, they also journey toward maturity. The growth story of the Tillermans makes excellent young adult reading.

Name_____ Date_____

Winesburg, Ohio by Sherwood Anderson

Place a T before each true statement and an F before each false statement.

_____   1. Wing Biddlebaum was driven out of Ohio for severely beating one of his students.

_____   2. Doctor Reefy married the girl whose life he saved.

_____   3. Elizabeth Willard's father promised his daughter a large sum of money if she married Tom.

_____   4. George and his mother communicated freely and easily.

_____   5. Jesse Bentley believed in a God of love and gentleness.

_____   6. David Hardy was terrified when he heard his grandfather praying in the woods.

_____   7. Edward and Tom King severely beat Joe Welling when Joe tried to explain his ideas to them.

_____   8. Ned Currie abandoned Alice Hindeman when he found out that Alice was involved with another man.

_____   9. Wash Williams was a handsome man who never married.

_____   10. Kate Swift had been George Willard's school teacher.

_____   11. Seth Richmond and George Willard were both attracted to the same girl.

_____   12. Tandy Hard received her name from her father.

_____   13. Reverend Curtis Hartman watched Kate through the broken corner of a stained glass window.

_____   14. Curtis Hartman and Kate Swift became secret lovers.

_____   15. George Willard understood all that Kate Swift said when the teacher urged him to become a writer.

_____   16. Enoch Robinson returned to Winesburg after the "secret people" in his room were destroyed.

_____   17. Belle Carpenter used George Willard to make Ed Handby jealous.

_____   18. Elmer Cowley decided to remain in Winesburg and work in his father's department store.

_____   19. Ray Pearson shared with Hal Winters his real feelings about marriage.

_____   20. George Willard persuaded Helen White to run away with him to the city.

© 1991 J. Weston Walch, Publisher   *100 More Great Books: Synopses, Quizzes, and Tests*

Name _____ Date _____

Winesburg, Ohio by Sherwood Anderson

Answer the following questions in two or three complete sentences.

1. Why were the lives of both Louise Bentley and Elizabeth Willard frustrated and incomplete?

_____

_____

_____

2. How did Curtis Hartman succeed in his struggle for faith? How did Jesse Bentley fail?

_____

_____

_____

3. How did Dr. Reefy help Elizabeth Willard?

_____

_____

_____

4. Why is the title "Sophistication" ironic?

_____

_____

_____

5. Why are Wing Biddlebaum and Wash Williams men who are both physically and mentally grotesque?

_____

_____

_____

Challenge Question

Write an essay discussing the role of George Willard as both observer of and participant in the life of Winesburg.

© 1991 J. Weston Walch, Publisher   *100 More Great Books: Synopses, Quizzes, and Tests*

Name_____   Date_____

Midnight Hour Encores by Bruce Brooks

Select the letter of the word or phrase which correctly completes each sentence.

_____ 1. Sib Spooner's name was (A) given to her by her father (B) given to her by her mother (C) picked by Sib herself (D) the name of a famous musician.

_____ 2. They began the journey to meet Sib's mother (A) because Sib asked to go (B) because Taxi insisted (C) because Sib's mother called (D) because Sib planned to go to school in California.

_____ 3. Sib first hears Dzyga play (A) on television (B) at a concert (C) on an old phonograph record (D) at a cello audition.

_____ 4. Sib and Taxi plan to travel west (A) in an old van (B) by train (C) by plane (D) by bus.

_____ 5. Sib wins cello competitions in all of the following places *except* (A) Prague (B) New York (C) Rome (D) San Francisco.

_____ 6. Sib practices on the trip (A) when they stop for the night (B) using a special stool that Taxi made (C) in local concert halls (D) by listening to records.

_____ 7. Gustavus was (A) her uncle (B) her brother (C) her teacher (D) Taxi's real name.

_____ 8. All Taxi's efforts are geared toward (A) making Sib dislike her mother (B) making Sib choose Taxi over her mother (C) helping Sib understand her mother (D) making Sib accept the values of the hippie culture.

_____ 9. Sib knows that Dzyga is in California by (A) the note she receives from the Institute (B) seeing his picture in the paper (C) finding one of his newest records (D) getting a phone call from him.

_____ 10. In addition to playing the cello, Sib (A) played the violin (B) taught piano lessons (C) wrote music (D) collected old recordings.

_____ 11. When she gets to California, Sib finds that her mother has (A) become well known and wealthy (B) remarried (C) stayed in the hippie culture (D) refused to let Sib into her house.

(continued)

© 1991 J. Weston Walch, Publisher

100 More Great Books: Synopses, Quizzes, and Tests

Name_____ Date_____

Midnight Hour Encores by Bruce Brooks

_____ 12. Sib's first romance took place at a competition in (A) Moscow (B) Paris (C) Prague (D) Rome.

_____ 13. As his tribute to Sib's talent, Milosz (A) gave her flowers (B) played the "Star-Spangled Banner" (C) bowed to her (D) gave Sib the award he had won.

_____ 14. Martin was (A) her mother's assistant (B) one of Sib's fellow students (C) Taxi's cousin (D) a brilliant cellist.

_____ 15. For Sib's mother, one of the most important parts of the audition is (A) how Sib plays (B) how her hair looks (C) whether she is on time (D) what she wears.

_____ 16. Sib's mother's name is (A) Connie (B) Jean (C) Betty (D) Alice.

_____ 17. Taxi (A) does not want Sib to stay with her mother (B) attends Sib's audition (C) leaves Sib behind in California (D) refuses to attend the audition.

_____ 18. Sib ends her audition with (A) Haydn (B) Brahms (C) Beethoven (D) a composition of Taxi's.

_____ 19. Dzyga responds to Sib's playing by (A) becoming completely involved in her music (B) weeping (C) sitting with his eyes closed (D) all of the above.

_____ 20. At the end of the novel, Sib (A) is enrolled in school in California (B) marries Martin (C) decides to stay with her mother (D) returns to New York with Taxi.

© 1991 J. Weston Walch, Publisher

Name _____ Date _____

Midnight Hour Encores by Bruce Brooks

Answer the following questions in two or three complete sentences.

1. Why did Sib's mother abandon her husband and child?

   _____

   _____

   _____

2. Why does Sib prefer music to literature?

   _____

   _____

   _____

3. Why does Sib search for Dzyga? How does she find him?

   _____

   _____

   _____

4. What are some of the ways Taxi uses to introduce Sib to the hippie culture that he and Connie were once part of?

   _____

   _____

   _____

5. Why does the author choose Sib herself to be the narrator of this novel?

   _____

   _____

   _____

Challenge Question

Sib is a musician and an unusually sensitive person. How is this sensitivity a gift for her? How is this sensitivity painful?

© 1991 J. Weston Walch, Publisher   *100 More Great Books: Synopses, Quizzes, and Tests*

Name_____ Date_____

The Stranger by Albert Camus

Place a T before each true statement and an F before each false statement.

_____ 1. Meursault's mother died in a nursing home.

_____ 2. All his mother's friends attended her funeral.

_____ 3. After his mother's death, Meursault experienced deep feelings of remorse because he had not cared for her himself.

_____ 4. The Arabs who followed Meursault and Raymond were relatives of the girl Raymond had abused.

_____ 5. Raymond and Meursault worked in the same office.

_____ 6. Meursault was very pleased when his employer offered him a transfer to Paris.

_____ 7. Celeste was the owner of the restaurant where they ate frequently.

_____ 8. Meursault shot the Arab after the other man shot at him.

_____ 9. The shooting took place on a deserted stretch of beach.

_____ 10. Masson and his wife were both witnesses to the killing.

_____ 11. The police inspector often beat Meursault severely while questioning him.

_____ 12. Raymond hired the lawyer who defended Meursault at his trial.

_____ 13. While he was in jail, Meursault made time pass by remembering the contents of his room.

_____ 14. His lawyer was anxious to have Meursault testify as a witness in his own defense.

_____ 15. After he was sentenced to death, Meursault was anxious to see a priest.

_____ 16. Marie came to visit him in jail only once.

_____ 17. The prosecutor claimed that Meursault had indirectly murdered his mother.

_____ 18. The newspapers took very little interest in Meursault's case.

_____ 19. Meursault was finally freed from prison after Raymond changed his testimony.

_____ 20. Meursault was taken to be executed at daybreak.

© 1991 J. Weston Walch, Publisher

Name _____   Date_____

The Stranger by Albert Camus

Answer the following questions in two or three complete sentences.

1. How does Meursault show a lack of feeling when his mother dies?

    _____

    _____

    _____

2. In what way is Meursault involved in the quarrel between Raymond and the Arabs?

    _____

    _____

    _____

3. How does Camus use the weather to create the mood in this novel?

    _____

    _____

    _____

4. How does the inspector try to make Meursault feel guilty?

    _____

    _____

    _____

5. At the end of the novel, how does Meursault feel about dying?

    _____

    _____

    _____

Challenge Question

Discuss the ways in which Meursault is "The Stranger," or the outsider.

Name_____ Date_____

David Copperfield by Charles Dickens

Match each description in Column A with the correct name in Column B.

Column A	Column B
_____ 1. The "umble" villain	A. Tom Traddles
_____ 2. Victim of the base desires of others	B. Dora Spenlow
_____ 3. Cruel schoolmaster	C. Aunt Betsey
_____ 4. Spoiled by his vain and selfish mother	D. Creakle
_____ 5. Would "never desert" her husband	E. Agnes Wickfield
_____ 6. David's child-wife	F. Clara Peggotty
_____ 7. Simple-minded, but good friend to David and his aunt Betsey	G. Emily
_____ 8. Saved Emily Peggotty by reuniting her with her uncle	H. Julia Mills
_____ 9. Finally became a magistrate in Australia	I. Dr. Strong
_____ 10. Scholar and loving husband	J. Murdstone
_____ 11. David's lawyer friend from his school days	K. Uriah Heep
_____ 12. Helped Dora and David meet without anyone's knowledge	L. Ham
_____ 13. Died trying to save another from a shipwreck	M. Mrs. Micawber
_____ 14. Relative who became David's guardian and benefactor	N. Mr. Dick
_____ 15. Woman with a scarred face	O. Dr. Mell
_____ 16. David's nurse and childhood friend	P. Steerforth
_____ 17. Kind teacher who was humiliated by Steerforth	Q. Rosa Dartle
_____ 18. Was in love with Dr. Strong's wife	R. Martha
_____ 19. Real love of David's mature life	S. Jack Mardon
_____ 20. Cruel stepfather who whipped David for no real cause	T. Mr. Micawber

© 1991 J. Weston Walch, Publisher

Name _____ Date_____

David Copperfield by Charles Dickens

Answer the following questions in two or three complete sentences.

1. How is Dickens's frequent theme of the abused child shown in *David Copperfield*?

   _____

   _____

   _____

2. Why is Steerforth not really a good friend to David?

   _____

   _____

   _____

3. How does Dickens show Martha and Emily as victims, rather than evil women?

   _____

   _____

   _____

4. How is David's relationship with Dora different from his relationship with Agnes?

   _____

   _____

   _____

5. In what ways is Betsey Trotwood a positive and consistent force in David's life?

   _____

   _____

   _____

Challenge Question

As a novelist, Charles Dickens is master of the caricature, the personality exaggerated for effect. Discuss some of the caricatures that are so well presented in *David Copperfield*.

© 1991 J. Weston Walch, Publisher   *100 More Great Books: Synopses, Quizzes, and Tests*

Name_____   Date_____

Oliver Twist by Charles Dickens

Select the letter of the word or phrase which correctly completes each sentence.

_____ 1. As a child, Oliver is abused by all of the following *except* (A) Mr. Bumble (B) Mr. Grimwig (C) Noah Claypole (D) Mrs. Sowerberry.

_____ 2. Oliver is apprenticed to (A) a baker (B) a carpenter (C) a blacksmith (D) an undertaker.

_____ 3. Jack Dawkins is skilled as (A) a forger (B) a housebreaker (C) a pickpocket (D) an attacker of children and old ladies.

_____ 4. Fagin is (A) the leader of the criminal ring (B) a child abuser (C) a housebreaker (D) a magistrate.

_____ 5. Oliver is rescued from false imprisonment by (A) Mr. Bumble (B) Mr. Brownlow (C) Harry Maylie (D) Nancy and the Dodger.

_____ 6. Oliver does not return to Brownlow's house because (A) he is kidnapped (B) he intends to run away (C) he gets lost in the narrow streets (D) he wants to return to Fagin's gang.

_____ 7. When the burglary fails, Sikes (A) is arrested (B) dumps Oliver in a ditch (C) hides at Fagin's (D) turns himself in.

_____ 8. Rose refuses to marry Harry Maylie because (A) she does not love him (B) her aunt does not approve (C) there is a stain on her name (D) she knows that Harry loves somebody else.

_____ 9. While with the Maylies, Oliver sees Fagin (A) on the street (B) looking in his window (C) in the local tavern (D) in the garden.

_____ 10. The man who most desires Oliver's return to the criminal world is (A) Mr. Bumble (B) Fagin (C) Sikes (D) Monks.

_____ 11. Nancy wishes to help Oliver (A) because she has a great deal of good in her (B) to save him from a life of crime (C) but she will not betray Bill (D) all of the above.

(continued)

© 1991 J. Weston Walch, Publisher

Name _____ Date_____

Oliver Twist by Charles Dickens

_____ 12. Mr. Bumble meets his disaster through (A) marriage (B) child abuse (C) theft (D) embezzlement.

_____ 13. The person first holding the evidence of Oliver's real identity is (A) Mrs. Sowerberry (B) Old Sally (C) Mrs. Bumble (D) Monks.

_____ 14. The Artful Dodger (A) has been trained by Fagin (B) is Jack Dawkins's nickname (C) is imprisoned for theft (D) all of the above.

_____ 15. Nancy does not keep her first appointment with Rose because (A) she is ill (B) she has changed her mind (C) Bill will not let her out (D) Rose does not come.

_____ 16. Bolter is the name given to (A) Charley Bates (B) Monks (C) Mr. Grimwig (D) Noah Claypole.

_____ 17. Mr. Brownlow wants to adopt Oliver because (A) he is the boy's grandfather (B) he had loved the boy's mother (C) the boy's father had been his close friend (D) he always took pity on orphans.

_____ 18. The most brutal episode in this novel is (A) the death of Nancy (B) the treatment of Oliver as a child (C) the execution of Fagin (D) the death of Sikes.

_____ 19. The location of the proof of Oliver's inheritance is supplied by (A) Mrs. Bumble (B) Monks (C) Fagin (D) Nancy.

_____ 20. The sadness in Oliver's good fortune comes from (A) the death of Mr. Brownlow (B) the death of Dick (C) the death of Fagin (D) the death of Nancy.

© 1991 J. Weston Walch, Publisher

Name _____ Date_____

Oliver Twist by Charles Dickens

Answer the following questions in two or three complete sentences.

1. How does Dickens show society's cruelty to the helpless in *Oliver Twist*?

   _____

   _____

   _____

2. How does Oliver first become involved with Fagin's gang?

   _____

   _____

   _____

3. Why does Nancy refuse Rose's offer of sanctuary?

   _____

   _____

   _____

4. How does Mr. Bumble try to excuse his role in destroying the evidence of Oliver's birth?

   _____

   _____

   _____

5. How do both Sikes and Fagin get the punishment deserved for their criminal activities?

   _____

   _____

   _____

Challenge Question

Write an essay discussing the coincidences in this novel. In what important scenes does the plot development depend on chance encounters or events?

© 1991 J. Weston Walch, Publisher

100 More Great Books: Synopses, Quizzes, and Tests

Name _____ Date_____

Maddy's Song by Margaret Dickson

Select the letter of the word or phrase which correctly completes each sentence.

_____ 1. In the opening chapter of the novel, the first victim of Jack Dow's violence was (A) Allison (B) Vinnie (C) Stephen (D) Philip.

_____ 2. Which of the following was the only position in Freedom that Jack Dow did *not* hold? (A) school board member (B) church deacon (C) town treasurer (D) church treasurer

_____ 3. When Jack was a child, he was forced to work (A) as a farm worker (B) in a coal mine (C) in a fish factory (D) on a road-building crew.

_____ 4. Aunt Ann Packard met Aunt Bea (A) at a family reunion (B) in the hospital (C) at church (D) when Aunt Ann came to work for her.

_____ 5. Maddy's musical talent was (A) something her father was proud of (B) inherited from her mother (C) shared by two of her brothers (D) really nothing out of the ordinary.

_____ 6. Maddy's feelings for her mother could best be described as (A) hate (B) indifference (C) love (D) protectiveness.

_____ 7. Jack Dow's mother and the babies died in (A) a fire (B) a blizzard (C) an automobile accident (D) a scarlet fever epidemic.

_____ 8. Maddy hid the notebook in which she wrote her music in (A) the piano bench (B) her bedroom (C) her locker at school (D) the pocket of her dress.

_____ 9. When the Heberts planned to buy a computer, Jack Dow was afraid because he (A) thought that he did not have the intelligence to learn to use a computer (B) was afraid that the money he had stolen would be noticed (C) thought that he might lose his job (D) didn't believe computers were worth the money.

_____ 10. The Dow house was all of the following *except* (A) run-down (B) isolated (C) large (D) painted white.

(continued)

© 1991 J. Weston Walch, Publisher

100 More Great Books: Synopses, Quizzes, and Tests

Name_____ Date_____

Maddy's Song by Margaret Dickson

_____ 11. Eleanor Hebert may best be described as a lady who (A) lost her temper easily (B) liked to spend her husband's money (C) wanted to manage everything (D) neglected her children.

_____ 12. Jonah Sears welcomed the solitude he found in Freedom so that he could (A) finish his thesis (B) find out how he really felt about his relationship with Audrey (C) catch up on his reading (D) recover his health.

_____ 13. Jack Dow was afraid that one of his children would (A) be sick (B) fail in school (C) escape (D) embarrass him in front of the church people.

_____ 14. The Freedom choir won the competition because the choristers (A) learned to feel the music (B) all had trained voices (C) looked nice in the costumes Eleanor made (D) replaced Jonah as the director.

_____ 15. All of the following are true of Aunt Ann Packard *except* (A) she was thin and sickly (B) she loved to cook (C) she saved Aunt Bea's life (D) she had once been in love.

_____ 16. The climax of the novel centered around (A) Elaine's baby (B) the musical competition (C) Vinnie's crippled hand (D) Maddy's cutting her hair.

_____ 17. Which of the following stood up for Maddy against her father's rage? (A) Vinnie (B) Allison (C) Jessica (D) Stephen

_____ 18. The character whose situation was most hopeless at the end of the novel was (A) Maddy (B) Elaine (C) Jessica (D) Jonah.

_____ 19. Jonah wanted Maddy to (A) help him with his thesis (B) go to music school (C) continue playing for the Freedom chorus (D) become one of his students in Portland.

_____ 20. Which of the following did not die in the fire? (A) Vinnie (B) Jack (C) Allison (D) Stephen

© 1991 J. Weston Walch, Publisher

Name _____   Date _____

Maddy's Song by Margaret Dickson

Answer the following questions in two or three complete sentences.

1. Describe the contrast between Jack Dow's public image and the reality of the Dows' home life.

   _____

   _____

   _____

2. Why are Aunt Bea and Aunt Ann glad when Jonah comes to live with them?

   _____

   _____

   _____

3. How did Jack Dow's boyhood influence the way he treated his family?

   _____

   _____

   _____

4. How did Maddy's mother, Vinnie, try to help her? Why did Vinnie fail?

   _____

   _____

   _____

5. In what ways does Jonah help Maddy? How does Maddy help Jonah?

   _____

   _____

   _____

Challenge Question

Discuss how the Dow family tragedy affects the entire town of Freedom. What do the people learn from this experience?

Name_____ Date_____

Silas Marner by George Eliot

Match each description in Column A with the correct name in Column B.

Column A

_____ 1. The aging church clerk and authority on all local matters

_____ 2. Silas's fiancée who married his friend

_____ 3. Advised Silas on the proper way to bring up a child

_____ 4. Opium addict who died in the snow

_____ 5. Minister in Raveloe

_____ 6. Accused of a theft committed by his friend

_____ 7. Pub and center for town gossip

_____ 8. Became very angry when he thought his sons were wasting his money

_____ 9. Neighborhood beauty loved by Godfrey Cass

_____ 10. Childhood playmate, later Eppie's husband

_____ 11. Was named for Silas's dead sister

_____ 12. Scoundrel, liar, who stole Silas's gold

_____ 13. Plain sister who never married

_____ 14. Town from which Silas fled in disgrace

_____ 15. Examined Molly and pronounced her dead

_____ 16. Killed while trying to jump over a high hedge

_____ 17. Nancy's favorite aunt

_____ 18. Caught between his sense of duty and his passions

_____ 19. Friend who betrayed Silas

_____ 20. Played the fiddle at the Raveloe dances

Column B

A. Dolly Winthrop

B. Nancy Lammeter

C. Priscilla

D. Silas Marner

E. William Dane

F. Lantern Yard

G. Aaron Winthrop

H. Solomon

I. Squire Cass

J. Molly

K. Dunstan Cass

L. Godfrey Cass

M. Mr. Macey

N. Wild Fire

O. Mrs. Osgood

P. Dr. Kimble

Q. Mr. Crackenthorp

R. Eppie

S. Sarah

T. Rainbow

© 1991 J. Weston Walch, Publisher

Name_____ Date_____

Silas Marner by George Eliot

Answer the following questions in two or three complete sentences.

1. Why did Silas Marner come as a fugitive to Raveloe?

_____

_____

_____

2. How did Dunstan Cass rationalize the theft of Silas Marner's gold?

_____

_____

_____

3. Why was Molly's death a relief to Godfrey?

_____

_____

_____

4. How does Dolly Winthrop help Silas?

_____

_____

_____

5. Why does Eppie refuse Godfrey's offer of wealth and social position?

_____

_____

_____

Challenge Question

Describe Silas Marner's character development. How did his love for Eppie change his life?

© 1991 J. Weston Walch, Publisher

Name_____ Date_____

Them That Glitter and Them That Don't
by Bette Greene

Place a T before each true statement and an F before each false statement.

_____ 1. Carol Ann is the oldest child in her family.

_____ 2. To help feed the family, Carol Ann has had to drop out of school.

_____ 3. Carol Ann has never felt close to her father.

_____ 4. Painter was often cheated by those he trusted.

_____ 5. Amber's mother helps Amber get Carol Ann dressed to sing at the school assembly.

_____ 6. After she sings, Carol Ann is booed by the other students.

_____ 7. Dirt and clutter do not bother Carol Ann because she is used to being poor.

_____ 8. Carol Ann's father is also a gypsy.

_____ 9. Mrs. McCaffrey recognizes that Carol Ann has a special gift.

_____ 10. Carol Ann sees nothing wrong with the illegal actions of her mother.

_____ 11. Amber comes with Carol Ann to their trailer.

_____ 12. By helping Carol Ann, Amber proves to be a genuine friend.

_____ 13. Painter sold his house and land for money to buy liquor.

_____ 14. Carol Ann helps her father steal the coffin for Baby Belinda.

_____ 15. In her dreams, Carlotta Dell will have the money to solve all the Delaney family's problems.

_____ 16. Carol Ann's mother absolutely refuses to let her marry Will Bellows.

_____ 17. Carol Ann constantly fears that her family will abandon her.

_____ 18. Her mother wants to use Carol Ann's musical abilities as a front to cheat people.

_____ 19. Will agrees to help Carol Ann with her musical career.

_____ 20. Mrs. McCaffrey travels with Carol Ann to Nashville.

© 1991 J. Weston Walch, Publisher   *100 More Great Books: Synopses, Quizzes, and Tests*

Name_____   Date_____

Them That Glitter and Them That Don't
by Bette Greene

Answer the following questions in two or three complete sentences.

1. What are the greatest differences between Carol Ann Delaney and Miss Carlotta Dell?

_____

_____

_____

2. Describe the love/hate feelings Carol Ann has toward her family.

_____

_____

_____

3. How does Amber Huntington show her cruel nature?

_____

_____

_____

4. How does Carol Ann's mother justify the "Baby Belinda" scheme?

_____

_____

_____

5. How is Carol Ann's high school graduation the turning point in her life?

_____

_____

_____

Challenge Question

Write an essay discussing how Carol Ann's difficult experiences have made her a person who will survive.

© 1991 J. Weston Walch, Publisher

Name_____ Date_____

A Portrait of the Artist as a Young Man
by James Joyce

Select the letter of the word or phrase which correctly completes each sentence.

_____ 1. The story is told (A) by Stephen's mother (B) through Stephen's developing consciousness (C) by Father Arnall (D) by a third-person narrator.

_____ 2. Stephen's earliest memories related to the sense of (A) taste (B) sight (C) sound (D) smell.

_____ 3. Stephen was unfairly punished at Clongowes when (A) he went to the infirmary (B) the master thought Stephen was someone else (C) Stephen broke his glasses (D) Stephen was pushed into a ditch.

_____ 4. The argument between Aunt Dante and Uncle Charles took place (A) at Christmas dinner (B) in a restaurant (C) on Stephen's birthday (D) on Sunday after Mass.

_____ 5. One critical experience in Stephen's boyhood was (A) his father's bankruptcy (B) his mother's death (C) the birth of his baby brother (D) his first day at school.

_____ 6. Stephen became a hero at school when (A) he got the highest grades (B) he stole food for the other boys (C) he told the rector that he had been unjustly punished (D) he won a track meet.

_____ 7. In his first term at Belvedere, Stephen was (A) praised for good work (B) reprimanded for having heresy in an essay (C) accused of cheating (D) the center of a large group of friends.

_____ 8. Stephen's first poetry (A) was religious (B) was published in the school magazine (C) was written to a girl he was in love with (D) was dedicated to Parnell.

_____ 9. At Belvedere College, Stephen (A) became an actor (B) was the fastest runner in the school (C) decided to become a priest (D) studied literature.

_____ 10. Stephen's college major was (A) law (B) art and music (C) engineering (D) medicine.

(continued)

© 1991 J. Weston Walch, Publisher

Name_____   Date_____

A Portrait of the Artist as a Young Man
by James Joyce

_____ 11. When he visited Cork with his father, Stephen was saddened by (A) his father's lost youth (B) the run-down condition of the city (C) the beauty of the Irish language (D) the memory of a girl he had loved.

_____ 12. Stephen's chief sin was (A) laziness (B) lust (C) anger (D) stealing.

_____ 13. The subject of the priest's sermon during the retreat was (A) the Crucifixion (B) the call to the priesthood (C) hell and coming judgment (D) the love of God.

_____ 14. Stephen finds absolution for his sins (A) in the college chapel (B) during his conference with the dean (C) in a small church where no one knows him (D) from his own father.

_____ 15. After his confession, Stephen (A) rejects the church entirely (B) drops out of school (C) no longer writes (D) becomes extremely religious.

_____ 16. As he thinks about his life as a priest, Stephen feels (A) trapped (B) excited (C) spiritually exalted (D) unworthy.

_____ 17. The friend who represents the ideas of Irish nationalism is (A) Wells (B) MacCann (C) Davin (D) Lynch.

_____ 18. Stephen's rejection of the church comes when (A) his mother wants him to attend Mass (B) he leaves college (C) he first decides to become a writer (D) he can't find any relief for his feelings of sinfulness.

_____ 19. Stephen talks out his problems with (A) his father (B) Cranly (C) Davin (D) the rector.

_____ 20. Even as he leaves home, Stephen still wants the blessing of (A) his father (B) the Catholic Church (C) Ireland (D) all of the above.

© 1991 J. Weston Walch, Publisher

Name_____ Date_____

A Portrait of the Artist as a Young Man
by James Joyce

Answer the following questions in two or three complete sentences.

1. As a small child, how does Stephen show unusual sensitivity?

   _____

   _____

   _____

2. What differences of opinion cause the quarrel among Aunt Dante, Uncle Charles, and Mr. Casey?

   _____

   _____

   _____

3. In his guilt and repentance, how does Stephen show the extremes of his personality?

   _____

   _____

   _____

4. Why does Stephen reject the dean's invitation to become a priest?

   _____

   _____

   _____

5. How does Stephen's idealized view of women play an important role in his developing consciousness?

   _____

   _____

   _____

Challenge Question

Write an essay describing the ways in which the same impulses which draw Stephen toward religion also help him decide to become a writer.

© 1991 J. Weston Walch, Publisher

Name _____ Date _____

Carrie by Stephen King

Place a T before each true statement and an F before each false statement.

_____   1. Carrie's special powers were inherited.

_____   2. Ralph White was a positive influence in his daughter's childhood.

_____   3. From the time she was young, Carrie could easily find a relationship with a gentle, loving God.

_____   4. Stella Horan remembered that only Carrie's house was pelted by a shower of stones.

_____   5. Carrie was a skilled seamstress.

_____   6. Tommy Ross helped Chris Hargensen plan the final cruel joke on Carrie.

_____   7. Mr. Garyle, the principal, refused to allow Chris's father to intimidate him.

_____   8. Margaret White often abused Carrie physically.

_____   9. Carrie's was the only case of telekinesis ever reported.

_____   10. Carrie had a good time at church camp when she was in junior high.

_____   11. Sue Snell survived the disaster because she ran out through one of the back fire doors.

_____   12. Tommy Ross was the first victim of the Prom Night catastrophe.

_____   13. The female in any family was believed to be the carrier of the TK gene.

_____   14. Carrie practiced using her powers by moving objects in her bedroom.

_____   15. All the homes in Chamberlain were destroyed in the fire.

_____   16. The fire was started by a combination of water and electrical current.

_____   17. Carrie's mother dies because Carrie calls down fire on her.

_____   18. At the end of the novel, the town of Chamberlain is beginning to rebuild.

_____   19. Sue Snell is with Carrie when Carrie dies.

_____   20. The novel's ending agrees with the commission's conclusion that these events are not likely to happen again.

© 1991 J. Weston Walch, Publisher

100 More Great Books: Synopses, Quizzes, and Tests

Name _____ Date_____

Carrie by Stephen King

Answer the following questions in two or three complete sentences.

1. How is Mrs. White's treatment of Carrie a reflection of the mother's own guilt feelings?

   _____

   _____

   _____

2. What unusual events were noticed by the neighbors when Carrie was three?

   _____

   _____

   _____

3. Why is Miss Desjardin unsuccessful in her efforts to help Carrie?

   _____

   _____

   _____

4. Why does Sue want Tommy to take Carrie to the prom?

   _____

   _____

   _____

5. How does Carrie lose control of her own powers in the climax of the novel?

   _____

   _____

   _____

Challenge Question

Write an essay describing how Carrie develops strength of character. Discuss how that strength leads to destruction.

© 1991 J. Weston Walch, Publisher

Name_____   Date_____

I Will Call It Georgie's Blues
by Suzanne Newton

Place a T before each true statement and an F before each false statement.

_____   1. Neal is a straight A student.

_____   2. Mrs. Talbot was one of the few outsiders who lived in Gideon.

_____   3. Neal began his musical career by playing the piano for the church services.

_____   4. Neal is closer to his mother than to his father.

_____   5. Aileen is anxious to go to college so that she can get away from home.

_____   6. Neal both plays and composes music.

_____   7. Georgie is convinced that his father is the only real person left in the family.

_____   8. Neal tells his parents about the strange ideas Georgie has.

_____   9. Mrs. T. tells Neal's parents about Neal's musical gifts.

_____   10. Pete Cauthin repeatedly gets Neal into trouble.

_____   11. Neal's Sunday school teacher is a very close friend.

_____   12. Aileen was the source of the rumors that Reverend Sloan was emotionally unstable.

_____   13. Mrs. T. came to live in Gideon after her husband died.

_____   14. Neal found out that his father shared many of his feelings of insecurity.

_____   15. Mr. MacNally tells Neal's father that Neal was playing the piano in the church.

_____   16. Neal finds Georgie hiding on the Captain's boat.

_____   17. Aileen runs away from home to marry Pete.

_____   18. When Neal finds Georgie's hideout, Georgie does not recognize Neal.

_____   19. At the end of the novel, the reader learns that Georgie has died.

_____   20. Neal finally plays his special melodies for Georgie.

© 1991 J. Weston Walch, Publisher   *100 More Great Books: Synopses, Quizzes, and Tests*

Name_____ Date_____

I Will Call It Georgie's Blues
by Suzanne Newton

Answer the following questions in two or three complete sentences.

1. How do Neal's and Aileen's reactions to their home situations differ?

_____

_____

_____

2. How does Mrs. T.'s house become Neal's real home?

_____

_____

_____

3. Why is Georgie the real victim of the family crisis?

_____

_____

_____

4. Why does Neal hide his musical talent?

_____

_____

_____

5. Explain the meaning of the novel's title, *I Will Call It Georgie's Blues*.

_____

_____

_____

Challenge Question

Explain how Neal Sloan's musical gifts help him cope with family crisis and grow toward maturity.

© 1991 J. Weston Walch, Publisher   *100 More Great Books: Synopses, Quizzes, and Tests*

Name _____   Date _____

Jacob Have I Loved by Katherine Paterson

Select the letter of the word or phrase which correctly completes each sentence.

_____ 1. The story in the novel is told by (A) a third-person narrator (B) Caroline (C) Cal (D) Louise.

_____ 2. The time when the story opens is (A) 1945 (B) 1941 (C) 1950 (D) 1918.

_____ 3. When Louise asks her mother for details of Louise's own birth, her mother (A) doesn't answer (B) can't remember (C) tells Louise to ask her grandmother (D) becomes angry.

_____ 4. Louise first sees Hiram Wallace (A) at the general store (B) on his boat (C) when he gets off the ferry (D) at his home.

_____ 5. Louise is convinced that Hiram is (A) a German spy (B) a relative (C) an island native (D) dangerous.

_____ 6. Caroline has great talent in (A) writing poetry (B) dramatics (C) singing (D) dancing.

_____ 7. Caroline and Louise have their deepest moment of closeness (A) during the hurricane (B) when Auntie Braxton dies (C) when they hear of the attack on Pearl Harbor (D) just before Caroline leaves for school.

_____ 8. Cal and Louise become friends because (A) they are the same age (B) both of them like to read (C) both of them dislike Caroline (D) both of them are lonely.

_____ 9. The only one who sleeps through the hurricane is (A) the Captain (B) Caroline (C) the grandmother (D) Louise.

_____ 10. According to island gossip, Hiram Wallace left Rass because (A) he was a coward (B) he had stolen money (C) he had gone bankrupt (D) he had no place to live.

_____ 11. Louise shows her sensitivity by (A) caring about the Captain (B) writing poems (C) having feelings that are easily hurt (D) all of the above.

(continued)

© 1991 J. Weston Walch, Publisher

Name_____   Date_____

Jacob Have I Loved by Katherine Paterson

_____ 12. The Captain marries (A) Louise's grandmother (B) Auntie Braxton (C) Louise (D) a lady from the mainland.

_____ 13. The money for Caroline's musical education is provided by (A) her parents (B) a scholarship (C) the Captain (D) her grandmother.

_____ 14. Caroline helps the Captain (A) rebuild his home (B) take care of his sick wife (C) get rid of all the unwanted cats (D) learn music.

_____ 15. Louise is happiest when she is (A) on the water (B) reading (C) away from the island (D) keeping her grandmother company.

_____ 16. Cal (A) is killed in the war (B) marries Louise (C) marries Caroline (D) never returns to the island.

_____ 17. The main religion on the island is (A) Catholic (B) Baptist (C) Methodist (D) Christian Scientist.

_____ 18. When Caroline is married, Louise (A) refuses to attend the ceremony (B) lets her parents go alone (C) stays with her grandmother (D) all of the above.

_____ 19. After her graduation, Louise (A) becomes a doctor (B) never marries (C) lives in a small mountain community (D) returns to the island.

_____ 20. After she assists at the birth of twins, Louise (A) rejoices in the approaching birth of her own child (B) understands her feelings for Caroline (C) is freed from her hatred and anger (D) all of the above.

Name _____   Date_____

Jacob Have I Loved by Katherine Paterson

Answer the following questions in two or three complete sentences.

1. Describe briefly the island of Rass, which is such an important part of Louise's life.

   _____

   _____

   _____

2. Why does Louise feel closer to her father than to any other member of her family?

   _____

   _____

   _____

3. Why does Louise feel that her parents love Caroline more than they love her?

   _____

   _____

   _____

4. Why does Louise believe that she is in love with the Captain?

   _____

   _____

   _____

5. Why must Louise leave the island in order to find her own sense of identity?

   _____

   _____

   _____

Challenge Question

Discuss some of the incidents and people in Louise Bradshaw's life which are important in helping her to grow up.

© 1991 J. Weston Walch, Publisher   *100 More Great Books: Synopses, Quizzes, and Tests*

Name_____ Date_____

Davita's Harp by Chaim Potok

Select the letter of the word or phrase which correctly completes each sentence.

_____ 1. Davita's parents moved frequently because (A) they could not pay the rent (B) the neighbors objected to their political meetings (C) the father was in poor health (D) the landlord found out that they were Jewish.

_____ 2. Her father's family (A) was Jewish (B) refused to attend her parents' wedding (C) lived in New York (D) approved of their son's political activities.

_____ 3. The first country Davita became aware of was (A) Germany (B) Russia (C) Spain (D) Ethiopia.

_____ 4. Jakob Daw was (A) very sensitive and gentle (B) a writer (C) a friend of Davita's mother (D) all of the above.

_____ 5. Davita first met David Dinn (A) on the beach near their cottage (B) at school (C) at the synagogue (D) at Ruthie's house.

_____ 6. Davita first visited a synagogue when (A) her mother took her (B) she followed David and his father (C) her father died (D) David had his bar mitzvah.

_____ 7. The symbol of evil in Davita's dreams was (A) the black bird (B) the wild horses (C) Baba Yaga (D) a snake.

_____ 8. The little bird in Jakob Daw's story finally found rest (A) inside the harp (B) in an oak tree (C) on the side of a great mountain (D) in the picture of the horses.

_____ 9. Davita built the sand castle (A) to have something to do (B) to amuse David (C) to protect the beach from evil (D) to show off for Jakob Daw.

_____ 10. Davita's father was killed (A) trying to save a life (B) at Guernica (C) covering a story for his newspaper (D) all of the above.

_____ 11. After Michael's death, Davita's mother tried to (A) commit suicide (B) use party politics to forget (C) return to Poland (D) find her religious faith again.

(continued)

© 1991 J. Weston Walch, Publisher   *100 More Great Books: Synopses, Quizzes, and Tests*

Name_____ Date_____

Davita's Harp by Chaim Potok

_____ 12. Davita defied Jewish custom when she (A) ate with Ruthie's family (B) said Kaddish for her father (C) studied with the boys (D) decided to go to public school.

_____ 13. The event which shattered Davita's world was (A) her brother's death (B) her mother's remarriage (C) Jakob Daw's death (D) the invasion of Poland.

_____ 14. Davita's mother left the Communist party when (A) Germany invaded Russia (B) her husband died (C) she remarried (D) the Communists joined forces with the Fascists.

_____ 15. Annie's marriage to Ezra Dinn results in (A) the establishment of a normal home life (B) the return of Davita's mother to her faith (C) the birth of another child (D) all of the above.

_____ 16. Ruthie contrasts with Davita because she is (A) not Jewish (B) of average intelligence (C) older (D) more beautiful.

_____ 17. Davita's mother returns to the synagogue (A) to say Kaddish for Michael (B) because her new husband insists (C) to write articles about the Jewish faith (D) to pray for her grandfather.

_____ 18. Davita does not receive the top academic award, even though she has the highest average, because (A) her father was not Jewish (B) she is a girl (C) her mother has been a Communist (D) she cheated on an exam.

_____ 19. The greatest influence on Davita's developing imagination was (A) her father (B) her mother (C) Aunt Sarah (D) Jakob Daw.

_____ 20. Davita comes to terms with her anger through (A) a dream about her father (B) telling off the teacher (C) a letter from Aunt Sarah (D) discussing the problem with David.

Name_____ Date_____

Davita's Harp by Chaim Potok

Answer the following questions in two or three complete sentences.

1. How does the reader know that Davita is an extraordinarily sensitive child?

_____

_____

_____

2. Why had both of Davita's parents abandoned their faith?

_____

_____

_____

3. How does the child Teresa become, for Davita, a symbol of the war?

_____

_____

_____

4. How do the stories that Jakob Daw tells fire Davita's imagination?

_____

_____

_____

5. What are Davita's feelings about her new father and her step-brother David?

_____

_____

_____

Challenge Question

Write an essay describing Ilana Davita's growth as presented by Chaim Potok through the plot of *Davita's Harp*.

© 1991 J. Weston Walch, Publisher   *100 More Great Books: Synopses, Quizzes, and Tests*

Name _____ Date_____

Words by Heart by Ouida Sebestyen

Place a T before each true statement and an F before each false statement.

_____   1. Lena beats Tater in the Bible memory contest.

_____   2. Mr. Kelsey expects Lena to win the contest.

_____   3. Lena's father has explained to her the true nature of racial prejudice.

_____   4. The community Lena lives in is almost entirely black.

_____   5. Bullet was shot through the head.

_____   6. Lena leaves school to work for Mrs. Chism.

_____   7. Mrs. Chism is greatly loved by her children.

_____   8. Lena's father warns her that she must not let other people know how intelligent she is.

_____   9. Lena gets Mrs. Chism's permission to borrow some of her books.

_____   10. Claudie is more aware of the realities of life than Lena is.

_____   11. Mr. Haney hates Lena's father because he does better work than Haney does.

_____   12. Lena enjoys having the other children torment Tater at school.

_____   13. All Mrs. Chism's children come when she invites them for dinner.

_____   14. Lena's father agrees to mend Mrs. Chism's fences if Mrs. Chism will lend Lena her books.

_____   15. Claudie goes to look for Pa when he doesn't come home.

_____   16. Lena's father is dead when she finds him.

_____   17. Lena is able to save Tater's life.

_____   18. Claudie decides that the family will move back south.

_____   19. Lena feels no sympathy for the Haney family.

_____   20. At the end of the novel, Haney seems to want to help Lena's family.

© 1991 J. Weston Walch, Publisher

Name_____ · _____ Date_____

Words by Heart by Ouida Sebestyen

Answer the following questions in two or three complete sentences.

1. What events ruin Lena's pleasure in having won the contest?

_____

_____

_____

2. In what ways does Lena show her intelligence and sensitive nature?

_____

_____

_____

3. Why is Claudie afraid for the family?

_____

_____

_____

4. What does Lena learn from working at Mrs. Chism's?

_____

_____

_____

5. Why does Lena's father tell her that she must help Tater?

_____

_____

_____

Challenge Question

Discuss the development of Lena's character. How do the words she has learned from the Bible go to her heart?

Name_____   Date_____

Homecoming by Cynthia Voigt

Place a T before each true statement and an F before each false statement.

_____ 1. The Tillerman children have been living with their father and mother near Provincetown.

_____ 2. Dicey senses that their mother is seriously troubled.

_____ 3. Maybeth is the most talkative of the Tillerman children.

_____ 4. The children wait overnight in the car for their mother to return.

_____ 5. Most of their journey takes place during the spring and summer.

_____ 6. Windy and Stewart are college students in Bridgeport.

_____ 7. Dicey feels that it is all right to steal food and money because the kids are so hungry.

_____ 8. James falls, but is not seriously injured.

_____ 9. Cousin Eunice can't look after the Tillermans because she has three children of her own.

_____ 10. Dicey decides to head for Maryland because she is afraid that her brothers and sister will be separated.

_____ 11. James earns money in Bridgeport by working as a window washer.

_____ 12. Dicey is able to telephone their grandmother when they arrive in Annapolis.

_____ 13. When they cross Chesapeake Bay, Dicey helps to sail the boat.

_____ 14. The circus people turn the children over to the sheriff.

_____ 15. Dicey enjoys traveling with the circus much more than the younger children do.

_____ 16. The Tillermans learn that their mother is dead.

_____ 17. Their grandmother lives on a run-down farm overlooking the water.

_____ 18. Will and Claire come to the farm to see how the children are doing.

_____ 19. Dicey stays with Maybeth while she takes tests for school.

_____ 20. Gram and the children will live and gain courage from each other.

© 1991 J. Weston Walch, Publisher

Name _____ Date _____

Homecoming by Cynthia Voigt

Answer the following questions in two or three complete sentences.

1. List the ages and main characteristics of each Tillerman child.

   _____

   _____

   _____

2. What are some of the greatest obstacles they encounter in their travels?

   _____

   _____

   _____

3. Why does Dicey decide to leave Cousin Eunice and to search for her grandmother?

   _____

   _____

   _____

4. List some of the people who help the Tillermans.

   _____

   _____

   _____

5. Why does Gram at first not want the children to stay with her? Why does she later change her mind?

   _____

   _____

   _____

Challenge Question

Dicey's mother had told her that determination was in her blood. Write a paragraph showing how Dicey's actions in this story show that determination.

© 1991 J. Weston Walch, Publisher

Answer Keys

Winesburg, Ohio by Sherwood Anderson

True or False:

1. F	6. T	11. T	16. T
2. T	7. F	12. F	17. T
3. F	8. F	13. T	18. F
4. F	9. F	14. F	19. F
5. F	10. T	15. F	20. F

Short Answers:

1. Both women married men whom they did not love. Both desired to live a greater life than was possible in Winesburg. Both had sensitive sons with whom the mothers could not communicate.

2. Hartman broke the window to free himself from his passion for Kate Swift. The minister experienced emotional freedom. Jesse Bentley failed to hear the voice of God. The old man could not communicate his vision of reality to his grandson David.

3. Just before Elizabeth died, Reefy gave her the love that restored her youth. Because of released frustration, Elizabeth could welcome death.

4. George's feelings for Helen White are the passions of a young man experiencing first love. Expressing their feelings makes both George and Helen "excited little animals."

5. Wing's hands are the outward expressions of deep feelings that no one understands. Wash Williams resembles an ape because his love has been twisted into hatred.

Challenge Question:

George is the listener. The "grotesques" come to him when they wish to talk. The author frequently uses dramatic irony. The reader of the novel understands what lies behind the words, but George does not. As a newspaperman, George is a neutral observer who does not pass judgment on those who visit him.

George participates as he deals with his own feelings. He struggles with his relationship with his mother and his reaction to her death. He experiences developing sexual awareness in his feelings for Louise Trunion and Helen White. George must in the end leave Winesburg in order to understand both the town and himself.

Midnight Hour Encores by Bruce Brooks

Multiple Choice:

1. C	6. B	11. A	16. A
2. A	7. C	12. D	17. B
3. C	8. C	13. B	18. D
4. A	9. A	14. A	19. D
5. B	10. C	15. D	20. D

Short Answers:

1. Because Connie was immature, wanted to continue to experiment, was not ready for the responsibility of a child.

2. Because literature is the same once it is written. Music can be improvised and changed.

3. Because he had won the same contests she had. Because his playing had such a special quality. She finds his playing on an old record. She learns from a letter from the institute that he is in California.

4. He buys records, travels and camps as the hippies did, takes her to meet people who were involved in the hippie culture.

5. The reader gets the flashbacks—her experiences at the competition, her feelings about music—from her point of view. The reader can go inside Sib's mind, where much of the significant action takes place.

Challenge Question:

Her sensitivity is positive because she can hear music in her head, she plays brilliantly, she has deep feelings, she grows and learns through her experiences. The negative aspects of her sensitivity are her inflated ego and the risk of being hurt. The ego is in part a defense against this hurt.

The Stranger by Albert Camus

True or False:

1. T	6. F	11. F	16. T
2. F	7. T	12. F	17. T
3. F	8. F	13. T	18. F
4. T	9. T	14. F	19. F
5. F	10. F	15. F	20. T

Short Answers:

1. Meursault does not want to see his mother's body. He doesn't even know for certain on what day she died. He sheds no tears. After the funeral, he only wants the physical pleasures of food, sex, and sleep.

2. Meursault writes the letter for Raymond that gets the girl to come back. She is beaten as a result of this visit. When Meursault goes with Raymond to Masson's home on the beach, the Arabs follow them. Raymond gives Meursault the gun when they confront the Arabs. After Raymond is injured, Meursault goes back to the beach carrying Raymond's revolver. When the Arab attacks him, Meursault kills the man.

3. During his mother's funeral, the intense heat affects Meursault's senses. On the beach, the heat is also intense. Response to this heat overwhelms any other feelings that the character has.

   In jail, Meursault remembers the sights and sounds of summer. This sensory experience is much more valid to him than any sense of right and wrong.

4. The police officer uses a crucifix to create in Meursault the guilt of having broken God's law. Meursault feels vexation rather than guilt.

5. The chaplain also tries to make him seek God as he faces death. His response is that everyone must die sometime. Living only for existence, Meursault resists any attempt to link him with the abstract. Death means freedom. All that he asks for at his death is a large crowd of spectators.

Challenge Question:

Meursault is the stranger who observes many scenes in which he does not participate. He watches his mother's funeral but feels no emotional identification with the other mourners. He stands on his balcony and watches others experience life, but never joins them. Even at his trial, he is a man watching his own life. No other person's life touches his. When Marie visits him in prison, she is separated from him by a wide gulf. As they make love, she is an experience for him, not a person.

The Stranger does not relate to anything beyond his own sensory awareness. Meursault is an indifferent person in an indifferent universe.

David Copperfield by Charles Dickens

Matching:

1. K	6. B	11. A	16. F
2. G	7. N	12. H	17. O
3. D	8. R	13. L	18. S
4. P	9. T	14. C	19. E
5. M	10. I	15. Q	20. J

Short Answers:

1. David is abused by the cruel Murdstone. The boys in the warehouse are victims of social cruelty. Mr. Creakle abuses his students and teaches them nothing.

2. Steerforth takes advantage of David at school by taking his money to protect him. Steerforth leads David into drunkenness and bad company. David is also too blind to see Steerforth's seduction of Emily until after the damage has been done.

3. Emily and Martha are led astray by the passions of men. Each girl is blamed by society as if she alone were to blame. Each girl is also eventually redeemed by unselfish love.

4. David loves Dora with boyish passion. His feelings for her never mature. Because Dora is so childish herself, she is never able to help David become a better man. Agnes is his "good star." Her love helps David become a stronger person. Their marriage at the end of the book is the union of two adults.

5. Aunt Betsey gives David his first real home. She refuses to surrender him into Murdstone's clutches. Aunt Betsey gets David started in life by giving him the money to begin his law career. She helps keep David's marriage to Dora on course. She nurses Dora when she is ill. Aunt Betsey also finally helps David realize his feelings for Agnes and pushes him toward a marriage that will last.

Challenge Question:

Dickens's caricatures in *David Copperfield* range from the comic to the devilish. Mr. and Mrs. Micawber are humorous in their constant indebtedness. Simple-minded Mr. Dick personifies goodness. Mrs. Steerforth and Rose Dartle think only of their own feelings and cannot feel any sorrow for others. Mr. Peggotty is the personification of self-sacrificing love. At the other end of the scale are the thoroughly evil Uriah Heep, who has not one positive trait, and the cruel Mr. Murdstone.

Physical descriptions also add to caricature: Traddles's hair that will never stay down, the striking scar on Miss Dartle's face, Heep's constant writhing motions.

Oliver Twist by Charles Dickens

Multiple Choice:

1. B	6. A	11. D	16. D
2. D	7. B	12. A	17. C
3. C	8. C	13. B	18. A
4. A	9. B	14. D	19. C
5. B	10. D	15. C	20. C

Short Answers:

1. Society's cruelty is shown in the treatment of the children and the paupers. Mr. Bumble is the agent of this careless abuse. Ironically, he ends life as a pauper himself.

2. He meets the Artful Dodger on the street. Dodger takes him to Fagin. Monks discovers Oliver's identity by his appearance, and plots to bind the boy to a life of crime.

3. Nancy will not incriminate those with whom she has lived. She will not leave Bill because she loves him.

4. Bumble says that his wife did it all, that he is in no way responsible.

5. Sikes hangs himself when he slips trying to escape. Fagin is sentenced and hanged.

Challenge Question:

Chance encounters include the following:

Old Sally overhears the last words of Oliver's mother.

Oliver meets Dodger, who takes the boy to Fagin.

Oliver is recognized by Monks.

Oliver is helped by a man who knew his family. He is startled by the portrait of his mother.

The house they break into turns out to be the residence of Oliver's aunt.

Oliver happens to run into Monks in the tavern, so that Monks is able to tell Fagin where the child is.

Noah and Charlotte happen to enter the Three Cripples.

Maddy's Song by Margaret Dickson

Multiple Choice:

1. C	6. D	11. C	16. A
2. A	7. A	12. B	17. C
3. A	8. D	13. C	18. B
4. B	9. B	14. A	19. B
5. B	10. A	15. A	20. D

Short Answers:

1. The community sees Jack Dow as the perfect father, husband, and businessman. In reality he is cruel and abusive. This contrast is established in the opening chapter between the way Jack treats his wife and children on Sunday mornings and the way the community perceives the Dow family at church.

2. The two old ladies are lonely. Jonah brings music back into Aunt Bea's life, something that has been missing since her husband died. Jonah gives Aunt Ann someone to cook for and fuss over. Both aunts enjoy being needed.

3. As a boy, Jack was sexually and emotionally abused. Having an unstable mother, Jack was forced to look after his younger brothers and sisters. He never had a home or any respect from others until he killed his family and escaped. Jack Dow's childhood experiences made him an emotional monster who was doubly dangerous because he appeared so normal.

4. Vinnie tried to give Maddy the gift of music and to help her develop her performing and composing gifts. Vinnie failed because she was so crippled and imprisoned by Jack that she could not get away. If Vinnie had not had the courage to teach Maddy, however, she never would have realized the musical gift that finally enabled her to escape to freedom.

5. Jonah helps Maddy by helping her realize how special her talent is, and that she is a worthwhile person. Jonah is the positive influence for Maddy, whereas her father had been a negative one. Teaching Maddy helps Jonah come to terms with his own feelings. He can begin to cope with his work and with his relationship with his wife.

Challenge Question:

The Dow family tragedy includes the entire town, which failed to see reality. Every person suffers guilt because all were too preoccupied to see beneath the surface. Eleanor Hebert's perfect world falls apart when Jack kills Elaine's child. Judy Hebert finds joy in her husband and son. Those surviving realize anew the value of living.

After their parents die, the Dow children are taken in by the whole town. Aunt Bea and Aunt Ann become their guardians, but the entire community opens its heart. Freedom has become a more caring town, but too late to save the innocent.

Silas Marner by George Eliot

Matching:

1. M	6. D	11. R	16. N
2. S	7. T	12. K	17. O
3. A	8. I	13. C	18. L
4. J	9. B	14. F	19. E
5. Q	10. G	15. P	20. H

Short Answers:

1. Silas had been wrongly accused of theft by his friend William Dane. He was cast out from his chapel fellowship. He came to Raveloe to escape all memory of the past.

2. He felt that he would "borrow" the money to pay for the horse that he had destroyed. Dunstan had little or no moral sense. He felt no guilt at stealing the property of another man.

3. With Molly dead and Dunstan gone, Godfrey did not have to face the consequences of his secret marriage to Molly. He was free to court and marry Nancy.

4. Dolly urged Silas to rejoin the community by taking part in the social and religious life of Raveloe. She also helped Silas care for Eppie. Dolly was a substitute mother for the child.

5. Eppie loves Silas. He is the only father she has ever known. She prefers Silas's cottage and the common people she loves to the wealth and privilege of the Cass mansion.

Challenge Question:

After his flight from Lantern Yard, Silas is a complete recluse whose only pleasure is his gold. Eppie brings love back into his life. At first the weaver's focus is solely on the child. Silas first ventures into Raveloe's public life when he goes to the Cass mansion for help after finding Eppie on his hearth. Then he begins to relate to the other members of the community. He goes to church and finds himself able to have faith again in his fellows. With Dolly's help and by visiting Lantern Yard, Silas is able to put the past behind him. At the novel's end, when Eppie marries Aaron, Silas is a healed man.

Them That Glitter and Them That Don't
by Bette Greene

True or False:

1. T	6. F	11. T	16. F
2. F	7. F	12. F	17. T
3. F	8. F	13. T	18. T
4. T	9. T	14. F	19. F
5. T	10. F	15. T	20. F

Short Answers:

1. Carol Ann is an outcast. She lacks the basic necessities of food, clothing, and shelter. No one even knows her real name. Carlotta Dell is a star. She is known by everyone and has enough of everything. Carlotta can provide for the Delaney family all the things that Carol Ann cannot. Carlotta will be accepted by those who have rejected Carol Ann.

2. She loves her parents, but she hates the way they force her to live and the illegal things her mother wants to do. She loves her father but knows that Painter is a weak man who forces his daughter to take the responsibility for the family.

3. Amber pretends to be Carol Ann's friend and then uses Carol Ann to satisfy her sick curiosity about gypsies.

4. Her mother says that the Delaneys need the coffin and need the money. She sees nothing wrong in taking money from those who are gullible enough to fall for their schemes. She rationalizes the desecration of the grave by saying that they buried the body in true gypsy fashion.

5. At graduation, Carol Ann experiences the abandonment of her family. She sees that marriage to Will would be the end of her dreams. Carol Ann decides that she must leave them all and stand on her own.

Challenge Question:

Carol Ann Delaney, from the time she was a baby, learned to fight for her place in the world and to stand on her own feet. Caring for her brother and sister taught Carol Ann responsibility. Amber taught her not to trust everyone who seemed to be a friend. Mrs. McCaffrey taught her that her talent was special and must be used. Will taught her that marriage with the wrong man could be more of a trap than a security. Carol Ann will succeed in Nashville because she has learned these lessons well. Experience has made her a survivor.

A Portrait of the Artist as a Young Man
by James Joyce

Multiple Choice:

1. B	6. C	11. A	16. A
2. D	7. B	12. B	17. C
3. C	8. C	13. C	18. A
4. A	9. A	14. C	19. B
5. A	10. D	15. D	20. D

Short Answers:

1. Stephen is aware of sights, sounds, and smells. He is curious about everything. He senses conflict between the adults in his family. He is highly imaginative and frequently projects the dreams and feelings of others.

2. Charles and Casey take the side of Parnell, the hero of the Irish nationalists. Aunt Dante takes the side of the Irish priesthood, which rejected Parnell because he was an adulterer.

3. When in sin, he feels utterly guilty. Every word in the sermon applies to him. After Stephen receives absolution, he also becomes extremely religious and seeks to serve God completely. He then rejects the church to enter the service of art.

4. Being a priest would give Stephen power, but would destroy his freedom. He cannot give up his individuality.

5. The Virgin Mary is the symbol of his religious adoration. His desire for women becomes the cause of his sin. Woman also becomes the inspiration for his writing.

Challenge Question:

Stephen's love of the mystical and his sensitivity to beauty draw him toward the church. He personalizes everything intensely. This makes both his religious ardor and his love of writing unique to him. Stephen sees himself, the artist, like God the creator. As did his dedication to religion, his dedication to his writing becomes the absolute center of his life.

Carrie by Stephen King

True or False:

1. T	6. F	11. F	16. T
2. F	7. T	12. T	17. F
3. F	8. T	13. F	18. F
4. T	9. F	14. T	19. T
5. T	10. F	15. F	20. F

Short Answers:

1. Carrie was born out of wedlock. Margaret's own guilt makes her view Carrie's coming to puberty as evil. Carrie represents for Margaret the physical evidence of her own sin. She uses her own warped feelings to make her daughter feel guilty.

2. The house was pelted first with pieces of ice. Then huge stones punched holes in the roof. This happened only to the Whites' house.

3. Things had gone too far. Carrie had been abused too often, had been the object of too many practical jokes before the teacher tried to intervene. Miss Desjardin also does not know the abnormality of Carrie's home life.

4. Sue feels guilty for her part in the locker-room episode. Although she lacks the courage to defy Chris openly, Sue sees the good in Carrie and desires to help her.

5. Carrie consciously locks the kids in the school. Her path of destruction through the town, opening gas pumps and destroying buildings, was the result of a force, not unlike an avalanche, which could not be stopped.

Challenge Question:

Carrie develops the strength to defy her mother and go to the prom with Tommy. Part of this strength comes as she practices developing her powers. She refuses her mother's attempts to push her into the closet. Carrie's fighting back makes her mother afraid.

The power Carrie has developed turns destructive as she is completely humiliated. When the other kids laugh at her as she is covered with blood, something inside Carrie breaks and the catastrophe is let loose.

I Will Call It Georgie's Blues

by Suzanne Newton

True or False:

1. F	6. T	11. F	16. F
2. T	7. F	12. F	17. F
3. F	8. F	13. T	18. T
4. T	9. F	14. F	19. F
5. F	10. T	15. F	20. T

Short Answers:

1. Aileen runs away with Pete. She fights her father openly and rebels against his expectations. Neal tries to be the perfect son and stay out of the conflict. He escapes into the world of his music.

2. Neal feels at home with Mrs. T. He can relax and be honest. He can play to his heart's content and forget his family problems for at least a little while. Neal can also talk with Mrs. T. about everything that really matters to him.

3. Aileen and Neal both have a way to escape. Georgie has no way to escape, except into a world of fantasy. He doesn't know how to protect himself against his father's anger.

4. Neal wants his music to be his private means of expression. He doesn't want his father to control his playing or composing.

5. After Georgie's breakdown, Neal dedicates the music that he has written to his little brother. Neal tries to express in music the hurt and confusion that Georgie could find no words for.

Challenge Question:

Neal finds release from his problems in playing the piano. As he works through the process of making his own music, Neal also works on dealing with his family problems. The crisis comes when Neal sees that Georgie can't cope at all. Neal has learned to be his own person. He frees himself when he dares to play in public. The gifts are no longer for himself, but can benefit others. The reader feels that Neal's new freedom will help provide healing for his parents and for Georgie.

Jacob Have I Loved by Katherine Paterson

Multiple Choice:

1. D	6. C	11. A	16. C
2. B	7. C	12. D	17. C
3. B	8. D	13. C	18. D
4. C	9. B	14. C	19. C
5. A	10. A	15. A	20. D

Short Answers:

1. It is a simple community of fishermen, isolated from the mainland, physically beautiful, very humble in its religion and culture, a place where people live very close to the forces of nature.

2. They share a common love of the water. She feels everyone else prefers Caroline.

3. They make more of a fuss over her, remember every detail of her birth, think that everything Caroline does is wonderful, make a great fuss if Caroline is sick.

4. Louise experiences normal adolescent love when she is in the boat with the Captain after the storm. Her jealousy when he marries Auntie Braxton makes her believe she loves him.

5. Cal is no longer there. She cannot be a waterman. Nothing really exists for her, she has no way to use her special talents.

Challenge Question:

Louise matures through her relationship with her father, her first feelings of love, her friendship with Cal, her close relationship with the world of nature, her profession of midwife, her marriage, and the approaching birth of her own child.

Davita's Harp by Chaim Potok

Multiple Choice:

1. B	4. D	7. C	10. D	13. C	16. B	19. D
2. B	5. A	8. A	11. B	14. D	17. A	20. A
3. D	6. B	9. C	12. B	15. D	18. B	

Short Answers:

1. She is able to move in her imagination into pictures, the picture of the horses and later the painting of the massacre at Guernica. She is sensitive to nature. As a narrator she describes the beauty of nature. She senses the feelings of others. She has premonitions through dreams, both of the death of her father and of the death of Jakob Daw.

2. Annie felt abandoned by her father, who left his family and caused his wife and children to be victims of the pogroms in Poland. Michael was embittered by witnessing the mutilation of a mill worker in Oregon.

3. Teresa is the first person Davita meets who has experienced the war personally. She puts herself into Teresa's place.

4. She dreams about the bird and the girl who could no longer gather flowers. Davita's imagination puts her into the settings of Jakob's stories.

5. Mr. Dinn represents security and stability. David is her competition in school. His growth also reflects Davita's own feelings about her maturing body and mind.

Challenge Question:

At the beginning of the novel, Davita is a child. She experiences her surroundings without realizing why things are happening. She learns first from Aunt Sarah and then from Jakob Daw about the meaning of faith. Her curiosity draws her to find out about her parents' experience. The trauma of death—first her father's and then Jakob Daw's—leads her to seek her Jewish heritage by learning to read Hebrew. As she comes to be a teenager, she knows of the evil and injustice in the world. She is prepared to fight these evils by passing on the good to her little sister.

Words by Heart by Ouida Sebestyen

True or False:

1. F	6. T	11. T	16. F
2. F	7. F	12. F	17. T
3. F	8. F	13. F	18. F
4. F	9. F	14. T	19. F
5. F	10. T	15. F	20. T

Short Answers:

1. Lena's pleasure is destroyed because the prize was a boy's, because of the threat of the knife through the bread, and the death of Bullet.

2. They are shown in her ability to memorize, her feelings for the love poetry from the Bible, her love for her father, her desire for books, her sensitivity to Mrs. Chism's needs, her sympathy for Tater when the others torment him.

3. She has experienced violence in the south. She fears that the racial hatred in the community will destroy the family.

4. She learns through the old lady's loneliness without her husband and children, her feeling for the death of the bird, her father's willingness to place his life in danger so that she could have books.

5. Her father can't be saved, but Tater can. Lena must learn the meaning of the words she has memorized.

Challenge Question:

She learns the nature of the hatred her father has sheltered her from. She learns what love is from her father and from Claudie. She learns that hating in return will only hurt her. Her life must give her father's death meaning.

Homecoming by Cynthia Voigt

True or False:

1. F	6. F	11. F	16. F
2. T	7. F	12. F	17. T
3. F	8. T	13. T	18. T
4. F	9. F	14. F	19. F
5. T	10. T	15. F	20. T

Short Answers:

1. Dicey, age thirteen, is mature for her age, able to see the needs of her brothers and sister and to plan for them. Her main desire is to keep her family together. James, age ten, is very intelligent for his age, has a great desire to know the "why" of everything. Maybeth, age seven, is shy and gentle, slow but not mentally handicapped. Sammy, age six, is constantly looking for his mother. His greatest need is for love and security.

2. They face the lack of money for food, the need to find shelter, the danger of walking on busy roads, the difficulty in crossing water, and the fear of those who would harm or separate them.

3. She fears that they will be split up. They need to go to their grandmother so that they can remain a family.

4. Windy and Stewart, the Yale students; Father Joseph, the priest in New Haven; Sergeant Gordo, who finds their mother; Sister Bernice, who wants to help Maybeth; Will and Claire, the circus people.

5. Gram is still lonely and bitter over the deaths of her son and husband. She has built a wall around her feelings, and does not want to care for anyone again. She changes her mind when she realizes that she needs the children and the children need her.

Challenge Question:

Dicey is determined that they will make it. She never gives up. She finds ways to provide in impossible situations. She insists that the others keep going. She is clever in finding ways to get food. She works hard for Cousin Eunice. She stays on at Gram's and continues to work in the hope that Gram will finally accept them.

Unit 3

History in Fiction

Synopses

The Ox-Bow Incident

by Walter Van Tilburg Clark

Random House, New York, 1940.

The Ox-Bow Incident is a story of mob violence in the small western town of Bridger's Wells. The story is told by Art Croft, a cowboy who has just come to town after the spring roundup. As the atmosphere is charged with rumors of cattle rustling, an excited rider brings the news that Kinkaid, one of Drew's ranch hands, has been murdered.

Farnley, the murdered man's buddy, stirs the town to revenge. Although Davies, an elderly store owner, tries to make the men observe due process of law, a lynch mob quickly forms. Tetley, a former Confederate officer, leads the chase into the mountain pass to catch the killers.

In the Ox-Bow, a narrow mountain valley, the men capture three travelers. Although Donald Martin, leader of the three, protests that he and his men know nothing about the killing, Tetley and Farnley insist on a hanging. Davies tries again to stop this injustice, but no one will listen.

Minutes after the victims are killed, the man who was supposedly murdered arrives. Each man in the group then begins to blame Tetley to avoid taking responsibility for the murders. Davies is shattered by his failure to stop the killings. Both Tetley and his son commit suicide.

The Ox-Bow Incident describes how a mob functions. The author also clearly defines the moral responsibility of those who are guilty because they do nothing. Clark has created an excellent portrait of the old West, with an incident which could take place anywhere that human emotions get out of control.

The Robe
by Lloyd C. Douglas

Riverside Press, Cambridge, Massachusetts, 1942.

Marcellus Gallio, an intelligent but unmotivated Roman tribune, offends Gaius, regent of the Emperor Tiberius. As punishment, Marcellus is sent to command the Roman forces at the remote station of Minoa in Palestine. Marcellus is served well by his faithful Greek slave, Demetrius. While on duty in Jerusalem, Marcellus is ordered to officiate at the crucifixion of Jesus.

The tribune wins Christ's robe, but the memory of the events deeply disturbs Marcellus's mind. Diana, the noblewoman who loves him, is able to persuade the Emperor to recall Marcellus from exile. The Gallio family sends their son to Athens, in the hope that rest will restore his mind. Healed by the very robe that he had thought to be cursed, Marcellus returns to Palestine, seeking knowledge of the man he crucified.

Escorted by Justus, a man who had known Jesus, Marcellus travels the country and hears wonderful stories of Jesus's words and miracles. The Christian movement grows as many come to believe that the crucified one still lives. Marcellus finds his personal faith when he sees the faith of the young Greek, Stephanos, and talks with Peter.

Returning to Capri, Marcellus gives his report to the Emperor. He and Diana are reunited temporarily. He flees from the royal barge, and spends time working with the common people. Marcellus shares with them the story of Jesus. As opposition to the Christian cause increases, Demetrius must rescue Diana, who is imprisoned on Capri by the mad emperor Caligula. Rome is now an insane city, where little goodness exists.

Marcellus and Demetrius return to Rome, where Demetrius almost dies but is saved by Peter. After Marcellus and Diana marry, they openly declare their faith and are sentenced to death by Caligula.

The robe, a source of strength, is saved for the Christian community. This novel presents a powerful picture of the early years of the Christian church, and of men and women who risked their lives for their faith.

Drums Along the Mohawk

by Walter D. Edmonds

Little, Brown and Company, Boston, 1936.

Drums Along the Mohawk recounts the American Revolution as fought by the frontier people in the Mohawk Valley of western Massachusetts and New York. The action takes place between 1776 and 1784. The most feared enemies are the savage Indians in the pay of the British. The war becomes very personal as the settlers struggle to save the farms they have carved from the wilderness.

As newlyweds, Gil and Lana Martin clear land in Deerfield. After the farm is destroyed, Gil works for Mrs. McKlennar, who treats the couple like her own children. Other neighbors such as the Weavers, the Realls, and the Demooths must also face personal confrontation with the enemy. The men of the community fight throughout the course of the war: first at Oriskany, later at Onondaga, and finally in sight of their own land.

Courage in this novel has many faces. Mary and John Weaver face separation and death in the first year of their marriage. Mrs. McKlennar makes the Indian raiders save her bed. Blue Back, the noble Indian, saves his white friends from death. Nancy Schuyler finds happiness with an Indian brave. Gil and Lana, whose experiences form the main plot line, have a life together between battles.

Edmonds gives his readers a comprehensive account of a community's struggle for survival. The novel provides an exciting look at an important phase of American history.

The Sun Also Rises

by Ernest Hemingway

Charles Scribner's Sons, New York, 1954.

The Sun Also Rises is the story of American expatriates in France and Spain during the 1920's. These wanderers, called by Gertrude Stein the "lost generation," watch life but never participate in it. Jake Barnes, an American newsman living in Paris, is one of several men attracted to Lady Brett Ashley. All relationships in the novel remain unfulfilled. Robert Cohn, a Jewish writer, follows Brett from Paris to Spain. Michael, who intended to marry Brett, goes bankrupt. Pedro Romero, a young bullfighter, loves Brett, but abandons her. Each quest for a thrill, even to watch bullfighting, comes up empty. The only relief Jake finds from sterility comes on a fishing trip into the Spanish Pyrenees, when he briefly rejoices in nature. Even during the great fiesta, Jake and his friends are spectators, not participants.

The Sun Also Rises is an autobiographical account of the way Hemingway and his friends tried to make sense of life. Each experience provides momentary excitement but never seems to satisfy. Action has no lasting value. The novel dramatizes the hopelessness of people without cultural or spiritual roots, and would make excellent reading for students interested in the America of the 1920's.

Across Five Aprils

by Irene Hunt

Follett Publishing Company, New York, 1964.

Across Five Aprils tells of Jethro Creighton's journey from boyhood to manhood during the Civil War. The family lives close to the border between Illinois and Kentucky. Only nine when the war comes, Jethro watches his brothers choose sides. Bill becomes a Confederate soldier; Tom and John join the Union forces. Jethro becomes the man of the family after his father, Matt, has a heart attack.

Jethro learns to understand the great events that are taking place around him. The boy must also cope with the hostility of the neighbors because Bill has gone South. War becomes very personal when Jethro must decide whether to help his cousin, a deserter. Although he never sees combat, Jethro grows up as he learns the meaning of love, suffering, and sacrifice.

Based on the author's memories of her grandfather, *Across Five Aprils* contains well-drawn characters and beautiful description.

Babbitt

by Sinclair Lewis

Harcourt Brace Jovanovich, New York, 1922.

Babbitt is Sinclair Lewis's ironic condemnation of mindless middle-class America in the 1920's. George Babbitt, real estate broker and model citizen of Floral Heights, lives a perfect nonthinking existence. He is one of the fellows who enthusiastically supports the Booster's Club and the Republican Party. Having no convictions of his own, George Babbitt lets his beliefs be formed by others. While hypocritically preaching honesty, he is not above taking his cut from a shady real estate deal.

George is troubled by a "dream girl" who lures him toward freedom. Babbitt becomes dissatisfied with his ideal life. He is also devastated when his closest friend, Riesling, who can no longer stand the confines of domestic life, goes to prison after shooting his wife.

Finally rebelling against social standards, Babbitt finds his own brand of freedom with the exotic Tanis Judique and her free-thinking "Bunch" of wild associates. Drinking and smoking too much, Babbitt begins to question his own prejudices against labor and liberalism. After refusing to join the bigots of the Good Citizen's League, Babbitt sees his business and his marriage falling apart.

Mrs. Babbitt's attack of appendicitis brings George back to the fold of conformity. He quickly sheds his free-thinking ideals and is again accepted by his associates. As the novel ends, the old Babbitt can only give hearty, if hollow, advice to his son Ted.

Sinclair Lewis uses a great deal of ironic humor to show his readers how shallow the "great man" really is. George F. Babbitt is the model of the complete conformist.

Gone With the Wind

by Margaret Mitchell

The Macmillan Company, New York, 1936.

Gone With the Wind is both a saga of the American Civil War and a character study of Scarlett O'Hara, one of literature's most fascinating women. Scarlett is a manipulator and a survivor, but part of her longs to be a lady like her mother Ellen. Scarlett is dominated by her desire for money and power as well as by an idealistic love for Ashley Wilkes. The one man who knows exactly what she is and admires her for it is Rhett Butler, another opportunist and scoundrel. The action covers ten years of Scarlett's life, between the ages of eighteen and twenty-eight. The period of Southern history is 1860–1870.

Melanie Wilkes, a survivor whose life is guided by a set of standards that Scarlett cannot comprehend, stands in contrast to Scarlett. When Melanie dies at the end of the novel, the South's grandeur dies with her.

Margaret Mitchell has created a fascinating set of characters: Mammy, Aunt Pittypat, Gerald O'Hara, Frank Kennedy. The action includes the siege of Atlanta, Scarlett's personal battle to keep Tara, and the invasion of the South by the Yankees and carpetbaggers. The novel is really the story of what one woman became as she responded to the demands of living.

Gone With the Wind contains a much wider plot line than the famous movie version presented. The reader understands Scarlett better, since the author tells the story primarily through her thoughts and actions. This novel would be a perfect reading assignment for history students.

The Mask of Apollo

by Mary Renault

Random House, New York, 1966.

Set in Greece in the fourth century B.C., *The Mask of Apollo* is told by Nikeratos, a tragic actor during the Golden Age of Greek theater. He finds himself in the eye of a political hurricane as he experiences drama both onstage and off. The inspiration for Niko's life becomes an ancient mask of Apollo, the god of his profession.

Dion, friend and student of the philosopher Plato, attempts to defeat Dionysios, the dictator of Syracuse. He is caught between Plato's image of the ideal society and the practical realities of a corrupt society. After Dion succeeds in driving out the corrupt ruler, he in turn is betrayed and assassinated by one of his own generals.

Niko's own character develops from a child star to one of the great protagonists of the era. The actor also has two loves: his young protegé Thettalos and the girl Axiothea, the female philosopher in a male world.

In *The Mask of Apollo*, Mary Renault has given her readers a wonderful inside look at the Greek theater. Through Niko's eyes, the reader learns how it felt to perform at the great festivals of Delphi and Athens. The actor also finds out that life can be more complex than anything the theater invents. This novel would make excellent outside reading for anyone studying Greek drama.

The Jewel in the Crown

by Paul Scott

William Morrow and Company, New York, 1966.

The Jewel in the Crown is a sweeping novel of India during the last years of British rule. On August 9, 1942, Daphne Manners, an English hospital worker, was raped in the Bibighar Gardens of Mayapore. The subsequent arrest of several young Indian men triggered riots, which were put down by military force. The "Manners affair" widened the gulf between the natives and the British; moreover, reaction fueled the fires of the Indian independence movement.

The Jewel in the Crown is also the tragic personal story of Daphne and her Indian lover Hari Kumar. Educated in England, Kumar was rejected by his boyhood friends and forced into a society which he loathed. Hari became the selected victim of Ronald Merrick, the sadistic chief of police whose proposals Daphne had rejected.

Many characters whose lives were touched by the fires which burned India speak in *The Jewel in the Crown*. Miss Crane was a mission teacher attacked by rioters. Robin White, the British civilian commander, differed with Reid, the military brigadier, on how best to control an explosive situation. Lili Chatterjee was an Indian aristocrat caught between her love for Daphne and her race. Giving each of these characters a voice in the novel, the author presents many aspects of a complex historical period. *The Jewel in the Crown* is an excellent fictional view of a significant era in modern history.

The Gates of Zion

by Bodie Thoene

Bethany House Publishers, Minneapolis, 1986.

The Gates of Zion is a turbulent story set during the birth of Israel. In 1947, when the United Nations votes for the partition of Palestine, Ellie Warne, a young American photographer, finds herself in the middle of the Jewish-Arab conflict. A mysterious scroll brought by two Bedouins involves her in the Jewish resistance movement. Ellie is also confused by her feelings for two men in her life: Moshe, the archaeologist and secret agent; and David, the daring flyer. The enemy is Hassan, the fanatical Arab terrorist, who also has a personal grudge against Moshe.

The sights and sounds of the conflict are vivid as Jerusalem becomes a battleground. Ellie is able to help the cause of the freedom fighters through her pictures for *Life* magazine. She also risks her own life to help Yacov, a Polish boy living with his grandfather in Old Jerusalem. As the supporters of the fanatical Arab Mufti commit horrible acts of terror against innocent civilians, Ellie also must risk her life for her faith.

The Gates of Zion is both a statement of faith and an exciting action story about those who dared to risk everything for their beliefs.

A Connecticut Yankee in King Arthur's Court

by Mark Twain

Penguin Books, New York, 1971.

A Connecticut Yankee in King Arthur's Court is the adventure of Hank Morgan, a nineteenth-century shop foreman, who receives a blow on the head which sends him back to fifth-century Camelot. Hank's Yankee wit saves him from being burned at the stake. The Yankee is established as "Sir Boss," the greatest magician in the kingdom. He outwits Merlin by dynamiting a tower and restoring a magic spring. The king learns to understand the problems of his people when he and Hank travel the land disguised as peasants. Having been sold as slaves, Hank and King Arthur are rescued by Clarence, Hank's clever assistant. Hank directly attacks the prejudices of chivalry; he defeats all Arthur's knights in combat by using a lasso and a revolver. The Yankee marries Sandy, the young lady he has won in combat. Hank tries to modernize England by building railroads and telephone lines. Desiring to establish a republic, Hank feels that the greatest enemies to freedom are the aristocracy and the established Church. The republic dies in one final battle. Technology produces death as multitudes of knights are blown up or electrocuted. Hank is put to sleep by Merlin's magic; this spell will last until Hank awakens in his own time.

A *Connecticut Yankee* contains some of Mark Twain's most bitter social satire. Hereditary institutions, both religious and political, are the enemies of freedom. Twain believes that men are bound by traditions which promote ignorance and stupidity. Even Hank's advanced technology fails when his trained technicians revert to their superstitious training. Although his plot occasionally becomes lost in social and political commentary, Mark Twain's genius in character creation shines through.

Battle Cry

by Leon Uris

Putnam Publishing Group, New York, 1953.

Battle Cry is the author's tribute to the Sixth Division of the United States Marine Corps, otherwise known as "Huxley's Whores." Made up of ordinary men from all levels of American life, the unit played a vital part in the campaign against the Japanese during World War II. While presenting a realistic picture of combat experience, Leon Uris sees war through the total experience of individuals: Mac, the tough sergeant; Danny, whose wife waited at home; Marion, the bookish scholar; Seabags, the farm boy from Iowa. During boot camp in San Diego, the men become a Marine unit. Individual differences help the group work together.

When the unit leaves for field exercises in New Zealand, Major Sam Huxley, the commander, knows that his men must hike, train, and suffer together if they are to survive combat. More difficult than the struggle against the enemy is the conflict with disease, loneliness, and boredom. Huxley builds the men's pride and welds them into a fighting force.

First on Guadalcanal and later in the Gilbert Islands, the men fight and die for their buddies and for their country. Mac describes the tortured march across twenty-five islands to gain a beachhead. The last victory cost many lives, including the life of the commander.

Leon Uris joined the United States Marines when he was seventeen. Based on his personal experience as an enlisted man, *Battle Cry* pictures a war in which the generals may get the credit, but the ordinary soldiers are the heroes.

Queen Dolley

by Dorothy Clarke Wilson

Doubleday, Garden City, New York, 1987.

Queen Dolley is a biographical novel of the life and times of Dolley Madison, great first lady and Washington hostess. Dolley's life spanned the administrations of twelve presidents. However, her loving marriage to fourth President James Madison formed the core of Dolley's life.

Brought up as a Quaker, Dolley was briefly married to John Todd, who died in a fever epidemic. Marrying Madison, who was seventeen years older than she, moved Dolley into the spotlight. First as secretary of state and then as president, Madison helped to shape the infant nation's policies. As the perfect hostess, Dolley herself often helped shape national policy when politicians of opposing opinions were invited to her "drawing rooms."

After they left the White House, the Madisons continued to entertain the world's celebrities at Montpelier, their beautiful Virginia home. After James died, Dolley returned to Washington to become an important figure on the social scene.

Wilson's novel pictures both the public and the personal aspects of "Queen Dolley." While entertaining at great receptions, she also grieved for the wasted life of her son Payne, the child of Dolley's first marriage to John Todd. Bravely remaining at the White House as the British army advanced on Washington, she saved great works of art by cutting them from the frames. Since Dolley and James were unable to have children, Dolley "mothered" a large group of nieces and nephews.

A very readable book, *Queen Dolley* pictures the evolution of American society between 1776 and 1840 as seen through the experiences of a great lady who always lived at the center of activity.

Name _____ Date _____

The Ox-Bow Incident
by Walter Van Tilburg Clark

Select the letter of the word or phrase which correctly completes each sentence.

_____ 1. The story takes place in (A) spring (B) summer (C) fall (D) winter.

_____ 2. Gil and Farnley fight over (A) Rose Mapen (B) buying whiskey (C) the outcome of a poker game (D) stealing a horse.

_____ 3. News of Kinkaid's murder is brought to town by (A) Croft (B) Bartlett (C) Greene (D) Davies.

_____ 4. The man of common sense who tries to prevent the town from becoming a mob is (A) Smith (B) Davies (C) Bartlett (D) Wingpen.

_____ 5. Amigo tells the men that the rustlers have (A) been caught (B) traveled through the pass into the mountains (C) stolen Colonel Tetley's horses (D) crossed the border into Mexico.

_____ 6. Gerald Tetley is (A) a victim of his father's cruelty (B) a hired killer (C) determined that the men will hang (D) one of the rustlers.

_____ 7. Which of the following is *not* a representative of law and order who fails to make the men listen? (A) the storekeeper (B) the minister (C) the judge (D) the sheriff

_____ 8. The chase into the mountains takes about (A) two days (B) two weeks (C) a month (D) three weeks.

_____ 9. Art Croft is wounded by (A) his pal Gil (B) one of the rustlers (C) Gerald Tetley (D) a stray bullet fired by the stagecoach guard.

_____ 10. Gil finds out that Rose Mapen is (A) dead (B) married (C) living in Chicago (D) engaged to one of the rustlers.

_____ 11. The Ox-Bow was (A) a river (B) a wide range for pasturing cattle (C) a deserted mountain meadow (D) a new breed of farm animal.

_____ 12. When the posse caught Martin and his men, they were (A) cleaning their guns (B) eating supper (C) attempting to change the brands on Drew's cattle (D) asleep.

(continued)

© 1991 J. Weston Walch, Publisher   *100 More Great Books: Synopses, Quizzes, and Tests*

Name_____ Date_____

The Ox-Bow Incident
by Walter Van Tilburg Clark

_____ 13. Which of the following was *not* a piece of circumstantial evidence used by the mob to "convict" Martin and his men? (A) no bill of sale for the cattle (B) Kinkaid's gun (C) the testimony of a witness to Kinkaid's death (D) Drew's habit of never selling cattle in the spring

_____ 14. Which of the following men had seen a hanging before? (A) Gil (B) Croft (C) Davies (D) Bartlett

_____ 15. As a last request, Martin asks permission to (A) eat a good meal (B) take a bullet out of his leg (C) write a letter to his wife (D) make out his will.

_____ 16. In a desperate attempt to stop the killing, Davies (A) grabs Farnley's gun (B) shoots Tetley (C) shows Martin's letter to one of the other men (D) cuts the ropes that bind Martin's arms and legs.

_____ 17. Tetley tries to make a man out of his son by forcing Gerald to (A) hang Martin (B) shoot Martin (C) cut down and bury Martin's body (D) drive the stolen cattle back to town.

_____ 18. Martin finally (A) is hanged (B) escapes (C) admits his guilt (D) is shot by Farnley.

_____ 19. The mob learns that they have hanged an innocent man when (A) Greene changes his testimony (B) Kinkaid arrives with the sheriff (C) Davies reads them Martin's letter (D) the Mexican admits that he is the guilty man.

_____ 20. To cover their guilt feelings, the members of the lynch mob (A) leave town (B) get drunk (C) collect money for Martin's widow (D) turn and fight each other.

Name_____ Date_____

The Ox-Bow Incident
by Walter Van Tilburg Clark

Answer the following questions in two or three complete sentences.

1. How does the poker game in the opening chapter prepare the reader for the remainder of the action?

_____

_____

_____

2. What arguments does Davies use in his attempt to prevent the killings?

_____

_____

_____

3. By what circumstantial evidence do the men determine Martin's guilt?

_____

_____

_____

4. How does the author show that Farnley is a violent, irrational man?

_____

_____

_____

5. Is Art Croft, the narrator, a developing character, or is he one who remains unchanged by his experiences?

_____

_____

_____

Challenge Question

Write an essay explaining who, in your opinion, is responsible for the deaths of Martin and his men.

© 1991 J. Weston Walch, Publisher   *100 More Great Books: Synopses, Quizzes, and Tests*

Name _____ Date_____

The Robe by Lloyd C. Douglas

Match each description in Column A with the correct name in Column B.

Column A   **Column B**

_____ 1. Girl loved by Demetrius   A. Peter

_____ 2. Farmer who befriended Marcellus and Diana   B. Miriam

_____ 3. Guided Marcellus on his tour of Palestine   C. Marcellus

_____ 4. Crippled girl with a beautiful voice   D. Kaeso

_____ 5. Aged, insane emperor   E. Arpino

_____ 6. Marcellus's second-in-command at Minoa   F. Paulus

_____ 7. Young man with talent as a sculptor   G. Antony

_____ 8. Faithful Christian steward of the Gallio family   H. Sarpedon

_____ 9. Had his mind restored by touching the robe   I. Theodosia

_____ 10. Was healed by Simon Peter   J. Jonathan

_____ 11. Marcellus's sister   K. Tiberius

_____ 12. Tribune with a grudge against Demetrius   L. Quintus

_____ 13. Small boy who learned generosity by giving away his donkey   M. Justus

_____ 14. Came to share the faith of the man that she loved   N. Stephanos

_____ 15. Insane ruler who made his horse a consul   O. Demetrius

_____ 16. Woman who was healed when she touched Jesus's robe   P. Caligula

_____ 17. Had a vision of Jesus as he died   Q. Marcipor

_____ 18. Was miraculously delivered from prison   R. Lydia

_____ 19. Physician who betrayed Marcellus to the authorities   S. Diana

_____ 20. Community where people's lives were changed by the message   T. Lucia
          of Jesus that Marcellus taught

© 1991 J. Weston Walch, Publisher

Name_____ Date_____

The Robe by Lloyd C. Douglas

Answer the following questions in two or three complete sentences.

1. How was the relationship between the slave Demetrius and his master Marcellus unusual?

_____

_____

_____

2. How was Marcellus first affected by the robe? How was his mind restored?

_____

_____

_____

3. After he met people who had known Jesus, how did Marcellus change?

_____

_____

_____

4. How did Demetrius help Diana to escape from the Emperor?

_____

_____

_____

5. Why did Marcellus and Diana refuse to renounce their faith, even though this refusal cost them their lives?

_____

_____

_____

Challenge Question

In what ways does *The Robe* show the effect Christianity had on the Romans?

© 1991 J. Weston Walch, Publisher   *100 More Great Books: Synopses, Quizzes, and Tests*

Name_____   Date_____

Drums Along the Mohawk by Walter D. Edmonds

Select the letter of the word or phrase which correctly completes each sentence.

_____ 1. The novel begins with (A) Gil's boyhood (B) the battle of Lexington (C) Gil and Lana's wedding (D) the arrival at the farm in Deerfield.

_____ 2. Gil and Lana first see the British agent Caldwell (A) leading a tribe of raiding Indians (B) in the tavern (C) at the trial of John Wolff (D) among the dead bodies on the battlefield.

_____ 3. For Lana, the symbol of home is (A) the peacock feather (B) her mother's silver (C) their marriage certificate (D) a beautifully carved bureau.

_____ 4. When the Indians are on the way to burn Deerfield, the settlers are warned by (A) a bell (B) a cannon (C) John Weaver (D) Blue Back.

_____ 5. For Lana, the most serious consequence of the Deerfield attack is the loss of (A) the peacock feather (B) the house (C) the wheat crop (D) her child.

_____ 6. The person in the novel who is treated most unjustly by the colonial soldiers is (A) Butler (B) Caldwell (C) Wolff (D) Thompson.

_____ 7. Which of these was the only person to be killed and scalped by the Indians? (A) Reall (B) Weaver (C) Bellinger (D) Martin

_____ 8. Mrs. McKlennar did all of the following *except* (A) tend her animals (B) work in the fields (C) sew and cook (D) help to protect her home from invaders.

_____ 9. The officer who gave the militia the best leadership was (A) Herkimer (B) Demooth (C) Arnold (D) Butler.

_____ 10. In order to prevent an attack, the militiamen were ordered to (A) send their families to Boston or New York (B) burn all Indian homes and crops (C) kill large groups of defenseless Indian civilians (D) dynamite the roads which led to the Indian village.

_____ 11. The father of Nancy Schuyler's child was (A) Jurry McLonis (B) Captain Demooth (C) Adam Helmer (D) John Butler.

(continued)

Name_____ Date_____

Drums Along the Mohawk by Walter D. Edmonds

_____ 12. Which of the following women was *least* suited to life on the frontier?
(A) Lana (B) Nancy (C) Mrs. Demooth (D) Emma Weaver

_____ 13. John Weaver really fell in love with Mary Reall when (A) they played
together as children (B) he saw her working in the fields (C) he took her
home to meet his mother (D) he comforted her after her father died.

_____ 14. The frontiersmen were cheated by the government in (A) taxes (B) pay
(C) food rations (D) all of the above.

_____ 15. Gil Martin helped Mary Weaver (A) write a letter to get John's battle pay
(B) build a cabin for herself and her child (C) find John's grave on the battlefield (D) get John's mother settled in a new home.

_____ 16. Adam Helmer excelled as a (A) runner (B) husband (C) farmer (D) horse
tamer.

_____ 17. The settlers tried to make the fort look as though it had more defenders by
(A) putting up straw figures (B) having each man shoot two guns (C) having
the women wear soldiers' coats and hats (D) setting up a smoke screen.

_____ 18. Gil and Lana Martin have how many children? (A) three (B) two (C) five
(D) none

_____ 19. Which officer risks a court-martial to give farmers seed grain for planting?
(A) Demooth (B) Bellinger (C) Herkimer (D) Dayton

_____ 20. At the end of the novel, the Martins are living (A) on Mrs. McKlennar's
farm (B) on their own land in Deerfield (C) in Albany (D) with Mary
Weaver and her child.

© 1991 J. Weston Walch, Publisher

100 More Great Books: Synopses, Quizzes, and Tests

Name _____ Date_____

Drums Along the Mohawk by Walter D. Edmonds

Answer the following questions in two or three complete sentences.

1. Why do the farmers in the Mohawk Valley receive so little help from the American government?

_____

_____

_____

2. How do Mrs. McKlennar and the Martins help each other?

_____

_____

_____

3. How does Blue Back represent the "good Indian" in the novel?

_____

_____

_____

4. Compare the relationship of Gil and Lana with that of Mary and John Weaver.

_____

_____

_____

5. In what ways are Nancy Schuyler and John Wolff both victims of circumstances beyond their control?

_____

_____

_____

Challenge Question

Write an essay discussing how Gilbert and Lana Martin represent the strengths necessary for frontier survival.

© 1991 J. Weston Walch, Publisher

Name_____   Date_____

The Sun Also Rises by Ernest Hemingway

Select the letter of the word or phrase which correctly completes each sentence.

_____ 1. The story is told by (A) Brett (B) an outside narrator (C) Robert Cohn (D) Jake Barnes.

_____ 2. Cohn has been all of the following *except* (A) a Harvard professor (B) married (C) a writer (D) a magazine editor.

_____ 3. Jake can't make love to Brett because (A) he has been injured in the war (B) she is not Catholic (C) he is already married (D) she reminds him of his ex-wife.

_____ 4. The other men dislike Cohn because he is (A) American (B) divorced (C) a writer (D) Jewish.

_____ 5. Jake's companion on the fishing trip to Spain is (A) Robert (B) Bill (C) Michael (D) Harris.

_____ 6. Montoya is (A) a hotel owner (B) a bullfighting fan (C) a friend of Jake's (D) all of the above.

_____ 7. Brett's husband (A) had divorced her (B) was dead (C) had abandoned her for another woman (D) was a member of the British House of Lords.

_____ 8. The only real contact that Jake has with life is (A) on a fishing expedition (B) at the fiesta (C) on the Left Bank in Paris (D) in the hotel room with Brett.

_____ 9. An *aficionado* is (A) a Spanish nobleman (B) a bullfighter (C) a good marksman (D) a fan of bullfights.

_____ 10. During the fiesta, Jake and his companions spend most of their time (A) watching the bullfights (B) quarreling and drinking (C) observing the local Spanish customs (D) praying in the cathedral.

_____ 11. Jake watches the bull run from (A) his balcony (B) the bar (C) inside a car (D) the top of the fight ring.

(continued)

© 1991 J. Weston Walch, Publisher

100 More Great Books: Synopses, Quizzes, and Tests

Name_____ Date_____

The Sun Also Rises by Ernest Hemingway

_____ 12. Hemingway makes the sharpest contrast between (A) Jake and Robert (B) Romero and Belmonte (C) Montoya and Bill (D) the Spanish and the Americans.

_____ 13. Brett reacts to the violence and blood of the bullring with (A) fascination (B) horror (C) ridicule (D) avoidance.

_____ 14. After Romero won the fight, he gave Brett (A) his cape (B) his lance (C) the bull's ear (D) the bull's tail.

_____ 15. Romero is savagely beaten by (A) Bill (B) Michael (C) Jake (D) Robert.

_____ 16. The excitement of the fiesta included all of the following *except* (A) dancing (B) fireworks (C) musical concerts (D) religious pageantry.

_____ 17. Brett runs away with (A) Romero (B) Robert (C) Jake (D) Michael.

_____ 18. After the fiesta, Jake decides to go for some rest to (A) Bayonne (B) San Sebastian (C) Pamplona (D) Madrid.

_____ 19. The attitude of the Americans toward the man who was trampled to death in the bullring was (A) indifference (B) horror (C) sympathy for his family (D) curiosity regarding how the accident happened.

_____ 20. At the end of the novel, Brett intends to (A) go and live with Robert (B) return to her husband's family in England (C) go back to Michael (D) live with Jake as his mistress.

Name_____   Date_____

The Sun Also Rises by Ernest Hemingway

Answer the following questions in two or three complete sentences.

1. In what ways is Jake Barnes a typical expatriate American?

    _____

    _____

    _____

2. Why is Brett Ashley so attractive to any man who meets her?

    _____

    _____

    _____

3. Why are the other men so disgusted with Robert Cohn?

    _____

    _____

    _____

4. Why are bullfights so intriguing to the Americans?

    _____

    _____

    _____

5. As you finish the novel, how do you know that life for Jake and Brett will not really change?

    _____

    _____

    _____

Challenge Question

Write an essay in which you discuss the ways that the characters in *The Sun Also Rises* observe life rather than participate in it.

© 1991 J. Weston Walch, Publisher   *100 More Great Books: Synopses, Quizzes, and Tests*

Name_____   Date_____

Across Five Aprils by Irene Hunt

Place a T before each true statement and an F before each false statement.

_____   1. Jethro was his parents' youngest son.

_____   2. Shad, the schoolteacher, was in love with Jethro's sister Mary.

_____   3. Matt Creighton encouraged his children to get all the education they could.

_____   4. Cousin Wilse Graham strongly believed that slavery should be abolished.

_____   5. The men Jethro heard talking about the war were certain that the North could beat the South in no time.

_____   6. Matt Creighton prevented the men from lynching Travis Burdow.

_____   7. Eb and Tom were both killed in combat.

_____   8. Shad tried to help Jethro and Jenny understand what was happening in the outside world.

_____   9. Ross Milton had been wounded in the War of 1812.

_____   10. Dave Burdow saved Jethro from being injured or killed.

_____   11. Matt Creighton died of a heart attack.

_____   12. Shad was wounded at the Battle of Gettysburg.

_____   13. One of the neighbor's sons brought the news that Bill had been killed in battle.

_____   14. Jethro wrote to President Lincoln for advice on how to help Eb.

_____   15. Men who hated Bill for going South burned the Creightons' house to the ground.

_____   16. Shad's aunt took care of him after he was wounded.

_____   17. Matt and Ellen refused to allow Jenny to make the trip to Washington to marry Shad because they felt their daughter was too young.

_____   18. Ed Turner and the other neighbors helped Jethro to rebuild after the fire.

_____   19. The family never had any news of Bill after he entered the army.

_____   20. Shad and Jenny saw Lincoln in Washington just before the president was assassinated.

Name _____ Date_____

Across Five Aprils by Irene Hunt

Answer the following questions in two or three complete sentences.

1. Why was Bill's departure so difficult for Jethro?

   _____

   _____

   _____

2. How had Matt Creighton saved Dave Burdow's son? How did Dave save Jethro?

   _____

   _____

   _____

3. Why was Shad an important influence in Jethro's life?

   _____

   _____

   _____

4. In what way was Matt's heart attack a turning point for Jethro?

   _____

   _____

   _____

5. How did President Lincoln become very real for Jethro?

   _____

   _____

   _____

Challenge Question

Discuss the character development of Jethro Creighton from ages nine to thirteen. What rapid changes force Jethro to grow up very quickly?

© 1991 J. Weston Walch, Publisher

Name_____ Date_____

Babbitt by Sinclair Lewis

Select the letter of the word or phrase which correctly completes each sentence.

_____   1. Babbitt once wanted to be a (A) doctor (B) minister (C) lawyer (D) baseball pitcher.

_____   2. The organization that Babbitt does *not* belong to is (A) the Union Club (B) the Booster's Club (C) the Athletic Club (D) the Good Citizen's League.

_____   3. The character trait most admired by the people of Floral Heights is (A) intelligence (B) honesty (C) clever conversation (D) conformity.

_____   4. Lewis reveals Babbitt's character by analyzing the contents of his (A) briefcase (B) pockets (C) letter files (D) glove compartment.

_____   5. Babbitt first gains a reputation as a speech maker at (A) his church (B) the Athletic Club (C) the real estate convention (D) the Booster's Club dinner.

_____   6. Babbitt is most hypocritical in his dealings with (A) Stan Graff (B) Henry Thompson (C) Paul Riesling (D) his son Ted.

_____   7. Babbitt first departs from the routine of his life when (A) he gives up smoking (B) he meets Paul in Chicago (C) he goes with Paul to Maine (D) he refuses to join the Good Citizen's League.

_____   8. Paul Riesling tries to escape from his problems by (A) playing the violin (B) having an affair with another woman (C) shooting his wife (D) all of the above.

_____   9. Babbitt has the opportunity to have an affair with Tanis when Mrs. Babbitt is (A) sick (B) in Maine (C) visiting her sick sister (D) involved with the New Thought League.

_____   10. The Babbitts receive a great social snub from (A) Henry Thompson (B) the McKelveys (C) the Littlefields (D) Dr. Drew.

_____   11. Chum Frink's greatest contribution to literature was (A) a book of sonnets (B) an autobiography (C) a collection of magazine advertisements (D) a collection of short stories.

(continued)

© 1991 J. Weston Walch, Publisher

Name _____ Date_____

Babbitt by Sinclair Lewis

_____ 12. The most radical liberal in Zenith was (A) Paul Riesling (B) Seneca Doane (C) Ted Babbitt (D) Mr. Littlefield.

_____ 13. During his "fling" with Tanis and her friends, Babbitt does all of the following *except* (A) buy liquor illegally (B) lie to his wife (C) steal money from his company (D) drink and smoke too much.

_____ 14. Babbitt knows that his friends have rejected him when (A) he begins to lose business accounts (B) his secretary quits (C) people begin to pretend they do not see him (D) all of the above.

_____ 15. Babbitt rebels against the routine of his business life most by (A) having lunch with Tanis (B) meeting Paul secretly in Chicago (C) going to the movies in the daytime (D) refusing to have lunch at the Booster's Club.

_____ 16. Babbitt married his wife because (A) she was a great beauty (B) she was pregnant (C) her father had the money that Babbitt needed for his business (D) his father arranged the marriage.

_____ 17. Babbitt is brought back to the confines of his life when (A) Tanis rejects him (B) his wife becomes ill (C) his business starts to fail (D) Ted gets married.

_____ 18. The author intends the reader to believe that Ted and Eunice's marriage will be (A) happy (B) filled with intellectual conversation (C) opposed by the girl's parents (D) just like the Babbitts' marriage.

_____ 19. George knows that his friends have accepted him again when (A) they visit his wife in the hospital (B) his secretary comes back to work (C) he is allowed to join the Good Citizen's League (D) he is welcomed back into his church.

_____ 20. George Babbitt's most important values are (A) social (B) material (C) spiritual (D) intellectual.

Name_____ Date_____

Babbitt by Sinclair Lewis

Answer the following questions in two or three complete sentences.

1. Why is Babbitt troubled by his "dream girl"?

   _____

   _____

   _____

2. In what ways is Myra Babbitt a carbon copy of her husband?

   _____

   _____

   _____

3. Why is Babbitt's relationship with Paul Riesling so special?

   _____

   _____

   _____

4. How does meeting Tanis change Babbitt's life?

   _____

   _____

   _____

5. Why does Babbitt return completely to the values and opinions his rebellion had caused him to reject?

   _____

   _____

   _____

Challenge Question

Write an essay discussing how Lewis shows us that George Babbitt is a weak man whose actions simply reflect the opinions of others.

© 1991 J. Weston Walch, Publisher

Name _____ Date _____

Gone With the Wind by Margaret Mitchell

Select the letter of the word or phrase which correctly completes each sentence.

_____ 1. The steadying influence on Scarlett while she was growing up was
(A) Gerald (B) Ellen (C) Mammy (D) Ashley.

_____ 2. All of the following men ask to marry Scarlett *except* (A) Rhett (B) Frank
(C) Ashley (D) Charles.

_____ 3. Scarlett's model for morality and ladylike behavior is (A) Mrs. Meade
(C) Aunt Pittypat (C) Ellen (D) Melanie.

_____ 4. Scarlett goes to Atlanta for the first time because (A) she is depressed after
Wade is born (B) she hates Tara (C) she is trying to recover from her mother's
death (D) she wants to visit Melanie.

_____ 5. Atlanta is important to both the Yankees and the Confederates because of
its (A) factories (B) railroads (C) hospitals (D) food supplies.

_____ 6. Scarlett shocks Atlanta society for the first time when (A) she drives alone
to the lumber mill (B) she does business with the carpetbaggers (C) she
dances while she is still in mourning (D) she steals her sister's beau.

_____ 7. Scarlett is most directly responsible for the death of (A) Charles (B) Gerald
(C) Bonnie (D) Frank.

_____ 8. Scarlett believes that the most important thing in life is (A) love (B) money
(C) social reputation (D) land.

_____ 9. When Scarlett visits Rhett in jail, he catches her in the lies that she tells
because of (A) her clothes (B) her hands (C) her shoes (D) the style of
her bonnet.

_____ 10. Scarlett is saved from rape through the intervention of (A) Rhett
(B) Ashley (C) Big Sam (D) Frank.

_____ 11. After she moves to Atlanta, Scarlett trusts the management of Tara to
(A) Pork (B) Will (C) her father (D) Ashley.

(continued)

© 1991 J. Weston Walch, Publisher   *100 More Great Books: Synopses, Quizzes, and Tests*

Name_____   Date_____

Gone With the Wind by Margaret Mitchell

_____ 12. The woman who becomes Scarlett's enemy when she learns the truth about Scarlett and Ashley is (A) Mrs. Meade (B) Aunt Pittypat (C) India Wilkes (D) Melanie.

_____ 13. The "good" character in an unrespectable profession is (A) Frank (B) Belle (C) Johnny Gallagher (D) Mrs. Merriwether.

_____ 14. Rhett asks Scarlett to marry him (A) for fun (B) right after Charles dies (C) on the road from Atlanta to Tara (D) right after Atlanta falls to the Yankees.

_____ 15. After Bonnie's death, Rhett is helped in his grief by (A) Melanie (B) Ashley (C) Mammy (D) Belle.

_____ 16. Whenever Scarlett faces any difficulty, she (A) drinks (B) puts off thinking about it (C) goes home to Tara (D) asks Mammy for advice.

_____ 17. Rhett is determined to get back into the Old Guard of Atlanta society for the sake of (A) his daughter (B) his wife (C) his reputation (D) his business.

_____ 18. Scarlett O'Hara's most outstanding character trait is her (A) intelligence (B) determination (C) sense of proper behavior (D) love of fun.

_____ 19. Probably the weakest of the main characters in the novel is (A) Ashley (B) Frank (C) Charles (D) Archie.

_____ 20. The title of the novel refers to (A) the death of Ellen (B) the death of the South (C) the collapse of Tara (D) the siege of Atlanta.

© 1991 J. Weston Walch, Publisher   *100 More Great Books: Synopses, Quizzes, and Tests*

Name_____ Date_____

Gone With the Wind by Margaret Mitchell

Answer the following questions in two or three complete sentences.

1. Why are Rhett Butler and Scarlett a perfect match?

_____

_____

_____

2. How does her return to Tara after the burning of Atlanta change Scarlett's personality?

_____

_____

_____

3. In what ways does Scarlett's behavior after the war shock Atlanta society?

_____

_____

_____

4. Why is Bonnie's death one of the most senseless tragedies of the novel?

_____

_____

_____

5. How are Gerald O'Hara and Miss Pittypat Hamilton both symbols of a civilization that is gone?

_____

_____

_____

Challenge Question

Write an essay defending the following statement: "Even though Scarlett O'Hara is the heroine of the novel, Melanie Wilkes represents the moral and social creed that the author values."

Name_____   Date_____

The Mask of Apollo by Mary Renault

Match each description in Column A with the correct name in Column B.

Column A   **Column B**

_____ 1. First woman to enter Plato's Academy   A. Myrmidons

_____ 2. Military stronghold of the dictators of Syracuse   B. Kallippos

_____ 3. First stage role Niko played as a child   C. Lenaia

_____ 4. Failed in his attempt to be both philosopher and general   D. Astyanax

_____ 5. Wrote a philosophical book describing the ideal state   E. Philistos

_____ 6. General who was the real power behind the weak, corrupt   F. Thettalos
        Dionysios
                                                                                                       G. Dion
_____ 7. Good actor who worked with Niko playing the second roles
        in Syracuse   H. Priam

_____ 8. Play presented in Delphi when Niko wore the mask of Apollo   I. Rupilius

_____ 9. Role for which Niko won his first acting prize as a leading man J. Ortygia

_____ 10. Young actor taught and trained by Niko   K. Menekrates

_____ 11. Ruler who also wrote plays   L. Alexander

_____ 12. Great drama festival held every year in Athens   M. Axiothea

_____ 13. Dion's killer   N. Herakleider

_____ 14. Roman officer who became Niko's friend   O. Theodoros

_____ 15. Led the people of Syracuse in civil war against Dion   P. Plato

_____ 16. Plato's nephew and assistant   Q. Corinth

_____ 17. Future ruler who visited Niko after a performance   R. Dionysios

_____ 18. Fellow actor and friend   S. Archon

_____ 19. Home of many exiles from Syracuse   T. Speusippos

_____ 20. Title used by the dictator princes of the Greek city-states

© 1991 J. Weston Walch, Publisher   *100 More Great Books: Synopses, Quizzes, and Tests*

Name_____ Date_____

The Mask of Apollo by Mary Renault

Answer the following questions in two or three complete sentences.

1. How did the mask make Niko the servant of Apollo?

_____

_____

_____

2. By what steps did Niko advance in the theater?

_____

_____

_____

3. Why did Plato try to censor the theater?

_____

_____

_____

4. How did Philistos try to trick the actors and ridicule Dion?

_____

_____

_____

5. Why did Dion's plans for Syracuse fail?

_____

_____

_____

Challenge Question

Write an essay discussing how Niko's character developed, both as an actor and as a man.

© 1991 J. Weston Walch, Publisher   *100 More Great Books: Synopses, Quizzes, and Tests*

Name_____ Date_____

The Jewel in the Crown by Paul Scott

Match each description in Column A with the correct name in Column B.

Column A

Column B

_____ 1. Indian schoolteacher killed by the rioters

A. Sister Ludmilla

_____ 2. Founded a college to educate young Indians

B. Reid

_____ 3. Refused Hari Kumar the funds necessary for him to go to college

C. Robin White

D. MacGregor House

_____ 4. Cared for India's outcasts and dying

E. Hari Kumar

_____ 5. Mayapore club for whites only

F. Colin Lindsay

_____ 6. Lush park in the center of Mayapore

G. Chadhuri

_____ 7. Where Daphne lived with Lili Chatterjee

H. Roland Merrick

_____ 8. Decided to use military troops against the native population during the riots

I. Poulson

J. Gymkhana

_____ 9. Hari's boyhood friend, who later rejected him

K. Sir Nello Chatterjee

_____ 10. Tortured Hari as a means of striking back at Daphne

L. Shalini

_____ 11. Opposed the arrest of Indian leaders under the Defense of India Act

M. Gupta Sen

N. Lili

_____ 12. Became a mission teacher as a way of giving her own life meaning

O. Daphne

P. Anna Klaus

_____ 13. Doctor who examined Daphne after she was attacked

Q. Maiden

_____ 14. Garden built by an Indian prince for his mistress

R. Vidyasagar

_____ 15. Close friend of Lady Manners, also Daphne's substitute mother

S. Bibighar

_____ 16. Could not get a good job because he was "too English"

T. Miss Crane

_____ 17. British official who questioned Daphne after she was attacked

_____ 18. Wanted to visit a Hindu temple

_____ 19. Hari's aunt, who gave him a place to live after his return from England

_____ 20. Young Indian arrested for printing and distributing anti-government literature

© 1991 J. Weston Walch, Publisher

Name_____ Date_____

The Jewel in the Crown by Paul Scott

Answer the following questions in two or three complete sentences.

1. Explain whether Edwina Crane succeeded or failed in her work as a teacher.

   _____

   _____

   _____

2. Why was life difficult for Hari Kumar after his return to India?

   _____

   _____

   _____

3. How were Merrick and Kumar character foils in their relationships with Daphne?

   _____

   _____

   _____

4. What examples of British prejudice against the Indians are shown in *The Jewel in the Crown?*

   _____

   _____

   _____

5. How does the reader learn what really happened to Daphne Manners?

   _____

   _____

   _____

Challenge Question

Write an essay showing how the author of *The Jewel in the Crown* presents many different points of view of the events in his narrative. How does each narrator provide a new slant on the basic plot outline?

© 1991 J. Weston Walch, Publisher

Name_____   Date_____

The Gates of Zion by Bodie Thoene

Match each description in Column A with the correct name in Column B.

Column A   **Column B**

_____ 1. Faithful Arab housekeeper who was a victim of terrorism   A. Mufti

_____ 2. Got a contract with *Life* magazine   B. Judith

_____ 3. Had stayed alive, but had lost her self-respect   C. Ellie

_____ 4. Negotiated to buy German planes for the Israeli Air Force   D. Ben Yehuda

_____ 5. Israeli leader known as "The Old Man"   E. Michael

_____ 6. Had been an ally of Hitler during World War II   F. Haganah

_____ 7. Rabbi who was a traitor to his own people   G. Rebbe Akiva

_____ 8. Used his work as an archaeologist as a cover for defense activities   H. Ehud

_____ 9. British officer who wanted to help the Jews   I. Rachel

_____ 10. Lost an eye trying to save Ellie's life   J. Jihad

_____ 11. Killed Hassan   K. Ben Gurion

_____ 12. Was almost killed when he went back to retrieve the precious   L. David
           scrolls
                                                                                      M. Miriam
_____ 13. Jerusalem's luxury hotel
                                                                                      N. Yacov
_____ 14. Brave pilot and Ellie's American boyfriend
                                                                                      O. Rebbe Lebowitz
_____ 15. Grandfather of Yacov and Rachel
                                                                                      P. Howard
_____ 16. War cry of the Arab terrorists
                                                                                      Q. Moshe
_____ 17. Courageous boat owner who smuggled many Jews into Palestine
                                                                                      R. King David
_____ 18. Street where many innocent Jewish civilians were the victims of
           Arab terrorism   S. Shaul

_____ 19. Underground Jewish defense organization   T. Luke Thomas

_____ 20. Code name for smuggling weapons into the Old City

© 1991 J. Weston Walch, Publisher

Name_____   Date_____

The Gates of Zion by Bodie Thoene

Answer the following questions in two or three complete sentences.

1. What are Ellie's feelings about the scrolls when she first sees them? What does she later learn about the importance of these ancient writings?

_____

_____

_____

2. Describe Hassan's attitude toward all Jews. Why does he hate Moshe in particular?

_____

_____

_____

3. How does Miriam become an innocent victim of terrorist warfare?

_____

_____

_____

4. By what daring trick do Ellie and David save Moshe and Howard?

_____

_____

_____

5. How is Rachel reunited with her family?

_____

_____

_____

Challenge Question

Write an essay explaining how Ellie changes from an indifferent observer to an active participant in the Jewish struggle for a free Israel.

© 1991 J. Weston Walch, Publisher   *100 More Great Books: Synopses, Quizzes, and Tests*

Name _____ Date_____

A Connecticut Yankee in King Arthur's Court
by Mark Twain

Select the letter of the word or phrase which correctly completes each sentence.

_____ 1. Twain tells the reader that the source of this story is (A) an ancient manuscript (B) an old man that he met at Warwick Castle (C) Twain's personal experience (D) Malory's *Le Morte d'Arthur*.

_____ 2. The first person Hank met in Camelot was (A) Sandy (B) Merlin (C) King Arthur (D) Sir Kay.

_____ 3. Hank was saved from being burned at the stake by his knowledge of (A) electricity (B) astronomy (C) firearms (D) ancient history.

_____ 4. Clarence is (A) a page at Arthur's court (B) willing to help Hank modernize the nation (C) a bright young man who learns quickly (D) all of the above.

_____ 5. Hank travels with Sandy (A) to help a maiden in distress (B) on a diplomatic mission for Arthur (C) to carry a message to Queen Guinevere (D) to defeat Merlin's magic power.

_____ 6. Hank receives the title of (A) Prime Minister (B) Chief Magician (C) Sir Boss (D) Master of the Treasury.

_____ 7. The condition of the average Englishman in the fifth century that Hank finds most appalling is (A) ignorance and superstition (B) excessive religious zeal (C) poverty (D) starvation.

_____ 8. The greatest practical joker at the court of Camelot is (A) Sir Kay (B) Sir Dinaden (C) Sir Launcelot (D) Sir Gareth.

_____ 9. Hank finds his suit of armor (A) very practical (B) a good defense against his enemies (C) very hot and uncomfortable (D) very tight.

_____ 10. The inhabitants of Sandy's "enchanted castle" are really (A) enemy knights (B) pigs (C) peasants in disguise (D) secret agents of Merlin.

_____ 11. Hank believes that the greatest enemy to progress in Camelot is (A) King Arthur (B) Merlin (C) the French (D) the Church.

(continued)

© 1991 J. Weston Walch, Publisher

100 More Great Books: Synopses, Quizzes, and Tests

Name_____   Date_____

A Connecticut Yankee in King Arthur's Court
by Mark Twain

_____ 12. The woman who best represents the evils of chivalry is (A) Sandy (B) Morgan le Fay (C) Guinevere (D) Lady Lawrence.

_____ 13. Hank's greatest victory over Merlin is (A) building a railroad (B) winning the king's confidence (C) making the sacred fountain in the Valley of Holiness flow again (D) abolishing slavery.

_____ 14. Hank's proudest accomplishment is his (A) banking system (B) military college (C) telegraph (D) newspaper.

_____ 15. When Hank tries to disguise King Arthur as a peasant, he has the greatest difficulty with his majesty's (A) posture and attitudes (B) accent (C) clothing (D) hair style.

_____ 16. When he is sold as a slave, King Arthur is most angry about (A) the weight of his chains (B) the price that he brought (C) the brutality of the slave master (D) being thrown into prison.

_____ 17. Arthur and Hank are saved by (A) knights on bicycles (B) Sir Launcelot (C) Clarence's cleverness (D) all of the above.

_____ 18. Hank defeats all the knights in the tournament by using (A) dynamite (B) a lasso and a pistol (C) a new kind of armor (D) electrical wiring.

_____ 19. At the end of the novel, King Arthur (A) makes Hank his successor as king (B) orders Hank executed (C) dies in a civil war (D) comes back with Hank to the nineteenth century.

_____ 20. The real victor at the Battle of the Sand Belt is (A) Hank (B) Merlin (C) Mordred (D) fifth-century superstition.

© 1991 J. Weston Walch, Publisher

100 More Great Books: Synopses, Quizzes, and Tests

Name _____   Date_____

A Connecticut Yankee in King Arthur's Court
by Mark Twain

Answer the following questions in two or three complete sentences.

1. How does Mark Twain explain the source of his story?

   _____

   _____

   _____

2. What character traits made Hank Morgan a natural for success in Camelot?

   _____

   _____

   _____

3. How does Hank try to improve the condition of the average Englishman?

   _____

   _____

   _____

4. What does King Arthur learn when he travels through England disguised as a peasant?

   _____

   _____

   _____

5. How does the power of the Church destroy the progress that Hank has brought to the English people?

   _____

   _____

   _____

Challenge Question

A *Connecticut Yankee in King Arthur's Court* is a social satire. Write an essay discussing how Twain pictures, in fifth-century Camelot, the evils that he saw in nineteeth-century America.

Name _____ Date _____

Battle Cry by Leon Uris

Select the letter of the word or phrase which correctly completes each sentence.

_____ 1. The battle sequences in the novel are seen primarily from the viewpoint of (A) Huxley (B) Mac (C) Danny (D) General Phillips.

_____ 2. The story begins (A) in 1940 (B) near the end of the Pacific campaign (C) right after Pearl Harbor (D) with a brief summary of Marine history.

_____ 3. The novel includes the love stories of all of the following *except* (A) Mac (B) Danny (C) Andy (D) Marion.

_____ 4. The company spotlighted in the story worked in (A) heavy artillery (B) supplies (C) communications (D) aviation.

_____ 5. The main purpose of boot camp was to (A) test the men's physical strength (B) make them into a fighting unit (C) see which men would break psychologically (D) teach each man how to use a rifle.

_____ 6. When he returned home on furlough, Danny (A) told Kathy he no longer loved her (B) felt that joining the Marines had been a bad mistake (C) could no longer communicate with his father (D) got married.

_____ 7. The strangest relationship in the unit was between (A) Mac and Seabags (B) Danny and Norton (C) Marion and Joe (D) Seeway and Levin.

_____ 8. Pedro joined the Marines to get (A) money (B) medical training (C) away from his wife (D) experience in hand-to-hand combat.

_____ 9. The division saw its first real combat experience on (A) Guam (B) Wake Island (C) Midway (D) Guadalcanal.

_____ 10. All the following men had wives who were faithful to them *except* (A) Zvonski (B) Danny (C) Marion (D) Huxley.

_____ 11. The citizens of New Zealand were glad to see the Marines because (A) their own men were away fighting in the Middle East (B) they feared the Japanese threat from the North (C) they found the American men generally friendly (D) all of the above.

(continued)

© 1991 J. Weston Walch, Publisher

100 More Great Books: Synopses, Quizzes, and Tests

Name _____ Date_____

Battle Cry by Leon Uris

_____ 12. The bloodiest combat in the novel occurred on an island nicknamed (A) Cora (B) Sarah (C) Helen (D) Betty.

_____ 13. Huxley's men were angry because (A) they were always part of the mopping-up operation (B) they had to march so many miles (C) their supplies did not arrive on time (D) they felt that their commanders were cowards.

_____ 14. A fine example of loyalty in *Battle Cry* is (A) Bryce (B) Shapiro (C) Ziltch (D) Peterson.

_____ 15. On their march through the islands, the Marines were helped by all of the following *except* (A) the natives (B) severe rainstorms (C) nuns who acted as nurses (D) landing craft that brought them supplies.

_____ 16. Which of the following men was *not* part of the original boot camp group? (A) Danny (B) Ski (C) Levin (D) L. Q. Jones

_____ 17. Huxley told his wife not to come to Hawaii because (A) he would not take the comfort that he could not give to his men (B) he feared for her safety (C) his orders said that no women could be on the islands (D) he had fallen in love with someone else.

_____ 18. The only man who broke under the psychological pressure of combat was (A) Levin (B) Bryce (C) Seeway (D) Pedro.

_____ 19. Which of the following men came back alive? (A) Danny (B) Pedro (C) Norton (D) Marion

_____ 20. At the end of the novel, Mac (A) decided to retire (B) visited the widows of the men who have died (C) got married (D) was transferred to the European field of action.

Name_____ Date_____

Battle Cry by Leon Uris

Answer the following questions in two or three complete sentences.

1. How do the men change during their time in boot camp?

_____

_____

_____

2. What methods does Huxley use to transform his men into a crack fighting unit?

_____

_____

_____

3. Why does Andy feel that he has "come home" when he visits the Rogers' farm in New Zealand?

_____

_____

_____

4. How do the women who love Marines suffer while their men are away in combat?

_____

_____

_____

5. How does Levin prove his loyalty to the group?

_____

_____

_____

Challenge Question

Write an essay showing how the Marine experience described in *Battle Cry* minimizes individual differences, breaks down prejudices, and makes ordinary men become "larger than life."

© 1991 J. Weston Walch, Publisher   *100 More Great Books: Synopses, Quizzes, and Tests*

Name_____ Date_____

Queen Dolley by Dorothy Clarke Wilson

Match each description in Column A with the correct name in Column B.

Column A

_____ 1. Dolley's spoiled, negligent son by her first marriage

_____ 2. Friend whom Dolley appointed as guardian of her fatherless child

_____ 3. First president for whom Dolley acted as White House hostess

_____ 4. Sister who became the daughter Dolley did not have

_____ 5. Dolley's first husband

_____ 6. Designer who helped Mrs. Madison refurnish the White House

_____ 7. French chef and faithful servant who helped Dolley pack the White House silver when word came of an impending attack

_____ 8. Madison's black valet

_____ 9. Madison's Secretary of State and his successor in the White House

_____ 10. Plantation, once owned by Patrick Henry, where Dolley lived as a child

_____ 11. Dolley's sister, who married a nephew of George Washington

_____ 12. President when Dolley Madison died

_____ 13. First met Dolley when she raced a horse against him

_____ 14. Portrait painter whose work was saved from being burned by the British

_____ 15. Madison's beloved farm in Virginia

_____ 16. Controversial Spanish ambassador who married one of Dolley's close friends

_____ 17. Friend whose journals provide the greatest insights into the Madisons' personal lives

_____ 18. Jefferson's Virginia home, where the Madisons visited each year

_____ 19. British minister's wife who was angered by the lack of formal protocol at the White House

_____ 20. Where the Madisons lived on their return to Washington after the British burned the White House

Column B

A. Sioussat

B. Gilbert Stuart

C. Latrobe

D. Marquis d'Yrujo

E. John Todd

F. Montpelier

G. Lucy

H. Paul Jennings

I. Payne Todd

J. Octagon

K. Scotchtown

L. Anna Payne Cutts

M. James Madison

N. Aaron Burr

O. Monticello

P. Jefferson

Q. Merry

R. Zachary Taylor

S. Margaret Smith

T. James Monroe

© 1991 J. Weston Walch, Publisher

Name _____ Date_____

Queen Dolley by Dorothy Clarke Wilson

Answer the following questions in two or three complete sentences.

1. How was Dolley influenced by her Quaker upbringing?

   _____

   _____

   _____

2. In what ways did Dolley influence political events?

   _____

   _____

   _____

3. How did Dolley's "style" as a hostess differ from that of Martha Washington?

   _____

   _____

   _____

4. What personal griefs did the Madisons suffer during their years of public life?

   _____

   _____

   _____

5. What interests kept Dolley actively involved in life after James Madison's death?

   _____

   _____

   _____

Challenge Question

Write an essay contrasting Dolley Madison the public figure and hostess with Dolley Madison the private woman. How did these aspects of her personality complement each other?

© 1991 J. Weston Walch, Publisher

Answer Keys

The Ox-Bow Incident by Walter Van Tilburg Clark

Multiple Choice:

1. A	6. A	11. C	16. C
2. C	7. D	12. D	17. A
3. C	8. A	13. C	18. D
4. B	9. D	14. A	19. B
5. B	10. B	15. C	20. C

Short Answers:

1. The reader sees the tension in the town as the fight erupts between Gil and Farnley. These cowboys have been penned up all winter and are ready for action. Farnley is also shown as a violent man who will fight with little or no provocation.

2. Davies tries to make the men stop and think before they become killers. He urges them to act within the law and not to become a mob. When the chase begins, Davies goes with them in the hopes of preventing a killing. At the end of the novel, Davies feels guilty because he did not have courage enough to grab one of the guns and prevent the hanging.

3. The land that Martin claims to have bought has been settled by someone else. His Mexican companion has Kinkaid's gun. Martin has no bill of sale to prove that the cattle with Drew's brand have actually been sold to him.

4. Farnley is violent in the poker game. Gil remembers how Farnley attacked a steer that had killed his pony. Farnley urges the mob to violence. He will not listen to any kind of logic or wait for any evidence.

5. Croft is a passive participant in the action. The injustice that he sees bothers him, but he lacks the courage to face the other men and avert the tragic consequences. As Davies confesses his feelings of guilt, Croft becomes a neutral listener. At the end of the novel, Croft and Gil prepare to return to their jobs. Both have changed little through what they have experienced.

Challenge Question:

Some of the men sin through direct action. Farnley and Tetley bear the most direct responsibility. Farnley incites the mob. Tetley leads it because he enjoys the power of command. Tetley really loses the most in the long run. He kills himself after his son commits suicide.

Smith and Barlett are responsible for stirring the mob with speeches. Each man enjoys being prominent and having influence over others. These are little men who suddenly have big roles in the eyes of their peers.

Many are responsible by omission, by what they do not do. Gerald Tetley says that they are weak men because they fail to face the passions of the mob and stop the killings of the innocent. Art Croft is an example of this type of character. Davies talks to the men, but lacks the courage to use a gun to enforce his words. Those really guilty in this novel are the ones who let their feelings get out of hand, and the neutral ones who see injustice and do nothing.

The Robe by Lloyd C. Douglas

Matching:

1. I	6. F	11. T	16. R
2. D	7. G	12. L	17. N
3. M	8. Q	13. J	18. A
4. B	9. C	14. S	19. H
5. K	10. O	15. P	20. E

Short Answers:

1. A friendship grew between the two men. Demetrius cared for his master. They risked their lives for each other. They later came to share their faith.

2. He put the robe on at the banquet, and was driven to depression by the memories of the Crucifixion. His mind was healed when he touched the robe in Athens. After his conversion, the robe became a symbol of strength and faith.

3. From a skeptic with no belief and no direction, he became a man of deep faith who gave hope to others.

4. He disguised her as a boy, took her in a boat to land, and hid her at the villa of Kaeso.

5. They believed in a greater kingdom. They left a corrupt Roman world for real life with Jesus.

Challenge Question:

Marcellus, the military man, becomes the man of peace. The people of a small village learn the value of working together. Diana and Marcellus find mutual love with their faith. Demetrius finds his freedom, even though he remains a slave. Characters to whom physical things were most important find spiritual wealth of greater value.

Drums Along the Mohawk by Walter D. Edmonds

Multiple Choice:

1. C	5. D	9. A	13. D	17. C
2. B	6. C	10. B	14. D	18. A
3. A	7. A	11. A	15. C	19. B
4. D	8. C	12. C	16. A	20. B

Short Answers:

1. The people are far from the center of the war. The men of the regular army do not understand the Indian menace and are incompetent in fighting them. Overall, the Continental Congress felt that the people of the Mohawk Valley should be able to take care of themselves.

2. Mrs. McKlennar gives the Martins a home and land to farm after their property in Deerfield is destroyed. The Martins give her a family to care for. Her loving is symbolized best by the present of the cradle when Lana's first son is born.

3. Blue Back is much more civilized in his behavior than many of the white men. He saves the lives of the Deerfield residents by warning them that the attack is coming. He also acts as a guide for the militia on several expeditions. The Indian is also presented as a loving husband. Blue Back's characterization saves the novel from the danger of stereotyping, which presents all Indians as evil.

4. Despite all their separations and struggles, Gil and Lana survive the war and have a life together. John and Mary never get a chance to live. John is killed in battle and never sees his child.

5. Nancy is farmed out for money by her mother. She is used physically by the father of her child. She is abused by Mrs. Demooth. Ironically, Nancy finds tenderness and stability only from an Indian. John Wolff is railroaded to prison because the community needs to find expression for its anti-Tory feelings. He is only guilty of an independent spirit which wants to be left alone.

Challenge Question:

Gil and Lana are able to keep going in the hardest times. Their relationship is severely shaken when Lana loses their first child. However, Lana realizes her love for Gil when he goes off to war.

Coping means adapting to whatever happens. Lana is able to live through harsh winters, times of siege in the fort, and Indian attacks. Through their love for each other, Lana and Gil grow to face the times. Mrs. McKlennar is a key factor in that growth. After the Martins' farm is destroyed, the widow gives Lana and Gil something to hope and work for again. Mrs. McKlennar also becomes the grandmother the Martins' children don't have.

The peacock feather is the symbol of home for the Martins. When Blue Back returns the feather, it, like Gil and Lana, is battered but still whole.

The Sun Also Rises by Ernest Hemingway

Multiple Choice:

1. D	6. D	11. A	16. C
2. A	7. B	12. B	17. A
3. A	8. A	13. A	18. B
4. D	9. D	14. C	19. A
5. B	10. B	15. D	20. C

Short Answers:

1. Barnes has no roots or family obligations. He is an American living in Paris. Drinking is a primary means of escape. Jake and his friends are thrill seekers who travel from one excitement to another looking for relief from boredom.

2. An aristocrat, Brett knows how to lure men with her laughter and her eyes. They follow her like puppies. Whenever there is a party, Brett is the center of it. She gives a sense of life, even to the most sterile environment.

3. Cohn is too "nice." The others feel that he is weak. It seems unmasculine when he follows Brett because he is so completely captivated by her. Several of the characters also have an anti-Semitic strain and dislike Cohn because he is Jewish.

4. Jake and his friends are fascinated by the violence and the danger. Bullfights have a vitality which is lacking in the expatriates' lives.

5. Life continues on the same cycle. Brett is returning to Michael, the bankrupt. Jake continues to drink to shut out the life that he cannot bear. Madrid becomes just another curiosity. Each character remains in a rut. None has learned anything.

Challenge Question:

The people in this novel watch, but rarely act. Jake can pick up a woman in a café, but he cannot make love to her. Brett goes from one man to another without establishing a single meaningful relationship. Mike, who values only money, is bankrupt. Although the men travel a great deal, each place blurs into the next and none has any real significance. During the fiesta, they watch the pleasure of the peasants from a distance. Entering cathedrals, they cannot pray. These expatriates are "a small island of onlookers." In reality, life for them is like the emptiness of the town square when the fiesta is over. They continue to drink in an attempt to fill the void.

Across Five Aprils by Irene Hunt

True or False:

1. T	6. T	11. F	16. T
2. F	7. F	12. T	17. F
3. T	8. T	13. F	18. T
4. F	9. F	14. T	19. F
5. T	10. T	15. F	20. T

Short Answers:

1. Bill and Jethro had been very close since Jethro was small. After Bill left, Jethro missed being able to talk with his brother. Also, Jethro could not understand his brother's decision to join the Confederate Army.

2. After Travis Burdow shot Mary Creighton, the men of the town wanted to lynch him. Matt prevented the lynching. Dave Burdow, Travis' father, saved Jethro from being attacked by Guy Wortman as Jethro was driving home through the woods.

3. Shad was Jethro's teacher, who taught him about the world beyond the farm. Shad was also a role model for Jethro. The young teacher showed Jethro how to think for himself and what it meant to be a man.

4. Jethro became the man of the family when his father could no longer work. He planted the crops. He made the dangerous trips to town for supplies. His father's illness forced Jethro to grow up very quickly.

5. When Jethro did not know how to deal with Eb's desertion, he wrote to Lincoln. Lincoln's compassionate reply helped Eb and many other deserters to return to the army and regain their self-respect.

Challenge Question:

Jethro must cope with the farm work after his brothers have gone and his father becomes ill. He tries to understand the course of the war. He copes with hatred at home when his farm is attacked. He faces a big decision alone when he must decide whether to help Eb or turn him in. Jethro learns to control his emotions, the grief and strain he feels. Rather than leaning on his mother, Jethro must become a source of strength for his mother and Nancy. Jethro Creighton becomes much older than his years as his circumstances make him a man at an early age.

Babbitt by Sinclair Lewis

Multiple Choice:

1. C	5. C	9. C	13. C	17. B
2. A	6. A	10. B	14. C	18. D
3. D	7. C	11. C	15. C	19. C
4. B	8. D	12. B	16. C	20. A

Short Answers:

1. Although he enjoys dreaming about her, Babbitt's dream girl threatens his comfortable life. These desires lead him beyond the permissible patterns of his society. The discontent these dreams create will lead to the rebellion in his affair with Tanis.

2. Myra wants to do everything right according to the opinion of Floral Heights society. Entertaining must always take the same form. Like George, Myra almost never has an original idea.

3. Paul, Babbitt's college roommate, is the one person George really loves. Paul has the sensitivity Babbitt lacks; Babbitt tries to protect Paul's gentleness. As long as Babbitt has Paul to hang on to, George maintains his balance. When Paul is sent to prison, Babbitt turns to Tanis for the love he needs.

4. Tanis introduces Babbitt to passionate love he never knew with his wife. In loving her, he defies all social conventions. Babbitt sees a new side of life as he parties with her wild friends. However, Babbitt tries to keep the relationship secret and maintain his respectability.

5. His wife's illness renders him helpless. He needs the security of the group, and returns to its standards. Babbitt, the great rebel, becomes Babbitt the complete conformist. His dream girl has died forever.

Challenge Question:

Babbitt's ideas and habits are the same as those of the men he does business with. His remarks as a host are those he has made many times before. His language is shallow; every word from his mouth is an ad slogan, or someone else's idea. His relationship with Paul seems to be the only genuine thing in his life. George cannot care enough, however, to break the mold.

His affair with Tanis is typical of a middle-aged man attracted by a woman who is the opposite of his wife. During his rebellion with the "Bunch," his behavior is also typical as he joins in their wild antics. At the end of the novel, Babbitt has completed the cycle to become the model father and businessman.

Gone With the Wind by Margaret Mitchell

Multiple Choice:

1. C	6. C	11. B	16. B
2. C	7. D	12. C	17. A
3. C	8. D	13. B	18. B
4. A	9. B	14. A	19. B
5. B	10. C	15. A	20. B

Short Answers:

1. Scarlett and Rhett are both shrewd, clever, and passionate. Neither fits the model of Southern perfection. Both want the most from life on their terms. Both survive through their own wits. Both are tragic in a way since each realizes too late how valuable real love can be.

2. Scarlett sheds her mother's teachings. She learns to fight, to cope at any cost. Having faced starvation, she becomes obsessed with food and money. She grows determined never to be on the bottom again.

3. She transacts business in a nonwomanly way. She betrays the South by dealing with the enemy.

4. Bonnie's death ends Rhett's love for Scarlett. Scarlett realizes too late how much she needs that love. The child was the one force that might have brought the two together.

5. Neither Gerald nor Miss Pitty can cope with reality. Gerald lives in the shadow world before his wife died. Miss Pitty is still living in the genteel world of her girlhood.

Challenge Question:

Melanie has the nobility of character Scarlett lacks. She still believes in goodness, yet has the strength to take action against evil. She is the Old South. Melanie has the courage to risk having another child, even though this birth may mean her death. She absolutely refuses to think evil of those she loves.

The Mask of Apollo by Mary Renault

Matching:

1. M		5. P		9. H		13. B		17. L
2. J		6. E		10. F		14. I		18. O
3. D		7. K		11. R		15. N		19. Q
4. G		8. A		12. C		16. T		20. S

Short Answers:

1. Through the mask, the god communicated with Niko. Apollo gave Niko direction, such as when he was trying to decide if he would act in Dionysios's play. The mask was his inspiration. Niko meditated on the mask and offered incense to Apollo before each performance. The mask also became the means to smuggle letters out of Syracuse. The enemy soldiers did not search an object sacred to the god.

2. Niko began as a child actor working with his father. He then did walk-ons and extra parts. Eventually he became a third actor and went on tour with Lamprias's company. He next became a second actor, and finally a protagonist. After his acting career was launched, Niko became a director with a company of his own.

3. Plato believed that too many tragedies portrayed the corrupt side of man, actions which people ought not to imitate. He believed that drama should present only the good. Plato also objected to the unflattering and frequently immoral pictures of the gods. He believed that these humanized pictures of the deities made people lose their respect for religion. Therefore, in Plato's ideal state, the theater would be severely censored.

4. The mask, which arrived at the last minute, had Dion's face. As the play was originally acted, this character would be ridiculed by the god Dionysios. Through changing the interpretation of the action, Niko was able to present the character who represented Dion with honor.

5. Dion could not follow Plato's philosophical principles in a city where everyone around him was self-seeking and evil. The ideal republic supposed that men's hearts could be made good. Syracuse was so filled with treason and treachery that Dion was finally beaten and murdered by one of his own men.

Challenge Question:

Nikeratos begins life with the theater as the center of his world. After he meets Dion and Plato, he is forced to face a wider world. The "how" involved in the craft of acting gradually takes second place to the "why" of a man's being. Growth as an actor is paralleled by Niko's growth as a man. His own love relationship with Thettalos is like the relationship of Dion and Plato.

Niko's admiration for Dion involves him in political intrigue, first in carrying messages, then in the attempt to rescue Plato. For the first time, Niko carries a real sword and not just a stage prop.

Maturity means facing life off-stage: shipwreck, battle, and personal loss. Deep grief becomes a reality with Dion dead. As an old man, Niko senses greatness in the next generation when he meets the young Alexander. Niko's life finally assumes meaning far beyond the depth of tragedy. In reality, too, he is Apollo's servant.

The Jewel in the Crown by Paul Scott

Matching:

1. G	6. Q	11. C	16. E
2. K	7. D	12. T	17. I
3. M	8. B	13. P	18. O
4. A	9. F	14. S	19. L
5. J	10. H	15. N	20. R

Short Answers:

1. Miss Crane's work did not make any real difference in the children's lives. In spite of the mission's efforts to civilize them, the Indians still became an attacking mob. Miss Crane also found no meaning for her own life. The only really human contact that she had was with Miss DeSilva. After the old teacher's death, Miss Crane had no one with whom she could really communicate. Her death by fire became a final identification with the India that she had failed to change.

2. Hari left in England the only life that he had ever known. He was horrified by the crowded stench of the native quarter. In India, the British would have nothing to do with him because his skin was not white. Repeated rejection made Hari Kumar a bitter man. Merrick hated Hari because Hari was too proud to be the typical submissive native.

3. Merrick assumed that Daphne would accept him because he was a man of authority who was white. Perhaps Merrick could have better accepted Daphne's rejection if she had loved another white man. To be rejected for an Indian made Merrick savagely determined to get even. Daphne's journal implies that Merrick planted the bicycle as evidence of Hari's guilt.

   Raging against rejection, especially that of Colin Lindsay, Hari had difficulty believing that an English girl could love him. Finally his need for affection drove him to meet Daphne in the garden. Hari honored Daphne's love by refusing to speak in his own defense.

4. Prejudice in British India was evil because it was almost unconscious. Even Lili, the Indian aristocrat, could not get in to visit Miss Crane in the white ward of the

hospital. No Indian could ever enter the club. Hari and Daphne could not go to a restaurant or movie because of segregation regulations.

Under British rule, Indians had few civil rights. The Defense of India Law was an excuse for the government to punish and imprison at will. With a typical military attitude, Reid uses armed force with little regard for the human consequences.

5. In her own journal, Daphne relates what really happened. After she and Hari made love, she was attacked by thugs who had been watching them. As she fled, Daphne made Hari promise to say nothing. Because he loved her, Hari honored Daphne's secret.

Challenge Question:

Paul Scott uses first-person point of view for several narrative voices in *The Jewel in the Crown*. Lili Chatterjee tells the story of her position as the aristocratic outcast. General Reid and Robin White both discuss how the riots were handled. Vidyasagar's story gives the reality of imprisonment. Sister Ludmilla explains her involvement in Hari's and Daphne's lives. In the novel's powerful conclusion, Daphne, in her own words, tells what really happened.

Third-person point of view is used for Miss Crane and Hari Kumar in order that the reader may know the characters' thoughts.

These various voice changes are linked by narrative sections in which the author, doing research in 1964, describes the various settings of the action. This "frame" narrative gives a powerful reality to the narratives in the various journals.

The Gates of Zion by Bodie Thoene

Matching:

1. M	6. A	11. S	16. J
2. C	7. G	12. P	17. H
3. I	8. Q	13. R	18. D
4. E	9. T	14. L	19. F
5. K	10. N	15. O	20. B

Short Answers:

1. She thinks that they are fakes and that the old men are trying to sell something worthless. She learns that these scrolls date from the first century A.D. and are copies of the ancient writings of Isaiah.

2. His hatred motivates everything that he does. Hassan enjoys having Jews die. He especially hates Moshe because Moshe's brother refused to marry Hassan's sister because she was not Jewish.

3. She spends the night with her son at the hotel. All the people there die from a terrorist bomb. Miriam is not a soldier, only a simple woman destroyed by senseless killing.

4. David flies low over the Arabs who are searching for Moshe and Howard. Ellie throws bottles of soda water, which the Arabs think are bombs. The trick makes the Arabs run and gives David time to land to get Moshe and Howard out.

5. When Yacov comes to stay with them, Rachel finds out, by hearing their grandfather's name, that Yacov is her little brother. She finds her grandfather when she and Ellie go into the Old City to help smuggle weapons.

Challenge Question:

Ellie begins as a photographer working with her uncle on the dig. After she sees the people senselessly killed in the riot, Ellie must flee for her life. The pictures that she took help to present the Jewish cause to the world.

Ellie must also choose between her love for David and her feelings for Moshe. She does this as she recognizes and accepts Moshe's feelings for Rachel. Ellie knows she really cares for David.

Ellie's faith grows as she becomes willing to risk her life smuggling supplies to the freedom fighters. She is no longer a spoiled American. She now understands herself and has a cause to believe in.

A Connecticut Yankee in King Arthur's Court
by Mark Twain

Multiple Choice:

1. B	5. A	9. C	13. C	17. D
2. D	6. C	10. B	14. D	18. B
3. B	7. A	11. D	15. A	19. C
4. D	8. B	12. B	16: B	20. D

Short Answers:

1. While touring Warwick Castle, Twain meets a strange man who says that he put a hole in a fifth-century breastplate. The stranger later sends Twain a manuscript containing Hank Morgan's story. After he finishes reading, Twain goes to the stranger's room and finds the man dying. This device of the "found manuscript" makes the fiction seem real.

2. Hank brings all his Yankee characteristics to Camelot. He is technically clever. He knows a great deal about mechanics and electricity. Hank sizes up people and situations quickly and thinks on his feet in times of crisis. He values the common man and believes that people should think for themselves without accepting the values that have been imposed by tradition.

3. Hank wants to free people from brutalization by the landed aristocracy. He improves the standard of living by giving more to the common man. Electricity, railroads, telegraphs, and telephones help people communicate. He increases literacy through schools and newspapers.

4. Arthur learns how poverty and disease reduce people to the level of animals. He learns how unfair the upper classes are to the peasants, who have no rights at all. The king learns how the man at the bottom of the feudal ladder feels.

5. Hank is tricked into making a trip to France for his child's health. While he is away, civil war breaks out and the king is killed. The church and the powers of superstition take over. All Hank's technical improvements are destroyed. The people he has educated desert him. Even though Hank is able to kill many knights, he is trapped in a cave and placed under Merlin's spell.

Challenge Question:

Twain believes that men should succeed according to their abilities or energy, not according to inherited social status. Aristocracy and established religion are the enemies of freedom. Twain shows the extremes of superstition in two scenes: the enchanted aristocrats who are really pigs, and the monks in the Valley of Holiness who believe that being dirty has sacred value. Hank finds that goodness, in Camelot or anywhere, lies in the faithfulness and nobility of individuals like Sandy and Clarence.

The novel's final apocalypse, the end of the world, comes with the slaughter of a society at the Battle of the Sand Belt. Twain pessimistically believes that individual goodness is not enough to hold back the darkness. As night descends over Camelot, Hank sleeps, the victim of an enchantment. Clever goodness may attack the forces of ignorance, but defeat is certain.

Battle Cry by Leon Uris

Multiple Choice:

1. B	6. D	11. D	16. C
2. C	7. C	12. C	17. A
3. A	8. B	13. A	18. B
4. C	9. D	14. C	19. A
5. B	10. A	15. B	20. B

Short Answers:

1. Boot camp turns soft civilians into tough soldiers. The individual becomes part of the unit. Conflicts are resolved, rough edges smoothed from personalities, and men become buddies for life. They learn how to obey orders without question. Boot camp also builds pride as the new men become part of the Marine tradition.

2. Huxley makes his men do more than any of them think they can stand. After taking them on long forced marches, he makes them march back. Doing what they think is impossible prepares them for the strain of combat. Their anger against Huxley welds them into a unit; at the same time, the men gain pride in being demanded to do what others cannot. Huxley is a leader who thinks first of his men. Even after the major is killed, the unit continues to function in the way that he has trained them.

3. Victimized by child abuse, Andy grew up in foster homes and later in lumber camps. He had experienced sex with prostitutes, but had never known love. Pat and her family give him a sense of belonging. The New Zealand farm gives Andy something that he can finally call his own.

4. Women like Kathy and Rae suffer from loneliness and the terrors of knowing that their men are going into battle, never to return. Jean Huxley, the major's wife, has always had to share her husband with his marriage to the Marines. Some women, such as Elaine and Susan, can't stand the strain and turn to other men.

5. Levin is accepted by the men after he does all the dirty jobs that they hand him without complaining. He also takes all the fun they poke at him. Seeway, the anti-Semitic soldier from Texas, finally becomes the buddy who is with Levin when the young soldier dies. Levin becomes a hero when he sacrifices his life to keep a boat from running head-on into a line of Japanese fire.

Challenge Question:

For the men of the Sixth Marines, unity becomes more important than individual differences. Marion, the intellectual, and Joe Gomez, the clever thief, become buddies. All the men cover for and protect each other.

Pedro, the Mexican medic, sacrifices his life for the others. The Indian Lighttower becomes part of the group. Seeway, the Texan who hates Jews, holds the hand of the dying Levin.

Each man becomes part of a unit that moves forward to drive out the Japanese and have a small part in the larger Pacific victory. Mac, the sergeant telling the story, becomes the symbol for all the others. *Battle Cry* is a novel of brotherhood under fire. For Mac, each man has become one of "his boys."

The Marines do experience fear as they face the fury of the Japanese troops. However, their excellent training and their loyalty to each other overcome the terror and help the men do the impossible.

Queen Dolley by Dorothy Clarke Wilson

Matching:

1. I	5. E	9. T	13. M	17. S
2. N	6. C	10. K	14. B	18. O
3. P	7. A	11. G	15. F	19. Q
4. L	8. H	12. R	16. D	20. J

Short Answers:

1. Dolley was always guided by the Inner Light, God speaking within the individual. Always loving the beautiful, she found glory in God's creation. In her private speech, she frequently used the Quaker "thee" and "thou." Although she dressed grandly for formal occasions, her private attire was often the somber gray of a Quaker housewife.

2. Learning of a political problem, Dolley would invite the disagreeing politicians to have dinner. The conversations at those parties frequently provided solutions to the nation's problems. Dolley was also Madison's confidante and frequently his secretary. Her fine mind helped the President think through the nation's problems.

3. Martha Washington's receptions were very formal. At her "drawing rooms," Dolley did away with many of the formal rules of etiquette. She encouraged many different kinds of people to mingle and get to know each other. Dolley was in every sense of the word a democratic hostess, welcoming all who came.

4. The Madisons grieved because they could have no children of their own. Instead, they "adopted" and cared for a string of relatives. The conduct of Payne, Dolley's son, was a great problem. Madison was constantly being asked to pay the boy's drinking and gambling debts. Dolley greatly sorrowed for the financial problems of Richard Cutts, her dear sister Anna's husband. Completely unselfish, James and Dolley Madison constantly gave to those close to them, even when such giving meant great personal sacrifice.

5. Dolley returned to Washington and stayed very active in the city's social life. Her parties were as popular as events at the White House. Her main passion was the publication of Madison's political papers, so that James's work would not be lost to the nation.

Challenge Question:

Both in public and private, Dolley Madison cared for people. In the middle of a large reception, she might be concerned for one shy individual. She was equally at ease in a crowd of thousands or running a foot race with a niece or nephew. Dolley was never self-conscious. Though dressing grandly for state occasions, she would put on old clothes for digging in the gardens at Montpelier.

As a devoted wife, Dolley served James publicly as his first lady and privately as his secretary and nurse. When Madison was dying, Dolley never left his side.

Mrs. Madison was a "Queen" publicly in setting fashion for the entire nation. In private, she was a "Queen of Hearts" whose love flowed out to everyone.

Science Fiction, Fantasy, and the Supernatural

Synopses

Watership Down

by Richard Adams

Macmillan Publishing Company, New York, 1972.

Watership Down is a beautiful allegory of a community of rabbits struggling to establish an independent society. Fiver, a small mystic, senses danger for the warren. After he and Hazel fail to convince the chief rabbit that destruction is coming, Hazel leads a small group to establish a new society on Watership Down, a large plain suitable for rabbits.

The group has many adventures. They barely escape from Cowslip's warren, where the rabbits are fat, placid, and indifferent to the death that surrounds them. In order to find female rabbits to expand the warren, Hazel proposes a bold venture to free the hutch rabbits on Nuthanger Farm. When the rabbits save Kehaar, an injured seagull, the great bird becomes their flying ally.

The greatest struggle is against General Woundwort and the militaristic rabbits of the Efrafa warren. Led by the gallant Bigwig, the rabbits fight valiantly to save their society. Only when Hazel, at the risk of his life, turns a dog loose, are Woundwort's troops defeated.

The rabbits are cleverly personified and given character traits found in any community. These noble little animals also have spiritual values, represented by rabbit folk hero El-ahrairah. Firth, or God, is the ruler of all. *Watership Down* may be compared in style with George Orwell's novel *Animal Farm*. For Watership's rabbits, however, courage, cleverness, and goodness triumph.

Foundation

by Isaac Asimov

Gnome Press, New York, 1951.

Foundation is the first volume in Asimov's space trilogy about the end of the Old Empire and the beginning of the new. Hari Seldon is a psychohistorian, a scientist who can statistically plot the future. History, Seldon believes, consists of a single line of unavoidable crises. Psychohistory can help humanity survive at each successive crossroads.

Each generation meets its "Seldon Crisis," the moment of inevitability. On the remote plant Terminus, Seldon first establishes the Encyclopedists, scholars who will preserve civilization through the Dark Ages until the New Empire arises. During the next generation, politicians led by Salvor Hardin control events by establishing a religious cult centered around atomic energy. The Foundation is next controlled by merchant princes led by Hober Mallow. Money has replaced faith as the driving loyalty.

In Asimov's universe, power lies with the clever. The victor in each interplanetary struggle knows that "force is the last refuge of the incompetent." Seldon, Hardin, and Mallow preserve civilization for another generation by outwitting their enemies. *Foundation* is science fiction at its best. Asimov creates his imagined world from scientific possibility and proven principles of human behavior.

The Last Unicorn

by Peter S. Beagle

Ballantine Books, New York, 1968.

The Last Unicorn tells the fanciful journey of one unicorn, a mythical symbol of purity and goodness. This last unicorn leaves her enchanted forest in search of all the unicorns who have disappeared.

After being captured by Mommy Fortuna's Midnight Carnival, the unicorn is saved by Schmendrick, a well-intentioned but very incompetent magician. Schmendrick promises to help the unicorn free her people. They must travel to the castle of King Haggard to confront the Red Bull, who has imprisoned the other unicorns. On their quest, the unicorn and the magician are joined by Molly Grue, a coarse, good-hearted girl, who has lived in the forest with a band of outlaws led by Captain Cully and Jack Jingley.

Before approaching Haggard's castle, the travelers arrive first in Hagsgate, a town ruled by fear of a prophecy that says that one from their own town will destroy them. When the unicorn is attacked by the Red Bull, Schmendrick changes her into the beautiful Lady Amalthea. Prince Lir, Haggard's son, falls in love with the fair maiden.

In order to save the unicorns imprisoned in the sea, the maiden must again become a unicorn. She can save Prince Lir's life but she cannot love him. Good triumphs as the unicorns are freed and Haggard's castle is destroyed. The last unicorn returns to her forest; the prince now rules his kingdom.

The Last Unicorn has a simple plot showing the triumph of imagination and beauty over force and fear. This novel is a modern fairy tale in which ideals triumph.

The Martian Chronicles

by Ray Bradbury

Doubleday and Company, Garden City, New York, 1946.

The Martian Chronicles imagines what will happen when Earth colonizes Mars. Between 1999 and 2026, a civilization is established and destroyed. Bradbury's Martians are not monsters, but beings with special psychic powers who desire truth, beauty, and peace. The men of Earth are clearly inferior to the natives of the new planet.

The settlement of Mars is not easy. The first two expeditions are destroyed by the Martians. When the third expedition comes, Spender, one of the crew, recognizes that Earth's population will destroy Mars if given a chance. Finally, however, pioneers establish a beachhead and new towns begin to grow.

Wave on wave of immigrants comes as the situation on Earth becomes more desperate. Each group of travelers to Mars brings strengths and weaknesses typical of the human race. Benjamin Driscoll wants to plant trees. Father Peregrine seeks truth as he brings Christianity to Mars. Women come seeking husbands. The old bring memories of lost children.

The Martians are almost destroyed by the construction fever. Sam Parkhill believes that he can make a fortune by running a hot dog stand in the Martian wilderness. When war breaks out on Earth, however, all the colonists want to go home. At last the four survivors who remain become "Martians."

The Martian Chronicles has been called by one critic "a study of morality set against the mythical backdrop of the future." Bradbury's wonderful descriptions make Mars a real place populated by characters that we recognize easily. These people of the future are very much like us.

A Wrinkle in Time
by Madeleine L'Engle

Farrar, Straus and Giroux, Inc., New York, 1962.

A Wrinkle in Time is a fantasy which may be read on a child's level, or may be interpreted as an allegory with spiritual overtones. Meg Murry, a gentle girl with a deep sense of her own impatience and inadequacy, is concerned for her missing father. Meg has a special relationship with her sensitive brother, Charles Wallace, who has mystical powers beyond his years. Meg, Charles Wallace, and their friend Calvin journey through a tesseract, a fifth dimension of time and space. Assisted by three strange ladies, Mrs. Whatsit, Mrs. Who, and Mrs. Which, Meg, Charles Wallace, and Calvin become involved in a battle against evil. The children find their father on the planet Camazotz, a place that has surrendered to the dark forces.

IT, a brain containing the essence of evil, gains control of Charles Wallace. Although the others escape, Meg must return to Camazotz to save her brother. The force of love provides the key to freedom.

A Wrinkle in Time is easy reading, but has a beauty of style and a depth of theme that intuitive students will appreciate.

The Great Divorce
by C. S. Lewis

Macmillan Publishing Company, New York, 1946.

The Great Divorce is an allegorical journey from Hell to Heaven. A student might easily compare Lewis's work with Bunyan's *The Pilgrim's Progress*. After walking through a dark, dreary town, a dreamer joins a bus line. The passengers' constant quarreling among themselves reveals a very ugly side of human nature. The travelers journey to a beautiful land, where sights and sounds are beyond human toleration. An apple cannot be lifted; a leaf has a crushing weight.

The various "ghosts" who have come on the bus meet the Solid People, inhabitants of this beautiful land. Each "ghost" talks with someone he or she has known in life. The varied relationships (mother/son, husband/wife, brother/sister) reveal the inadequacy of human love. The traveler meets his Teacher, George MacDonald, an author whose works C. S. Lewis greatly admired. The Teacher explains the meaning of what the traveler sees. Heaven becomes the essence of selfless love; Hell is the embodiment of perfect selfishness. Each person is offered the greater love, which will transform him or her from a ghost into a Solid Person.

Refusing to relinquish their wills, the passengers return to the bus. Although the wonders of Heaven are available, the ghosts choose Hell instead.

This allegory beautifully combines description of the imagined Paradise with real insight into the imperfect motivation present in most human relationships. Goodness and beauty become possible only when a person accepts Divine Love rather than human love.

Z for Zachariah

by Robert C. O'Brien

Macmillan Publishing Company, New York, 1974.

Z for Zachariah tells the story of Ann Burden, a farm girl who has been living alone in her sheltered valley after a nuclear war. When she sees another person approaching, Ann is both excited and afraid. The man is John Loomis, who has been protected from radiation sickness by a "safe suit" made from a special plastic which Loomis helped to develop. After bathing in a polluted stream, Loomis becomes ill. Ann takes him into her house and nurses him back to health. When Loomis talks in his delirium, Ann learns that he has killed a man. Having a thorough knowledge of mechanics, Loomis helps Ann get the tractor going so that she can work the farm. Ann begins to dream of the life that she and Loomis could have together.

Then happiness turns to terror when Loomis tries to attack Ann. He seeks to control her by using her pet dog to track her down and by cutting off her food supply. To save her own life, Ann must steal the "safe suit," leave the valley, and search for life elsewhere.

A simply written survival novel, *Z for Zachariah* asks basic questions about human nature. If only one man and woman were left on earth, would goodness or selfishness prevail?

The Hollow Hills

by Mary Stewart

Doubleday and Company, New York, 1973.

The Hollow Hills, an account of King Arthur's birth and childhood, is really Merlin's story. Chosen by King Uther Pendragon as guardian for his heir, Merlin protects the young prince by using courage, magic, and common sense. Young Arthur is cared for by Ralf, his protector, and Count Ector, his foster father.

Merlin desires to restore his Sight, the special magic power to foretell the future. Traveling through the kingdom disguised as a doctor and a wandering musician, Merlin seeks the magic sword which had belonged to Macsen, the great emperor. Merlin is aided in his quest by the "Old Ones," ancient Britons who live in the "hollow hills." To protect the blade from those who would destroy Arthur's kingship, Merlin places the sword in a secret cave until Arthur can claim his throne.

Assuming the role of a hermit, Merlin becomes Arthur's tutor. He then takes the young prince to his father; the young man is publicly acknowledged as the next king. Magic for Merlin is a mixed blessing, since foreknowledge brings pain. He sees Arthur plant the seeds that will bring disaster to Arthur's dream.

This beautiful narrative of the birth of Camelot will appeal to students interested in the legends of chivalry. Although Arthur is the subject, the protagonist is really Merlin, who is the personification of courage, loyalty, and love.

The Other

by Thomas Tryon

Random House, New York, 1971.

The Other is a strange tale involving the psychic powers of twins, Niles and Holland Perry. A quiet, obedient child, Niles has inherited from his Russian grandmother Ada the mind-projecting ability to become another animal or person. At first, this power seems harmless as Niles and Ada together play "the game." In Holland, however, psychic power becomes motivated by evil. Causing destruction everywhere, Holland is responsible for death or injury to his father, his mother, his cousin Russell, and Mrs. Rowe, a neighbor.

The shock in the story comes as Ada shows Holland's grave to Niles. Who is the killer? Has Holland's evil spirit taken possession of Niles?

Final catastrophe stalks the Perry family when the sister Torrie's infant daughter is found drowned in a vat of wine. Grandmother Ada commits suicide because she cannot cope with the knowledge that the twins' power came from her. As the story ends, the surviving twin has been placed in an institution. Niles no longer exists; the spirit of Holland has taken over.

The Time Machine

by H. G. Wells

Bantam Books, New York, 1982.

The Time Machine is H. G. Wells' vision of a grim future. At a dinner for a group of assembled friends, the Time Traveler relates his adventures. Using his Time Machine, the Time Traveler arrives in a world where the human race has divided into two groups: the gentle Eloi and the vicious cannibalistic Morlocks.

With Weena, the gentle Eloi who has become his companion, the Time Traveler attempts to recover his machine from the Morlocks. Stealing matches from an abandoned museum, he starts a blaze which enables him to escape. Unfortunately Weena also perishes in the blaze.

After going forward one million years to a completely dead world, the Time Traveler returns to his own time. One of his friends waits to interview him. However, the Time Traveler again disappears, this time never to return.

H. G. Wells was not optimistic about man's progress. The evil in man, represented by the Morlocks, defeats the gentle Eloi. Wells's keen interest in science makes *The Time Machine* a novel which looks far into the future.

Things Invisible to See

by Nancy Willard ⹀⹀⹀⹀⹀⹀⹀⹀⹀⹀⹀⹀⹀⹀⹀⹀⹀⹀⹀⹀⹀⹀⹀

Alfred A. Knopf, New York, 1984.

Things Invisible to See takes place on two levels: the everyday physical world and the higher realm of the spiritual. Ben Harkissian accidentally hits Clare Bishop with a baseball. Although her body is paralyzed, Clare learns that she can move through the realm of the spirit world. She sees into the bodies of others, and learns that, when death comes, the lights go out in the soul. "The Ancestress" becomes Clare's guide to this higher reality.

Clare and Ben's love develops after he goes to see her at the hospital. She replaces baseball as the most important thing in Ben's life. Meanwhile, Ben's twin brother Willie courts Marsha, Ben's former girlfriend.

Although no one can determine why she is paralyzed, Clare eventually leaves the hospital. A séance, presided over by the figure of Death, produces information no one understands, that Cold Friday will cure Clare.

Shipwrecked on a raft in the South Pacific, Ben is visited by Clare in the form of a bird. Ben also makes a bargain with Death. If Ben and his baseball team can beat Death's team in a three-inning game, their lives will continue.

Before the game, Ben and his friends are injured. Their mothers must substitute for them. Cold Friday has been found. She removes the curse that was placed on Clare. Using her special powers, Clare brings Ben back to consciousness by the power of her love. Life defeats Death in the final inning.

This book is a strange tale of things beyond normal knowledge. The characters learn that the natural is separated from the supernatural by a very thin veil.

Name _____ Name _____ Date _____

Watership Down by Richard Adams

Select the letter of the word or phrase which correctly completes each sentence.

_____ 1. Fiver receives a sense of coming destruction for the Sandleford warren from (A) a patrol report (B) a dream (C) a sign board (D) Kehaar's flight results.

_____ 2. When Hazel tries to warn the chief rabbit, he is (A) put in prison (B) ignored (C) listened to carefully (D) severely punished.

_____ 3. Hazel becomes chief rabbit of the small group because of his (A) cleverness (B) physical strength (C) size (D) mystical visions.

_____ 4. The greatest enemy for the rabbits are (A) weasels (B) cats (C) other rabbits (D) men.

_____ 5. Bigwig accepts Hazel's leadership when (A) Hazel beats him in a fight (B) Hazel saves him from the snare in Cowslip's warren (C) Hazel helps them escape from Efrafa (D) Hazel turns the dog loose in the warren.

_____ 6. Fiver's vision of disaster is proven true by (A) Holly (B) Strawberry (C) Dandelion (D) Blackberry.

_____ 7. Silflay refers to (A) rabbit's natural enemies (B) feeding patterns (C) breeding habits (D) a special governing council for the warren.

_____ 8. The greatest single problem faced by the Watership warren is a lack of (A) food (B) good defenses (C) female rabbits (D) burrowing space.

_____ 9. General Woundwort's personality is best explained by his (A) childhood experiences (B) size (C) natural desire for power (D) contact with human beings.

_____ 10. The best natural storyteller in the warren is (A) Hazel (B) Strawberry (C) Blackberry (D) Dandelion.

_____ 11. The activity most unnatural to rabbits but most necessary to save their lives is (A) eating meat (B) swimming (C) talking with other animals (D) riding in a machine with human beings.

(continued)

© 1991 J. Weston Walch, Publisher

Name _____ Date _____

Watership Down by Richard Adams

_____ 12. Efrafa's greatest problem is (A) a lack of food (B) weak leadership (C) overcrowding (D) disease.

_____ 13. Hazel is injured by (A) a wire snare (B) a falling tree branch (C) a shotgun (D) a concrete bridge support.

_____ 14. The most accomplished officer of the Efrafa warren is (A) Campion (B) Avens (C) Rabscuttle (D) Chervil.

_____ 15. The rabbit folk hero El-ahrairah represents all of the following traits *except* (A) cleverness (B) mystical insight (C) strength (D) fearlessness.

_____ 16. General Woundwort controls the rabbits of Efrafa by (A) democratic government (B) powerful speaking (C) military force (D) food rationing.

_____ 17. The most heroic battle against General Woundwort is fought by (A) Hazel (B) Blackberry (C) Dandelion (D) Bigwig.

_____ 18. The rabbits of Watership talk with all of the following *except* (A) birds (B) mice (C) weasels (D) cats.

_____ 19. The Efrafans are routed when (A) the dog charges them (B) men dynamite the field (C) General Woundwort is killed (D) a strange disease kills many of their leaders.

_____ 20. At the end of the novel, all of the following are true of the Watership warren *except*: (A) Bigwig is training young rabbits (B) Hazel dies of old age (C) Campion has become the new chief rabbit (D) A new warren has been established in conjunction with the Efrafans.

100 More Great Books: Synopses, Quizzes, and Tests

Name _____ Date_____

Watership Down by Richard Adams

Answer the following questions in two or three complete sentences.

1. Why does Hazel's group decide to leave the Sandleford warren?

   _____

   _____

   _____

2. What special role does Fiver play in the group's decisions?

   _____

   _____

   _____

3. What dangers do they face in Cowslip's warren?

   _____

   _____

   _____

4. How do the rabbits escape from Efrafa?

   _____

   _____

   _____

5. What trick does Hazel use to defeat the Efrafan forces?

   _____

   _____

   _____

Challenge Question

Write an essay discussing Hazel's positive leadership abilities. What character traits make other rabbits follow him? How is Hazel's form of leadership contrasted with General Woundwort's dictatorship?

© 1991 J. Weston Walch, Publisher   *100 More Great Books: Synopses, Quizzes, and Tests*

Name_____   Date_____

Foundation by Isaac Asimov

**Select the letter of the word or phrase which correctly completes each
sentence.**

_____ 1. Gaal Dornick was (A) a native of Trantor (B) a spy for Seldon's enemies
(C) a new mathematician who wanted to join Seldon's group (D) really the
king of Terminus.

_____ 2. Before he gained political power, Salvor Hardin was (A) a newspaper editor
(B) an army general (C) a merchant trader (D) an atomic scientist.

_____ 3. The greatest weakness in Seldon's theory of psychohistory was that
(A) nothing could be changed (B) the behavior of the individual had no
significance (C) the theory couldn't be proven (D) religion and morals
had no value.

_____ 4. The real purpose of the Encyclopedia Foundation was (A) to write the
Encyclopedia Galactica (B) to give Seldon power (C) to build a population
center at the remote rim of the Empire (D) to protect the source of atomic
power.

_____ 5. The title taken by Hardin was (A) Grand Master (B) Mayor (C) Prince
Regent (D) Chancellor.

_____ 6. At times of crisis, words from Seldon came (A) from his writings (B) from
old tape recordings of his speeches (C) from an image of Seldon in the
Time Vault (D) from the *Encyclopedia*.

_____ 7. The chief power threat that Hardin had to repel came from (A) Trantor
(B) Anacreon (C) Korell (D) the Action party on Terminus itself.

_____ 8. The priests of the Foundation (A) possessed secret knowledge of atomic
energy (B) were descended from the original settlers of Terminus (C) never
shared atomic secrets with any other planet (D) were all killed by the traders
and politicians.

_____ 9. Which of the following was *not* true of young King Leopold of Anacreon?
(A) He died in a hunting accident. (B) He was controlled by Wienis. (C) An
atomic aura made his people believe that he was divine. (D) As soon as he
assumed real power, he intended to have Wienis killed.

(continued)

© 1991 J. Weston Walch, Publisher

Name_____   Date_____

Foundation by Isaac Asimov

_____ 10. Ponyets tricked the Grand Master of Askone with (A) an atomic ray gun (B) a device that turned iron into gold (C) a series of fake documents (D) counterfeit money.

_____ 11. Gonov had been imprisoned for (A) spying (B) treason (C) selling atomic weapons (D) an assassination attempt on the life of the Grand Master.

_____ 12. Mallow knew that other planets had atomic energy when he saw (A) the cooking devices on Korell (B) the guards' atomic ray guns (C) a radioactive necklace (D) the secret documents of the government.

_____ 13. The missionary on Korell was really (A) a priest of the Foundation (B) a religious representative of the New Empire (C) one of the traders (D) an agent of the Korell secret police.

_____ 14. The atomic aura which could protect a man from a bullet was called a (A) ray detector (B) force shield (C) UV light (D) mass coherence.

_____ 15. The total time frame of *Foundation* involves about how many generations? (A) four (B) one (C) six (D) eight

_____ 16. All of the following held power at some point *except* (A) the priests (B) the army (C) the politicians (D) the merchant princes.

_____ 17. Atomic energy was used by the Foundation for all of the following *except* (A) curing disease (B) blowing up alien planets (C) cooking food (D) tricking enemies.

_____ 18. Hari Seldon appeared (A) every century (B) every five hundred years (C) to each new leader (D) in each time of crisis.

_____ 19. By the end of the novel, religion (A) had been completely abolished (B) no longer appealed to the masses (C) had been gradually replaced by material greed (D) was in complete control of the civilization.

_____ 20. Asimov implies at the end of this first volume that (A) civilization will continue to exist only on Terminus (B) seeds of the Second Empire exist in another galaxy (C) Seldon will be resurrected to resume control (D) atomic energy will cease to be important for the future of civilization.

© 1991 J. Weston Walch, Publisher

Name_____ Date_____

Foundation by Isaac Asimov

Answer the following questions in two or three complete sentences.

1. According to Seldon, why is the settlement of Terminus essential to the survival of the human race?

_____

_____

_____

2. How does Hardin take power from the Encyclopedists?

_____

_____

_____

3. By what means does Hardin destroy the power of Wienis?

_____

_____

_____

4. Describe how the Foundation makes science a religion.

_____

_____

_____

5. What change in philosophy comes after the merchant princes take power?

_____

_____

_____

Challenge Question

Write an essay describing how the balance of power shifts as the leaders of the Foundation struggle to outwit their enemies.

Name_____ Date_____

The Last Unicorn by Peter S. Beagle

Place a T before each true statement and an F before each false statement.

_____   1. The unicorn could understand the speech of both plants and animals.

_____   2. Schmendrick used a strong magic spell to free the unicorn from Mommy Fortuna's carnival.

_____   3. Schmendrick was a master magician with great self-confidence.

_____   4. Jack Jingley and Captain Cully thought themselves excellent song writers.

_____   5. The unicorn's magic power was in her horn.

_____   6. Molly Grue decided to join the quest because she was falling in love with Schmendrick.

_____   7. The town of Hagsgate was as poor and barren as the rest of King Haggard's kingdom.

_____   8. The people of Hagsgate were too afraid to enjoy anything they had.

_____   9. The only child born in Hagsgate had been killed so that he could not fulfill the prophecy.

_____   10. The witch who built Haggard's castle became angry when King Haggard refused to pay her for her work.

_____   11. Haggard's castle was a shining building which could be seen from a great distance.

_____   12. Schmendrick knew that the unicorn would be safer if he turned her into a beautiful woman.

_____   13. Prince Lir was the son of King Haggard and the witch.

_____   14. As the travelers entered the castle, they could hear the roaring of the Red Bull.

_____   15. Even though Prince Lir loved the Lady Amalthea, every brave deed he attempted for her ended in failure.

_____   16. Schmendrick had to prove his ability as a magician in order to become immortal.

_____   17. All of the unicorn's people were imprisoned by the Red Bull in the dungeons of King Haggard's castle.

_____   18. The travelers leave time as they step through the face of a clock.

_____   19. The unicorn restores Prince Lir by touching him with her hoof.

_____   20. At the end of the novel, Molly and King Lir plan to be married.

© 1991 J. Weston Walch, Publisher

Name_____ Date_____

The Last Unicorn by Peter S. Beagle

Answer the following questions in two or three complete sentences.

1. What special powers does the unicorn have?

   _____

   _____

   _____

2. Why does Schmendrick agree to accompany the unicorn on her quest?

   _____

   _____

   _____

3. According to Schmendrick, in what way is the magic greater than the magician?

   _____

   _____

   _____

4. What does Prince Lir learn about his real origins?

   _____

   _____

   _____

5. How are the other unicorns set free?

   _____

   _____

   _____

Challenge Question

Write an essay discussing *The Last Unicorn* as a parable on the triumph of good over evil.

Name_____ Date_____

The Martian Chronicles by Ray Bradbury

Match each description in Column A with the correct name in Column B.

Column A	Column B
_____ 1. Planted trees to improve the oxygen level on Mars	A. LaFarge
_____ 2. Commander of the first Martian expedition	B. Peregrine
_____ 3. Priest who found beauty and truth among the Martians	C. Janice
_____ 4. Built the "House of Usher" to get even with those who would destroy the products of the imagination	D. Parkhill
	E. Biggs
_____ 5. Owner of the only hot dog stand on Mars	F. Belter
_____ 6. After his wife and children died, he built robot replacements	G. Mr. K
_____ 7. Saw Martians in the shapes he had known as a boy back in a small town in Illinois	H. Stendahl
_____ 8. Tried to stop the members of his expedition from destroying the beauty of Mars	I. Captain Black
	J. Proprietor
_____ 9. Found himself in a Martian insane asylum	K. Driscoll
_____ 10. Shot the first explorer who came from Earth to Mars	L. Wilder
_____ 11. Saw a Martian who took the form of his dead son Tom	M. Hathaway
_____ 12. Owner of the only luggage store on Mars	N. Gripp
_____ 13. Decided to remain the last bachelor on Mars rather than marry a woman who disgusted him	O. Mr. Xxx
	P. Williams
_____ 14. Committed suicide to destroy what he believed to be a hallucination	Q. Spender
_____ 15. The eldest son of the first family of new Martians	R. Timothy
_____ 16. Traveled to Mars to marry the man she loved	S. Gomez
_____ 17. Had a conversation with a lone Martian while traveling at night through a deserted landscape	T. Ward
_____ 18. Black man who almost missed the last rocket	
_____ 19. Returned to Mars after commanding a rocket expedition to Saturn and Jupiter	
_____ 20. Threw up in the Martian canals	

© 1991 J. Weston Walch, Publisher

Name_____ Date_____

The Martian Chronicles by Ray Bradbury

Answer the following questions in two or three complete sentences.

1. What special visionary or psychic powers do the Martians possess?

   _____

   _____

   _____

2. Why do the first three expeditions fail?

   _____

   _____

   _____

3. As the Earth people arrive in greater numbers, what happens to the Martian civilization?

   _____

   _____

   _____

4. Explain the symbolism of the automated house which destroys itself.

   _____

   _____

   _____

5. Why do most of the colonists who come to Mars eventually decide to return to Earth?

   _____

   _____

   _____

Challenge Question

Write an essay explaining how *The Martian Chronicles* illustrates that the good and evil in man will be carried to whatever planet the human race decides to explore.

© 1991 J. Weston Walch, Publisher   *100 More Great Books: Synopses, Quizzes, and Tests*

Name _____ Date_____

A Wrinkle in Time by Madeleine L'Engle

Place a T before each true statement and an F before each false statement.

_____   1. Meg is the oldest child in her family.

_____   2. Meg meets Mrs. Whatsit and Mrs. Who before Charles Wallace does.

_____   3. No one in the village knows that Meg's father is missing.

_____   4. Both of Meg's parents are scientists.

_____   5. Calvin has no parents or family.

_____   6. On their return, those who travel through a tesseract find that several years have passed.

_____   7. The travelers stop on the planet Uriel to rest before they continue their journey.

_____   8. Mrs. Which tells them that Earth has already been taken over by the forces of evil.

_____   9. Meg wants to protect both Calvin and Charles Wallace from harm.

_____   10. Mrs. Which tells them that their father is already dead and is beyond help.

_____   11. Mrs. Whatsit warns Charles Wallace that he is in more danger on Camazotz than any of the others.

_____   12. The three women go with the children to Central.

_____   13. Mrs. Who gives Meg her glasses.

_____   14. Calvin is more vulnerable to the forces of evil than any of the others.

_____   15. Meg and Calvin are able to free Meg's father from the forces of evil which have imprisoned him.

_____   16. After tessering off Camazotz, Calvin almost dies from being frozen at absolute zero.

_____   17. Meg is healed through Aunt Beast's warm touch.

_____   18. Calvin goes with Meg when she returns to IT to save Charles Wallace.

_____   19. Charles Wallace is saved by the power of love.

_____   20. At the end of the novel, Mrs. Whatsit and Mrs. Who return to live in the small house in the woods.

© 1991 J. Weston Walch, Publisher   *100 More Great Books: Synopses, Quizzes, and Tests*

Name_____ Date_____

A Wrinkle in Time by Madeleine L'Engle

Answer the following questions in two or three complete sentences.

1. In what ways is Charles Wallace a special child?

_____

_____

_____

2. Why does Calvin find the Murrys' home such a special place?

_____

_____

_____

3. What weakness in Meg's personality becomes the source of her greatest strength?

_____

_____

_____

4. How does IT control the people of Camazotz?

_____

_____

_____

5. How does Meg show courage as she returns to rescue her brother?

_____

_____

_____

Challenge Question

Discuss how *A Wrinkle in Time* is an allegory of the power of love to triumph over evil.

Name_____   Date_____

The Great Divorce by C. S. Lewis

Place a T before each true statement and an F before each false statement.

_____   1. In Hell, people live together in large groups and argue constantly.

_____   2. The driver of the bus brings light into the twilight of the town.

_____   3. The light grows brighter as the bus ascends.

_____   4. The dreamer meets his wife in Heaven.

_____   5. Each of the "ghosts" is met by someone he or she had known in life.

_____   6. The dreamer recognizes the people he sees in Heaven because they had been famous on earth.

_____   7. The ghosts of artists and writers were easily able to give up all the ideas they had on earth.

_____   8. The dreamer is able to move very easily from one place to another.

_____   9. The dreamer's senses gradually become more used to the bright land.

_____ 10. The woman ghost had ruined her husband's life to achieve her own ambitions.

_____ 11. One of the ghosts easily carries a basketful of apples back to the bus.

_____ 12. The "dwarf" is able to conquer the "Tragedian" who is leading him.

_____ 13. The lizard of the ghost's lustful desire is transformed into a magnificent lion.

_____ 14. All of the Solid People try to lead the "ghosts" of their loved ones toward the mountains.

_____ 15. None of the "ghosts" can have any changes made in his life unless the "ghost" permits the change.

_____ 16. Nonhuman objects in this vision of Heaven have the power to speak.

_____ 17. Many of the Solid People had made journeys to Hell in an attempt to redeem those they loved.

_____ 18. MacDonald explains to the dreamer the meaning of each encounter that he witnesses.

_____ 19. The story ends with the dreamer's return to Hell.

_____ 20. The dreamer awakens to see a bright, sunlit morning.

Name _____ Date_____

The Great Divorce by C. S. Lewis

Answer the following questions in two or three complete sentences.

1. How is Hell in the "twilight town" really the creation of the people who live there?

   _____

   _____

   _____

2. What changes occur as the bus rises?

   _____

   _____

   _____

3. Give examples of two "ghosts" whose love is really destructive possessiveness.

   _____

   _____

   _____

4. What "dangers" for the ghosts exist in the world of the Solid People?

   _____

   _____

   _____

5. How are the dreamer's senses affected in the beautiful land he visits?

   _____

   _____

   _____

Challenge Question

Explain how Lewis proves in *The Great Divorce* that Hell or Heaven is really the total sum of each person's choices.

Name_____ Date_____

Z for Zachariah by Robert C. O'Brien

Place a T before each true statement and an F before each false statement.

_____ 1. Ann's mother and father were killed when a bomb fell on the nearby town of Ogdentown.

_____ 2. Members of Ann's family had been early settlers in the valley.

_____ 3. Ann's ambition before the war had been to be a nurse.

_____ 4. As Loomis approaches the valley, Ann watches him through her binoculars.

_____ 5. Loomis becomes ill by eating contaminated food.

_____ 6. Loomis teaches Ann how to measure the radiation levels in the water.

_____ 7. Before the war, Ann had been deeply religious.

_____ 8. Edward had been a fellow scientist with whom Loomis worked at Cornell.

_____ 9. Loomis had wanted to go outside the shelter in the "safe suit" so that he could find out what had happened to his wife and children.

_____ 10. Ann dreams that she and Loomis may marry after he recovers from his illness.

_____ 11. When Loomis is well enough to walk, Ann shows him where her special cave is located.

_____ 12. Ann is able to get enough gas to run the tractor from the gas pumps in front of the store.

_____ 13. The scientists at Cornell were able to manufacture six special "safe suits" before atomic war struck.

_____ 14. As Loomis recovers from his illness, he becomes more secretive in his actions.

_____ 15. Ann and Loomis share the work of planting the beets and the corn.

_____ 16. Loomis thought that Ann was living in the Kleins' apartment above the store.

_____ 17. Ann tries to run over Loomis with the tractor.

_____ 18. Faro is shot by a stray bullet from Ann's rifle.

_____ 19. In an attempt to starve Ann into submission, Loomis sets fire to the house and the barn.

_____ 20. At the end of the novel, Ann plans to travel in search of other survivors.

© 1991 J. Weston Walch, Publisher   *100 More Great Books: Synopses, Quizzes, and Tests*

Name_____   Date_____

Z for Zachariah by Robert C. O'Brien

Answer the following questions in two or three complete sentences.

1. What had happened to Ann's family? How had she alone survived?

_____

_____

_____

2. How had Loomis survived and made his way to the valley?

_____

_____

_____

3. Describe the actions of Loomis that make Ann realize that the man is dangerous.

_____

_____

_____

4. How does Loomis use Faro to track Ann down?

_____

_____

_____

5. How does Ann escape from the valley?

_____

_____

_____

Challenge Question

Discuss Ann's inner conflict in her struggle with Loomis. How is this conflict resolved?

Name_____   Date_____

The Hollow Hills by Mary Stewart

Match each description in Column A with the correct name in Column B.

Column A	Column B

Column A

_____ 1. Publicly opposes Arthur's claim to succeed his father

_____ 2. Birthplace of Arthur

_____ 3. Merlin's loyal servant who guarded young Prince Arthur

_____ 4. Mother of Arthur's first child

_____ 5. Duke of Cornwall who became Arthur's ally

_____ 6. Arthur's mother

_____ 7. Name given to Arthur to hide his identity

_____ 8. Arthur's foster father

_____ 9. Island where Merlin hid the sword

_____ 10. Merlin's nurse, who looked after Arthur until the prince was four years old

_____ 11. Ancient conqueror whose magic sword was the symbol of kingship

_____ 12. Arthur's closest boyhood friend

_____ 13. Arthur's foster brother

_____ 14. The Great King, Merlin's father

_____ 15. Servant who returned with Merlin from his travels in the Middle East

_____ 16. Faithful servant who carried the infant Arthur to Merlin

_____ 17. The "Old One" who saved Merlin's life

_____ 18. Name given by Arthur to the magic sword

_____ 19. King who refused to acknowledge publicly the birth of his son

_____ 20. Taught Merlin to use the special magic powers of "Sight"

Column B

A. Bedwyr

B. Morgause

C. Emrys

D. Moravik

E. Ambrosius

F. Cador

G. Marcia

H. Tintagel

I. Llyd

J. Ector

K. Caliburn

L. Ralf

M. Galapas

N. Lot

O. Ygraine

P. Cel

Q. Macsen

R. Caer Bannog

S. Uther

T. Stilicho

© 1991 J. Weston Walch, Publisher   *100 More Great Books: Synopses, Quizzes, and Tests*

Name_____   Date_____

The Hollow Hills by Mary Stewart

Answer the following questions in two or three complete sentences.

1. How did Merlin protect Arthur until the young prince was acknowledged by his father?

_____

_____

_____

2. Describe the special "Sight" which Merlin possessed.

_____

_____

_____

3. Why did Merlin know that he must find the sword?

_____

_____

_____

4. What fears for Arthur's future tormented Merlin?

_____

_____

_____

5. How did Arthur prove himself worthy of being a king?

_____

_____

_____

Challenge Question

Write an essay explaining how Merlin as narrator combines the real world of human conflicts with the realms of myth and magic.

© 1991 J. Weston Walch, Publisher

Name _____ Name _____ Date_____

The Other by Thomas Tryon

Select the letter of the word or phrase which correctly completes each sentence.

_____ 1. The Perry family lives in (A) England (B) Alabama (C) Connecticut (D) Missouri.

_____ 2. The twins' hideout was located in (A) the attic (B) the apple cellar (C) the icehouse (D) the back storeroom.

_____ 3. Which of the following was *not* one of Holland's victims? (A) Mr. Angelini (B) Vining (C) Russell (D) Alexandra

_____ 4. Ada had come to America from (A) Germany (B) Russia (C) Argentina (D) Yugoslavia.

_____ 5. Russell was killed by (A) hanging (B) drowning (C) a pitchfork (D) a heart attack.

_____ 6. Niles tried to comfort his mother by (A) reading to her (B) playing games with her (C) playing the piano for her (D) going for walks with her.

_____ 7. The gold ring symbolizes (A) Ada's family ancestry (B) the powers of evil (C) the horoscope sign of Niles's birth (D) Grandfather Perry's Civil War regiment.

_____ 8. Ada tries to force Niles to face the fact of Holland's death after (A) Russell's death (B) the neighbors find Mrs. Rowe's body (C) Alexandra's accident (D) Eugenia's death.

_____ 9. Niles had cut off Holland's finger (A) to get the ring (B) because Ada told him to (C) as a souvenir of his dead brother (D) with Winnie's kitchen knife.

_____ 10. Miss Josceline-Marie was (A) the boys' schoolteacher (B) the librarian (C) a neighbor (D) a shop owner in the village.

_____ 11. When he was a child, Niles had tried to become (A) a rooster (B) a fish (C) a bat (D) a bee.

(continued)

© 1991 J. Weston Walch, Publisher

Name_____   Date_____

The Other by Thomas Tryon

_____ 12. Alexandra tries to (A) discover the contents of the tobacco tin (B) get Niles to admit that Holland is dead (C) report Holland's activities to the police (D) save Mrs. Rowe's life.

_____ 13. Holland's power works through Niles (A) by the sound of Holland's voice (B) only in the apple cellar (C) when Niles puts on the ring (D) because Holland is really still alive.

_____ 14. Aunt Fania (A) is poisoned (B) falls into the well (C) is paralyzed by a wasp sting (D) falls down the stairs.

_____ 15. Niles is sensitive to all of the following *except* (A) nightmares (B) thunder and lightning (C) Russian music (D) heat and cold.

_____ 16. In his last struggle against Holland's influence, Niles threatens to (A) dig up Holland's grave (B) kill Torrie's child (C) tell the truth about the murders (D) kill Ada.

_____ 17. The body of Torrie's baby is found (A) in its bed (B) in the wine vat (C) in the apple cellar (D) at the bottom of the well.

_____ 18. The evil is finally stopped by (A) Ada (B) Alexandra (C) Uncle George (D) Mr. Angelini.

_____ 19. "The Other" refers to the evil represented by (A) Niles (B) Holland (C) Ada (D) the Angel of Death.

_____ 20. At the end of the novel, (A) Niles is living alone in the family home (B) Holland's spirit has taken over Niles's body (C) Uncle George has also been killed (D) Niles is dead.

© 1991 J. Weston Walch, Publisher

Name _____   Date_____

The Other by Thomas Tryon

Answer the following questions in two or three complete sentences.

1. Contrast the personalities of Niles and Holland.

   _____

   _____

   _____

2. How is the power transmitted from Ada to Niles?

   _____

   _____

   _____

3. What do the deaths of Russell and Mrs. Rowe have in common?

   _____

   _____

   _____

4. How does Ada try to stop Niles? Why does she fail?

   _____

   _____

   _____

5. How is the evil power in the twins finally stopped?

   _____

   _____

   _____

Challenge Question

Write an essay discussing the ways in which the Perry twins represent the battle between good and evil.

© 1991 J. Weston Walch, Publisher

Name _____ Date_____

The Time Machine by H. G. Wells

Select the letter of the word or phrase which correctly completes each sentence.

_____ 1. Most of the novel is narrated by (A) the Time Traveler's friend (B) the Time Traveler himself (C) the Psychologist (D) the author.

_____ 2. The Fourth Dimension that the men discuss is (A) Time (B) Space (C) Height (D) Depth.

_____ 3. The Time Machine is activated by (A) pushing buttons (B) a series of levers (C) remote control (D) voice commands.

_____ 4. The only helpful item that the Time Traveler brings from his own time is (A) a camera (B) a gun (C) a crowbar (D) matches.

_____ 5. The Eloi are all of the following *except* (A) afraid of the dark (B) gentle and loving (C) meat eaters (D) small in stature.

_____ 6. The Time Traveler meets Weena when (A) she greets him as he arrives (B) he rescues her from drowning (C) he saves her from one of the Eloi (D) her family wants to sell her to the Time Traveler as a slave.

_____ 7. When the Time Traveler first sees the Morlock tunnels, he thinks that they are (A) ventilation shafts (B) ruins of television towers (C) subway entrances (D) storage caves for weapons.

_____ 8. The Morlocks are all of the following *except* (A) blind (B) hairy (C) mechanically inclined (D) brutal and vicious.

_____ 9. The meat the Morlocks are eating is (A) human flesh (B) beef (C) cooked on a huge spit (D) smoked and heavily salted.

_____ 10. The Time Traveler goes into the underground world because (A) Weena encourages him (B) he wants to get his Time Machine back (C) he wants to see what the Morlocks look like (D) he thinks that the Morlocks can help him get back to his own time.

_____ 11. The Palace of Green Porcelain had once been (A) a private home (B) a museum (C) a large department store (D) a royal residence.

(continued)

© 1991 J. Weston Walch, Publisher

Name_____ Date_____

The Time Machine by H. G. Wells

_____ 12. The most useful item that the Time Traveler finds in the palace is (A) a gun (B) old books (C) a box of matches (D) skeletons of abandoned animals.

_____ 13. The Morlocks try to trap the Time Traveler by (A) kidnapping Weena (B) using his Time Machine as bait (C) surrounding him in the forest (D) burying him alive.

_____ 14. The Time Traveler defeats the Morlocks by (A) starting a fire (B) killing their leader (C) blowing up their underground machinery (D) escaping in his time machine.

_____ 15. The total time that the Time Traveler spends in the land of the Eloi is about (A) six months (B) a week (C) a year (D) three hours.

_____ 16. After he leaves the land of the Eloi, the Time Traveler (A) returns to his own world (B) goes a million years into the future (C) dies immediately (D) never travels in time again.

_____ 17. The Time Traveler's second journey into the future sees a world which is (A) becoming more perfect (B) gradually dying (C) much like his own (D) ruled by animals instead of men.

_____ 18. When he returns to his friends, the Time Traveler's greatest desire is for (A) meat (B) fruit (C) rest (D) silence.

_____ 19. On his second voyage into time, the Time Traveler takes a (A) good supply of food (B) camera (C) rifle (D) tape recorder.

_____ 20. H. G. Wells believes all of the following *except* (A) time travel is a real possibility (B) man is getting better and better (C) technology can both harm and help the human race (D) scientific experimentation is fascinating.

Name_____   Date_____

The Time Machine by H. G. Wells

Answer the following questions in two or three complete sentences.

1. How does the Time Traveler first convince his friends that it is possible to journey through time?

   _____

   _____

   _____

2. Describe the differences between the Eloi and the Morlocks.

   _____

   _____

   _____

3. How does the Time Traveler escape from the Morlocks?

   _____

   _____

   _____

4. Of what significance are the flowers that the Time Traveler finds in his pocket?

   _____

   _____

   _____

5. What happens to the Time Traveler at the end of the novel?

   _____

   _____

   _____

Challenge Question

Write an essay discussing H. G. Wells's outlook for the future of man. In what ways are his opinions both pessimistic and optimistic?

© 1991 J. Weston Walch, Publisher

Name_____ Date_____

Things Invisible to See by Nancy Willard

Place a T before each true statement and an F before each false statement.

_____ 1. Willie is a better athlete than Ben.

_____ 2. Several people in Clare's family have extrasensory powers.

_____ 3. Ben did not see Clare when his ball hit her.

_____ 4. The first body that Clare enters is that of her cat.

_____ 5. The figure of Death always appears as a respectable gentleman in a three-piece suit.

_____ 6. Ben's father is a scientist who works for the war effort.

_____ 7. Marsha is a selfish girl who takes advantage of both Ben and Willie.

_____ 8. Grandpa and Grandma both live with Clare's family permanently.

_____ 9. At the séance, the voice of Mrs. Bishop's dead child comes through Davy's mouth.

_____ 10. The doctors determine that Clare's paralysis has been caused by extensive nerve damage.

_____ 11. Ben never writes to Clare after he goes off to war.

_____ 12. Ben is cast adrift at sea when his plane is shot down over the Pacific.

_____ 13. God, in this novel, is not involved in the experiences of the human race.

_____ 14. Ben agrees to gamble with Death in exchange for a long life.

_____ 15. Willie is not involved in Ben's baseball game.

_____ 16. The baseball players are injured in a bus accident.

_____ 17. Cold Friday has to burn the house down to save Clare from the Devil's curse.

_____ 18. Clare's love restores Ben to consciousness.

_____ 19. Death's team wins the baseball game.

_____ 20. Hal Bishop must give his life so that his daughter may walk again.

© 1991 J. Weston Walch, Publisher   *100 More Great Books: Synopses, Quizzes, and Tests*

Name _____   Date _____

Things Invisible to See by Nancy Willard

Answer the following questions in two or three complete sentences.

1. How is Ben's character contrasted with Willie's character?

   _____

   _____

   _____

2. Under what circumstances does Ben finally tell Clare that he caused her accident? Why does he tell her?

   _____

   _____

   _____

3. What does "the Ancestress" represent?

   _____

   _____

   _____

4. What bargain does Ben make with Death?

   _____

   _____

   _____

5. How does Clare help the living win the ball game?

   _____

   _____

   _____

Challenge Question

Describe some of the ways that *Things Invisible to See* places magic in daily life, and makes the supernatural seem real.

© 1991 J. Weston Walch, Publisher

Answer Keys

Watership Down by Richard Adams

Multiple Choice:

1. C	5. B	9. A	13. C	17. D
2. B	6. A	10. D	14. A	18. C
3. A	7. B	11. B	15. B	19. A
4. D	8. C	12. C	16. C	20. C

Short Answers:

1. Fiver sees the signboard and envisions the fields covered with blood. The chief rabbit refuses to pay any attention to the warning. The small group, with Hazel as leader, decides to flee to a safer place.

2. Fiver has special insight which lets him know the future. He also senses danger. The frail rabbit is the prophet of the society. In the beginning, some of the others scoff at Fiver's visions. However, after Bigwig is almost killed by the snare in Cowslip's warren, Fiver's warnings are never again ignored.

3. The danger is hidden death. All the rabbits seem fat and indifferent. They are being groomed for slaughter. This warren has no sense of community. Each rabbit will ignore the deaths of others as long as he is not a victim himself. Hazel's group is lured to this warren so that more victims may be provided for the man's snares.

4. Bigwig leads the group past the Efrafan sentries. As the rabbits flee toward the river, Kehaar attacks General Woundwort. After Hazel chews the mooring rope, the rabbits float down the river away from their enemies. They are finally forced to swim for their lives when the boat goes under a very low bridge.

5. Hazel, Dandelion, and Blackberry go to the farm. Hazel chews the rope to let the dog loose. The dog chases Dandelion out to where Blackberry is waiting. In turn, Blackberry leads the dog into the middle of the enemy forces. Without General Woundwort to lead them, the Efrafans are hopelessly confused and routed.

Challenge Question:

Hazel is a fair, democratic leader. He listens to the opinions of the other rabbits. He also knows how to use well the skills of each rabbit in his group. For example, Dandelion's story-telling skill helps keep the community calm in times of great pressure. Hazel is a clever rabbit. He fights by thinking up unique ideas. He uses the seagull Kehaar for reconnaissance and information. He turns the dog loose to defeat the enemy. As a leader, Hazel rises to meet each new situation. He becomes clearly identified with El-ahrairah, the great rabbit hero.

General Woundwort controls his society by force. His motive for ruling is the desire for power. No one's will or opinion counts in Efrafa except the General's. Hazel, in contrast, acts always for the good of the community. Even after Hazel is injured, he continues to take great risks on behalf of the warren. Showing consideration for the weak, Hazel will never leave the sick or wounded to the mercy of their enemies. Even the physically strong like Bigwig and Holly respect Hazel's leadership skills.

Foundation by Isaac Asimov

Multiple Choice:

1. C   3. B   5. B   7. B   9. A   11. C   13. D   15. A   17. B   19. C
2. A   4. C   6. C   8. A   10. B   12. B   14. B   16. B   18. D   20. B

Short Answers:

1. Since the Empire is on the verge of collapse, civilization must be preserved. Pretending to establish a group of writers, Seldon really establishes a protected power base on Terminus. These people will have the atomic power to repel any challenge to their society. Seldon's theory of psychohistory will program these people toward a single course of action. In reality, Seldon becomes the "god" who determines the fate of mankind.

2. The Encyclopedists viewed classifying the past as man's most important activity. Hardin looks toward the future and the real threat of invasion from Anacreon.

3. Hardin gets rid of Wienis and the puppet King Leopold by using the atomic power his enemies lack. Hardin wins, not by force, but by the mental ingenuity to outwit his foes. His motto is, "Force is the last refuge of the incompetent."

4. The priests are those who possess the secrets of atomic energy. Scientific information is given only to the initiated. The masses of people are controlled by this "mystical" power. The radioactive aura that surrounds King Leopold makes his people think that the king is divine. "The Great Galactic Spirit" is the personification of that atomic power.

5. The practical politicians had used the religion of science which the encyclopedists had invented. The traders and merchant princes secularized society; love of money replaced worship of the abstract. The merchants used atomic energy as a bartering chip for power. Control of factories and power plants became a more vital weapon than the control of man's imagination. Mallow realized, however, that the power of money might be replaced in a future time, just as the power of religion had been replaced in his own.

Challenge Question:

The first men of the Foundation were scholars. Their purpose was veneration of the past. Their writings protected society from total oblivion. Then the balance of power went from the scholars to the practical realists. Under Hardin, repelling invasion became crucial. The mayors lived in the present. Their focus, however, was still Terminus itself as the center of activity. Under the merchant princes, the Foundation widened its economic base by giving atomic power to other planets and then controlling those planets as an empire.

Asimov's *Foundation* parallels the history of Western civilization. The Church preserved culture during the Dark Ages. The politicians and traders of the Renaissance built a power base. The next generation of explorers from Italy and Spain then widened that power base into an empire.

The Martian Chronicles by Ray Bradbury

Matching:

1. K	4. H	7. I	10. G	13. N	16. C	19. L
2. T	5. D	8. Q	11. A	14. O	17. S	20. E
3. B	6. M	9. P	12. J	15. R	18. F	

Short Answers:

1. Martians can assume any shape projected by a person's imagination. They become the visualizations of dreams. They can see into the future. The Martians hear the songs of Earth before the Earth men come. A Martian can go into a man's mind to help him understand any language. They also possess the power to affect the force of gravity, to divert falling rocks or speeding bullets. Along with all these powers, the Martians for the most part have a moral goodness which the Earth men lack.

2. Nathaniel Ward, commander of the first expedition, is killed. Williams, of the second expedition, is destroyed when the Martians think he is insane. Captain Black and his men are killed by Martians who have assumed the shapes of their childhood memories.

3. All the Martian cities become ghost towns. The few Martian survivors go back to the hills. These remaining few no longer have any shape, but become instead light and energy. The Martians finally only appear to men in forms that come from the men's minds.

4. The automated house represents the triumph of technology. Without human presence, however, all technology has become meaningless. The house, destroyed by accidental fire, is powerless to save itself. Finally, it recites a useless date, since time also has become meaningless.

5. Mars has never really become home for these people. When war breaks out on Earth, they all decide to try to return. After everything is destroyed, two families manage to get away in their private rockets. Mars finally becomes a new Garden of Eden, a cradle for the human race to reproduce and survive.

Challenge Question:

Man's presence on Mars is both good and evil. The good in man goes to Mars with the priest who wishes to teach his faith. Driscoll plants trees to help the oxygen level. Inventive technology is positive when Hathaway builds robots to replace his dead family. Love also comes as Janice journeys to Mars to start a new life with Will. The forces seeking to control man's imagination are beaten by Stendahl who fights to preserve literature and creativity.

Greed and lust come from Earth as the miners and builders duplicate the wild boom towns of the old West. The gentle Martians are driven to the hills as the Earthlings take over. The builders have no regard or respect for the civilization which came before them.

After the war on Earth, only two families remain. These people will be the mixture of good and evil which, Ray Bradbury believes, makes us human.

The Last Unicorn by Peter S. Beagle

True or False:

1. T	5. T	9. F	13. F	17. F
2. F	6. F	10. T	14. T	18. T
3. F	7. F	11. F	15. F	19. F
4. T	8. T	12. T	16. F	20. F

Short Answers:

1. The unicorn, an immortal being, has the power to keep the forest around her as eternal spring. She can communicate with all plants and animals. Her horn has life-giving powers. She can appear and disappear at will. The unicorn has a strange beauty which enchants all who see her.

2. Schmendrick must prove himself as a magician so that he may be freed from a curse of immortality and allowed to live as a human being. He is fascinated by the unicorn's beauty. He goes with her to protect that beauty. He also wants his own life to find meaning in the adventure.

3. The magician is only the vehicle through which the magic comes. Schmendrick says that he never knows what his spells will do. He can perform tricks for children, but he never knows if he can do anything great until the hour of challenge comes. Magic in this fantasy is always a force for good. The magician allows the force to take effect.

4. Lir is not Haggard's son. Born in Hagsgate, the prince was the son of Drinn, who had spirited him away so that the town could be saved. The Red Bull cannot be defeated by magic. He must be confronted by Lir, who needs to prove his courage in this ultimate combat.

5. The travelers go through the clock to confront the Red Bull. Lir tries to do battle against the monster, but is killed. Schmendrick finds the full power of his magic, and turns the Lady Amalthea into the unicorn again. The unicorn confronts the Red Bull and drives him into the sea. Haggard's castle is toppled, and the other unicorns rush free from the foam.

Challenge Question:

The unicorn represents the goodness which must confront the threat of evil. She can't remain placidly in her forest while the Red Bull roars in triumph. Freeing her people is the most important thing she can do.

The people of Hagsgate represent the morally weak society which chooses to save itself by ignoring the presence of the evil force.

Only immortal strength can win the battle against the Red Bull. Lady Amalthea must again become a unicorn before the other unicorns can be set free. King Lir must find mortal love with another princess.

Schmendrick finds meaning in life only as he finds mortality through the exercise of his magic and his relationship with Molly. Although the unicorn's magical powers are wonderful, she will grieve because a unicorn can never know love. The greatest triumph is in living and being completely human. The price of such a victory, however, is mortality.

A Wrinkle in Time by Madeleine L'Engle

True or False:

1. T	6. F	11. T	16. F
2. F	7. T	12. F	17. T
3. F	8. F	13. T	18. F
4. T	9. T	14. F	19. T
5. F	10. F	15. T	20. F

Short Answers:

1. Charles Wallace can see into the minds and feelings of others. His mind is tuned to spiritual realities. He has mystical powers that others lack. This special confidence is also his weakness when the force of evil tries to control his mind.

2. Calvin's family does not want him. With Meg's family, Calvin gains a sense of meaning and purpose. Calvin is no longer alone. Because of his new sense of belonging, Calvin becomes a source of strength on their journey.

3. Meg's strength ultimately comes from her dissatisfaction with herself, her anger at injustice, her refusal simply to accept the things that she is told, her refusal to believe that her father is dead.

4. IT rules by total mind control. Greatest evil becomes total lack of individuality. Total conformity is needed for survival.

5. She goes back alone. She is willing to confront IT, and to fight evil to save the brother she loves.

Challenge Question:

Meg's love and determination represent the spiritual struggles of those who continually believe the best, who sacrifice energy and time as they willingly give themselves. Meg's love liberates. Her strength frees her father, Charles Wallace, and Calvin. The power of that love also liberates Meg herself. In time of crisis, she finds greater strength than she ever knew she possessed.

The Great Divorce by C. S. Lewis

True or False:

1. F	6. F	11. F	16. T
2. T	7. F	12. F	17. F
3. T	8. F	13. F	18. T
4. F	9. T	14. T	19. F
5. T	10. T	15. T	20. F

Short Answers:

1. By building new houses with a thought, they separate themselves from each other by choice. They are perfectly satisfied with living in twilight. They constantly quarrel with each other and insist on their own rights. Even after having visited the bright land and seen its wonders, they return to the bus by choice.

2. Light increases. The narrator sees the distorted faces of the other people. He then sees his own face.

3. Robert's wife and Michael's mother both really desire to control those they claim to love.

4. They are unable to walk. They may be crushed by a leaf or cut by a blade of grass. The ghosts are so "unsolid" that contact with any physical substance could seriously hurt them.

5. He gradually adjusts. At first his senses are overwhelmed, but as he leans on his Teacher, the dreamer walks more easily. His eyes tolerate the bright light. His ears become used to the sounds.

Challenge Question:

The Solid People have chosen to find reality by giving up themselves. The man possessed by the lizard of lust is freed when he allows that negative force to be changed into positive energy. The author found the real meaning of Truth when he chose to give up his pet ideas.

The "ghosts" who return to the bus do so because they allow wrong choices to control them. The dwarf is destroyed because he hangs on to his negative nature instead of accepting his wife's redeeming love.

Z for Zachariah by Robert C. O'Brien

True or False:

1. F	6. T	11. F	16. T
2. T	7. F	12. T	17. F
3. F	8. T	13. F	18. F
4. T	9. F	14. T	19. F
5. F	10. T	15. F	20. T

Short Answers:

1. The family had set out to see if others were alive. They had died, either from radiation sickness or gas poisoning. Ann stayed in the valley to guard the property. Because its weather patterns were not affected by the outside world, the valley was spared from contamination.

2. Loomis was in the underground laboratory when the war began. He had taken the "safe suit" made from polapoly, a radiation-proof plastic, and started out to see if other people were alive. Loomis killed Edward, his fellow scientist, to have the suit for himself. From a distance, he saw the line of green trees in the valley. He journeyed toward the green because he thought there would be life there.

3. He is secretive about being able to walk. He moves without his cane when he thinks Ann is not watching him. He first tries to grab her. Then, after he attacks her at night, she moves out of the house and back into the cave.

4. Loomis puts Faro on a leash and controls the dog's food supply. Faro knows Ann's scent; he also knows where the cave is. Loomis puts Faro on this track and then follows where the dog leads him.

5. She tricks Loomis into going to meet her at the other end of the valley. She steals the safe suit and the wagon with the equipment that she will need to be safe from radiation. She keeps Loomis away at gunpoint, but will not shoot him. Ann leaves Loomis alone in the valley; she starts out to see if she can find anyone else who is alive.

Challenge Question:

Even after Loomis attacks her, Ann wants to think the best of him. Ann romanticizes that she and Loomis, the last man and woman, could together revitalize the human race. Ann wants to believe that Loomis is just frightened or confused, not deliberately evil. After he burns her cave and tries to kill her, Ann realizes that she must save herself. She cannot kill Loomis; instead, she leaves the valley to him.

The Hollow Hills by Mary Stewart

Matching:

1. N	6. O	11. Q	16. G
2. H	7. C	12. A	17. I
3. L	8. J	13. P	18. K
4. B	9. R	14. E	19. S
5. F	10. D	15. T	20. M

Short Answers:

1. Merlin rescued Arthur at birth from Tintagel, carried him to Brittany, and provided Ector as his guardian. He left Ralf as a bodyguard, and finally escorted Arthur to Uther's camp.

2. It gave Merlin the ability to see across space events at which he was not present, to look back into the past and to see into the future.

3. The sword was the symbol of authority. Whoever claimed it would be a great emperor and would unify Britain. It was the symbol of Arthur's special destiny.

4. He saw the shadows of the events that would bring an end to the great dream of kingship: the dangers from the child born of Arthur's passion; the conflict over Guinevere; Arthur's death at age forty; and Merlin's own death.

5. Taking his father's sword, Arthur led the troops into battle. He proved himself on the field before his father proclaimed him heir to the throne.

Challenge Question:

The book gives a vivid description of Merlin's physical fights with those who would try to destroy Arthur and capture the sword. The wonderful landscape descriptions and accounts of Merlin's journeys are very real. Matched with these are Merlin's wonderful visions of things beyond human sight: the magic of the sword and the glories of the young king's future.

The Other by Thomas Tryon

Multiple Choice:

1. C	6. A	11. A	16. C
2. B	7. B	12. A	17. B
3. A	8. C	13. A	18. D
4. B	9. A	14. C	19. B
5. C	10. D	15. D	20. B

Short Answers:

1. Niles is good, obedient, loving. Holland is the mischief maker who is always in control. Niles is the protector; Holland is the killer.

2. Ada knew that she had psychic powers when she was twelve years old. Her moon pin symbolizes that power. She taught Niles to play "the game," to use the power to transfer his thoughts to other situations and objects. When Holland's evil power begins to take control, Ada realizes that the game has gone too far.

3. Both Mrs. Rowe and Russell have crossed or threatened Holland. Russell threatened to expose the secret. Mrs. Rowe was angry because Holland called her names. Both were eliminated because of these threats.

4. Ada tries to destroy Niles when she realizes that Holland has taken over. But she fails because the evil force is stronger and she dies in the fire.

5. Mr. Angelini knows what Niles has really been doing. He tells Uncle George, who has the boy institutionalized.

Challenge Question:

Niles is the "good boy"; Holland is "The Other," the evil force. After Holland's death, his finger and the ring become the forces that motivate Niles. Niles's psychic powers make Holland a real, physical presence. Each time the force of evil is threatened, it reaches out to destroy. When Alexandra learns the truth, "The Other" silences her. Ada is destroyed when she tries to end the evil influence. At the novel's end, evil has triumphed because only Holland exists.

The Time Machine by H. G. Wells

Multiple Choice:

1. B	6. B	11. B	16. B
2. A	7. A	12. C	17. B
3. B	8. A	13. B	18. A
4. D	9. A	14. A	19. B
5. C	10. B	15. B	20. B

Short Answers:

1. The men first discuss the ways that it is possible to travel in time as well as in space. Next, the Time Traveler activates a model of his Time Machine and sends it into the future. He finally shows his friends the full-sized machine in which he had traveled.

2. The Eloi are beautiful and gentle, the flower children of the race. They live above ground and eat only fruit and vegetables. The Morlocks represent man's technology gone wild. Living underground, these monsters are cannibals who prey on the Eloi. The evil of the Morlocks can be cleansed only by fire.

3. The Time Traveler, using the matches that he found in the ruined museum, sets the woods on fire. This blaze drives the Morlocks away, since they cannot stand heat and light. Although the Morlocks try to trap the Time Traveler inside the statue of the Sphinx, he is able to activate his machine and escape.

4. The flowers, given to the Time Traveler by Weena, prove the truth of his story. The faded blossoms also represent goodness and beauty in a world which seems dominated by darkness and evil.

5. The Time Traveler goes with his camera for another journey into time. His young listener waits for him to come back, but the Time Traveler never returns.

Challenge Question:

Wells sees clearly the dangers of technology in the wrong hands. He feels that man must struggle or he will become weak. The Eloi no longer have any strength because everything is too easy for them. Even creativity is lost when man must no longer work for anything. *The Time Machine* warns man to beware of the evil in human nature. The final vision of a dying world with no inhabitants seems to reflect Wells's belief that mankind will finally destroy itself.

However, the Time Traveler's love for Weena, symbolized by the flowers, shows the good in man also. If the destroyers must win in the end, at least human beings, as long as they survive, must have tenderness for each other.

Things Invisible to See by Nancy Willard

True or False:

1. F	6. F	11. F	16. T
2. T	7. T	12. F	17. F
3. T	8. F	13. F	18. T
4. T	9. F	14. T	19. F
5. T	10. F	15. F	20. F

Short Answers:

1. Ben is athletic and sensitive. He has an honest, loving nature. People easily take advantage of him. Ben's moral standards make him try to find Clare after the accident. Willie is an opportunist. He uses his flat feet as an excuse to stay out of the army. Willie wants to take everything that belongs to someone else. He goes to work for the black market. Lacking any ability to love, he becomes the perfect candidate for a pact with Death.

2. Ben tells Clare the truth when he is going into combat. He tells her the truth because he cannot face death with guilt on his conscience. Even after she knows, Clare assures Ben that she loves him.

3. "The Ancestress" is Clare's link with the psychic world. She comes to Clare in the hospital and teaches Clare how to use the spiritual power she possesses. She also guides Clare to Ben when Ben is lost at sea.

4. If the living lose the game, Death can claim them. If the living win, Death cannot have them until they are over a hundred.

5. Clare puts "stuff" on the balls that she pitches. These are thoughts about the wonders of life. The Dead Knights are attracted by these and long to be alive again. This distraction gives the game to the living.

Challenge Question:

The world of magic and reality meet as Clare is able to see and move into the bodies of birds and animals. Death appears as a businessman. Cooper's death is described in ordinary terms as he moves into another boat. The contest between life and death, between love and the forces of evil, is pictured in the ordinary metaphor of a sandlot baseball game. This contest parallels a greater game presided over by the Lord of the Universe.

Unit 5
Social Issues and Moral Challenge

Synopses

Go Tell It on the Mountain

by James Baldwin

Dial Press, New York, 1953.

Go Tell It on the Mountain, the story of the Grimes family of Harlem in the 1930's, is the work of James Baldwin, an important black novelist of the Harlem Renaissance group. Growing up black is felt through the soul of the sensitive son.

Religion plays a key role in the Grimeses' family life. Fourteen-year-old John is desperately seeking a special spiritual experience like that of his friend Elisha. The father, Gabriel, a preacher at the Tabernacle of the Fire Baptized, is a harsh father figure. Elizabeth, John's mother, repeatedly tells John that he must wait on God's will.

The Grimes family's experience has been shaped by the past. Using flashbacks, Baldwin tells the stories of Aunt Florence, Gabriel, and Elizabeth. All three had come North hoping to find the Promised Land. Each was disappointed. Florence had survived living with her alcoholic husband, Frank. Elizabeth had loved and lost Richard, John's real father. Gabriel fought his own private war with passion. After losing his first son, Royal, Gabriel married Elizabeth and promised to accept her son. Gabriel gave John food and clothing, but never the love that the child so desperately needed.

The last section of the novel records John's special spiritual experience. After coming to know God for himself, John finds the strength to stand up to his father.

The characters in this novel come to life. Each person lives in the pain and joy that experience has provided. Go Tell It on the Mountain provides important insight into black American culture.

Only Earth and Sky Last Forever

by Nathaniel Benchley

Harper and Row, New York, 1972.

Only Earth and Sky Last Forever is the story of Dark Elk, a Cheyenne boy who has been adopted by the Sioux. Longing for the chance to prove himself a warrior, Dark Elk wants to win the love of Lashuka by outwitting his rival, Running Deer. When Dark Elk goes to visit his adopted parents at the reservation, he sees how the white man has dehumanized his people. The boy goes to the sacred place, Paha Spa, to see a vision from the Great Spirit. He meets instead a prospector with a gun.

The Sioux become desperate when the white men begin to take the sacred Indian lands because gold has been discovered there. Joining the camp of Chief Crazy Horse, Dark Elk begins to find his manhood. The young man gets his first taste of battle when the Indian forces attack wagon trains in an attempt to get food and supplies needed for survival.

At the novel's conclusion, Crazy Horse's men defeat the white men at Little Big Horn. Dark Elk can find no joy in this victory because Lashuka is killed. His personal quest for freedom is over. For Dark Elk, the white man has won the battle.

Benchley has defined the nobility of the Indian warrior who will die for his people. Man will die; nature alone remains constant. "Only earth and sky last forever." This moving narrative presents western history from the Indian point of view.

Bury My Heart at Wounded Knee

by Dee Brown

Holt, Rinehart and Winston, New York, 1970.

Bury My Heart at Wounded Knee tells the tragic story of the white man's systematic destruction of the American Indian between 1860 and 1890. Although the narrative of the Indian author may not be completely objective, the documentation is complete. Eye-witness accounts, letters, and photographs bring the events to life.

The white man's greed drove the Indian from the lands that Indian nations had held for centuries. As each tract of tribal land became attractive to white settlers, miners, or cattlemen, ruthless government agents cheated the Indians into giving up their heritage. Promises were made which offered the Indians food and land. Treaty after treaty was broken as the whites needed more space.

Dee Brown relates the exploits of heroic Indians who fought back in a losing cause: Crazy Horse, Black Elk, Red Cloud, Geronimo, Sitting Bull. Usually portrayed as brutal savages, the Indians in Brown's account are shown as warriors who learned the art of atrocity from the white soldiers. The Indians copied the battle practices of the "Bluecoats."

The pattern of each tribal experience is the same. Only the names of the Indian victims and the white opportunists change to fit the circumstances. The whites discovered that Indian land was valuable. The land was taken by treaty or by conquest. The Indians were then forced to live on useless reservations. Those who rebelled were ruthlessly exterminated. Those who cooperated lost their will to live and died heartbroken on·the reservations.

Bury My Heart at Wounded Knee is an ugly chronicle of man's inhumanity to man. Vivid details of massacres and suffering do not make pleasant reading. The book is a record of Indian genocide, the systematic extermination of the red man by the white. History accounts and films frequently agree with General Sheridan that "the only good Indian is a dead Indian." In writing this book, Dee Brown wants to set the record straight.

Crime and Punishment

by Fyodor Dostoyevsky

Airmont Publishing Company, New York, 1967.

This classic Russian novel deals with crime and its consequences to the criminal. Raskolnikov, a brooding university student, murders an evil old pawnbroker. This killing occurs near the novel's beginning; the remainder of the plot chronicles the effects of crime on the killer, who has theorized that a few superior people may take the law into their own hands. Raskolnikov believes that the world would be better without the old woman, and that he has the right to eliminate her without consequence to himself. Unfortunately, Raskolnikov must also kill the woman's sister to cover his tracks. He is gradually driven mad by his guilt. Through sheer luck, he is able to escape from the scene of the crime undetected. He hides the money that he has stolen from the old woman's apartment.

In his delirium, Raskolnikov is cared for by his loving friend Razumihin. Raskolnikov's mother and sister Dounia arrive. Dounia is being courted and victimized by two unscrupulous men, the lawyer Luzhin and the lustful land-owner Svidrigailov. A foil to this evil pair is the gentle, caring Razumihin.

Raskolnikov becomes involved with the family of Marmeladov, a drunk whom he meets in a tavern. Marmeladov's stepdaughter Sonia, the heroine of the novel, has been forced into prostitution to provide for her brothers and sisters. Raskolnikov loves Sonia. He pays for her father's funeral and later looks after her. The complexity of human nature is revealed in the benign murderer.

Raskolnikov is obsessed with the crime he has committed. He confesses to Porfiry Petrovitch, the commissioner of police. The officer does not believe him, but later confronts the killer with the theory that proves his actions. Raskolnikov suffers frequent hallucinations and is obsessed with returning to the scene of the crime.

Believing that some "extraordinary men" are above the law, Raskolnikov commits his crime to prove his theory. His theory does not, however, provide for the sensitivity of his own nature. Ironically, this "killer" loves deeply and does much good for others. He is sharply contrasted to the other characters who hide their evil intent beneath cloaks of social respectability. In one of the book's most powerful scenes, Svidragailov's attempted rape of Raskolnikov's sister Dounia is contrasted to the loving scenes between Raskolnikov and Sonia.

Sonia convinces Raskolnikov that he must confess if he is to be redeemed. She offers to go with him into exile. Svidrigailov commits suicide. Sentenced to eight years in a Siberian prison, Raskolnikov atones for his guilt, finds true love for Sonia, and faith in God.

The complex plot and difficult Russian names make this novel very challenging reading. Dostoyevsky is a realist who has hope. This novel deals with both the evil in human nature and the possibility of redemption.

Intruder in the Dust

by William Faulkner

Random House, New York, 1948.

Lucas Beauchamp, a black man, is accused of murdering Vinson Gowrie, a poor white. Sixteen-year-old Charlie Mallison wants to help Lucas because Lucas saved Charlie's life. Lucas tells Charlie that a look at Gowrie's body will prove that Lucas is innocent. Assisted by his black friend Aleck Sander and a local eccentric, Miss Habersham, Charlie makes the dangerous journey to the cemetery. The body in the grave is not Vinson; nor was the man shot with Lucas's gun.

When Charlie returns to town, he persuades his uncle, the lawyer Gavin Stevens, to look at the grave. This time the coffin is empty. Stevens and Sheriff Hampton attempt to prevent the Gowrie clan from lynching Lucas. They find the body of Jake Montgomery, an unscrupulous lumber dealer, in a shallow grave near the cemetery. Vince's body is hauled out of the quicksand. The killer is not Lucas, but Crawford Gowrie. Crawford killed his brother in a dispute over stolen lumber.

Faulkner shows us a town ready to explode. Justice can only come through the efforts of two young boys and an old lady, who believe that a black man can tell the truth. The story explores one of Faulkner's frequent themes: Southern whites will pay a terrible price for prejudice, and redemption can come only through the young.

As Charlie narrates the story, the action is seen through his consciousness. Past and present become strangely merged. Charlie loses his innocence as he faces the reality of southern prejudice.

Farewell to Manzanar

by Jeanne Wakatsuki Houston

Houghton Mifflin Company, Boston, 1973.

Farewell to Manzanar is Jeanne Wakatsuki Houston's personal memoir. As Japanese-Americans during World War II, the author and her family lived for four years in an internment camp because the government considered them potentially dangerous aliens. Jeanne was seven when the Japanese bombed Pearl Harbor. Taken to the camp at Manzanar after her father was arrested as a dangerous alien, Jeanne and her family struggled to maintain humanity with humor.

The two greatest problems were the breakdown of traditional Japanese family values and the lack of privacy. Her brother Woody, who became the head of the family in their father's absence, tried to make their cubicle into a home. Jeanne's mother worked as a dietitian and made a home for her children. A curious child, Jeanne adjusted quickly to the strange, but often exciting, environment of the camp.

When the father, Wakatsuki Ko, was released and came to Manzanar to join his family, he had great difficulty adjusting. His determination to succeed and survive helped his daughter develop the strengths in her own character.

Although he opposed Jeanne's "Americanization," her father was nevertheless proud of his daughter's strength and independence.

After four years, the camp was closed and the war ended. Jeanne had then to cope with reentry into a society still hostile to Asians. She experienced prejudice as she found some doors closed to her simply because she was Japanese.

Thirty years later, Jeanne finally came to terms with her experience at Manzanar when she returned with her own children to look at the ruins on the campsite. Returning to the past helped her know who she had become.

Farewell to Manzanar is an important book which shares with the world the experience of Japanese-Americans who struggled to reconcile their American birthright with their Japanese heritage.

The Honorable Prison

by Lyll de Becerra de Jenkins

E. P. Dutton, New York, 1988.

This powerful novel is the story of Marta Maldonado's struggle for freedom. Her father is the editor of an opposition newspaper in a South American dictatorship. The General, whose brutal regime has crushed all opposition, exiles the family to a remote army base. Living in a wet climate under rough conditions, Marta's father succumbs quickly to lung disease. The "honorable prison" is really a place of slow death. Although the family members are isolated and starved, they are helped by loyal Pedro, who sacrifices his life to bring them food.

Marta and her brother Ricardo are caught in a conflict between their loyalty to their father and their own desire for freedom. Going to market once a week, Marta meets Fernando, the local schoolteacher, who is trapped by the authority of his uncle, the mayor of the village. Although she desires to run away, Marta remains loyal to her father's principles.

The Honorable Prison pictures life in a repressive society. The characters survive by will and family loyalty. Based on the author's experience, the plot makes the struggle for freedom a stark reality.

Skindeep

by Toeckey Jones

Harper and Row, New York, 1986.

Set in South Africa, this novel deals with apartheid on a deeply personal level, the relationship between a man and a woman. Rhonda meets Dave in a college cafeteria. The two are strongly attracted to each other, but Dave resists the risk of personal involvement.

Rhonda's parents are staunch white Africans to whom the blacks are nonpersons. Rhonda and Dave admit their love for each other. Rhonda then plans a vacation for the two of them in Capetown. During this vacation, Rhonda learns that Dave is a "pass-white," a person with colored blood who can pass as a white man. Even though she loves Dave, Rhonda is horrified at the depth of prejudice that she finds within herself. Her friends Joel and Lynn, who are anti-apartheid activists, try to help Rhonda cope. Her parents are horrified.

Written by a modern South African author, this book reflects the author's concern for the effects of race barriers on human relationships. Some scenes in this novel are sexually explicit and might make this book unsuitable for some students.

Fragments of Isabella

by Isabella Leitner

J. B. Lippincott Publishers, New York, 1978.

Fragments of Isabella is the memoir of a Hungarian Jewish woman who survived concentration camps. First in Auschwitz and then in Birnbaumel, Isabella and her three sisters struggled against the inhumane Nazi system to stay together and to remain human. Short, simply told episodes show these women hanging on to their mother's love of life. During a forced march in the snow, three of the women escape. Eventually they manage to come to their father in America.

A powerful piece of Holocaust literature, Isabella's story also shows that concentration camp horror continued to grip the lives of the survivors. The epilogue, written by Isabella's husband Irving, narrates a meeting in Paris thirty years later with Germans who could have been Isabella's captors.

The strength of this book lies in its brief, episodic style. Isabella starkly contrasts the normal lives of the German people and the beauty of nature with the horror of Nazi death camps. One profound question stirs the reader's conscience: "How could the world allow such atrocities to happen?"

Kaffir Boy

by Mark Mathabane

Macmillan Publishing Company, New York, 1986.

Mark Mathabane grew up in the slums of black South Africa. The horrors of apartheid, beatings and persecution, were part of his daily life. His earliest memories were of the Peri-Urban police who raided his home and abused his parents. The family lived in squalor and starvation.

Mark's father wanted his son to learn the tribal ways. His mother was determined that Mark would go to school so that he might have a better life. School proved to be another kind of horror when he was beaten because he could not afford proper uniforms. Still, his mother insisted that education was the only escape.

Through the Smiths, the family that his grandmother worked for, Mark learned that all white people were not brutes. He was introduced to books and tennis. This sport, together with Mark's excellent academic standing, proved to be his escape from apartheid. Mark still had to suffer rejection from both whites and blacks. Through the help of American friends, Mark left South Africa for a tennis scholarship at a college in South Carolina.

The graphic descriptions in this book leave the reader with no illusions regarding the horrors of apartheid. Mark Mathabane is a black South African who loves his country and has conquered the bitterness of his own experience. He writes to promote change in his country.

Other People's Houses

by Lore Segal

Fawcett Books, New York, 1986.

Other People's Houses recounts the author's childhood flight from Nazi terror. Born in Vienna, Lore spent the first ten years of her life protected by parents and grandparents. When Hitler marched into Austria, she was sent with other Jewish children to London. For the next ten years, Lore learned to survive change in several homes: the wealthy orthodox Levines, the crude but friendly Hoopers, and the philanthropists Miss Douglas and Mrs. Dillon. Lore's parents followed her to England. Their sad plight as refugee aliens formed a sharp contrast to Lore's ability to adapt easily.

After Lore's college graduation, she emigrated with her mother, first to the Dominican Republic and finally to New York. The Holocaust becomes a very personal tragedy as Lore recounts the deaths of her father, her grandfather, and her uncle's wife. A sensitive child, she fought her own battles against the forces that would take away her identity.

Other People's Houses presents an unusual angle on growing up during World War II. As Segal writes from an adult viewpoint, the author's memories of her experiences jump from the page with clarity and precision.

The Shoes of the Fisherman

by Morris L. West

William Morrow and Company, New York, 1963.

The Shoes of the Fisherman is a fictional look inside the Vatican, as the Roman Catholic Church struggles to relate faith to the real world. After long imprisonment in Siberia, Kiril Cardinal Lakota is released by Kamenev, his tormentor. Suddenly Kiril is elected pope, chosen to walk in "the shoes of the fisherman." Pope Kiril shakes conservatives like Cardinal Leone by his efforts to relate the church to the struggles of the ordinary man.

Fighting his own private battle against depression and loneliness, Kiril tries to understand the task he faces. His battles are shown through segments of his private journals. The pope finds a friend in Jean Telemond, a brilliant Jesuit who has been forbidden to publish because he is suspected of heresy.

Subplots include the private battle of George Faber, a newsman seeking love, and Ruth Lewin, who tries to find again the Jewishness she had rejected.

World concerns overshadow personal griefs and struggles. Seeking to avert a war, Pope Kiril becomes the diplomatic mediator between the president of the United States and Kamenev, now premier of the Soviet Union. *The Shoes of the Fisherman* shows the relationship between faith and doubt in the private lives of the men who shape public policy.

All the President's Men

by Bob Woodward and Carl Bernstein

Simon and Schuster, New York, 1974.

All the President's Men, the story of the Watergate break-in and cover-up, has been called "the most devastating detective story of the century." On June 17, 1972, Carl Bernstein and Bob Woodward, reporters at the *Washington Post*, covered a seemingly routine burglary at the Democratic Headquarters in Washington. In the following weeks the repercussions of this crime reached to the highest levels of the Nixon administration.

The reporters traced rumors and talked to frightened government employees who were reluctant to reveal the crime at the top. Woodward's contact, nicknamed "Deep Throat," confirmed that Nixon's men had used all kinds of dirty tricks to discredit the Democrats. Haldeman, Ehrlichman, Stans, and others would stop at nothing to achieve their own political ends.

At the trial of the Watergate burglars and later at the Senate Watergate hearings, everything that Woodward and Bernstein had discovered was proven. Resignations of the men closest to the president marked the end of an era.

All the President's Men is a fascinating account of the use and misuse of political power. This book is indispensable reading for the study of modern American history.

Name _____ Date_____

Go Tell It on the Mountain
by James Baldwin

Select the letter of the word or phrase which correctly completes each sentence.

_____ 1. The main plot of the novel begins on (A) Christmas (B) John's birthday (C) Roy's wedding day (D) Easter.

_____ 2. John seeks most the affection and approval of (A) his father (B) his mother (C) Roy (D) Aunt Florence.

_____ 3. John's chief job in the church is (A) preaching (B) playing the piano (C) teaching younger children (D) cleaning.

_____ 4. Roy is injured in (A) a knife fight (B) a store robbery (C) a gun battle (D) a car accident.

_____ 5. John's role model was (A) his father (B) Roy (C) Elisha (D) Richard.

_____ 6. During her childhood, Florence's closest friend was (A) Esther (B) Deborah (C) Mary (D) Elizabeth.

_____ 7. Florence felt rejected because (A) she was not pretty (B) she was not intelligent (C) Gabriel got all the attention (D) her mother died when she was a baby.

_____ 8. After Gabriel was converted, he (A) left home (B) became a preacher (C) married Esther (D) went to college.

_____ 9. Gabriel's first son was named (A) Royal (B) David (C) John (D) Richard.

_____ 10. Gabriel found that he no longer loved Deborah when (A) she became ill (B) he realized how very old she was (C) she refused to adopt his son (D) he found out that she could not have children.

_____ 11. Elizabeth left home (A) to get a better job (B) to escape from her mother (C) to have more freedom (D) all of the above.

_____ 12. Gabriel and Elizabeth met (A) at church (B) at the movies (C) on the train (D) at Florence's apartment.

(continued)

© 1991 J. Weston Walch, Publisher   *100 More Great Books: Synopses, Quizzes, and Tests*

Name _____ Date_____

Go Tell It on the Mountain
by James Baldwin

_____ 13. When Gabriel asked Elizabeth to marry him, he promised that he would (A) take her back to the South (B) give up preaching and get a better job (C) love and provide for John (D) send John to college.

_____ 14. John's real father (A) was intelligent and sensitive (B) loved Elizabeth deeply (C) killed himself (D) all of the above.

_____ 15. During John's vision, the boy feels as though he is (A) in a deep pit (B) in heaven (C) on fire (D) speaking in a different tongue.

_____ 16. John's religious experience takes place (A) during the Sunday service (B) in his bedroom (C) in a park (D) at a Saturday night meeting.

_____ 17. Gabriel had the greatest hopes for (A) Roy (B) John (C) Elisha (D) Ruth.

_____ 18. All of the following helped John "pray through" *except* (A) his mother (B) Elisha (C) Sister McCandless (D) Mother Washington.

_____ 19. John's praying took (A) under an hour (B) all night (C) all afternoon (D) three hours.

_____ 20. John makes a significant move toward manhood when he can (A) confront his father (B) pray like Elijah (C) preach (D) get over his feelings of jealousy toward Roy.

© 1991 J. Weston Walch, Publisher

Name _____ Date_____

Go Tell It on the Mountain
by James Baldwin

Answer the following questions in two or three complete sentences.

1. Describe the religion of the community of "Saints" to which John's family belonged.

   _____

   _____

   _____

2. How were Roy and John different in their behavior toward their father?

   _____

   _____

   _____

3. In what ways had Florence's experience made her bitter?

   _____

   _____

   _____

4. What internal battles did Gabriel continue to fight?

   _____

   _____

   _____

5. Why did Elizabeth feel closer to John than to any of her other children?

   _____

   _____

   _____

Challenge Question

Several characters in *Go Tell It on the Mountain* struggle to find meaning for their lives. Write an essay discussing the ways that each succeeds or fails in this quest.

© 1991 J. Weston Walch, Publisher   *100 More Great Books: Synopses, Quizzes, and Tests*

Name_____ Date_____

Only Earth and Sky Last Forever by Nathaniel Benchley

Place a T before each true statement and an F before each false statement.

_____ 1. Running Deer was Dark Elk's friend and companion.

_____ 2. Lashuka's father was exiled from his village after he killed a man who tried to cheat him.

_____ 3. Dark Elk felt that the Indians' only hope for survival lay in returning to the reservation.

_____ 4. "Washita" was the Sioux term for an Indian who had followed the ways of the white man.

_____ 5. Dark Elk intended to capture the great eagle by grabbing the bird by the legs.

_____ 6. Lashuka's grandmother approved of Dark Elk's friendship with her granddaughter.

_____ 7. Crazy Horse used Dark Elk as an advance scout when the young man went into his first battle.

_____ 8. Dark Elk's parents had been massacred by the whites.

_____ 9. The Indians believed that the Great Spirit lived in the hills of the high country.

_____ 10. The whites wanted the Indian lands because the area was rich in trees and wildlife.

_____ 11. When the whites met in council with the Indians, the tribal leaders were surrounded by white soldiers.

_____ 12. Dark Elk rescued Lashuka's grandmother after her village was attacked by the white soldiers.

_____ 13. The white man's "fire water" had terrible effects on the Indians.

_____ 14. The Indian chiefs broke every treaty they made with the white man.

_____ 15. A young brave's worth was measured by how many ponies he owned.

_____ 16. The sound of the owl was given by the young warriors as a signal that they were returning to camp.

_____ 17. Dark Elk and Lashuka ran away and got married without her grandmother's permission.

_____ 18. The Battle at the Little Big Horn lasted for four days.

_____ 19. Dark Elk was inducted into the Elk *akicita*, or warrior society.

_____ 20. As the story ended, Dark Elk saw the defeat of the Indians by the whites as inevitable.

Name _____ Date_____

Only Earth and Sky Last Forever by Nathaniel Benchley

Answer the following questions in two or three complete sentences.

1. What difficulties did Dark Elk face in proving himself an Indian warrior and winning the approval of Lashuka's grandmother?

   _____

   _____

   _____

2. How do the circumstances of Dark Elk's adoptive parents at the Red Cloud reservation show the white man's brutal treatment of the Indians?

   _____

   _____

   _____

3. Why does Dark Elk want to capture the eagle? Why does he fail?

   _____

   _____

   _____

4. What opportunities to become a man does Dark Elk find in the camp of Crazy Horse?

   _____

   _____

   _____

5. How does Dark Elk change after Lashuka is killed?

   _____

   _____

   _____

Challenge Question

Discuss the ways that the nobility of the American Indian is shown in the character of Dark Elk.

© 1991 J. Weston Walch, Publisher   *100 More Great Books: Synopses, Quizzes, and Tests*

Name _____   Date_____

Bury My Heart at Wounded Knee by Dee Brown

Match each description in Column A with the correct name in Column B.

Column A		Column B
_____	1. Cheyenne camp where Indians were massacred while standing under the American flag	A. Kit Carson
_____	2. White men who had married into the Cheyenne tribe	B. Satanta
_____	3. Samuel Parker, Iroquois who served as Indian commissioner under President Grant	C. Donehogawa
_____	4. Led the Nez Percé in their futile fight for survival	D. Crazy Horse
_____	5. Civil war hero who came west to organize the cavalry's battle against the Indian tribes	E. Sherman
_____	6. Made fortunes selling guns and whiskey to the Indians	F. Wovoka
_____	7. White plainsman who was greatly respected by the Navaho	G. Chief Joseph
_____	8. Blond officer who massacred the Black Hills Indians and was killed by them in revenge	H. Sitting Bull
_____	9. Oglala chief who won battles against the white man; he later worked for the government in persuading other Indians to go to the reservations	I. Little Big Man
_____	10. Leader of the Oregon Modoc tribe who was forced by his own braves to murder a white officer	J. Sand Creek
_____	11. Warrior whose heart was buried near Wounded Knee Creek	K. "Laramie Loafers"
_____	12. Led the Kiowa and the Comanche in their struggle to save the buffalo herds from extermination	L. Tom Jeffords
_____	13. Coined the saying "The only good Indian is a dead Indian."	M. General Sheridan
_____	14. Warned his people, the Sioux, not to sell their reservation lands to the greedy white men	N. George Armstrong Custer
_____	15. White friend of Cochise who tried to help the Apache save their land	O. Wounded Knee
_____	16. Last of the great Apache chiefs, forced to live as a renegade in Mexico	P. William and George Bent
_____	17. Indian chief who was legally declared a "person" by a federal judge	Q. Standing Bear
_____	18. Indian warrior who, as a prison guard, assisted as a white soldier killed Crazy Horse	R. Captain Jack
_____	19. Site of the final massacre which destroyed the last of the Sioux	S. Geronimo
_____	20. Self-proclaimed Indian "Messiah," whose ritual included "The Dance of the Ghosts"	T. Red Cloud

© 1991 J. Weston Walch, Publisher

Name_____ Date_____

Bury My Heart at Wounded Knee by Dee Brown

Answer the following questions in two or three complete sentences.

1. In what ways did the Indians learn brutality from the government soldiers?

_____

_____

_____

2. How did the Indians' beliefs about the land differ from the beliefs of the white men?

_____

_____

_____

3. How were Captain Jack and Chief Joseph forced to become warriors?

_____

_____

_____

4. List three white men who were true friends to the Indians.

_____

_____

_____

5. How was greed a factor in the destruction of the various Indian tribes?

_____

_____

_____

Challenge Question

In his preface to *Bury My Heart at Wounded Knee*, Dee Brown says that he intends to give the reader "a clearer understanding of what the American Indian is, by knowing what he was."

Write an essay discussing how the Indians were forced to exchange their independence and nobility for "poverty, hopelessness and squalor." What attributes of the Indians' natures made them easy victims?

© 1991 J. Weston Walch, Publisher   *100 More Great Books: Synopses, Quizzes, and Tests*

Name_____ Name_____ Date_____

Crime and Punishment by Fyodor Dostoyevsky

Match each description in Column A with the correct name in Column B.

Column A

_____ 1. A socialist who believed in free love without the commitment of marriage

_____ 2. Left the money which freed Raskolnikov's mother and sister from poverty

_____ 3. The most thoroughly good man in the novel

_____ 4. Setting for most of the story's action

_____ 5. Painter falsely accused of the crime

_____ 6. Paid for Marmeladov's funeral

_____ 7. Raskolnikov's mother

_____ 8. The maid who brought Raskolnikov his meals

_____ 9. Sonia's violent stepmother

_____ 10. Attempted to shoot Svidrigailov

_____ 11. Sonia's younger sister

_____ 12. Attempted to frame Sonia as a thief

_____ 13. Loved Raskolnikov and offered to share the cross of atoning for his guilt

_____ 14. Was crushed under the wheels of a carriage

_____ 15. Committed suicide

_____ 16. Setting for the novel's "Epilogue"

_____ 17. Second victim of Raskolnikov's crime

_____ 18. Doctor and friend of Razumihin

_____ 19. Old woman who violently abused her sister

_____ 20. Police officer who first recognized Raskolnikov's guilt

Column B

A. Raskolnikov

B. Alyona Ivanovna

C. Lizaveta

D. Razumihin

E. Katrina Ivanovna

F. Sonia

G. Porfiry Petrovitch

H. Dr. Zossimov

I. Dounia

J. Marfa Petrovna

K. Svidrigailov

L. Nilolay

M. Lebeziatnikov

N. Pulcheria Alexandrovna

O. Petersburg

P. Luzhin

Q. Natasha

R. Polenka

S. Siberia

T. Marmeladov

© 1991 J. Weston Walch, Publisher

Name _____ Date_____

Crime and Punishment by Fyodor Dostoyevsky

Answer the following questions in two or three complete sentences.

1. What "chance" happenings allow Raskolnikov to get away with killing the old pawnbroker?

   _____

   _____

   _____

2. How are both Dounia and Sonia victims of the evil of others?

   _____

   _____

   _____

3. What actions of Raskolnikov reveal the goodness in his nature?

   _____

   _____

   _____

4. Explain Raskolnikov's theory of "ordinary" and "extraordinary" people.

   _____

   _____

   _____

5. Explain why *Crime and Punishment*, in spite of its dark content, has a positive resolution.

   _____

   _____

   _____

Challenge Question

Defend the following statement: Dostoyevsky shows humanity as being a complex mixture of good and evil. Destruction and redemption are both real possibilities.

© 1991 J. Weston Walch, Publisher

Name_____ Date_____

Intruder in the Dust by William Faulkner

Supply the word or phrase which correctly completes each sentence.

1. The poor whites hated Lucas because _____ .

2. Lucas had saved Charlie's life by _____ .

3. The place where the Gowries live is named _____ .

4. Lucas asks Charlie to _____ .

5. Charlie travels to the cemetery on a _____ named _____ .

6. Miss Habersham goes with the boys because _____ .

7. Charlie wants to prevent _____ .

8. The man that Miss Habersham and the boys find in the grave is _____ .

9. When his uncle goes to the cemetery, they find that the grave _____ .

10. The two outstanding details of Miss Habersham's appearance are her _____ _____ and her _____ .

11. Aside from his uncle, the member of Charlie's family who becomes involved in helping Lucas is _____ .

12. As he travels back from the cemetery with his uncle, the countryside looks unusual to Charlie because _____ .

13. Lawyer Stevens refers to the blacks as _____ .

14. The body that the boys saw being carried on the mule was _____ .

15. Crawford shot his brother because _____ .

16. Vince Gowrie's body is found _____ .

17. The time covered by the main action of the novel is about _____ .

18. Aside from Stevens, the only other white man who tries to prove that Lucas is innocent is _____ .

19. As he tells the story, Charlie seems to suffer from _____ .

20. After Lucas is freed, he asks Stevens for _____ _____ .

© 1991 J. Weston Walch, Publisher

Name _____ Date_____

Intruder in the Dust by William Faulkner

Answer the following questions in two or three complete sentences.

1. What actions of Lucas's anger the white community?

   _____

   _____

   _____

2. How does Charlie know that the town is in a dangerous mood?

   _____

   _____

   _____

3. What evidence proved that Lucas could not have shot Vince?

   _____

   _____

   _____

4. Why was Lucas on the scene when Vince died?

   _____

   _____

   _____

5. During this experience, what does Charlie learn about his southern heritage?

   _____

   _____

   _____

Challenge Question

Faulkner often uses the narrative device of stream of consciousness, moving back and forth in time within the mind of a single character. Explain how Charlie condenses both time and space as he recounts his experiences.

© 1991 J. Weston Walch, Publisher   *100 More Great Books: Synopses, Quizzes, and Tests*

Name _____   Date_____

Farewell to Manzanar by Jeanne Wakatsuki Houston

Select the letter of the word or phrase which correctly completes each sentence.

_____ 1. When Pearl Harbor was bombed, Jeanne (A) had not been born (B) was seven years old (C) was a teenager (D) had just become engaged to be married.

_____ 2. Jeanne's father was arrested because (A) he had been in the Japanese army (B) he refused to sign the loyalty oath (C) he was suspected of giving information to the enemy (D) he had burned the American flag.

_____ 3. An "Issei" is (A) Japanese food (B) the Japanese word for "foreigner" (C) an American-born Japanese (D) a Japanese who emigrated to the United States.

_____ 4. A serious problem in their housing at Manzanar was caused by (A) sand (B) snow and ice (C) rats (D) fleas.

_____ 5. The most optimistic member of Jeanne's family during their camp experience was (A) her mother (B) her father (C) her brother Woody (D) her grandmother.

_____ 6. Jeanne's attitude on the journey to the camp may be best described as (A) fear (B) curiosity (C) anger (D) resignation.

_____ 7. Jeanne's father was (A) a proud dreamer (B) a heavy drinker (C) concerned with the honor of his family (D) all of the above.

_____ 8. At Manzanar, Jeanne participated in all of the following *except* (A) baton lessons (B) drama classes (C) ballet (D) church catechism lessons.

_____ 9. The others in the camp called Jeanne's father an "inu" or dog because (A) he was very ugly (B) he had a nasty temper (C) they thought he had collaborated with the enemy (D) he drank too much.

_____ 10. The riots at Manzanar were caused when (A) food was short (B) conditions became too crowded (C) three men were accused of stealing (D) anger was expressed against those who wanted to return to Japan.

_____ 11. Jeanne experienced her greatest difficulty in adjustment (A) when her father returned (B) when her brother joined the army (C) when she returned to school after leaving the camp (D) when her grandmother died.

(continued)

© 1991 J. Weston Walch, Publisher

100 More Great Books: Synopses, Quizzes, and Tests

Name_____ Date_____

Farewell to Manzanar by Jeanne Wakatsuki Houston

_____ 12. Her father most disapproved of Jeanne's (A) American dress (B) desire to join the Catholic Church (C) Caucasian boyfriend (D) American speech patterns.

_____ 13. Jeanne's brother Woody found his sense of heritage by (A) talking with his father (B) learning to speak Japanese (C) visiting his father's family in Japan (D) reading old Japanese manuscripts.

_____ 14. After the war, Jeanne's mother (A) died (B) became the financial provider for the family (C) divorced Jeanne's father (D) had a nervous breakdown.

_____ 15. When he learned that the camp at Manzanar was going to be closed, Jeanne's father (A) at first refused to leave (B) was anxious to get back to Los Angeles (C) decided to move to New Jersey (D) decided to take the bus back to Los Angeles.

_____ 16. When she returned to school, Jeanne found her greatest sense of acceptance (A) because she was a good student (B) in the Girl Scouts (C) as a majorette (D) when she was elected homecoming queen.

_____ 17. When Jeanne received a scholastic award, she (A) was ashamed of her parents at the ceremony (B) did not tell her parents (C) was refused the prize because she was Japanese (D) felt happy and proud.

_____ 18. Jeanne envied her friend Radine because (A) Radine was Caucasian (B) Radine's family was wealthy (C) Radine was accepted by everyone (D) Radine got better grades in school than Jeanne did.

_____ 19. When Jeanne and her family went back to Manzanar, they found (A) the camp exactly as they had left it (B) locked gates that they could not get through (C) a few ruined remains (D) several other families visiting at the same time.

_____ 20. Jeanne (A) blamed the government for her father's death (B) believed that her life was ruined by her experience in the camp (C) did not want to tell her children about Manzanar (D) saw herself as a child in the responses of her daughter.

Name_____ Date_____

Farewell to Manzanar by Jeanne Wakatsuki Houston

Answer the following questions in two or three complete sentences.

1. Why did the American government move the Japanese-Americans to camps like Manzanar?

   _____

   _____

   _____

2. What does the phrase "shikata ga nai" mean? How does this reflect Jeanne's mother's response to their internment?

   _____

   _____

   _____

3. What conditions in the camp presented the greatest difficulties? How did people learn to cope?

   _____

   _____

   _____

4. How was Woody, Jeanne's brother, finally able to understand his father?

   _____

   _____

   _____

5. Why was Jeanne's visit to Manzanar in 1972 helpful and necessary for her?

   _____

   _____

   _____

   _____

Challenge Question

Discuss how Jeanne Wakatsuki's story shows the ability of human beings to find dignity and goodness, even under great pressure.

100 More Great Books: Synopses, Quizzes, and Tests

Name_____ Date_____

The Honorable Prison by Lyll de Becerra de Jenkins

Place a T before each true statement and an F before each false statement.

_____ 1. Marta has a younger brother and sister.

_____ 2. Marta's father was once a supporter of the General.

_____ 3. Marta's mother participates with enthusiasm in her husband's political activities.

_____ 4. Colonel Ferreira, who commands the troops at the pueblo, is considerate of the needs of Marta's family.

_____ 5. The family decides to eat one meal each day at the base mess hall.

_____ 6. The General does not know that Marta's father is ill when he exiles the family to the remote base.

_____ 7. Under the General's regime, political executions are common.

_____ 8. Parades and festivals are used as a cover-up for the persecutions and murders that are really taking place.

_____ 9. Paulo, the soldier assigned to take Marta to the market, abuses Marta and makes fun of her.

_____ 10. Fernando's uncle is a captain in the General's army.

_____ 11. Honorio, Pedro's uncle, succeeds in his attempt to smuggle medicines to Marta's father.

_____ 12. Marta's father and mother identify with the needs of the peasant classes because both of them come from peasant backgrounds themselves.

_____ 13. Aspirin and alcohol are the only medicines available in the remote mountain town.

_____ 14. Marta works for several weeks as an assistant teacher in Fernando's school.

_____ 15. Although he appears to help them, Pedro is really an informer who reports all the family's activities to the army.

_____ 16. Fernando is beaten and killed by the soldiers.

_____ 17. When Marta's mother goes to see the colonel, he responds at once to her request for help.

_____ 18. The doctor sent to see Marta's father is unable to be of any real help because he lacks the proper equipment and medicine.

_____ 19. Marta decides to leave her family so that she can have a free life of her own.

_____ 20. As the novel ends, the General's regime has been overthrown.

© 1991 J. Weston Walch, Publisher   *100 More Great Books: Synopses, Quizzes, and Tests*

Name _____   Date _____

The Honorable Prison by Lyll de Becerra de Jenkins

Answer the following questions in two or three complete sentences.

1. How had Marta's father and his friends tried to fight the General's power?

_____

_____

_____

2. Why does the family's escape plan fail?

_____

_____

_____

3. Why does the pueblo become a death trap for Marta's father?

_____

_____

_____

4. Why do Pedro and the other peasants feel such a strong sense of loyalty to Marta's father?

_____

_____

_____

5. What contrast does the author make between Marta's father and Fernando's uncle?

_____

_____

_____

Challenge Question

Write an essay discussing the character development of Marta Maldonado. In what ways does she mature during her family's imprisonment?

Name _____   Date _____

Skindeep by Toeckey Jones

Place a T before each true statement and an F before each false statement.

_____   1. Rhonda and Dave meet at the local country club.

_____   2. In group discussions, Dave expresses strong antiapartheid sentiments.

_____   3. Rhonda's father agrees to send Rhonda to school in London.

_____   4. Rhonda's parents are in sympathy with the problems of black South Africans.

_____   5. Dave's appearance is made unusual by his complete lack of hair.

_____   6. Rhonda has not had a boyfriend before she meets Dave.

_____   7. Mark, Rhonda's brother, does not like Dave.

_____   8. Mark's dog is killed by a hit-and-run black driver.

_____   9. Rhonda pays for the trip to Capetown out of her own money.

_____   10. While in Capetown, Rhonda and Dave spend most of their time on a "Whites Only" beach.

_____   11. Mark's dog "Spoodie" got his name because he was a mixed breed.

_____   12. Dave tells Rhonda that his mother and brothers are dead.

_____   13. Sophie, the black maid, strongly disapproves of Rhonda's relationship with Dave.

_____   14. Mrs. Schwartz is Dave's adopted mother.

_____   15. Dave sees his real family on the street in Capetown.

_____   16. When she learns that Dave has black blood, Rhonda feels no sense of horror or disgust.

_____   17. Dave returns to Capetown to live as a black.

_____   18. Rhonda's father is more sympathetic than her mother when he learns of Rhonda's relationship with Dave.

_____   19. At the end of the novel, Rhonda has resumed her relationship with Dave.

_____   20. Dave has become very involved in antigovernment politics.

© 1991 J. Weston Walch, Publisher   *100 More Great Books: Synopses, Quizzes, and Tests*

Name_____   Date_____

Skindeep by Toeckey Jones

Answer the following questions in two or three complete sentences.

1. In what ways are the feelings of Rhonda's family typical of white South African attitudes?

   _____

   _____

   _____

2. What mysterious things about Dave make him attractive to Rhonda?

   _____

   _____

   _____

3. How do Joel and Lynn differ from Rhonda in their attitudes toward blacks?

   _____

   _____

   _____

4. What details of Dave's background does Rhonda learn from Mrs. Schwartz?

   _____

   _____

   _____

5. Why does Rhonda say at the novel's conclusion that she is afraid for Dave?

   _____

   _____

   _____

Challenge Question

Discuss the specific ways that Dave and Rhonda's relationship is doomed from its very beginning.

© 1991 J. Weston Walch, Publisher

Name _____ Date_____

Fragments of Isabella by Isabella Leitner

Supply the word or phrase which correctly completes each sentence.

1. Isabella's father tried to save his family by _____

   _____ .

2. The names of Isabella's three sisters were _____

   _____ .

3. Isabella and her family had lived in _____ .

4. The reaction of the Gentile neighbors to deporting the Jews was _____

   _____ .

5. The only member of Isabella's family to die in Auschwitz was _____ .

6. _____ was the officer who determined whether Jews would
   live or die.

7. The pact that the sisters made was that _____

   _____ .

8. Isabella failed as a "Kapo" because _____

   _____ , _____ .

9. The chief difference between Auschwitz and Birnbaumel was _____

   _____ .

10. The Germans marched their captives through the snowstorm because _____

    _____ .

11. The guards forced the prisoners out of hiding by _____

    _____ .

(continued)

© 1991 J. Weston Walch, Publisher   *100 More Great Books: Synopses, Quizzes, and Tests*

Name _____   Date _____

Fragments of Isabella by Isabella Leitner

12. Isabella and her sisters escaped when they _____
_____ .

13. The sister who failed to escape was _____ .

14. For the fugitives, the greatest find in the house was _____
_____ .

15. The women were finally liberated by _____ troops.

16. Isabella and her sisters came to America with the help of _____
_____ .

17. When she was first released, Isabella could not stand to use a mirror because ____
_____ .

18. Isabella wanted her mother's hope to live on through _____
_____ .

19. In Paris, Isabella was most deeply affected by _____
_____ .

20. Isabella had to leave the café because _____
_____ .

© 1991 J. Weston Walch, Publisher

Name_____   Date_____

Fragments of Isabella by Isabella Leitner

Answer the following questions in two or three complete sentences.

1. Why did Isabella's father fail in his attempt to rescue his family?

_____

_____

_____

2. How did Isabella's mother give strength to her daughters?

_____

_____

_____

3. How is Irma Grese the embodiment of Nazi cruelty?

_____

_____

_____

4. After their escape, how did the sisters survive until they were liberated?

_____

_____

_____

5. Why did Isabella return to Europe with her family after the war?

_____

_____

_____

Challenge Question

Write an essay discussing how *Fragments of Isabella* illustrates the determination of the human spirit to survive even the most horrible experiences.

© 1991 J. Weston Walch, Publisher

Name_____ Date_____

Kaffir Boy by Mark Mathabane

Place a T before each true statement and an F before each false statement.

_____ 1. Mark was the oldest child in his family.

_____ 2. Mark's parents were constantly in trouble with the authorities.

_____ 3. All the policemen who raided Mark's home were white.

_____ 4. Both Mark's parents were Christians who went to church regularly.

_____ 5. Predawn police raids were frequent when Mark was a child.

_____ 6. Mark's grandfather was an important stabilizing influence in his young life.

_____ 7. No physical punishment was permitted at the school Mark attended.

_____ 8. Mark's mother had to work long hours so that her son might have an education.

_____ 9. All Mark's school classes were conducted in English.

_____ 10. Mrs. Smith gave Mark his first tennis racket.

_____ 11. Tennis was the only sport that Mark played while he was in school.

_____ 12. Mark believes that his schooling saved him from a life of crime and street violence.

_____ 13. Mark's parents were both supportive of their son's efforts to free himself from apartheid.

_____ 14. Mark's despair almost led him to commit suicide.

_____ 15. Mark never personally participated in rioting and looting.

_____ 16. None of Mark's brothers and sisters had the opportunity to attend school.

_____ 17. Mark was blacklisted by blacks because he participated in white tournaments.

_____ 18. Stan Smith was Mark's grandmother's white employer.

_____ 19. Mark received the highest possible marks on his secondary school graduation exams.

_____ 20. Mark received a full tennis scholarship to Princeton University.

© 1991 J. Weston Walch, Publisher

Name _____   Date_____

Kaffir Boy by Mark Mathabane

Answer the following questions in two or three complete sentences.

1. What does the word "kaffir" mean? Why is it such a degrading term?

   _____

   _____

   _____

2. Why were Mark's mother and grandmother important in his life?

   _____

   _____

   _____

3. How was Arthur Ashe's visit significant for South Africa's black population?

   _____

   _____

   _____

4. How did Wilfred Harmon and Stan Smith help Mark's career?

   _____

   _____

   _____

5. Why did Mark believe that he had to leave South Africa?

   _____

   _____

   _____

Challenge Question

Write an essay describing the dehumanizing effects, shown in Mark Mathabane's autobiography, that apartheid has on the black population of South Africa.

Name _____   Date_____

Other People's Houses by Lore Segal

Place a T before each true statement and an F before each false statement.

_____   1. Lore has clear memories of the Nazis' first arrival in Austria.

_____   2. Lore's father and mother were both college professors.

_____   3. Lore's Uncle Paul was her special childhood friend.

_____   4. Lore's parents came to England about a year after Lore.

_____   5. Adapting was easy for Lore, regardless of where she had to live.

_____   6. Because she studied hard, Lore got top grades in her classes at the University of London.

_____   7. Lore's grandfather died in Austria and was buried near his family home.

_____   8. Albert Hooper and Lore hated each other.

_____   9. Both Lore's father and mother were interned in England as "hostile aliens."

_____   10. Lore's father died primarily because he could not adjust.

_____   11. Lore felt guilty because she believed that she had caused her father's death.

_____   12. Helene and Lore became close friends because both of them had been refugees as children.

_____   13. Miss Douglas and Mrs. Dillon refused to have Lore in their home when they found out that she was Jewish.

_____   14. Paul and Ilse were able to settle happily on the farming commune in the Dominican Republic.

_____   15. Lore's grandmother was difficult for the other members of the family to live with.

_____   16. After his wife's death, Paul went back to medical school.

_____   17. Lore taught English to diplomats in the Dominican Republic.

_____   18. Lore's grandfather and grandmother had several happy years living in New York together.

_____   19. Lore is both an artist and a writer.

_____   20. Lore's childhood experiences made a happy marriage impossible for her.

© 1991 J. Weston Walch, Publisher

Name_____ Date_____

Other People's Houses by Lore Segal

Answer the following questions in two or three complete sentences.

1. Why was Lore's friendship with her Uncle Paul so special?

   _____

   _____

   _____

2. What memories stand out of her trip to England on the "Children's Transport"?

   _____

   _____

   _____

3. In what ways was Lore's father a "war casualty"?

   _____

   _____

   _____

4. What difficulties did Lore have in the Dominican Republic as a displaced person?

   _____

   _____

   _____

5. Why does Lore describe her grandmother as "a formidable woman"?

   _____

   _____

   _____

Challenge Question

Explain in a well-developed essay specific ways that Lore Segal's experience as a child and young woman contributed to her development as a writer.

© 1991 J. Weston Walch, Publisher   *100 More Great Books: Synopses, Quizzes, and Tests*

Name _____ Name _____ Date_____

The Shoes of the Fisherman by Morris L. West

Select the letter of the word or phrase which correctly completes each sentence.

_____ 1. A new pope is selected by (A) the Rota (B) the Vatican Secretary of State (C) the College of Cardinals (D) a popular vote of all Catholics.

_____ 2. For Kiril Lakota, the most difficult part of his prison experience had been (A) Kamenev's interrogations (B) solitary confinement (C) not being able to say Mass (D) the Siberian cold.

_____ 3. Kiril was set free because (A) Kamenev needed him in the Vatican (B) the pope demanded it (C) Kiril's family was able to pay for his freedom (D) he was ill.

_____ 4. Kiril was proclaimed pope by (A) Telemond (B) Rinaldi (C) Leone (D) Semmering.

_____ 5. George Faber worked for (A) the Vatican (B) the Italian government (C) the American State Department (D) an American newspaper.

_____ 6. Pope Kiril met Ruth Lewin (A) in St. Peter's (B) in the room of a dying man (C) at a Vatican audience (D) at a press corps reception.

_____ 7. Campeggio agreed to (A) promote the Vatican foreign policy (B) carry a message to Kamenev (C) help George get evidence against Chiara's husband (D) interview Pope Kiril on the day of his coronation.

_____ 8. Pope Kiril was afraid that controversy in the church might be started by his (A) beard (B) accent (C) nationality (D) choice of a coat of arms.

_____ 9. As a coronation gift, Kamenev sent Pope Kiril (A) a cross (B) a book (C) his congratulations (D) a package of sunflower seeds.

_____ 10. Georg Wilhelm Forster was (A) the German ambassador to the Vatican (B) Kamenev's messenger to Kiril (C) Kiril's servant (D) a man who attempted to kill the pope.

_____ 11. Ruth Lewin found her faith again by (A) helping deformed children (B) working with poor Roman Jews (C) talking with the pope (D) all of the above.

(continued)

© 1991 J. Weston Walch, Publisher

Name_____ Date_____

The Shoes of the Fisherman by Morris L. West

_____ 12. When Kiril left the Vatican to mix with the ordinary people of Rome, he (A) forgot to take any money (B) got lost in the city (C) was seriously injured (D) was disgusted by what he saw.

_____ 13. Which of the following was *not* a change that Pope Kiril felt needed to be made? (A) Changing the church liturgy to the language of the people (B) Allowing priests to marry (C) Greater compassion from the church courts (D) Translation of church documents into the native languages of those who were studying for the priesthood

_____ 14. To gain Chiara's divorce, Faber stooped to (A) bribery (B) blackmail (C) libel (D) attempted manslaughter.

_____ 15. Calitri changed his testimony to the church court because he (A) wanted to further his own political ambitions (B) fell in love with somebody else (C) felt guilty for the way he had treated his wife (D) was advised to do so by his confessor.

_____ 16. After he became pope, Kiril's greatest need was for (A) rest (B) wise political advice (C) an Italian translator (D) a close friend.

_____ 17. Telemond struggled between (A) the church and science (B) faith and doubt (C) obedience and the desire for knowledge (D) Eastern Orthodox and Roman Catholic theology.

_____ 18. The greatest blow to Kiril was (A) the decision of the Holy Office to censor Telemond's books (B) Leone's refusal to support his political policies (C) Telemond's death (D) Rinaldi's retirement.

_____ 19. George Faber finds (A) love with Ruth (B) happiness with Chiara (C) political success in the Vatican (D) a new job with a Paris newspaper.

_____ 20. Kiril's proposal to travel to various countries in search of peace (A) is rejected by the Russians (B) is supported by the College of Cardinals (C) includes plans for a trip to China (D) will not include Africa or South America.

© 1991 J. Weston Walch, Publisher

Name_____   Date_____

The Shoes of the Fisherman by Morris L. West

Answer the following questions in two or three complete sentences.

1. Describe the process by which a new pope is chosen.

   _____

   _____

   _____

2. Why did the other cardinals feel that Kiril Lakota was the man to lead the church in a troubled world?

   _____

   _____

   _____

3. What struggle was shared by George Faber and Ruth Lewin?

   _____

   _____

   _____

4. Why were Telemond's ideas unacceptable to the church censors?

   _____

   _____

   _____

5. How did Pope Kiril hope to help the cause of world peace?

   _____

   _____

   _____

Challenge Question

Write an essay describing the private struggles of a man in a very public position which are narrated in *The Shoes of the Fisherman*.

© 1991 J. Weston Walch, Publisher

Name _____ Name _____ Date_____

All the President's Men
by Bob Woodward and Carl Bernstein

Match each description in Column A with the correct name in Column B.

Column A	Column B
_____ 1. Managing editor who supervised the publication of the Watergate stories	A. Kalmbach
	B. Ziegler
_____ 2. Former member of Nixon's election campaign who was willing to talk openly with the reporters	C. "Deep Throat"
_____ 3. President Nixon's press secretary who hated the *Washington Post*	D. Democratic National Committee
_____ 4. Democrat whose campaign was wrecked by the "Canuck letter"	
_____ 5. Nixon's personal lawyer, "paymaster" for the undercover agents	E. CREEP
_____ 6. Owner and publisher of the *Washington Post*	F. Muskie
_____ 7. Woodward's secret contact within the Nixon administration	G. McCord
_____ 8. Did extensive research on Edward Kennedy	H. Mitchell
_____ 9. In charge of wrecking the campaigns of various Democratic candidates by using an assortment of dirty tricks	I. Bradlee
	J. Bernstein
_____ 10. Nixon's chief of staff who supervised the Watergate cover-up	K. Katharine Graham
_____ 11. Judge at the Watergate trial	
_____ 12. Nixon's attorney general	L. Sloan
_____ 13. Organization formed to elect Nixon to a second term	M. Martha Mitchell
_____ 14. Watergate burglars were attempting to "bug" their offices	
_____ 15. FBI director who deliberately destroyed files of evidence	N. Segretti
_____ 16. First of the Watergate defendants to give evidence to the Senate investigating committee	O. Woodward
	P. L. Patrick Gray
_____ 17. Insisted that her husband resign as head of Nixon's campaign	Q. Haldeman
_____ 18. Kept insisting to the press that he was not a crook	R. Sirica
_____ 19. College drop-out who had gone to work for the *Washington Post* when he was sixteen	S. Nixon
	T. Howard Hunt
_____ 20. Met an informer in a parking garage in the middle of the night	

© 1991 J. Weston Walch, Publisher   *100 More Great Books: Synopses, Quizzes, and Tests*

Name_____ Date_____

All the President's Men
by Bob Woodward and Carl Bernstein

Answer the following questions in two or three complete sentences.

1. How were Woodward and Bernstein foils to each other in their personalities and in their methods of researching the Watergate story?

   _____

   _____

   _____

2. What checks did Bradlee insist upon before information could be published?

   _____

   _____

   _____

3. Describe Woodward's relationship with "Deep Throat." Why was this contact important in covering the story?

   _____

   _____

   _____

4. Why could Hugh Sloan be characterized as a courageous man?

   _____

   _____

   _____

5. How did Nixon's men try to prevent the *Washington Post* from printing the truth about their secret activities?

   _____

   _____

   _____

Challenge Question

Write an essay describing the "mushroom effect" of the Watergate affair, which began as a simple break-in and resulted in the downfall of a president.

© 1991 J. Weston Walch, Publisher

100 More Great Books: Synopses, Quizzes, and Tests

Answer Keys

Go Tell It on the Mountain by James Baldwin

Multiple Choice:

1. B	5. C	9. A	13. C	17. A
2. A	6. B	10. D	14. D	18. A
3. D	7. C	11. D	15. A	19. B
4. A	8. B	12. D	16. D	20. A

Short Answers:

1. The "Saints" are those to whom God has spoken. Each has had a special experience in which he or she "prayed through." The church gives meaning and excitement to their otherwise drab and dreary lives. The leaders of the church are responsible for the moral supervision of the congregation, especially the young.

2. Roy rebels outwardly and openly defies his father by participating in activities that are against their religious beliefs. He finally curses his father. John does everything to please his father, but never receives the affection he desires. Like his mother, John keeps all his feelings inside. No one knows what he feels or suffers.

3. Florence had been rejected by her mother in favor of her wild brother Gabriel. She finally walks away to seek a better life in New York. She never finds love, but instead becomes involved in an unhappy marriage with Frank, an alcoholic. Nearing the end of her life, Florence prays in a desperate attempt to resolve her anger at Gabriel and to find inner peace.

4. As a young man, Gabriel drank heavily and was involved with many women. After his unhappy marriage to Deborah, he had a passionate affair with Esther. His religion became a struggle to control his lust. His struggle made him harsh toward everyone, especially John, the child who was another man's son.

5. John was the child of Elizabeth's love relationship with Richard. Elizabeth saw in her son all his father's sensitivity. The mother hurt for John too because she knew that his sensitivity and intelligence would make the world a painful place for him.

Challenge Question:

Florence's struggles began in her childhood. A very intelligent child, Florence left home when her mother seemed fully focused on Gabriel, the worthless brother. She never found the happiness she sought. Her marriage to Frank ended when he walked out on her. Near the end of her life, Florence was left with only disease and bitterness. Her only victory lay in getting even with Gabriel by exposing her brother's sin to Elizabeth.

Gabriel had grand visions of establishing a "royal line" through a son. When Deborah could not have children, Gabriel had a child by Esther. Gabriel was never able to acknowledge Royal. The bitterness was greatest when he found out that his wife had known all along. Gabriel continued to make Elizabeth feel the guilt that he carried himself.

His son Roy also disappointed him. Gabriel's supreme grief was that the best child was John, the son who was not his.

Elizabeth had exchanged love for security. Because she loved Richard so much, she refused to insist on marriage, even when she learned that she was carrying Richard's child. Gabriel gave her food and shelter, but always made her feel guilty because of her love for Richard. The greatest irony for Elizabeth came when she found out that Gabriel, the perfect one, had committed the same sin.

Only John had hope for the positive resolution of his struggle. After his religious experience, he does not know what his future challenges will be. John's victory comes immediately, however, when he is able to look his father in the face and smile without fear. Having won this victory, John can take the next step forward toward finding an identity of his own that no one can take from him.

Only Earth and Sky Last Forever by Nathaniel Benchley

True or False:

1. F	4. F	7. F	10. F	13. T	16. F	19. T
2. T	5. T	8. T	11. F	14. F	17. F	20. T
3. F	6. F	9. T	12. T	15. T	18. F	

Short Answers:

1. His parents had been killed, so Dark Elk had to live at the reservation. He had no opportunity to prove himself in combat or to get the ponies necessary to purchase a wife.

2. Food was scarce and of poor quality. Indians drank too much liquor. By leaving their own ways of life, the Indian men lost their sense of self-respect. Indians no longer trusted each other.

3. Dark Elk wanted the eagle's feathers as a gift for Lashuka. He could not hold on when the eagle bit his wrist with its beak.

4. Dark Elk can fulfill the functions of an Indian male. He helps the tribe hunt for buffalo. He learns how a warrior must function under pressure: by handling the horses, by serving as a scout, and by participating in the attack on the wagon train. He finally qualifies for full membership in the society of warriors.

5. Lashuka is his reason for living. After her death, he fights blindly, not caring whether he lives or dies. When he no longer has her, he submits mentally, and later physically, to the white man's system.

Challenge Question:

Dark Elk puts loyalty to his tribe above any personal fears. He will fight for that which he values. He is close to nature. His sense of integrity stands in contrast to the white man's continual treachery. The young hero of this novel becomes a symbol of primitive goodness which is destroyed by the avarice of civilization.

Bury My Heart at Wounded Knee by Dee Brown

Matching:

1. J	6. K	11. D	16. S
2. P	7. A	12. B	17. Q
3. C	8. N	13. M	18. I
4. G	9. T	14. H	19. O
5. E	10. R	15. L	20. F

Short Answers:

1. Scalping and physical mutilation were first practiced by the soldiers at battles like Sandy Creek. The whites also killed innocent women and children along with the warriors. The Indians copied what they saw the whites do.

2. For the Indian, the land was sacred. No one had a right to own it. The whites used the land to satisfy their greed. The Indian hunted only the animals that he needed. The whites massacred the animals so that whole tribes starved.

3. Both chiefs tried to live peacefully and were willing to make concessions to the whites. Both chiefs were forced into hostilities when the soldiers attacked them.

4. George and William Bent married Indians. Both acted as interpreters in trying to get the Indians a fair deal in treaty dealings with the whites. Major Edward Wynkoop tried to get his superior officers to stop brutalizing the Indians. He was replaced by someone who would do the killing. General Crook tried to help Standing Bear and the Poncas keep their land. He failed when government officials passed laws to preserve the corrupt reservation system.

5. The whites wanted gold in the Black Hills, oil in Oklahoma, farmland in Texas and Colorado. They needed the railroads to carry goods and settlers. Greed for these things overshadowed all human considerations in the whites' dealings with the Indians.

Challenge Question:

Each tribe is pictured as having a unique way of life which was threatened by white encroachment. Occasionally the Indian chiefs won temporary victories. Soon, however, the superior forces of the whites made further resistance futile.

Dee Brown also pictures the Indians as noble and trusting. They tried to cooperate with the whites, but were the victims of broken agreements. Those who adopted the ways of the white man became weak as they were forced to surrender their way of life. Indians frequently betrayed other Indians to the whites in exchange for promises of food and protection. The tribal system was destroyed. The Indians, deprived of their hunting lands, were forced to live on reservations, always established on worthless land that the white man did not want. In the author's opinion, the Indian's greatest catastrophe is that he has been robbed of his heritage. Thirty years of systematic destruction, 1860–1890, made the Indians the downtrodden and frustrated race that they are today.

Crime and Punishment by Fyodor Dostoyevsky

Matching:

1. M	4. O	7. N	10. I	13. F	16. S	19. B
2. J	5. L	8. Q	11. R	14. T	17. C	20. G
3. D	6. A	9. E	12. P	15. K	18. H	

Short Answers:

1. The porter is not in the lodge. Raskolnikov can hide in the empty apartment. No one sees him enter or leave the building. He overhears a conversation which lets him know the exact time when the victim will be alone.

2. Dounia has been forced into an engagement with Luzhin. Both he and Svidrigailov try to make her a financial prisoner. Sonia is also forced to sell her body to survive.

3. His care for Marmeladov, his love for his mother and sister, his love for Sonia and concern for her family.

4. Ordinary people must obey the law and are responsible for the crimes that they commit. "Extraordinary" people become their own law and are not bound by any moral code. Napoleon becomes Raskolnikov's model of the "extraordinary" man.

5. Confession and acceptance of suffering bring redemption. Realizing that he is an "ordinary" man, Raskolnikov finds love and peace only when he accepts the moral responsibility for his actions.

Challenge Question:

Human nature is portrayed in the complexity of Raskolnikov's character. He loves and hates. He is gentle in his love for Sonia, yet completely amoral when he kills. Evil is cloaked with respectability in the characters of Luzhin and Svidrigailov. Sonia, although she is outside society's moral code, is a woman of selfless goodness. The same love for a woman destroys Svidrigailov, redeems Sonia and Raskolnikov, and brings happiness to Dounia and Razumihin. Lust turned inward destroys. Love turned toward others redeems.

Intruder in the Dust by William Faulkner

Fill-ins:

1. he refuses to act like a Negro
2. pulling him out of the creek
3. "Beat Four"
4. dig up the body
5. horse, Highboy
6. Lucas worked for her
7. a lynching
8. Jake Montgomery
9. is empty
10. gloves, hat, shoes
11. his mother
12. he didn't see any Negroes
13. Sambo
14. Jake
15. Vin stole from him
16. in the quicksand
17. forty-eight hours
18. Sheriff Hampton
19. lack of sleep
20. a receipt for the money that Lucas paid Stevens

Short Answers:

1. Lucas is proud. He will never beg or crawl. He is always well-dressed. He refuses to shuffle and call the white men "master" or "sir." He is independent and refuses to accept charity from anyone.

2. The square is packed with cars. People are waiting for the Gowries to come. The sheriff has put a guard at the jail door. The blacks are all hiding in fear.

3. The man had been shot with a Luger. Lucas owned a Colt .45.

4. Lucas was out walking when he saw the lumber being stolen. When Lucas reported this, Crawford offered to pay him to identify the thieves. Lucas was supposed to meet Crawford in the woods. Instead, Vinson came and Crawford shot him. Lucas found the body.

5. Charlie learns that hatred against blacks is the evil in his southern heritage. He also learns that a man can be noble, regardless of the color of his skin.

Challenge Question:

Intruder in the Dust uses extensive flashbacks. The style of the novel is difficult. The reader must stop frequently to ask where Charlie is, in both place and time. His thoughts are mingled with the story line.

The story begins when Lucas is arrested. Charlie goes back in time to tell how Lucas saved him. His visit to Lucas's home and Lucas's refusal to take his money explain Lucas's pride. A flashback also gives us Miss Habersham's background. The internal narrator in the present gives us Charlie's thoughts. He is afraid as he travels to the cemetery. Place is also condensed. Charlie's mind moves from one scene to another as he imagines Miss Habersham's trip home. His mind probes the fear of the blacks as they believe that the whites may go on a rampage.

Farewell to Manzanar by Jeanne Wakatsuki Houston

Multiple Choice:

1. B	5. C	9. C	13. C	17. A
2. C	6. B	10. D	14. B	18. C
3. D	7. D	11. C	15. A	19. C
4. A	8. B	12. B	16. C	20. D

Short Answers:

1. The government believed that leaving the Japanese on the West Coast presented a security threat. They were afraid that people who had relatives in Japan or who had been born there would give information to the enemy.

2. The phrase means "it cannot be helped" or "it must be done." Jeanne's mother coped with the circumstances. She stored her furniture and adjusted to the hardships of the camp. She put up with her husband's drinking and submitted even when he tried to beat her.

3. Primitive living conditions and lack of privacy were the greatest problems. People made the barracks into homes. They made beauty from piles of rocks. Those who had skills shared them with others. They practiced their culture and traditions. People remained human by sharing and helping each other.

4. Returning to Japan with the occupation forces, Woody visited with Aunt Toyo, his father's sister. Woody was able to understand his father better and also to gain an appreciation of his own Japanese heritage.

5. Jeanne visited Manzanar to understand herself as she was when she lived there. This understanding, which is reflected in her writing this book, helped her to move out from her past, to finally leave Manzanar behind her forever.

Challenge Question:

Jeanne's mother preserved her dignity when she broke her china rather than allow herself to be cheated. People at the camp coped in simple ways: using cardboard to give themselves privacy, sharing cooking skills to improve the poor food, sharing with others whatever they had, preserving the Japanese tradition of polite manners. The older people passed their knowledge on to the children. One old lady tried to teach ballet to give her life some meaning.

Jeanne's father, even though he had failed at so much, continued to dream. He needed to assert his authority and to remain the head of his family. Although arguments sometimes erupted, there was still tenderness between Jeanne's parents. Her father's final expression of his dignity came when he bought a car because he refused to be shipped back on the bus. Jeanne learned from her father. Gaining strength through her Manzanar experience, she became a strong person in spite of rejection.

The Honorable Prison by Lyll de Becerra de Jenkins

True or False:

1. F	6. F	11. F	16. F
2. T	7. T	12. F	17. F
3. F	8. T	13. T	18. T
4. F	9. F	14. F	19. F
5. F	10. F	15. F	20. T

Short Answers:

1. Marta's father printed the paper as long as he could. After the presses were shut down, the paper was printed and distributed secretly. The political group that Marta's father belonged to also tried to help those who were being politically persecuted by the General. This group of freedom fighters was trying to overthrow the oppressive dictatorship.

2. All their money was withdrawn from the bank to pay for the escape. Someone at the bank told the authorities. The family was arrested before they could get to the car that was to take them to freedom.

3. The General intends to kill Marta's father slowly by placing him in a climate that will destroy his health. Slow starvation, a wet climate, and lack of proper medical attention all contribute to his lung disease. The father and husband is also worn down emotionally as he watches his family suffer. Marta's father, however, is a strong man who holds to his ideals, even as he is dying. Marguerite, Marta's mother, is the one who breaks under the strain of the imprisonment.

4. Marta's father understood the suffering of the peasants because he was also a *campesino*, one who came from peasant stock. He had left the country to go to law school so that he could fight for the common man. Having his own father murdered by the authorities made Señor Maldonado feel that he was one with the people.

5. Marta's father fights for his ideals. He will hang on to his beliefs, even when loyalty means death. He continued to risk his life printing his paper rather than take an easy diplomatic post in Europe. The mayor, Fernando's uncle, has no principles other than self-preservation. He will be loyal to whichever regime happens to be in power.

Challenge Question:

Marta's conflict is between her loyalty to her family and her own need for self-expression. Fernando makes her conflict more complicated when he offers her an easy way out, a chance to run away with him. Marta's attraction to Fernando is part of her adolescent development. Finally, however, she chooses family loyalty over her fascination with him.

At first she hates what this imprisonment has done to her family. She asks, "Is any ideal worth this?" However, as she sits by her dying father, Marta realizes the strength he possesses. He becomes for her the "indispensable man," the one who sacrifices himself for others. Imprisonment matures Marta and helps her choose her father's unselfish route; she places others, her brother and her mother, above self-interest. The death of Pedro, the young soldier who risked his life to feed the family, is a turning point which teaches Marta what courage really is.

Skindeep by Toeckey Jones

True or False:

1. F	5. T	9. T	13. F	17. T
2. F	6. F	10. F	14. T	18. F
3. F	7. F	11. T	15. T	19. F
4. F	8. F	12. T	16. F	20. T

Short Answers:

1. They fear violence from the blacks. They view the blacks as subhumans, seeing them only as servants. They take white superiority for granted. They want to protect their privileged way of life.

2. Answers might include: his sharp, keen eyes; the mystery about his hair; his lack of willingness to talk about himself.

3. Joel and Lynn are activists, see blacks as people, and want to work for the abolition of apartheid. They are willing to help Rhonda when she wants to be with Dave. They also shelter her when she learns the truth.

4. Dave's mother wanted her son to pass for white so that he could have a better education and way of life. Mrs. Schwartz adopted him to give him that chance.

5. Dave has made the choice to return to being black. He faces violence from his own brother. He is in danger from the police.

Challenge Question:

Rhonda is a product of the white South African system. Dave has chosen to live as a black. She cannot do this. Also, their relationship was based on a lie from the beginning. When the truth was revealed, it was more than either of them could handle.

Fragments of Isabella by Isabella Leitner

Fill-ins:

1. obtained papers for them to come to America
2. Rachel, Chicha, Cipi
3. Kisvarda, Hungary
4. indifference or relief
5. her mother
6. Joseph Mengele
7. all four would stay alive together
8. she could not beat other prisoners
9. Birnbaumel had no crematoriums
10. the Germans were fleeing from the approaching Russian army
11. the smell of cooking potatoes
12. took shelter in an abandoned house during a snowstorm
13. Cipi
14. an abundance of food
15. Russian
16. the American attaché in Odessa
17. the mirror reminded her of the Nazis' shiny boots and the smoke from the ovens
18. her sons, Peter and Richard
19. the memorial to the concentration camp dead
20. she could not stand being with the Germans

Short Answers:

1. His attempt to save his wife and children was blocked by the outbreak of World War II. The family did not get the papers until after Hitler occupied Hungary; then they could not leave.

2. She gave her children a belief in love and human dignity. Her vision was that man is capable of good. Their mother's belief gave support to Isabella and her sisters. Isabella was determined to teach her own sons to respect man and to hate war.

3. Irma was the spit-and-polish Nazi, "the beautiful monster," who enjoyed tricking the prisoners when they were forced to stand in long inspection lines. Her cruel nature was apparent when she forced Rachel to kneel and hold rocks in her hands.

4. In the abandoned house, the family had left everything behind. The sisters found food. They were able to wear warm clothes and stay hidden until the Russian troops arrived.

5. She went to Europe to find a new sense of her Jewish heritage and to restore the fragments of her broken life. She could deal with reality only by facing it. Isabella and her husband also wanted their sons to understand what had happened during the Nazi era.

Challenge Question:

Isabella and her sisters took strength from each other and also from their brother Philip. They remained human in ministering to other people and in burying the dead. Each time they escaped the ovens, they found the courage to live for one more day. When Isabella was in the hospital, her sisters came to give her the will to live. The sisters saw strength in the other prisoners. One good example of courage was the Gentile woman who was in the camp for helping her Jewish friends. These people were survivors because they never forgot their mother's positive teachings and they never gave up hope of living.

Kaffir Boy by Mark Mathabane

True or False:

1. T	4. F	7. F	10. T	13. F	16. F	19. F
2. T	5. T	8. T	11. F	14. T	17. T	20. F
3. F	6. F	9. F	12. T	15. F	18. F	

Short Answers:

1. "Kaffir" is the Afrikaans equivalent of "nigger," used by whites to refer to all blacks. The term indicates a being who is one step above an animal and below a human being.

2. His mother protected him from his father's rages. She worked so that he could have an education and get out of the ghetto. His grandmother took him into the white man's world; Mark learned that not all whites were vicious brutes. The love that young Mark received came from these two women.

3. Ashe became a symbol of hope for all black South Africans, especially athletes. His achievements in the white man's world made other blacks believe that they could also make it out of the slums.

4. Harmon gave Mark an opportunity to use the tennis facilities on his ranch and to play tennis with white athletes. Stan Smith treated Mark as an equal. Smith also worked to get Mark a tennis scholarship so that he could come to America.

5. Mark could not compromise with apartheid. His bank job would have paid well, but Mark would still have been a second-class citizen in his own land. He needed to live in America, a country which to him represented a life where every individual had an equal opportunity.

Challenge Question:

Blacks had no privacy. Their homes could be invaded at any time. The legal procedure was unfair. Blacks were beaten and imprisoned for violating laws that they could not control or understand. The educational system was geared to make the black man a servant to the white. The black man must never cross the line of the white restrictions. Mark was almost arrested for putting his foot on the steps of a white bus. The most dehumanizing effect of apartheid was the abject humility that the black must always use in the presence of his white "superiors."

Other People's Houses by Lore Segal

True or False:

1. T	5. T	9. F	13. F	17. T
2. F	6. F	10. T	14. F	18. F
3. T	7. F	11. T	15. T	19. T
4. T	8. T	12. F	16. F	20. F

Short Answers:

1. Paul read to her, told her stories, gave her a sense of excitement and life. He encouraged her to draw and paint. He listened to her and let her know that he cared for her.

2. Answers might include: the packed trains, the cold, the sausage that she could not get rid of, the masses of other refugee children, and the different adults who wanted to help. The sense of being helplessly shuffled from one place to another.

3. He lost his work as an accountant. He could not become a servant. Because people were hostile to him in England, Herr Groszmann lost first his self-respect and then his health.

4. She had to live with her grandparents. She had no boyfriends. She did not understand the culture, and could not use her university degree to get a job for which she was trained. Lore had no cultural roots.

5. Omama insulted everyone. She meant the best for her family, but was very possessive of everyone. She tried to run the lives of everyone in the house. Lore resented her constantly telling everyone what to do.

Challenge Question:

Lore was made observant by the variety of living situations in which she found herself. She learned contrast, the difference between the Levines and the Hoopers. Even as a child traveling to England, she discovered an innate talent for studying specifics. A sharp memory gave her a wonderful ability to remember and record in detail the faces of her companions and her natural surroundings.

Life in England and in the Dominican Republic taught her to see through hypocrisy. She was not easily fooled.

The Shoes of the Fisherman by Morris L. West

Multiple Choice:

1. C	6. B	11. D	16. D
2. B	7. C	12. A	17. C
3. A	8. A	13. B	18. C
4. C	9. D	14. B	19. A
5. D	10. B	15. A	20. B

Short Answers:

1. The electing cardinals are locked in the Sistine Chapel in the Vatican. Each time a vote is taken, the ballots are burned. If no pope is chosen, the ballots are burned with wet straw and the smoke is black. If someone is elected, the ballots are burned dry and the smoke is white. A two-thirds majority is necessary for election.

2. Suffering and imprisonment made Kiril able to understand the problems of the common man. The cardinals believed that he would bring to the Vatican new ideas that were badly needed in a changing world.

3. George and Ruth both struggled for love and individuality. Having succeeded professionally, George needed human affection on a personal level. Having abandoned her Jewish faith and then lost her husband, Ruth too was locked in a life without meaning. Faith and meaning for both people came in their love for each other.

4. Father Telemond linked man with the evolution of the world. This was heresy to the church, which saw man as created in the image of God. Because the expression of the ideas was suspect and the vocabulary unclear, Cardinal Leone and the Holy Office refused to grant Telemond permission to publish.

5. By traveling first to France and then to other countries, Pope Kiril hoped to relate the church to the needs of the world. Also he was pledged to act as a mediator between the United States and Russia in an attempt to avert war.

Challenge Question:

Pope Kiril was a man who had suffered greatly. He often had to battle with the memories of his imprisonment. Needing to be with people, Kiril also felt the loneliness of his position. When Telemond, who was his only friend, died, Kiril felt the loneliness even more keenly.

As a public man, Pope Kiril had vowed to uphold the traditions which were essential to Christian faith. He also desired to propose change which would make that faith relevant to twentieth-century life. Many counselors offered Pope Kiril advice. His Russian nationality and his past relationship with Kamenev made the Italians in the church cautious and suspicious.

Since his decisions were absolute, he must finally listen to God and his conscience for direction.

All the President's Men
by Bob Woodward and Carl Bernstein

Matching:

1. I	5. A	9. N	13. E	17. M
2. L	6. K	10. Q	14. D	18. S
3. B	7. C	11. R	15. P	19. J
4. F	8. T	12. H	16. G	20. O

Short Answers:

1. Woodward was "Ivy League," extremely organized, with contacts high in government. Bernstein was a college drop-out. Woodward usually did the first draft of every story, which Bernstein then edited. Woodward was more thorough and methodical, while Bernstein worked on sudden bursts of inspiration. Woodward was cautious, Bernstein more apt to take risks.

2. Bradlee made the two men promise that they must agree on any piece of information before it could be included in any story. Every item must be verified by two separate primary sources. Secondhand evidence was not admitted.

3. "Deep Throat" was a high official in the Nixon administration. Knowing exactly what was going on, he gave Woodward direction for the investigation. "Deep Throat" also confirmed whether the reporters were on the right track. He could never, however, be quoted as a primary source of information.

4. Sloan resigned from CREEP when he learned about the "slush money" and the other dirty tactics of the Nixon men. At a risk to himself and his family, Sloan was willing to talk to reporters and to the courts. In the beginning, Sloan was the only source that Woodward and Bernstein could count on to be absolutely candid.

5. Under the leadership of Ziegler, the Nixon administration tried to smear the reputation of the *Post* and to call its reporters liars. Officials, when questioned, lied to the *Post* about their knowledge and activities. CREEP, Nixon's election committee, also filed a civil suit against the reporters and tried to subpoena all their notes. When the truth was revealed, Ziegler was forced to apologize.

Challenge Question:

The Watergate affair became something more than a petty crime when the reporters learned that huge sums of money were being paid to assorted operatives for secret activities. The break-in was only part of a larger plan.

At first McCord and Liddy were ready to take the rap for the others. With the involvement of Dwight Chapin and Segretti, the criminal activities were traced to the White House itself. Haldeman, Ehrlichman, and Mitchell, all close friends of the president, were indicted. The biggest single question, never answered, was whether Nixon himself was involved in the "dirty tricks" campaign. The whole plan, in which politicians tried to put themselves above the law, ended in the only presidential impeachment in American history.

Unit 6
Success and Achievement

Synopses

Giant Steps
by Kareem Abdul-Jabbar and Peter Knobler

Bantam Books, New York, 1983.

Giant Steps is the career story of one of basketball's greats. Lew Alcindor, who upon becoming a Muslim took the name of Kareem Abdul-Jabbar, grew up in Harlem. As the only child in a middle-class black family, Lew was a shy boy who loved books and music. His Catholic school education also introduced him to sports. As Lew grew taller than most boys his age, the great love of his life became basketball.

Kareem sparked three championship teams: Powers High School, UCLA, and the Milwaukee Bucks of the National Basketball Association. Although a success on the court, Kareem had problems being close to people. After several people let him down, Kareem withdrew into his private world.

Islam played an important role in Kareem's life. He believes that only the Muslim faith came directly from its founder and accepts any person as an individual. After those to whom he turned for spiritual leadership failed him, Kareem again had to find his own way.

Kareem's story gives an inside look at professional basketball as seen through the life experience of one of its greatest champions.

Yankee From Olympus
by Catherine Drinker Bowen

Little, Brown and Company, Boston, 1945.

The Holmes family of Boston produced three distinguished Americans: clergyman and historian Abiel Holmes; physician and poet Dr. Oliver Wendell Holmes; judge and constitutional analyst Oliver Wendell Holmes, Jr. From 1800 to 1935, their lives were blended with the growth of the American nation. The Holmes women, Sally Wendell, Amelia Jackson, and Fanny Dixwell, were also important influences in their husbands' lives. Changes in the nation brought changes to which each of the Holmeses had to adapt. Abiel met the challenge presented to his Calvinist ideals by the rise of liberal Unitarianism. Dr. Holmes revolutionized medical practice by insisting that doctors employ proper sanitation methods. Justice Holmes made the Constitution a living document by issuing legal opinions relating law to life.

This superb family biography also shows the great men as human beings. Abiel was forced to resign his pulpit because he refused to compromise with the free-thinkers in his congregation. Dr. Holmes searched the battlefields of the Civil War for his wounded son. Justice Holmes emerged from the shadow of his famous father only after Dr. Holmes's death.

Yankee From Olympus would be valuable outside reading for American history students because events in the Holmes family are placed in the larger historical framework. The War of 1812, the Civil War, and World War I are described in terms of their effects on this remarkable family. Bowen's readable style makes her book very much within the reach of the average or above-average student.

Captains and the Kings

by Taylor Caldwell

Doubleday and Company, New York, 1972.

Captains and the Kings chronicles the rise of a fictional Irish immigrant, Joseph Armagh. Arriving in America in the 1840's, Joseph sees his mother die in horrible poverty. He determines to protect his brother Sean and his sister Regina. Leaving his family in a convent, Joseph begins making his fortune in the oil fields of western Pennsylvania. Befriended by unscrupulous businessman Ed Healey, Joseph quickly learns about the power that accompanies wealth. As he rises in the business world, Joseph quickly learns who can be trusted. Harry Zeff, whose life Joseph saves, and Mr. Montrose, a mysterious southern gentleman, work with Joseph to build his power base. Joseph also learns of the hidden banking cartel, men manipulating rulers and nations for their own profit.

After he inherits Mr. Healey's enterprises, Joseph's business successes sharply contrast with his personal catastrophe. Sean and Regina both reject Joseph's plan for their lives. Idolizing Katherine, the wife of powerful Governor Tom Hennessey, Joseph promises Katherine that he will marry her daughter Bernadette. The marriage is loveless. Because Hennessey had brutalized Katherine, Joseph destroys the governor and drives him to suicide.

Taking his place among the world's most powerful men, Joseph destroys all who oppose him. He finds the only happiness in his life with Elizabeth, Hennessey's second wife. Ironically, as Joseph's might increases, everything that he cares for crumbles. The Armagh family has been cursed by Senator Bassett, an honest man who was driven to suicide by Joseph's manipulations. Joseph's sons Rory and Kevin are murdered by the very establishment Joseph supports. His daughter Ann Marie is the victim of a tragic love affair. At the novel's end, just before World War I, Joseph is dead. The economic power cartel, however, continues to manipulate world history.

Captains and the Kings has a brilliant cast of characters. Caldwell presents a chilling but plausible explanation for much recent history. Are all nations indeed pawns of the powerful few who can manipulate the many?

Sister Carrie

by Theodore Dreiser

Doubleday and Company, New York, 1900.

Sister Carrie is the story of Carrie Meeber, a country girl who has come to find happiness in Chicago. Passion for Carrie shapes the lives of two men, Charles Drouet and George Hurstwood. Drouet, a traveling salesman with an eye for pretty girls, meets Carrie when she first arrives. After persuading Carrie to live with him and to pose as his wife, Drouet introduces her to Hurstwood, a middle-aged man who becomes infatuated with Carrie's youth and beauty. Finding a new interest in acting, Carrie stars in an amateur theatrical. Believing that he cannot live without Carrie, Hurstwood tricks her into running away with him.

First in Montreal and then in New York, Hurstwood is a fugitive. He has stolen money from the company he worked for. His wife has divorced him. His fortunes steadily decline until the former dandy is an unemployed bum, who finally reaches the nadir of despair and commits suicide.

Carrie finds new interest in the great city. She loves the social life of the idle rich. Needing work to support Hurstwood, Carrie returns to the theater and rises to stardom. Even in her moment of success, Carrie continues to long for the happiness that always seems to lie somewhere else.

The world of this novel is without pity or sympathy. Dreiser's characters enact Darwin's theory of the survival of the fittest. Carrie is amoral, thinking only of herself. Hurstwood and Drouet orbit around Carrie's star. Although this novel shocked the reading public in 1900, today the story provides a realistic picture of ruthless ambition.

Pentimento

by Lillian Hellman

Little, Brown and Company, Boston, 1973.

Pentimento, an episodic biography, is a memory of significant people in the life of Lillian Hellman, America's most important woman playwright. Hellman draws her title from pentimento, the process of seeing the lines of an original painting after another has been superimposed on the canvas. The book is a series of flashbacks rather than a straight chronology.

Lillian remembers her eccentric relatives: the cousin whose boyfriend was a Mafia boss; Uncle Willy, a gunrunner, and the first love of Lillian's life; her independent aunts, Jenny and Hannah.

As Hellman recalls her experiences in theater and film, significant moments emerge like photographs. Different accounts have varied moods. The reader feels the mounting tension in the episode where Hellman aids her friend Julia by smuggling money into Nazi Germany. Memory is colored with laughter as Lillian tells how Dashiell Hammett, the great love of her life, helps Lillian kill a snapping turtle. Her affair with Arthur Cowan, an offbeat millionaire, also shows the reader that this playwright's life has been anything but dull.

The sensitive reader will relate to the author's memories as Hellman peels away the layers of the past and remembers the reality of her experience.

Up the Down Staircase

by Bel Kaufman ═══════════════════════════════

Prentice-Hall, Englewood Cliffs, NJ, 1964.

Up the Down Staircase narrates, with humor and realism, the trials of a first-year English teacher in a New York City high school. Fresh from classes in Chaucer and educational theory, Sylvia Barrett comes to Calvin Coolidge High filled with enthusiasm. Her ideals are quickly shattered as she must cope with overcrowding, an authoritarian administrator, broken equipment, and impossible students.

Bel Kaufman's unique style makes this book engrossing reading. The story unfolds through memos from the administration, notes from other faculty members, and comments from the students' suggestion box. Sylvia's personal conflicts are told through her letters to her college classmate, Ellen. The young teacher has to cope with the death of Evelyn Lazar, who tries to induce an abortion, and the suicide attempt of Alice Blake, who cannot cope with her English teacher's cruel rejection. Sylvia tries to help Joe Ferone, who defies every rule the school makes.

Miss Barrett's choice between leaving and continuing to teach has faced many young instructors. Saved by her sense of humor, Sylvia's real affirmation comes from the growth she sees in her students. High school students and teachers will find themselves in the pages of *Up the Down Staircase.*

Profiles in Courage

by John F. Kennedy ═══════════════════════════════

Harper and Row, New York, 1964.

Profiles in Courage recounts the personal valor of eight United States senators who risked political and personal defeat to follow the leadings of conscience. These senators were often abused by the press and rejected by the people who had elected them. Acts of courage span the history of America, from John Quincy Adams, whose fight for an embargo bill made him hated in New England, to Robert Taft who questioned the constitutionality of the Nazi war trials and was called a traitor. Each man fought for his principles; he did not bend to the pressure of his constituents or his peers. These episodes show the greatness of our constitutional system, which provides for expression of differing opinions.

The 1964 edition of *Profiles in Courage,* published after President Kennedy's death, has an introduction by Robert Kennedy telling of the courage in John Kennedy's own life. Courage, according to Kennedy, is what we live for as well as what we die for. This book is a new look at America's history and at the author who was a part of that history.

Anna and the King of Siam

by Margaret Landon

Washington Square Press, New York, 1943.

Anna and the King of Siam is the biography of Anna Leonowens, a Welsh teacher at the royal court of Siam (now Thailand) between 1862 and 1867. Left widowed with two small children, Anna found a challenge in the royal household. Her strong personality frequently brought her into conflict with King Mongkut and his prime minister, the Kralahome. Her first fight was for a house of her own. As time passed, the teacher became the crusader against oppression and slavery, especially for the women of the harem. Anna made friends with the members of the king's household and helped many who were in trouble.

Although she left Siam in 1867, the teacher had left a great mark on the land and its people. Anna had the greatest influence on Crown Prince Chulalongkorn. The young man became the monarch who brought Siam into the twentieth century.

Margaret Landon's research included articles written by Anna herself and material on Siam of that time period. Anna's is a story of personal determination set against a backdrop of court intrigue and romance. *Anna and the King of Siam* is a fascinating glimpse of oriental life.

Eleanor and Franklin

by Joseph P. Lash

W. W. Norton, New York, 1971.

Eleanor and Franklin is an in-depth biography of Mrs. Eleanor Roosevelt, one of the most outstanding women of the twentieth century. Anna Eleanor Roosevelt was a shy child of an aristocratic but unstable family background. The opening chapters discuss the significant events of Eleanor's early life: losing both parents, personality development at Allenswood School in England, marriage to her cousin Franklin.

As a young wife and mother, Eleanor was first introduced to the political scene when Franklin was elected to the New York state senate. Her shyness made coping difficult. Eleanor also had to deal with Sarah Roosevelt, her overbearing mother-in-law. She first entered the Washington scene in 1913 when Franklin was appointed assistant secretary of the Navy under President Wilson.

During those early Washington years, two traumatic events influenced Eleanor's life: the discovery of her husband's affair with her secretary, Lucy Mercer; and Franklin's developing polio. Both circumstances built Eleanor's character.

Eleanor entered politics first as a lobbyist for the League of Women Voters. Not really desiring public life, she nevertheless participated in all her husband's campaigns. During the Depression, Eleanor championed the poor and minority groups. During World War II she became her husband's traveling ambassador, visiting troops all over the world.

Based on Mrs. Roosevelt's private papers, Lash's book pictures a private woman forced to lead a very public life. The narrative balances her private problems with her children and her role as first lady. The author obviously admires his subject very much. Although several sections of the narrative become a bit heavy with names and dates, *Eleanor and Franklin* is excellent reading for any student of twentieth-century U.S. history.

The Natural

by Bernard Malamud

Farrar, Straus and Giroux, New York, 1952.

The "Natural" is Roy Hobbs, a baseball player whose natural abilities are exceptional. Roy, with his special bat Wonderboy, intends to conquer the sports world at the age of fifteen. Then Roy is shot by a half-crazed woman. His major league debut is postponed by fifteen years.

When Roy finally does join the sagging New York Knights, the team is in the league cellar. Owned by ruthless Judge Goodwin and managed by Pop Fisher, the Knights game is a comedy of errors. Roy's wonderful play, however, gives Pop and his team hope again.

Although Roy is brilliant on the field, he personally struggles against several antagonists. Roy's nemesis is Pop's niece Memo. The star's passions for her almost destroy him until he finds another girl, Irene, who believes in him. Max Mercy, a ruthless sports columnist, struggles to discover the secrets in Roy's past. When the Knights make it all the way to the playoffs, the Judge pays Roy not to hit and to sacrifice his team.

In *The Natural*, Malamud gives his reader an inside look at the craziness of baseball. The hero myth, in which the good guys win in the ninth inning, also has an interesting reversal in this story. *The Natural* is a sports novel that is well worth reading.

West With the Night

by Beryl Markham

North Point Press, San Francisco, 1983.

In the 1920's and 1930's, Beryl Markham's life adventures in Africa were stranger than fiction. At the age of four, she came from England to her father's farm in Kenya. Beryl's life was a love affair with Africa. As a teenager, she hunted with the natives. She recognized nothing of the racial barriers so common in Africa. As an adult, Beryl had a double career: as a horse trainer and as Africa's first woman aviator.

Markham's writing shows her love of Africa's landscape and people. The reader shares Beryl's feelings as she assists at the birth of a colt, flies to rescue a downed flier or uses her plane to stalk elephants for safari hunters. She also relates the significant relationships in her life: her father, her native assistant Arab Ruta, her flying teacher Tom Black, the great game hunter Baron Blixen.

The title *West With the Night* comes from Markham's last great adventure, an attempt to fly solo from England to New York. She crossed the Atlantic, but crash-landed in Nova Scotia.

The wonder of *West With the Night* is the book's style. A teacher could well use many of Markham's paragraphs as examples of descriptive writing. The sights and sounds of Africa come alive. The student should read this book slowly to enjoy its wonderful imagery.

A Man Called Peter

by Catherine Marshall

McGraw-Hill Book Company, New York, 1951.

Peter Marshall, a young immigrant from Scotland, came to America in 1927. Sensing a call to the ministry, Peter went to Atlanta, Georgia, where friends sponsored his education. While pastoring in Atlanta, Peter met and married Catherine Wood.

The Marshalls moved to Washington, where Peter became pastor of New York Avenue Presbyterian Church and chaplain of the United States Senate. The Marshalls overcame personal difficulties, including Catherine's battle with TB. Peter's ability to make God real to everyone touched all who knew him. Death at 46 cut short his ministry, but he left a rich legacy.

Mrs. Marshall's loving biography of her husband shows Dr. Marshall's faith in God and his loving warmth as a human being. This biography shows the great strength of personal faith in God.

The Bell Jar

by Sylvia Plath

Harper and Row, New York, 1971.

The protagonist of *The Bell Jar* is Esther Greenwood, an intelligent, sensitive girl for whom life has become a prison. Esther's story is her battle against mental illness, represented by the enclosing "bell jar."

Spending a month on the staff of a New York fashion magazine opens Esther's eyes to the brutal realities of life and men. Her mind battles to understand the experience. Marco attempts to rape Esther. She rejects the love of Constantin because she fears he will sink into an ordinariness that she cannot accept. The author's portrait of the false New York publishing world is brilliant. Plath creates many unforgettable characters: the sensual Doreen; Jay Cee, the fashion editor; Lenny, the womanizer; Marco, the brute.

Returning to Boston, Esther is increasingly unable to cope with reality. She becomes obsessed with taking her own life. After a suicide attempt almost succeeds, Esther is placed in a state hospital. She is saved from the horrors of this institution by her college benefactress, Philomena Guinea, who pays for Esther's further treatment.

In a private hospital where she is treated as a human being, Esther struggles to escape from the bell jar in her mind which stifles reality. Dr. Nolan, her psychiatrist, becomes her ally. Ironically, Joan, the girl Esther most looked up to, commits suicide. At the novel's end, Esther is about to be released. The ending, however, is clouded by Plath's own uncertainty. Esther tells the reader that the "bell jar" may descend again.

The Bell Jar reveals an inner world, Esther's often warped perception of reality. The novel's first-person narrative is powerful, poetic, and sensitive. Caution might be used in assigning or recommending this novel, since its content might be disturbing to some students, and the author of this thinly disguised autobiography did, in fact, commit suicide. *The Bell Jar* is, however, a brilliant study of personality breakdown.

I Am Third

by Gale Sayers with Al Silverman

Viking Press, New York, 1970.

I Am Third is the personal story of Gale Sayers, great football running back for the Chicago Bears. Growing up in Omaha, Nebraska, Gale had a difficult home life. He discovered happiness with his special talent for running. Although excelling in track and football, Gale was not very interested in academics. When Gale went to the University of Kansas to play college ball, he had severe problems passing his courses. Being very shy also caused him difficulties.

Marriage to Linda helped Gale become more sure of himself. With her support and encouragement, he set records for rushing and yards gained in a single game. Other special college relationships included instructor Jesse Milan and Gale's coach Jack Mitchell.

During his college senior year, Gale made some difficult choices. Although several teams wanted to sign Gale, he chose to play professional ball for the Chicago Bears. After Gale's career was threatened by a knee injury in 1968, he experienced the loneliness of recuperation. Gale's friendship with Brian Piccolo was very special. Piccolo's death from cancer made Gale seek new meaning for his own life.

Sayers discusses the highlights of his football career as well as the meaning of each experience. The title of this book explains Gale Sayers's priorities. The motto was taken from his college track coach: "The Lord is first; my family is second; I am third."

Beverly: An Autobiography

by Beverly Sills and Lawrence Linderman

Bantam Books, New York, 1987.

America's leading opera singer, Beverly Sills began her career as a child star in Brooklyn. She began touring with an operetta company when she was a teenager.

Beverly's public career led her to the stages of Europe's major opera houses. She was finally established as an international star with the New York City Opera Company. After her retirement as a singer in 1984, Sills became the managing director of the company. She was the first woman ever to hold such a post. Her leadership helped put American opera on the map.

In private life, Beverly and Peter Greenough have experienced happiness and tragedy. A deaf daughter and a retarded son have both been loved and cared for. Beverly also experienced ugly prejudice from her husband's friends because she was Jewish.

This frank autobiography gives the opinions of a very outspoken, intelligent woman. The reader also gets a fascinating look at the development of an opera star and the growth of the American musical theater.

Madame Sarah

by Cornelia Otis Skinner

Houghton Mifflin Company, Boston, 1967.

Madame Sarah is the fascinating life of actress and stage legend Sarah Bernhardt. Born to a Jewish mother and a French father, the shy, thin girl survived a terrible childhood during which she was badly neglected. Sarah began her acting career at the renowned Thèâtre Française, home of the French National Theater Company. Throughout her sixty-year career, Bernhardt stunned the world with her brilliant voice. She toured in many great roles, most of them including spectacular death scenes. The great of the world who paid her homage ranged from the faithful "court" of her acting company to the Prince of Wales. Even after a leg amputation in her seventies, Sarah continued to dazzle her adoring public.

Bernhardt was really several women: doting mother to her son Maurice; temperamental *prima donna*; hard-working theater manager and director; nurse to wounded veterans; and eccentric collector of odd people, animals, and art objects. Refusing to conform to society's rules, Sarah gained as much attention for her off-stage exploits as she did for her acting roles. Throughout her career, stories of her antics were front-page news. The public never knew what she would do next.

In writing *Madame Sarah*, Cornelia Otis Skinner has given her readers a wonderful look at a theatrical legend. This biography would be of particular interest to any student interested in the theater.

The Gift of Music

by Jane Stuart Smith and Betty Carlson

Crossways Books, Westchester, Illinois, 1987.

In *The Gift of Music*, Smith and Carlson summarize over three centuries of classical music through the biographies of thirty-six great composers. The book's organization shows the place of each musician in the Christian tradition which forms the basis of western culture. Each short biography also narrates the personal experiences which influenced each composer's musical style.

During the seventeenth century, the Baroque music of Bach, Vivaldi, and Handel presented a positive resolution of joy. Music was based on faith; solid forms were an expression of belief. In the eighteenth century, Haydn and Mozart developed many of the musical forms that are so familiar today, such as the symphony and the concerto.

Moving toward more individualized expression, the romantics of the early nineteenth century used music to express profound personal feelings. Schubert, Liszt, and Chopin all made great contributions to musical literature.

As music moved toward modern times, the sound and the form became more individualized. Composers such as Schönberg and Stravinsky horrified audiences by a total break with tradition.

Nationalism was a very important force in music. Many composers were influenced by the folk melodies of their native lands: Chopin in Poland, Bartók in Hungary, Ives in America. Personal unhappiness also brought many of these geniuses to the edge of despair. The sufferings of Mozart, Schumann, Rachmaninoff, and Prokofiev reveal that creativity in conflict with reality can be very painful.

The Gift of Music will interest any student musician. Young talent always needs to understand the roots of music as an art form. Smith and Carlson have provided a fine summary of these origins.

The Agony and the Ecstasy

by Irving Stone

Doubleday and Company, New York, 1961.

The Agony and the Ecstasy brings to life Michelangelo Buonarroti, sculptor, painter, and genius of the Italian Renaissance. Ridiculed by his father for his desire to be an artist, Michelangelo found patronage in the sculpture garden of Lorenzo de' Medici, Florence's benevolent dictator and patron of all artists. Living in Lorenzo's palace, Michelangelo was treated as a son. He learned about classical culture from the great scholars of Lorenzo's court. The young sculptor began to find inspiration in blocks of marble. Despite the political turmoil that followed the death of Lorenzo, Michelangelo continued to sculpt: the "Battle of the Centaurs," the "Madonna and Child," and finally the "David," which became a symbol for his beloved Florence.

Summoned to Rome, Michelangelo found his art dependent on the patronage of several very unpredictable popes. Julius II insisted that the sculptor become a painter to do the ceiling of the Sistine Chapel. Clement II, son of Lorenzo de' Medici, commissioned a statue of Moses, but never paid for the work. All through his life, Michelangelo fought the prejudices of politicians, popes, and artists with limited vision. He studied anatomy, even dissected corpses, to glorify the human body. Yet his nude figures horrified many.

Michelangelo knew the love of Contessina, Lorenzo's daughter, and of Clarissa Saffi, a noblewoman of Bologna. He fought to provide for his father and brothers, whose constant financial needs drained Michelangelo's resources.

More important than meeting material needs was meeting his own need to fulfill his private artistic vision. The crowning glory of that vision, when the artist was in his seventies, was designing the dome of St. Peter's Cathedral.

Irving Stone's portrait of the great artist also brings to life the exciting Renaissance world in which one man was painter, sculptor, engineer, poet, and statesman. This book would be of special value for students in European history classes.

Oprah

by Robert Waldron

St. Martin's Press, New York, 1987.

Waldron's biography of talk show hostess Oprah Winfrey discusses Oprah as a real person. Oprah's rise to stardom has been a phenomenon. She was the first black woman to have her own syndicated talk show. Oprah can identify with people who have problems: the overweight, the victims of rape and child abuse. Oprah has lived through such experiences. The book discusses her career, beginning with radio and television work as a college student. She moved upward from Nashville to Baltimore to finally have her own show in Chicago. Oprah, however, remains very human in spite of her success.

The book provides an inside look at a celebrity who is a very special human being. One high point is the account of her performance in the film *The Color Purple*. Her biography is a story of frustrations as well as successes. In spite of her popularity, Oprah knows how loneliness feels. The author's account is easy to read. Oprah's narratives of her own experiences help the reader understand the factors which have shaped her very special personality.

The Picture of Dorian Gray

by Oscar Wilde

Ward, Lock and Company, London, 1891.

The Picture of Dorian Gray is Oscar Wilde's tale of a man who sells his soul to evil forces in exchange for eternal youth. After Basil Hallward paints a beautiful portrait of handsome Dorian Gray, Dorian wishes that he might remain young and handsome forever. The young man, influenced by Lord Henry Wotton, begins to sink into decadence. Dorian destroys the woman who loves him and finally destroys the painter of the portrait itself. Dorian's youthful beauty remains unstained. Instead, the portrait, reflecting the man's crimes, becomes increasingly hideous.

Finally, Dorian seeks escape in the sordid opium dens of the London waterfront. He becomes a killer to protect his ugly secret. When Dorian cannot be found, his servants search the house. They find an ugly corpse and a slashed portrait.

Oscar Wilde explores the power of evil to destroy beauty. This novel also gives insight into an aristocracy without morals, whose lifestyle consisted of taking pleasure without any thought of consequences.

Name_____   Date_____

Giant Steps by Kareem Abdul-Jabbar
and Peter Knobler

Match each description in Column A with the correct name in Column B.

Column A

_____ 1. Kareem's high school basketball coach

_____ 2. Young player whom Kareem helped to carry on the Lakers' tradition

_____ 3. High school Kareem attended

_____ 4. Great guard who played on the Milwaukee team with Jabbar

_____ 5. Basketball pro who greatly influenced Jabbar as a teenager

_____ 6. Kareem's first wife

_____ 7. Harlem tournament for all black basketball players

_____ 8. Kareem's spiritual guide who trained him in the principles of Islam

_____ 9. Girl who helped Kareem recover after others had failed him

_____ 10. Great basketball coach at UCLA

_____ 11. Taught Kareem self-control through the martial arts

_____ 12. Friend who played both college and professional ball with Kareem

_____ 13. Played trombone and loved classical jazz

_____ 14. Man Kareem beat up on the court

_____ 15. Catholic grammar school that Kareem attended

_____ 16. Last professional team Kareem played for

_____ 17. Leader of the Black Muslim group

_____ 18. Kareem's eldest son

_____ 19. Team that drafted Kareem after he graduated from college

_____ 20. Insisted that her son attend church and come home early

Column B

A. Bruce Lee

B. Powers

C. Kent Benson

D. Rucker

E. St. Jude's

F. Donohue

G. Milwaukee

H. Wooden

I. Wilt Chamberlain

J. Cheryl

K. Ferdinand Lewis Alcindor

L. John Worthy

M. Lucius Allen

N. Oscar Robertson

O. Cora Alcindor

P. Amir

Q. Habiba

R. Lakers

S. Malcolm X

T. Hamaas

© 1991 J. Weston Walch, Publisher

Name_____ Date_____

Giant Steps by Kareem Abdul-Jabbar
and Peter Knobler

Answer the following questions in two or three complete sentences.

1. What interests and activities were important in Kareem's childhood?

_____

_____

_____

2. How did going to UCLA change Kareem's outlook?

_____

_____

_____

3. Why did Kareem become a Muslim?

_____

_____

_____

4. What difficulties did Kareem have communicating with the public and the press?

_____

_____

_____

5. What personal experience did Kareem have with racial prejudice?

_____

_____

_____

Challenge Question

Write an essay discussing the ways in which significant people in Kareem Abdul-Jabbar's life both helped and hurt his growth as a human being.

Name_____   Date_____

Yankee From Olympus by Catherine Drinker Bowen

Match each description in Column A with the correct name in Column B.

Column A

Column B

_____ 1. Philosopher and close personal friend of Oliver Wendell Holmes, Jr.

_____ 2. Author of *The Autocrat of the Breakfast Table*

_____ 3. Liberal minister and founder of Unitarianism

_____ 4. Jewish Supreme Court justice

_____ 5. Bachelor uncle who persuaded Wendell Holmes to marry

_____ 6. Author of *The Annals of America*

_____ 7. Was wounded three times during the Civil War

_____ 8. President of Harvard who changed the curriculum to include the study of law and modern languages

_____ 9. Abiel Holmes's spirited wife

_____ 10. Gave Wendell Holmes his chance as a partner in a law firm

_____ 11. Returned home to care for her aged father

_____ 12. Wendell Holmes's teacher who later became his father-in-law

_____ 13. Charmed President Roosevelt at her first White House dinner

_____ 14. Tried to help her shy son when she saw that the son was dominated by his father

_____ 15. Governor who urged the people of Boston to prepare for the Civil War that he saw approaching

_____ 16. Bakery owner whose case tested the right of an employer to determine the hours of his employees

_____ 17. Younger brother who was much more outgoing than Wendell Holmes

_____ 18. Author whose work shook the foundations of New England Calvinism

_____ 19. Lived with his daughter's family and greatly influenced his grandchildren

_____ 20. Commander of the Twentieth Massachusetts

A. John Holmes

B. Henry Abbott

C. John Andrew

D. William James

E. Judge Wendell

F. Sally Wendell

G. Charles Darwin

H. Louis Brandeis

I. John Dixwell

J. William Ellery Channing

K. Amelia Jackson Holmes

L. Abiel Holmes

M. Dr. Holmes

N. George Shattuck

O. Oliver Wendell Holmes, Jr.

P. Fanny Dixwell Holmes

Q. Charles Eliot

R. Lockner

S. Ned Holmes

T. Amelia Holmes Sargent

© 1991 J. Weston Walch, Publisher

Name _____   Date_____

Yankee From Olympus by Catherine Drinker Bowen

Answer the following questions in two or three complete sentences.

1. How did growing up in Boston influence each of the Holmes men?

   _____

   _____

   _____

2. Why was Wendell Holmes overshadowed by his father for a good portion of Wendell's adult life?

   _____

   _____

   _____

3. How was each man's wife a source of help and strength to her husband?

   _____

   _____

   _____

4. How was Wendell Holmes affected by his war experiences?

   _____

   _____

   _____

5. Why was the Northern Securities case a significant landmark in Holmes's judicial career?

   _____

   _____

   _____

Challenge Question

Write an essay explaining the ways in which Abiel, Dr. Oliver, and Judge Wendell Holmes were innovators in American society.

© 1991 J. Weston Walch, Publisher   *100 More Great Books: Synopses, Quizzes, and Tests*

Name_____   Date_____

Captains and the Kings by Taylor Caldwell

Select the letter of the word or phrase which correctly completes each sentence.

_____ 1. Joseph Armagh's attitudes were largely shaped by the death of (A) his father (B) his mother (C) the old priest (D) Mr. Healey.

_____ 2. Joseph paid for his trip to Titusville by stealing money from (A) Bill Strickland (B) Mr. Healey (C) Tom Hennessey (D) Mr. Squibbs.

_____ 3. The man most loyal to Joseph throughout Armagh's entire life was (A) Harry (B) Charles (C) Timothy (D) Mr. Spaulding.

_____ 4. Joseph's first important job for Mr. Healey involved (A) gun running (B) importing slaves (C) bootlegged liquor (D) prostitution.

_____ 5. Joseph first saw Katherine Hennessey (A) in the yard of her home (B) at the orphanage (C) through a train window (D) at the opera.

_____ 6. Joseph married Bernadette because (A) he loved her (B) he had promised her father (C) she reminded Joseph of his sister (D) he had promised Katherine.

_____ 7. Joseph inherited the base of his fortune from (A) his uncle (B) Mr. Montrose (C) Mr. Healey (D) Tom Hennessey.

_____ 8. Which of the following was murdered by the powerful "International Committee of Foreign Studies"? (A) President Lincoln (B) Kevin (C) Rory (D) all of the above

_____ 9. The novel's most tragic lovers were (A) Joseph and Bernadette (B) Anne Marie and Courtney (C) Rory and Marjorie (D) Claire and Luanne.

_____ 10. Joseph's business assistants included (A) Harry Zeff (B) Timothy Dineen (C) Charles Devereaux (D) all of the above.

_____ 11. According to this novel, the cause of war is (A) political (B) social (C) economic (D) communistic.

(continued)

© 1991 J. Weston Walch, Publisher

100 More Great Books: Synopses, Quizzes, and Tests

Name_____ Date_____

Captains and the Kings by Taylor Caldwell

_____ 12. The only real love of Joseph's life was (A) Katherine (B) Elizabeth (C) Bernadette (D) Miss Emmy.

_____ 13. The members of the cartel believed that the most difficult nation for them to control would be (A) England (B) France (C) Russia (D) the United States.

_____ 14. The greatest obstacle to Rory's becoming president was (A) his religion (B) his family (C) his looks (D) his lack of money.

_____ 15. Courtney Hennessey (A) was shot (B) joined the army (C) was really Joseph's son (D) became a monk.

_____ 16. Probably the most completely destructive character in this novel is (A) Bernadette (B) Joseph (C) Claudia (D) Mr. Spaulding.

_____ 17. Rory agreed to end his marriage to Marjorie because (A) he no longer cared about her (B) his mother insisted (C) Marjorie told Rory that she no longer loved him (D) he was madly in love with Claudia.

_____ 18. The American president who was most completely the puppet of the cartel was (A) Lincoln (B) Garfield (C) Taft (D) Wilson.

_____ 19. The man who most destroyed Joseph Armagh was (A) Regan (B) Bassett (C) Hennessey (D) Chisholm.

_____ 20. At the end of the novel, Joseph (A) decided to run for the Senate (B) died of a heart attack (C) moved to England (D) committed suicide.

Name_____   Date_____

Captains and the Kings by Taylor Caldwell

Answer the following questions in two or three complete sentences.

1. How did Joseph Armagh's childhood experience influence the man that he later became?

_____

_____

_____

2. How did Mr. Healey shape Joseph's career?

_____

_____

_____

3. How was Joseph's relationship with his wife Bernadette contrasted with his relationship with Elizabeth?

_____

_____

_____

4. According to this novel, what events in American politics were "arranged" by the powerful banking elite?

_____

_____

_____

5. Which of Rory Armagh's actions result in his elimination?

_____

_____

_____

Challenge Question

Write an essay describing the view of history that Taylor Caldwell presents in *Captains and the Kings.*

© 1991 J. Weston Walch, Publisher

Name_____   Date_____

Sister Carrie by Theodore Dreiser

Select the letter of the word or phrase which correctly completes each sentence.

_____ 1. Carrie first meets Drouet (A) in the store where she works (B) on the street (C) on the train (D) at her sister's house.

_____ 2. When Carrie is able to find a job, she loses it when (A) she becomes ill (B) she can't keep up with her work (C) she rejects the attentions of the boss (D) she is late too often.

_____ 3. Drouet first helped Carrie when he (A) carried her luggage (B) paid her rent (C) bought her the clothes she needed (D) took her to the theater.

_____ 4. Julia Hurstwood may best be described as (A) selfish (B) ambitious (C) ruthless (D) all of the above.

_____ 5. Hurstwood believes that he must have Carrie after (A) they have dinner together (B) he sees her in the play (C) he meets her for the first time in the park (D) his wife rejects him.

_____ 6. Carrie does most of her dreaming (A) in her rocking chair (B) in front of the mirror (C) in the doorway (D) when she goes to the theater.

_____ 7. Hurstwood steals his company's money (A) by knocking out the bookkeeper (B) when the safe is accidentally left open (C) after weeks of careful planning (D) so that he can send money to his wife.

_____ 8. Hurstwood gets Carrie on the train by (A) telling her Drouet is sick (B) promising that he will get her into the theater (C) telling her what a wonderful place New York is (D) threatening to send her back to her sister.

_____ 9. Hurstwood decides to leave Montreal for New York because (A) he thinks he can make more money (B) Carrie will be happier there (C) they can live more cheaply in New York (D) he thinks that he is less likely to run into someone he knows.

_____ 10. During the first year of their life in New York, (A) Hurstwood can't find work (B) Carrie is contented (C) Carrie sees Drouet again (D) Carrie begins her career as an actress.

(continued)

© 1991 J. Weston Walch, Publisher   *100 More Great Books: Synopses, Quizzes, and Tests*

Name_____   Date_____

Sister Carrie by Theodore Dreiser

_____ 11. The person who opens Carrie's eyes to the riches of city life is (A) Hurstwood (B) Lola Ogden (C) Mrs. Vance (D) Minnie.

_____ 12. Carrie's stage name, Madena, was first given to her by (A) Drouet (B) Hurstwood (C) Ames (D) Mr. Dooley.

_____ 13. Hurstwood loses his job in New York when (A) the building burns down (B) his partner dies (C) the building is sold (D) he becomes too drunk to work any longer.

_____ 14. Hurstwood's deteriorating life is best seen by the change in (A) his appearance (B) his eating habits (C) his treatment of Carrie (D) the kind of friends he has.

_____ 15. When Carrie finally walks out on Hurstwood, she (A) doesn't tell him where she is going (B) leaves twenty dollars for him (C) moves in with Drouet (D) goes to Europe with Mr. and Mrs. Vance.

_____ 16. The only job that Hurstwood can find is working as (A) a cabdriver (B) a bartender (C) a strikebreaker (D) a liquor salesman.

_____ 17. When Carrie meets Drouet in New York, she (A) has dinner with him (B) decides to marry him (C) refuses to see him (D) sends Drouet to find Hurstwood.

_____ 18. Hurstwood dies (A) of pneumonia (B) of starvation (C) of gas fumes (D) from an attack by the strikers.

_____ 19. At the end of the novel, Carrie (A) is still alone (B) plans to continue her career in the theater (C) is still unsatisfied (D) all of the above.

_____ 20. The character in the novel who changes most radically is (A) Carrie (B) Drouet (C) Hurstwood (D) Mrs. Vance.

© 1991 J. Weston Walch, Publisher

Name_____   Date_____

Sister Carrie by Theodore Dreiser

Answer the following questions in two or three complete sentences.

1. Why does Carrie leave her sister's home?

_____

_____

_____

2. What traits make Carrie attractive to both Drouet and Hurstwood?

_____

_____

_____

3. What role does chance play in Hurstwood's flight from Chicago?

_____

_____

_____

4. How does Carrie's friendship with Mrs. Vance change her view of life?

_____

_____

_____

5. Despite her success, why is Carrie still unsatisfied?

_____

_____

_____

Challenge Question

Write an essay explaining the parallel plot lines of *Sister Carrie*, how Carrie's star rises as Hurstwood's life is ruined.

Name_____ Date_____

Pentimento by Lillian Hellman

Place a T before each true statement and an F before each false statement.

_____ 1. Hellman was born in Boston.

_____ 2. Lillian was closer to her cousin Bethe than any other member of her family was.

_____ 3. Lillian understood what was happening when she went to the restaurant with Bethe and her boyfriend.

_____ 4. Uncle Willy was her father's brother.

_____ 5. Lillian got most of her information from Caroline Ducky, her great-aunt's maid.

_____ 6. Lillian inherited from her aunts a briefcase of papers dealing with her family history.

_____ 7. Lillian was married to Hammett for ten years.

_____ 8. *Toys in the Attic* was Hellman's first successful play.

_____ 9. *Pentimento* contains few references to Hellman's experiences with the McCarthy committee.

_____ 10. Lillian and Julia were schoolmates.

_____ 11. Lillian went to Vienna to study with Sigmund Freud.

_____ 12. Lillian smuggled Julia's money into Germany by concealing the currency inside her hat.

_____ 13. Julia lost an arm while she was fighting for the underground.

_____ 14. Lillian found Julia's daughter and took the child back to America.

_____ 15. Hellman's first play was a great success.

_____ 16. Hellman recalls that she created many of her own difficulties while working in Hollywood.

_____ 17. Arthur Cowan was Hellman's second husband.

_____ 18. Hammett buried the big turtle after he and Lillian killed it.

_____ 19. Helen was Lillian's aunt.

_____ 20. All Hellman's work was received by the public with equal enthusiasm.

© 1991 J. Weston Walch, Publisher

Name _____   Date_____

Pentimento by Lillian Hellman

Answer the following questions in two or three complete sentences.

1. Why were both Cousin Bethe and Uncle Willy romantic figures for Lillian as a child?

   _____

   _____

   _____

2. How did Lillian show her courage and her love for Julia?

   _____

   _____

   _____

3. How did Hellman's relationship with Dashiell Hammett help her as a writer?

   _____

   _____

   _____

4. How does Hellman's writing show her sense of humor?

   _____

   _____

   _____

5. How did politics and international events influence Lillian's life?

   _____

   _____

   _____

Challenge Question

Discuss three significant people who shaped Hellman's life. What is special about her memory of each of them?

Name_____ Date_____

Up the Down Staircase by Bel Kaufman

Select the letter of the word or phrase which correctly completes each sentence.

_____ 1. Sylvia had intended to begin her first homeroom period by (A) taking attendance (B) having a good discussion on first impressions (C) putting a seating chart on the board (D) telling the students about her own school experience.

_____ 2. Sylvia's closest friend on the faculty is (A) Sadie Finch (B) Paul Barringer (C) Henrietta Pasterfield (D) Bea Schachter.

_____ 3. Which of the following quickly becomes Sylvia's "enemy"? (A) McHabe (B) Dr. Clarke (C) Grayson (D) Dr. Bester

_____ 4. The events in the book take place between (A) February and June (B) September and February (C) June and September (D) one September and the next.

_____ 5. Henrietta Pasterfield tries to teach English by (A) not giving any homework (B) making everything a game (C) enforcing strict discipline (D) getting other teachers to do her work for her.

_____ 6. Open School was supposed to provide Sylvia with an opportunity to (A) meet with the parents (B) let the kids run her classes (C) visit the classrooms of other teachers (D) talk freely with the principal.

_____ 7. According to Mr. McHabe, the most important thing that a student can do is (A) get good grades (B) be polite (C) make friends easily (D) follow all the rules.

_____ 8. Sylvia feels guilty when Evelyn Lazar dies because (A) she did not report Evelyn's pregnancy to the nurse (B) she couldn't stop to talk with Evelyn (C) she had not notified Evelyn's parents (D) she did not know who Evelyn was.

_____ 9. "The Ghost Walks" refers to a visit from (A) Mr. Bester (B) Dr. Clarke (C) Mr. McHabe (D) Paul Barringer.

_____ 10. The most thoroughly unpleasant student in Sylvia's class seems to be (A) Linda Rosen (B) Harry Kagan (C) Vivian Paine (D) Edward Williams.

(continued)

© 1991 J. Weston Walch, Publisher

Name _____   Date _____

Up the Down Staircase by Bel Kaufman

_____ 11. Jose Rodriguez (A) is Puerto Rican (B) has been to court (C) gains self-respect through a mock trial (D) all of the above.

_____ 12. Vivian Paine's biggest accomplishment is (A) learning to read Shakespeare (B) losing weight (C) writing poetry (D) learning how to use punctuation.

_____ 13. Sylvia says that she envies her friend Ellen because Ellen (A) is married (B) has a child (C) lives in the real world (D) has more time to herself.

_____ 14. Sylvia almost loses her job when she (A) fails to hand in her grades on time (B) lets a student go to the lavatory without an escort (C) can't control her classes (D) doesn't know enough English to teach well.

_____ 15. Edward Williams's greatest difficulty comes from (A) his age (B) his family background (C) his race (D) his learning disability.

_____ 16. Alice Blake tries to kill herself when (A) the other students make fun of her (B) she becomes pregnant (C) Barringer corrects her grammar and punctuation (D) she fails English.

_____ 17. Sylvia's greatest personal challenge comes from (A) Alice Blake (B) Mr. McHabe (C) Joe Ferone (D) Dr. Bester.

_____ 18. Bea urges Sylvia to (A) take the job at Willowdale (B) stay at Calvin Coolidge (C) transfer to another high school (D) get out of teaching entirely.

_____ 19. Sylvia is injured by (A) a student attacker (B) glass from a broken window (C) a falling piece of scenery (D) a drunk driver.

_____ 20. The novel ends (A) with Sylvia's decision to return to Coolidge (B) in homeroom 304 (C) at the beginning of the second semester (D) all of the above.

© 1991 J. Weston Walch, Publisher

Name _____   Date_____

Up the Down Staircase by Bel Kaufman

Answer the following questions in two or three complete sentences.

1. Why is Sylvia completely unprepared for her first day at Calvin Coolidge?

   _____

   _____

   _____

2. Which of the staff seem most out of touch with the needs of the teachers and the students?

   _____

   _____

   _____

3. Why does writing to Ellen meet a great need for Sylvia?

   _____

   _____

   _____

4. How are Evelyn Lazar and Alice Blake victims of "the system"?

   _____

   _____

   _____

5. Why does Sylvia want so much to reach Joe Ferone?

   _____

   _____

   _____

Challenge Question

One measure of a teacher's success is in the growth of the students. Rate Sylvia Barrett as a teacher. Discuss specific points of success and failure during her first semester at Calvin Coolidge High School.

Name _____   Date _____

Profiles in Courage by John F. Kennedy

Match each description in Column A with the correct name in Column B.

Column A

_____ 1. Orator from Massachusetts who loved the Union more than he feared slavery

_____ 2. President who missed being impeached by only one vote

_____ 3. Supported an embargo proposed by the man who had defeated his father

_____ 4. Only his vote saved a president from being removed from office

_____ 5. Great southern compromiser who wanted to avoid secession and war

_____ 6. Powerful speaker called the "czar" of the House of Representatives

_____ 7. Opposed Wilson's plan to arm U.S. ships prior to World War I

_____ 8. Defended the soldiers accused in the Boston Massacre

_____ 9. Opposed silver as the basis for United States currency

_____ 10. A southern sympathizer whose career was ended when he voted against the expansion of slavery into the new territories

_____ 11. Rejected by the people of Texas when he refused to support secession from the Union

_____ 12. First Catholic candidate for president of the United States

_____ 13. "Mr. Republican" who failed to get his party's nomination for president

_____ 14. Secretary of war whom President Johnson attempted to dismiss

_____ 15. Leader of the Radical Republicans who wanted to punish the South

_____ 16. Believed that his brother was also a great example of courage

_____ 17. Ill senator carried to his seat to vote in the impeachment proceedings

_____ 18. Believed that courage was required both to die and to live

_____ 19. President during a very corrupt administration

_____ 20. Spoke in defense of an unpopular congressional pay raise

Column B

A. Edmund Ross

B. Thomas Harte Benton

C. George Norris

D. Andrew Johnson

E. Sam Houston

F. Henry Clay

G. Robert Kennedy

H. John Adams

I. Joseph Cannon

J. Ulysses S. Grant

K. John C. Calhoun

L. Daniel Webster

M. Robert A. Taft

N. John F. Kennedy

O. Al Smith

P. James W. Grimes

Q. Lucius Lamar

R. John Quincy Adams

S. Thaddeus Stevens

T. Edwin Stanton

© 1991 J. Weston Walch, Publisher

100 More Great Books: Synopses, Quizzes, and Tests

Name _____ Date _____

Profiles in Courage by John F. Kennedy

Answer the following questions in two or three complete sentences.

1. Why has the United States Senate been an important arena for displaying courage?

    _____

    _____

    _____

2. How did both Webster and Benton place the national interest above state or sectional considerations?

    _____

    _____

    _____

3. How did the courage of Edmund Ross change the course of American history?

    _____

    _____

    _____

4. How did Sam Houston's status change from hero to outcast?

    _____

    _____

    _____

5. What did John Quincy Adams and Robert A. Taft have in common?

    _____

    _____

    _____

Challenge Question

Kennedy writes that courage is present when "a man does what he must—in spite of personal consequences, in spite of obstacles and dangers and pressures." Explain how the senators discussed in *Profiles in Courage* are examples of this statement.

Name_____ Date_____

Anna and the King of Siam by Margaret Landon

Match each description in Column A with the correct name in Column B.

Column A		Column B
_____	1. Took the name of Harriet Beecher Stowe and set her slaves free	A. Tuptim
_____	2. Dangerous half-brother of the prime minister	B. Mae Pia
_____	3. Assisted Anna in teaching the king's children the alphabet	C. Bangkok
_____	4. Powerful prime minister	D. Fa-ying
_____	5. Brought Anna to Siam on board his ship	E. Phra Alak
_____	6. Died a terrible death rather than reveal the names of those who had helped her escape from the palace	F. Beebe
_____	7. The king's head wife	G. King Mongkut
_____	8. Faithful nursemaid to Anna's children	H. Klun Thao Ap
_____	9. Frenchman who plotted to steal Siamese provinces	I. Son Klin
_____	10. Had a braid of his hair removed in an elaborate public ceremony	J. Chulalongkorn
_____	11. King's favorite child who died of cholera	K. Kralahome
_____	12. Sacrificed her tongue to rescue her beloved mistress	L. L'Ore
_____	13. Had been a Buddhist monk before he ascended the throne	M. Louis
_____	14. Woman freed when Anna "purchased" her from a brutal mistress	N. Singapore
_____	15. Capital city of Siam	O. Captain Orton
_____	16. City where Anna established her first school	P. Sir John Hay
_____	17. Chief judge in the king's harem	Q. Lady Thiang
_____	18. The king's private secretary	R. Aubaret
_____	19. Anna's only daughter	S. Avis
_____	20. English diplomat to the court of Siam	T. The Interpreter

© 1991 J. Weston Walch, Publisher

Name_____   Date_____

Anna and the King of Siam by Margaret Landon

Answer the following questions in two or three complete sentences.

1. How did Anna's childhood prepare her for her life in Siam?

   _____

   _____

   _____

2. What difficulties did Anna encounter when she first came to Bangkok?

   _____

   _____

   _____

3. Why was King Mongkut a difficult employer?

   _____

   _____

   _____

4. Which of the Siamese women were examples of courage in places of great difficulty?

   _____

   _____

   _____

5. How did Anna's teachings make a permanent difference for the Siamese people?

   _____

   _____

   _____

Challenge Question

Write an essay discussing the character strengths that helped Anna Leonowens survive in Siam and assist the people with whom she worked.

© 1991 J. Weston Walch, Publisher

Name_____ Date_____

Eleanor and Franklin by Joseph P. Lash

Match each name in Column A with the letter of the correct description in Column B.

Column A

_____ 1. Malvina Thompson

_____ 2. Campobello

_____ 3. Joseph Daniels

_____ 4. Hall Roosevelt

_____ 5. Admiral Halsey

_____ 6. Earl Miller

_____ 7. Missy LeHand

_____ 8. Youth Congress

_____ 9. Harry S Truman

_____ 10. Hyde Park

_____ 11. Lucy Mercer

_____ 12. Louis Howe

_____ 13. Theodore Roosevelt

_____ 14. Elliot Roosevelt

_____ 15. Arthurdale

_____ 16. Sarah Roosevelt

_____ 17. Mlle Souvestre

_____ 18. Val-Kill

_____ 19. Alfred Smith

_____ 20. King George VI and Queen Elizabeth

Column B

A. Franklin's nurse and companion

B. Gave Eleanor away at her wedding

C. Eleanor's younger brother

D. Trusted secretary and friend

E. Domineering mother-in-law

F. Headmistress of Allenwood

G. Organization Eleanor supported which turned out to be a Communist front

H. Roosevelt family home

I. Eleanor's private cottage retreat

J. Opposed Eleanor's visits to the troops in the South Pacific

K. Secretary who fell in love with Franklin

L. Roosevelt summer home

M. First Catholic candidate for president

N. Eleanor persuaded the convention to accept him as third-term VP

O. Franklin's boss at the Navy Department

P. Eleanor's personal security guard

Q. Eleanor's unstable father

R. Failed Depression housing experiment

S. Royal guests

T. Presidential advisor who helped Eleanor enter the world of politics

© 1991 J. Weston Walch, Publisher

Name _____   Date_____

Eleanor and Franklin by Joseph P. Lash

Answer the following questions in two or three complete sentences.

1. Why was Eleanor's childhood difficult?

   _____

   _____

   _____

2. What problems did Eleanor have with her mother-in-law?

   _____

   _____

   _____

3. How did Franklin's relationship with Lucy Mercer affect the Roosevelts' marriage?

   _____

   _____

   _____

4. What causes did Eleanor champion during the 1920's and 1930's?

   _____

   _____

   _____

5. What contributions did Eleanor make to the morale of the fighting men during World War II?

   _____

   _____

   _____

Challenge Question

Write an essay discussing Eleanor Roosevelt as a woman who put aside her own wishes to serve others.

© 1991 J. Weston Walch, Publisher

Name _____   Date_____

The Natural by Bernard Malamud

Select the letter of the word or phrase which correctly completes each sentence.

_____   1. The first city in which Roy was scheduled to play major league baseball was (A) New York (B) Chicago (C) Philadelphia (D) Pittsburgh.

_____   2. Roy carried a bassoon case because he (A) wanted to protect his bat (B) was an amateur musician (C) did not want his equipment stolen (D) did not trust Sam.

_____   3. Sam Simpson (A) was a former major league player (B) had discovered Roy's talent (C) wanted the Cubs to give him a regular salary again (D) all of the above.

_____   4. Roy first saw Harriet Bird (A) in the dining car (B) in the stands at the ball park (C) as she was getting on the train (D) through an open door to a hotel room.

_____   5. When Harriet shot Roy, his name did not get into the papers because (A) Roy had amnesia (B) the team's publicity office covered up the episode (C) Roy was carrying Sam's wallet (D) the police did not bother to investigate the episode.

_____   6. Roy's bat Wonderboy (A) was made for Roy by his brother (B) was heavier than the average bat (C) was made from a special tree (C) helped him win the world series for the Knights.

_____   7. Roy's major league career lasted (A) ten years (B) fifteen years (C) five years (D) one season.

_____   8. Pop Fisher (A) cared about his players (B) owned stock in the Knights (C) had failed in his own playing career (D) all of the above.

_____   9. Bump was killed when he (A) was shot by a jealous husband (B) hit the wall while chasing a fly ball (C) was drinking and driving (D) played a nasty practical joke on another player.

_____   10. All of the following are true of Roy Hobbs *except* (A) he did not begin to play professional ball until he was thirty (B) he was a powerful home run hitter (C) he had a small appetite and could never eat before a game (D) he first played baseball in high school.

(continued)

© 1991 J. Weston Walch, Publisher   *100 More Great Books: Synopses, Quizzes, and Tests*

Name_____   Date_____

The Natural by Bernard Malamud

_____ 11. Pop benched Roy at the beginning of the season because Roy (A) refused to be hypnotized (B) turned his ankle (C) hit badly in batting practice (D) argued with the umpire too often.

_____ 12. When Roy asked the Judge for a raise, the team's owner (A) turned him down (B) gave him a salary equal to what Bump had been making (C) told him to ask Pop (D) fired Roy.

_____ 13. Roy came out of his long batting slump when (A) Memo told him that she loved him (B) he got a new bat (C) Iris stood up in the stands to encourage him (D) the Knights returned to their home ball park.

_____ 14. Roy was hospitalized for (A) overeating (B) a pulled leg muscle (C) appendicitis (D) a nervous breakdown.

_____ 15. Roy's main objective in his relationship with Memo was to (A) marry her (B) make her forget Bump (C) get her away from the Judge's influence (D) help her forget an unhappy childhood.

_____ 16. Max Mercy is determined to (A) uncover the secret of Roy's past (B) expose Roy as a drug user (C) have Roy marry Iris (D) get Roy fired from the team.

_____ 17. In his last game with the Knights, Roy does all of the following *except* (A) break his bat (B) hit a home run (C) strike out (D) walk.

_____ 18. The end of Roy's baseball career comes when (A) he tells off the Judge (B) Max prints the story about Roy's youth (C) Roy buries Wonderboy in the outfield (D) Memo leaves him.

_____ 19. Roy takes the payoff money the Judge has given him and (A) throws it in the Judge's face (B) invests in a sports equipment company (C) buys stock in another team (D) marries Iris.

_____ 20. At the end of the novel, Roy (A) is a hero (B) is teaching baseball techniques to young kids (C) has been publicly accused of selling out his team (D) has a son of his own who is interested in playing baseball.

Name_____ Date_____

The Natural by Bernard Malamud

Answer the following questions in two or three complete sentences.

1. Why was Roy's major league success so important to Sam?

_____

_____

_____

2. How had Pop Fisher been a failure in his own major league career?

_____

_____

_____

3. Why is Bump's death a major break in Roy's career?

_____

_____

_____

4. How are Memo and Iris contrasting influences in Roy's life?

_____

_____

_____

5. Why does the Judge want his own team to lose in the playoffs?

_____

_____

_____

Challenge Question

Write an essay discussing Roy Hobbs as a hero. In what ways does Roy not measure up to the usual qualities of a hero in fiction? To what degree is he heroic?

© 1991 J. Weston Walch, Publisher   *100 More Great Books: Synopses, Quizzes, and Tests*

Name_____ Date_____

West With the Night by Beryl Markham

Supply the word or phrase which correctly completes each sentence.

1. The great plain in East Africa was named the _____ .

2. The Elkington lion was unusual because _____

   _____ .

3. Kibii, Beryl's childhood playmate, was later named _____ .

4. _____ was the name of the first horse that Beryl had as her own.

5. _____ the dog was Beryl's childhood companion.

6. Beryl left her father's farm because _____

   _____ .

7. When Beryl was a child, the natives nicknamed her _____ .

8. _____ was a special horse who won a race against all odds.

9. _____ taught Beryl how to fly.

10. _____ , a friend of Beryl's, was a flier and hunter who was killed in a plane crash.

11. Beryl considered _____ the greatest hunter in Africa.

12. The _____ is the most difficult and dangerous animal to stalk for the hunt.

13. On safari, Blix and Winston were almost killed when _____

    _____ .

14. _____ , the native guide, was greatly respected by hunters.

15. In case of a crash, Beryl always carried a bottle of _____ .

16. The greatest difficulty on Beryl's flight from Kenya to England came from _____

    _____ .

17. She is sad as she leaves Africa because _____ .

18. Beryl's attempt to fly the Atlantic solo was financed by _____ .

19. The plane she flew on the transatlantic trip was named _____ .

20. The plane crashed in Nova Scotia because _____ .

© 1991 J. Weston Walch, Publisher

Name _____ Date _____

West With the Night by Beryl Markham

Answer the following questions in two or three complete sentences.

1. How did Beryl's childhood experiences give her a great love for Africa?

   _____

   _____

   _____

2. Describe some of the dangers facing a lone pilot in the African bush.

   _____

   _____

   _____

3. How does Beryl Markham bring the animals of Africa to life in her book?

   _____

   _____

   _____

4. Why was the relationship between Beryl and Arab Ruta so special?

   _____

   _____

   _____

5. What were some of Beryl's greatest difficulties during her solo Atlantic crossing?

   _____

   _____

   _____

Challenge Question

How does Beryl Markham's writing show her to be a woman who met many challenges by refusing to accept limitations in life?

© 1991 J. Weston Walch, Publisher

100 More Great Books: Synopses, Quizzes, and Tests

Name_____ Date_____

A Man Called Peter by Catherine Marshall

Supply the word or phrase which correctly completes each sentence.

1. Peter Marshall came to America from _____ .

2. The most difficult experience of Peter's childhood was _____
   _____ .

3. Peter's first jobs in America included _____
   _____ .

4. _____ paid Peter's way to come to America.

5. Catherine and Peter met while she was a student at _____ .

6. The other ministers nicknamed Peter _____ because
   he used _____ .

7. New York Avenue Presbyterian was also called _____
   _____ .

8. A hard time in the Marshalls' life came when _____ .

9. The housekeeper who came to help the Marshalls was _____ .

10. On their honeymoon, the Marshalls went to _____ .

11. The Marshalls' son was nicknamed _____ .

12. Peter preached at the U.S. Naval Academy just before _____
    _____._____ .

13. The Marshalls' summer home on _____ was named _____ .

14. The initials GGP after Peter's name meant _____ .

15. Peter Marshall felt that the greatest honor of his life was _____
    _____ .

16. After Peter's first heart attack, Catherine tried to get him to _____ .

17. Peter's closest friend in the Senate was _____ .

18. Peter called his death his _____ .

19. Peter's last words to his wife were _____ .

20. The little boy Donald paid his last tribute to Peter Marshall by _____
    _____ .

© 1991 J. Weston Walch, Publisher

Name _____   Date_____

A *Man Called Peter* by Catherine Marshall

Answer the following questions in two or three complete sentences.

1. In what ways did Peter Marshall's boyhood influence his later work as a minister?

   _____

   _____

   _____

2. Why was Catherine Marshall so nervous when they moved to Washington?

   _____

   _____

   _____

3. How did Peter Marshall show that he was a good father?

   _____

   _____

   _____

4. What lessons did both Peter and Catherine learn from Catherine's illness?

   _____

   _____

   _____

5. Why was Peter Marshall's ministry as chaplain so meaningful to the members of Congress?

   _____

   _____

   _____

Challenge Question

Discuss the specific traits of Peter Marshall's character which made him a very real human being as well as a great man of faith.

Name_____ Date_____

The Bell Jar by Sylvia Plath

Select the letter of the word or phrase which correctly completes each sentence.

_____ 1. When the novel opens, Esther's age is approximately (A) twelve (B) nineteen (C) thirty (D) twenty-five.

_____ 2. During her month in New York, Esther works (A) for a newspaper (B) in a senator's office (C) for a ladies' magazine (D) in a stockbroker's office.

_____ 3. Esther's friend who takes life least seriously is (A) Joan (B) Susan (C) Doreen (D) Betsy.

_____ 4. When she returns from New York, Esther receives a blow when (A) her father dies (B) she fails to gain admission to a writing course (C) she can't get a job (D) her scholarship is canceled.

_____ 5. Esther considers killing herself by every means *except* (A) shooting herself (B) taking an overdose of pills (C) drowning (D) slitting her wrists.

_____ 6. The man whom Esther comes closest to really loving is (A) Buddy (B) Irwin (C) Marco (D) Constantin.

_____ 7. Esther rejects her New York experiences by (A) running away (B) throwing away her wardrobe (C) refusing to go to the office (D) leaving Doreen lying in the hall.

_____ 8. Buddy (A) dated Esther in college (B) has TB (C) expects that Esther will marry him (D) all of the above.

_____ 9. The person who helps Esther least is (A) Dr. Gordon (B) Dr. Nolan (C) Dr. Quinn (D) Philomena Guinea.

_____ 10. Esther's life is saved when she is found by (A) Joan (B) Valery (C) Doreen (D) her mother.

_____ 11. Esther describes most of her experiences in terms of (A) touch (B) taste (C) sound and light (D) strange ghostly visions.

_____ 12. At the hospital, Esther's ideal role model is (A) Joan (B) Dee Dee (C) Valery (D) Mrs. Norris.

(continued)

© 1991 J. Weston Walch, Publisher

100 More Great Books: Synopses, Quizzes, and Tests

Name _____ Date_____

The Bell Jar by Sylvia Plath

_____ 13. Esther's mother may be best described as (A) cruel (B) indifferent (C) helpless (D) brilliant.

_____ 14. Esther sees the outside world entirely (A) through her own feelings (B) through books (C) through the feelings of other people (D) through her memories.

_____ 15. Esther's sexual experience with Irwin may be best described as (A) exciting (B) brutally painful C) loving (D) boring.

_____ 16. One of the novel's greatest ironies lies in (A) Buddy's indifference (B) Joan's death (C) Esther's recovery (D) Doreen's sexuality.

_____ 17. Esther's most open expression of emotion occurs (A) in New York (B) on the beach (C) in Dr. Nolan's office (D) at her father's grave.

_____ 18. Esther learns of the publicity that surrounded her suicide attempt from (A) her mother (B) Joan (C) Buddy (D) Dr. Nolan.

_____ 19. Esther asserts her own identity (A) at Joan's funeral (B) by publishing a book (C) in an interview with her doctor (D) when she is released from the hospital.

_____ 20. The novel ends (A) with Esther's future unresolved (B) on a hopeful note (C) as Esther is about to leave the hospital (D) all of the above.

© 1991 J. Weston Walch, Publisher

Name_____   Date_____

The Bell Jar by Sylvia Plath

Answer the following questions in two or three complete sentences.

1. What experiences during her month in New York influence Esther most?

   _____

   _____

   _____

2. How is the first-person point of view used in *The Bell Jar*?

   _____

   _____

   _____

3. In what ways does Esther's physical strength help her to survive her emotional difficulties?

   _____

   _____

   _____

4. Why does Esther refuse to marry Buddy?

   _____

   _____

   _____

5. What is the symbolism of the bell jar?

   _____

   _____

   _____

Challenge Question

   Discuss how Esther's role as the narrator brings the reader into Esther's experiences as the protagonist of the novel.

Name_____ Date_____

I Am Third by Gale Sayers
with Al Silverman

Place a T before each true statement and an F before each false statement.

_____ 1. Gale Sayers suffered several severe injuries during his high school athletic career.

_____ 2. Gale feels that his mother cared more for his brothers than she cared for him.

_____ 3. Sayers has difficulty talking with reporters and television newspeople.

_____ 4. In both high school and college, English was Gale's best subject.

_____ 5. Gale's father polished cars for a living.

_____ 6. Linda and Gale were married while they were both still in high school.

_____ 7. The Sayerses have two children.

_____ 8. Gale does not allow playing football to affect his disposition.

_____ 9. Gale never experienced racial prejudice during his career as a college athlete or as a professional player.

_____ 10. Gale's friend Break played both high school and college football with Sayers.

_____ 11. When Sayers and Brian Piccolo first became roommates, they had a hard time learning to get along with each other.

_____ 12. Piccolo was a much more talkative man than Sayers.

_____ 13. Piccolo was given the "Most Courageous Player" award in 1970.

_____ 14. Sayers's career almost ended in 1968 when he broke his shoulder during a game.

_____ 15. Sayers is very fond of music.

_____ 16. George Halas was Gale Sayers's high school football coach.

_____ 17. Gale Sayers scored seven touchdowns in a single game and set a football record.

_____ 18. Gale Sayers is a stockbroker as well as a football player.

_____ 19. Sayers has never become involved in civil rights demonstrations.

_____ 20. Linda Sayers writes that Gale has much more self-confidence than he had when she married him.

© 1991 J. Weston Walch, Publisher   *100 More Great Books: Synopses, Quizzes, and Tests*

Name_____ Date_____

I Am Third by Gale Sayers
with Al Silverman

Answer the following questions in two or three complete sentences.

1. How did Gale Sayers compensate for his difficult home life?

   _____

   _____

   _____

2. How are injuries regarded differently in professional football than in high school or college play?

   _____

   _____

   _____

3. Why was his relationship with Brian Piccolo important to Gale Sayers?

   _____

   _____

   _____

4. In what ways did Linda Sayers help her husband's career?

   _____

   _____

   _____

5. How has Gale Sayers worked to help all black Americans?

   _____

   _____

   _____

Challenge Question

Write an essay discussing how Gale Sayers has become a more mature person off the football field.

© 1991 J. Weston Walch, Publisher

100 More Great Books: Synopses, Quizzes, and Tests

Name_____   Date_____

Beverly: An Autobiography
by Beverly Sills and Lawrence Linderman

Match each name in Column A with the letter of the correct description in Column B.

Column A	Column B
_____ 1. Lily Pons	A. Set designer for Sills's operas
_____ 2. New York City Opera	B. Made Sills a child star
	C. Great female conductor
_____ 3. Peter Greenough	D. New York arts complex
_____ 4. Sarah Caldwell	E. Opera that made Sills an international star
_____ 5. Major Bowes	F. Eccentric soprano
_____ 6. La Scala	G. Company Sills managed
_____ 7. Donizetti	H. Comic with whom Sills did a television special
_____ 8. Muffy	I. Voice teacher and friend
_____ 9. Estelle Liebling	J. Ran Sills's first road tour
_____ 10. *Julius Caesar*	K. Composer of three operas about English queens
_____ 11. Norman Triegle	L. New York City Opera conductor
_____ 12. Rosa Ponselle	M. Italy's leading opera house
_____ 13. Carol Burnett	N. Soprano whose records Beverly listened to
_____ 14. Tito Capolianco	O. Beverly's son
_____ 15. La Traviata	P. Bass, Beverly's friend
_____ 16. Lincoln Center	Q. Talk show host for whom Beverly was a frequent guest
_____ 17. J. J. Schubert	R. Most frequent role Sills has sung
_____ 18. Julius Rudell	S. Sills's daughter
_____ 19. Johnny Carson	T. Sills's husband
_____ 20. Bucky	

© 1991 J. Weston Walch, Publisher

100 More Great Books: Synopses, Quizzes, and Tests

Name_____   Date_____

Beverly: An Autobiography
by Beverly Sills and Lawrence Linderman

Answer the following questions in two or three complete sentences.

1. How did the experiences of Beverly's childhood influence her career?

_____

_____

_____

2. Name three significant performances which led to her rise to stardom.

_____

_____

_____

3. Why was Beverly's life in Cleveland so terrible?

_____

_____

_____

4. Why did Beverly decide to retire as a singer?

_____

_____

_____

5. Which roles does Beverly regard as her outstanding achievements?

_____

_____

_____

Challenge Question

Having read her story, discuss some of the reasons that Beverly Sills is one of America's most illustrious women.

© 1991 J. Weston Walch, Publisher

100 More Great Books: Synopses, Quizzes, and Tests

Name _____   Date_____

Madame Sarah by Cornelia Otis Skinner

Match each description in Column A with the correct name in Column B.

Column A   **Column B**

_____ 1. Sarah's spoiled son

_____ 2. English manager of Sarah's first American tour

_____ 3. Playwright who created many roles exclusively for Sarah

_____ 4. Sarah's indifferent mother

_____ 5. Sarah's substitute mother and kind advisor

_____ 6. Sarah's granddaughter, from whom the author received much information for this biography

_____ 7. National theater from which Sarah resigned to tour on her own

_____ 8. Great English actor who became Sarah's close friend

_____ 9. Actress Sarah slapped when she pushed Sarah's sister

_____ 10. Play which was the greatest single success of Bernhardt's career

_____ 11. Father of Sarah's child

_____ 12. Left Bank theater where Sarah gained her greatest following

_____ 13. Victor Hugo drama which made Sarah a star

_____ 14. Bernhardt's good-for-nothing husband

_____ 15. Sarah's summer estate in Brittany

_____ 16. Actress who wrote a slanderous book to get even with Sarah

_____ 17. Sarah's first great leading man

_____ 18. Sarah's most famous role in the French classical theater

_____ 19. Sarah's last leading man, who was thirty years younger than she was

_____ 20. First called Sarah "his little actress"

A. Madame Guerard

B. Edward Jarrett

C. *Ruy Blas*

D. Jacques Damala

E. Comédie Française

F. Odéon

G. Mounet-Sully

H. Madame Nathalie

I. Phèdre

J. *La Dame aux camélias*

K. Maurice

L. Marie Columbier

M. Judith Bernhardt

N. Alexandre Dumas

O. Sir Henry Irving

P. Victorien Sardou

Q. Lou Tellegen

R. Lysiane

S. Belle Isle

T. Prince Henri de Ligne

© 1991 J. Weston Walch, Publisher

100 More Great Books: Synopses, Quizzes, and Tests

Name_____   Date_____

Madame Sarah by Cornelia Otis Skinner

Answer the following questions in two or three complete sentences.

1. What difficulties did Sarah have as a child which influenced her becoming an actress?

_____

_____

_____

2. In what ways did Bernhardt both entertain and shock her audiences in Paris?

_____

_____

_____

3. What made Sarah Bernhardt's acting so special?

_____

_____

_____

4. How was Sarah victimized by those she loved the most?

_____

_____

_____

5. How did Sarah Bernhardt show tremendous courage in the last years of her life?

_____

_____

_____

Challenge Question

Write an essay discussing some of the ways in which "The Divine Sarah" became a legend during her lifetime.

Name_____   Date_____

The Gift of Music
by Jane Stuart Smith and Betty Carlson

Match each description in Column A with the correct name in Column B.

Column A   **Column B**

_____ 1. Completely changed the sound of twentieth-century music by using an atonal form

_____ 2. Greatest composer of tragic Italian opera

_____ 3. German-born composer who had his greatest successes in England

_____ 4. Optimistic composer of *The Four Seasons*

_____ 5. Crushed by Communist oppression in Stalin's Russia

_____ 6. Husband-and-wife team of great romantic musicians

_____ 7. His operas were based on a world mythology which ended in total chaos

_____ 8. Composer of the first modern ballet

_____ 9. Ideally joined musical form with biblical text in his *St. Matthew's Passion*

_____ 10. Happy composer of over one hundred symphonies

_____ 11. Searched for the meaning of death and resurrection, but never found the answer

_____ 12. National composer of Poland who wrote only for the piano

_____ 13. Escaped from Russia at the time of the Bolshevik revolution by traveling across Finland in a snowstorm

_____ 14. Collected English folk songs and used many of them in his compositions

_____ 15. No mourners attended his funeral when he was buried in a pauper's grave

_____ 16. French composer who wrote his autobiography

_____ 17. National composer of Hungary

_____ 18. American black genius of "ragtime"

_____ 19. Romantic composer who had the strongest roots in the classical tradition

_____ 20. Found some of his greatest romantic inspiration in the sights and sounds of the sea

A. Wagner

B. Handel

C. Bartók

D. Rachmaninoff

E. Bach

F. Mozart

G. Schönberg

H. Chopin

I. Debussy

J. Hayden

K. Verdi

L. Prokofiev

M. Joplin

N. Vivaldi

O. Vaughn Williams

P. Schumanns

Q. Berlioz

R. Mahler

S. Brahms

T. Stravinsky

© 1991 J. Weston Walch, Publisher   *100 More Great Books: Synopses, Quizzes, and Tests*

Name_____   Date_____

The Gift of Music
by Jane Stuart Smith and Betty Carlson

Answer the following questions in two or three complete sentences.

1. Explain the term "baroque." How did this ideal contribute to the musical forms of the seventeenth century?

   _____

   _____

   _____

2. Which composers, while writing beautiful music, were not easy to live with as people?

   _____

   _____

   _____

3. How did folk music influence the development of classical music?

   _____

   _____

   _____

4. In what ways were composers dependent on the patronage of the wealthy for the development of their musical talents?

   _____

   _____

   _____

5. Why did the composers of the early twentieth century find difficulty in getting audiences to listen to their music?

   _____

   _____

   _____

Challenge Question

Write an essay explaining the concept that genius is a gift from God which also has a high price tag. What sacrifices did these composers make to give great music to the world?

© 1991 J. Weston Walch, Publisher

Name_____ Date_____

The Agony and the Ecstasy by Irving Stone

Match each description in Column A with the correct name in Column B.

Column A   **Column B**

_____ 1. Michelangelo's patron and second father

_____ 2. Fiery monk whose preaching almost destroyed Florentine art

_____ 3. Family of artisans who gave Michelangelo his love for marble

_____ 4. Pope who commissioned the painting of the Sistine Chapel

_____ 5. Gave Michelangelo the opportunity to study anatomy by dissecting corpses

_____ 6. Michelangelo's father

_____ 7. First love of Michelangelo's life

_____ 8. Artist with whom Michelangelo tried to compete in fresco painting

_____ 9. Michelangelo's faithful servant in Rome

_____ 10. Young man loved by the aging Michelangelo

_____ 11. Town which served as major source of marble

_____ 12. Work of art on which the sculptor carved his own name

_____ 13. Statue which became a symbol of freedom for the people of Florence

_____ 14. Boyhood apprentice and close friend for all of Michelangelo's life

_____ 15. Broke Michelangelo's nose in a quarrel

_____ 16. Michelangelo's teacher in the Medici sculpture gardens

_____ 17. Woman whom Michelangelo loved briefly, but passionately

_____ 18. Pope who commissioned the "Last Judgment" fresco

_____ 19. Architect whom Michelangelo defeated in the competition to design the dome of St. Peter's

_____ 20. Mayor of Florence who helped Michelangelo get the commission for the "David"

A. Leonardo da Vinci

B. "David"

C. Torrigiani

D. Prior Bichiellini

E. Clarissa

F. Savonarola

G. Paul III

H. Argiento

I. Sangallo

J. Lodovico

K. Contessina de' Medici

L. "Pietà"

M. Lorenzo de' Medici

N. Gonfaloniere Soderini

O. Carrara

P. Julius II

Q. Tommaso de' Cavalieri

R. Topolino

S. Bertoldo

T. Granacci

© 1991 J. Weston Walch, Publisher

Name _____   Date_____

The Agony and the Ecstasy by Irving Stone

Answer the following questions in two or three complete sentences.

1. In what ways did Michelangelo's family make his life difficult?

   _____

   _____

   _____

2. Describe the education Michelangelo received at the court of Lorenzo de' Medici.

   _____

   _____

   _____

3. Why did Michelangelo believe that he had to study human anatomy?

   _____

   _____

   _____

4. Describe the battle of wills between Michelangelo and Pope Julius II.

   _____

   _____

   _____

5. How does Michelangelo's biography show that he was a man of many talents?

   _____

   _____

   _____

Challenge Question

Write an essay describing some of the sacrifices in terms of "normal living" that Michelangelo made in order to fulfill his potential as an artist.

Name_____ Date_____

Oprah by Robert Waldron

Place a T before each true statement and an F before each false statement.

_____ 1. As a small child, Oprah was raised by her mother.

_____ 2. Oprah showed early talent as a mimic and actress.

_____ 3. Oprah was often beaten as a child.

_____ 4. Oprah today is bitter toward the people who brought her up.

_____ 5. Oprah's father was the real stabilizing influence in her early life.

_____ 6. In college, Oprah decided to major in speech and dramatics.

_____ 7. Oprah's first job was in a television station.

_____ 8. Oprah was a great success as a news reporter in Baltimore.

_____ 9. Oprah won a beauty contest while she was in high school.

_____ 10. Oprah got married while she was living in Baltimore.

_____ 11. The move to Chicago was the real beginning for Oprah's career.

_____ 12. Oprah's guests are mostly celebrities.

_____ 13. Oprah won an Oscar for her role in *The Color Purple*.

_____ 14. Oprah's main competition in the talk show field came from Phil Donahue.

_____ 15. Oprah is always orderly and very well organized.

_____ 16. Oprah made a bet with Barbara Walters about losing weight.

_____ 17. Today, Oprah Winfrey is a millionaire.

_____ 18. Oprah's show is distributed by the CBS television network.

_____ 19. Stedman Graham is Oprah's business manager.

_____ 20. Oprah dislikes shopping and lets members of her staff buy her wardrobe for her.

© 1991 J. Weston Walch, Publisher   *100 More Great Books: Synopses, Quizzes, and Tests*

Name_____   Date_____

Oprah by Robert Waldron

Answer the following questions in two or three complete sentences.

1. What childhood experiences most directly influenced the development of Oprah's character?

   _____

   _____

   _____

2. What did she learn during her early years in radio and television that helped her later career?

   _____

   _____

   _____

3. What weaknesses make Oprah very human to her audiences?

   _____

   _____

   _____

4. Why was Barbara Walters Oprah's idol?

   _____

   _____

   _____

5. Why was her role in *The Color Purple* a high point in Oprah's career?

   _____

   _____

   _____

Challenge Question

Write an essay explaining Oprah Winfrey's special appeal to her audiences. Why has she become so popular?

© 1991 J. Weston Walch, Publisher   *100 More Great Books: Synopses, Quizzes, and Tests*

Name_____   Date_____

The Picture of Dorian Gray by Oscar Wilde

Select the letter of the word or phrase which correctly completes each sentence.

_____ 1. When the novel opens, Basil (A) is anxious for Lord Henry to meet Dorian (B) has just started the portrait (C) has just finished the portrait (D) is considering suicide.

_____ 2. Dorian's greatest asset is (A) his money (B) his intellect (C) his social status (D) his beautiful face.

_____ 3. Basil does not want Lord Henry to meet Dorian because (A) he is afraid Lord Henry will corrupt him (B) he wants to keep Dorian's friendship for himself (C) he knows that Dorian will be easily influenced (D) all of the above.

_____ 4. Dorian first sees Sibyl Vane in the role of (A) Juliet (B) Lady Macbeth (C) Rosamund (D) Ophelia.

_____ 5. Sibyl knows Dorian (A) as Lord Henry's friend (B) as Prince Charming (C) as the subject of Basil's painting (D) by his real identity.

_____ 6. The person most anxious to protect Sibyl is (A) her mother (B) Dorian (C) Jim (D) the Jew who is her manager.

_____ 7. Dorian notices the first change in his portrait after (A) he rejects Sibyl (B) he refuses to let Basil exhibit the painting (C) he goes to the theater with Lord Henry (D) he moves the portrait to an upstairs room.

_____ 8. Dorian was most influenced to evil by (A) Basil (B) Lord Henry (C) Jim Vane (D) Lord Kelso.

_____ 9. Sibyl Vane (A) married Lord Henry (B) killed herself (C) died in a fire (D) went to Australia with her brother.

_____ 10. Dorian rejected Sibyl when (A) she did a bad job of acting (B) he found her with another man (C) he fell in love with Lord Henry's sister (D) Basil told him to have nothing more to do with her.

_____ 11. Lord Henry sent Dorian a book dealing with (A) lives of famous painters (B) Dorian's family tree (C) how to expand sensual experience (D) how to pose for a portrait.

(continued)

© 1991 J. Weston Walch, Publisher

Name _____ Date_____

The Picture of Dorian Gray by Oscar Wilde

_____ 12. Dorian hid the painting because (A) he did not want anyone to know its value (B) he did not want Basil to know that the portrait had been damaged (C) he did not want his sins revealed (D) he did not want the portrait to be stolen.

_____ 13. Dorian murders Basil (A) so that Basil can't exhibit the portrait (B) after Basil sees how the portrait has changed (C) when Basil finds out that Dorian killed a man (D) so that Basil can't leave England.

_____ 14. Dorian forces Alan Campbell to (A) help him bury Basil (B) carry the painting to a new location (C) destroy Basil's body (D) find out the identity of Sibyl's brother.

_____ 15. Dorian's deeds most sharply contrast with (A) his looks (B) his reputation (C) his reading habits (D) his thoughts.

_____ 16. The character in the novel who changes least is (A) Basil (B) Dorian (C) Lord Henry (D) Jim Vane.

_____ 17. Jim Vane is (A) killed in a train wreck (B) murdered by Dorian (C) never seen again in England (D) shot by accident.

_____ 18. Dorian is most afraid when (A) he sees Jim Vane's face (B) he learns that Sibyl is dead (C) he sees blood on the hands of the portrait (D) his servants find the portrait.

_____ 19. Dorian kills himself by (A) gunshot (B) slashing the portrait (C) taking poison (D) an overdose of opium.

_____ 20. Dorian's body is identified by (A) fingerprints (B) rings (C) the likeness to the portrait (D) Lord Henry.

Name _____ Date _____

The Picture of Dorian Gray by Oscar Wilde

Answer the following questions in two or three complete sentences.

1. Why does Basil not want Lord Henry to meet Dorian?

_____

_____

_____

2. How does Lord Henry influence Dorian?

_____

_____

_____

3. What specific events cause the greatest changes in the portrait?

_____

_____

_____

4. How does Dorian hide the portrait?

_____

_____

_____

5. Describe the contrast between Dorian Gray's appearance and his actions.

_____

_____

_____

Challenge Question

Discuss the theme of moral responsibility in *The Picture of Dorian Gray*. How does Lord Henry contribute to Dorian's downfall? How is Dorian himself responsible?

© 1991 J. Weston Walch, Publisher

100 More Great Books: Synopses, Quizzes, and Tests

Answer Keys

Giant Steps by Kareem Abdul-Jabbar and Peter Knobler

Matching:

1. F	6. Q	11. A	16. R
2. L	7. D	12. M	17. S
3. B	8. T	13. K	18. P
4. N	9. J	14. C	19. G
5. I	10. H	15. E	20. O

Short Answers:

1. He liked books and music, especially jazz. He learned to like basketball early, and spent much time practicing the shots that later became his trademark.

2. He left home and the rigid influence of his Catholic upbringing. He experienced for the first time the swinging life of California with its drugs and wild parties. He soon divorced himself from this scene, however, and concentrated almost entirely on basketball. At UCLA, he also experienced real racial prejudice that for a time made him bitter.

3. He felt that Islam was the most directly revealed faith, coming directly from Mohammed. He needed something to believe in. Islam gave him a sense of identity, and helped to free him from the prejudice that he had developed against whites and Jews.

4. Because he hated some of the press comments about him, Kareem withdrew from talking to the press. The reporters thought that he was very difficult to interview. On several occasions, losing his temper gave him a bad name in the press. Kareem feels that sometimes, because he was a star, both the media and the public were out to get him.

5. As a high school student, Kareem went to Virginia and discovered the meaning of segregation. Later in the 1960's he witnessed the race riots in Harlem. During his college years, Kareem did not play in the Olympics, which he felt were dominated by whites. As a pro, Kareem felt that fouls were called on him that were not called on white players for the same offense.

Challenge Question:

His father and mother shaped his early life. He was later separated from them when he became a Muslim. Both Donohue in high school and Wooden at UCLA helped his development as a player. Donohue, however, hurt Kareem by calling him a "nigger."

In his religious life, he was influenced by Hamaas. Later, when Kareem began to think for himself, Hamaas could not tolerate Kareem's independence of thought. When Hamaas himself went berserk, Kareem drifted away from his strict Muslim faith.

His first marriage to Habiba failed because they really did not know each other as people. Cheryl, his second wife, loved him both in success and failure. She was important to him because she gave him support even in the lowest moments of his life.

Yankee From Olympus by Catherine Drinker Bowen

Matching:

1. D	4. H	7. O	10. N	13. P	16. R	19. E
2. M	5. A	8. Q	11. T	14. K	17. S	20. B
3. J	6. L	9. F	12. I	15. C	18. G	

Short Answers:

1. Answers might include: participation in the social life of the community, attending Harvard College, family background which had roots back to Puritan times, involvement in the exciting intellectual life of New England, and knowing personally the great men of their time.

2. The father was famous and outgoing; the son was very shy. The son was embarrassed when his father wrote publicly about private family matters. The son was forced to depend financially for many years on his father.

3. Sally provided a cheerful influence for her Puritan husband. Amelia helped to prevent a serious breach between father and son. Fanny supported Wendell in his law career. She drew him out when he tended to retreat too much into himself.

4. He would not talk about his experiences and launched into serious study of law. He was in serious danger of totally cutting himself off from human relationships.

5. It was Holmes's first significant dissent as a Supreme Court justice, and the beginning of his interpretation of the Constitution in terms of human experience.

Challenge Question:

Abiel wrote the first significant history of the first century of America. He recorded the changes as he lived them. Dr. Holmes related medicine to life. He was also America's first poet with a great sense of humor. Justice Holmes was one of the first to teach law at the university level. His legal interpretations breathed life into the Constitution. He often defied the political establishment and based his opinions more on individual cases than on theory.

Captains and the Kings by Taylor Caldwell

Multiple Choice:

1. B	4. A	7. C	10. D	13. D	16. A	19. B
2. D	5. B	8. D	11. C	14. A	17. C	20. B
3. A	6. D	9. B	12. B	15. D	18. D	

Short Answers:

1. The death of his mother and his father's incompetence made Joseph bitter. The poverty of his childhood made him determined to be rich at any cost.

2. He introduced Joseph to the men of power, showed Joseph how money ruled politics, gave Joseph early lessons in tests of loyalty, and made Joseph heir to his fortune.

3. Joseph was indifferent to Bernadette's love for him. Elizabeth was the strength and love of Joseph's life.

4. The Civil War, the assassinations of Lincoln and Garfield, the Spanish-American War, World War I.

5. Rory defied the wishes of the "Elite." He was killed when he tried to tell the truth to the press and to the public.

Challenge Question:

Modern history's events have been controlled by an invisible but powerful financial elite. This group manipulated public opinion by control of the press. Any politician could be bribed or intimidated. The good have been helpless against the power of the strong. Those who have learned of this group and who have opposed its aims have been systematically eliminated. Although the Armagh family is fictional, the events described in this novel are very real. Taylor Caldwell challenges her readers to think. Is such world domination a terrifying possibility?

Sister Carrie by Theodore Dreiser

Multiple Choice:

1. C	6. A	11. C	16. C
2. A	7. B	12. A	17. A
3. C	8. A	13. C	18. C
4. D	9. D	14. A	19. D
5. B	10. B	15. B	20. C

Short Answers:

1. She has lost her job. Her brother-in-law disapproves of her. They have told her that she will have to return to Wisconsin. She has seen some of life's pleasures, and she wants more.

2. Carrie's attractive simplicity and helplessness make both men want to protect her. She is sensual and rouses the passionate nature in both. She makes the men feel young.

3. Hurstwood steals the money that costs him his job because the safe happens to be open. His wife finds out about his relationship with Carrie through a chance meeting with a friend. He runs from Montreal because of a chance meeting with an acquaintance from Chicago.

4. Carrie sees what fashionable life on Broadway is like. Her interest in the theater is renewed. She goes to fashionable restaurants. Carrie contrasts the men she sees in these places with the declining Hurstwood.

5. Carrie always wants something more; money, clothes, and stardom do not satisfy her. At the end of the novel, she intends to move on to act in tragedy. The future for her is always greater; the present is never enough.

Challenge Question:

As Hurstwood's concern for his appearance declines, Carrie's desire for finery increases. She goes to work because he cannot find employment. Carrie moves into luxury as Hurstwood is dying of starvation. He is living in a flophouse on the Bowery, while she lives at the Waldorf. Hurstwood commits suicide and his body is sent to an unmarked grave. Carrie's name is in lights; she dreams of moving on to greater success.

Pentimento by Lillian Hellman

True or False:

1. F	4. F	7. F	10. T	13. F	16. T	19. F
2. T	5. T	8. F	11. F	14. F	17. F	20. F
3. F	6. F	9. T	12. T	15. T	18. F	

Short Answers:

1. Relating to Bethe, Lillian was in love with love; she saw the romance of the situation but not the dangers. Willy was also a romantic figure. In her trips with him to Cajun country, Lillian experienced her first romantic feelings for a specific person.

2. Answers might include: smuggling the money into Germany, her visit to Julia in the hospital, the search for Julia's child.

3. Their love gave her strength. His critical judgment strengthened her work.

4. Her sense of humor is evident in her ability to laugh at her own weaknesses, such as being sick when her play went on. Funny episodes with Samuel Goldwyn and Tallulah Bankhead and the episode with the turtle show great humor.

5. There are anti-Nazi feelings in her desire to help Julia. Several of her works were political dramas, especially *The Watch on the Rhine*. She gave benefit performances for those who were fighting the Fascists.

Challenge Question:

Hammett's influence was the greatest, in spite of their turbulent relationship. Caroline Ducky, her great-aunt's black maid, gave her insight into the realities of her family. These insights later appeared in *The Little Foxes*. Julia is an example of deep love; Helen, her faithful housekeeper and morale builder.

In doing this essay, the student may also write about Uncle Willy, Bethe, Cowan, or any of the other major characters Hellman profiles.

Up the Down Staircase by Bel Kaufman

Multiple Choice:

1. B	5. B	9. A	13. C	17. C
2. D	6. A	10. B	14. B	18. B
3. A	7. D	11. D	15. C	19. C
4. B	8. B	12. B	16. C	20. D

Short Answers:

1. As an idealist, Sylvia is not prepared for overcrowding or inadequate facilities. She does not understand the personal difficulties that frequently prevent her students from learning.

2. The librarian will not let them take out books. Dr. Clarke, the principal, thinks in complex language removed from the real world. McHabe issues long directives that can't possibly be followed. The nurse and the school secretary are completely tangled up in paperwork and memos.

3. The letters provide an outlet for Sylvia's frustrations. She can "think through" crisis events. Writing to Ellen gives Sylvia a sense of perspective.

4. Evelyn dies because no one has time to listen. Alice is hurt by the insensitivity of one teacher.

5. Sylvia sees beyond Joe's negative attitude and misbehavior. She sees his ability and the person that he could become.

Challenge Question:

Jose Rodriguez gains self-respect. Vivian Paine is helped by using Sylvia as a role model. The kids' writing papers show that many of them have begun thinking for themselves or have gained a new appreciation of literature through Sylvia's teaching. Many of the students come to trust her enough to sign their names to their suggestion box notes.

Evelyn and Alice are failures because Sylvia can't reach them in time to help. Joe Ferone is a big, unanswered question. Did Sylvia reach him in time?

During one semester, Miss Barrett's positive experiences outweigh the negative ones enough for her to return instead of taking a job at fashionable Willowdale Academy.

Profiles in Courage by John F. Kennedy

Matching:

1. L	6. I	11. E	16. G
2. D	7. C	12. O	17. P
3. R	8. H	13. M	18. N
4. A	9. Q	14. T	19. J
5. F	10. B	15. S	20. K

Short Answers:

1. The Senate has considered key issues in American history. People elected as senators have had to consider whether they would put their own interests or the good of the country first. Those who have stayed true to their principles have shown great courage.

2. Webster was a Northerner who placed the Union above the interests of the anti-slavery forces. Benton placed the preserving of the Union above his own Southern interests.

3. Only Ross's vote prevented the impeachment of a president. The anti-Southern powers in Congress were stopped because Johnson stayed in office.

4. He was the hero of the Mexican War and the first president of the Republic of Texas. As governor of the state of Texas, Houston was rejected when he refused to support secession.

5. Both were overshadowed by the presidencies of their fathers. Both were rebels within their own parties. However, although Adams later became president, Taft never did.

Challenge Question:

Because of their courage, several of these senators lost their seats: Adams, Houston, Benton, Webster. Others stayed in office, but were violently abused by the people in their own states: Ross, Lamar, and Norris. Taft probably could have been president if he had not spoken out so strongly for his principles. For each man, courage proved very costly.

Anna and the King of Siam by Margaret Landon

Matching:

1. I	4. K	7. Q	10. J	13. G	16. N	19. S
2. T	5. O	8. F	11. D	14. L	17. H	20. P
3. M	6. A	9. R	12. B	15. C	18. E	

Short Answers:

1. She lived in India and saw what colonialism had done to the natives there. Anna developed a strong sympathy for Asian peoples. She saw them not as inferior beings but as people who could control their own destinies. Anna's childhood also taught her self-reliance and the ability to survive under difficult circumstances.

2. Anna did not understand the Siamese language or customs. She could not even get to see the king for weeks. When she began her work, Anna made enemies of those who feared that she would have too much influence in the royal household.

3. The king was excessively temperamental. She never knew what kind of mood he would be in. He seemed to want the best for his people, but could be very dangerous

if his will was questioned or disobeyed. He might call her to the palace in the middle of the night for the most trivial reasons.

4. Lady Son Klin remained faithful to the king, even after he rejected her. Lady Thiang was loyal as the head wife, who arranged his majesty's meals and tasted all his food. Tuptim was the bravest of all. She escaped from the palace to be with the man she loved. When Tuptim was caught, she refused to betray the servants who had helped her.

5. When Prince Chulalongkorn became king, he made Siam a free nation. The sensitive young prince understood Anna's teachings and passed those lessons on to his people. Lady Son Klin also set her own slaves free.

Challenge Question:

Anna was a stubborn woman who did not give up, even when faced with great difficulties. She would not compromise what she thought to be right. Anna believed in the dignity of the individual. A great admirer of Abraham Lincoln, she fought in the court of Siam to help victims of injustice. She admired the king's desire to fight for what was his against the Europeans who plotted to take away his country. Her greatest strength was that she stood up to both the king and his prime minister and would not be bullied by unreasonable authority.

Anna was also a good teacher who helped enlarge her students' minds. She was eager to understand the Siamese people and to help the royal children fulfill their potential.

Eleanor and Franklin by Joseph P. Lash

Matching:

1. D	4. C	7. A	10. H	13. B	16. E	19. M
2. L	5. J	8. G	11. K	14. Q	17. F	20. S
3. O	6. P	9. N	12. T	15. R	18. I	

Short Answers:

1. Eleanor was shy and physically unattractive; her father was unstable; she lived a sheltered life with her stern grandmother.

2. Sarah wanted to run things, even at the White House. She furnished Eleanor's home, always sat at the head of the table, used Eleanor's children against her, and generally tried to possess Franklin.

3. Their marriage was no longer a love relationship, but a union of respect. Eleanor stayed because she believed in Franklin's ideals. She could not give Franklin the affection he needed. This episode helped Eleanor move toward being her own person.

4. Answers might include: the League of Women Voters, legislation for the poor, equal employment for blacks and youth, fair housing.

5. She traveled to England, Australia, and the South Pacific, visited hospitals, answered all letters personally. She felt concern for each serviceman; she saw each as an individual.

Challenge Question:

Eleanor overcame shyness to support her husband as senator, governor, and president. She served as hostess to thousands when she would rather be with a few. She subordinated her opinions to her husband's wishes, and supported Franklin for third and fourth terms when she would rather have retreated into private life. She set aside her own position in a society of wealth and privilege to become the champion of the poor.

The Natural by Bernard Malamud

Multiple Choice:

1. B	4. C	7. D	10. C	13. C	16. A	19. A
2. A	5. C	8. D	11. A	14. A	17. B	20. C
3. D	6. C	9. B	12. A	15. B	18. C	

Short Answers:

1. Sam's own life had been a failure, both as a player and as a scout. The Cubs had revoked Sam's salary because he had failed to turn up any new talent. By bringing Roy to the Cubs, Sam hoped to gain back his standing as a first-class scout with a regular salary.

2. In a key World Series game, Pop Fisher had fallen while running the bases, a fall that became known as "Fisher's Flop" or "Fisher's Folly." Pop believed that, by managing the Knights to a pennant victory, he would make amends for his own failure as a player. Roy was his hope for this redemption.

3. When Bump dies after running into the wall, Roy takes his place in the field and in the batting order. Given this chance, Roy becomes the hero whose batting and fielding skills lead the team to success.

4. Memo is the temptress who seeks to destroy Roy's playing ability and his self-confidence. She also tempts him to take the Judge's offer of a sellout. She is associated with evil in the last scene of the novel. Standing at the side of the sinister Judge, Memo watches the game from the tower.

   Iris represents the positive female influence on the hero. She stands in the bleachers to encourage Roy. Even after she is hit with a fly ball, Iris urges Roy to do his best. Ironically, his effort for her is too little and too late.

5. The Judge wants to end Pop Fisher's career as a manager and to control the Knights himself. He also wants to beat the gambling interests who heavily favor the Knights. The Judge wants the Knights eliminated before they lose disgracefully in the World Series against the Yankees.

Challenge Question:

The Knight in shining armor, he carries a magic bat instead of a lance. Before he can go into battle, however, Roy is unheroically shot by a crazed woman in a hotel room.

When Roy finally does make the major leagues, his magnificent season is marred by lack of self-control. Both his appetite for food and his passion for Memo take Roy out of the game when his team has a chance at the pennant.

Although Iris's love is a positive influence on the hero, Roy cannot win for her. When he tries to win the game for the team, he can only strike out. The Knight ends his career by burying his lance in the outfield.

Roy Hobbs wants to be a great man. Although his quest is a failure, Roy makes a supreme effort for one season. He is a hero to the extent that he will not take the Judge's bribe. He rejects Memo when he sees her for the evil that she represents. Human effort for Roy, however, falls short; he can't win the game. His career ends, not in a triumphant procession, but in a blaze of scandal. The sad postscript to Roy's career comes in a comment by one fan: "He could have been a king."

West With the Night by Beryl Markham

Fill-ins:

1. Serengeti
2. he lived uncaged near human habitations
3. Arab Ruta
4. Pegasus
5. Buller
6. her father lost the farm through bankruptcy
7. Lakwani
8. Wise Child
9. Tom Black
10. Denys Finch-Hatton
11. Baron Blixen
12. elephant
13. they were stranded in a flood
14. Makula
15. morphine
16. the Italian military authorities
17. Africa will never again be the same
18. J. C. Carberry
19. "The Gull"
20. the fuel line was clogged with ice

Short Answers:

1. The land and animals were part of her life. The jungle was just beyond their front porch. She was taught to hunt by the natives, and had no fear of animals. As Beryl became a woman, she learned to love Africa and not to destroy it.

2. There were few landing fields and lights, and no landmarks by which to get direction. Fliers ran the risk of crash-landing far from help, of running out of fuel, or of having equipment failure.

3. She gives the animals human personalities. The reader experiences a scene as the animal would feel it. Markham does this with the lions, the horses, the dog, and the zebra. Her writing makes the animals a vital part of the African world.

4. She hunted with him when they were children. He later became her loyal helper. Ruta took special care of her animals, her airplanes, and of Markham herself.

5. She suffered from loneliness and darkness, and had problems with bad weather late in the year. She lost her sense of direction, and was concerned that she might have to crash-land over water.

Challenge Question:

Beryl Markham did things others would not try to do. She beat the odds in horse racing. She was the first woman pilot to fly into the bush, the first to stalk elephants from a plane, the first to attempt the flight from England to America. She lived in a constant spirit of adventure and with a complete absence of fear.

A Man Called Peter by Catherine Marshall

Fill-ins:

1. Scotland
2. the death of his father
3. construction work, digging ditches
4. Jim Broadbent
5. Agnes Scott College
6. "Twittering Birds Marshall," many nature images
7. The Church of the Presidents or Lincoln's Church
8. Catherine had tuberculosis
9. Alma Deane, AD
10. Scotland
11. "Wee Peter"
12. the attack on Pearl Harbor
13. Cape Cod, Waverly
14. Great Game Player
15. becoming chaplain of the Senate
16. slow down, not work so hard
17. Arthur Vandenburg
18. graduation
19. "See you in the morning"
20. going across the street to view Dr. Marshall's body

Short Answers:

1. It was in his youth that he gained his understanding of hard work and ordinary people, his love of nature, his sense of a personal God.

2. Because of the heavy responsibility of their position and her lack of social experience.

3. He spent time with his son, played with him, disciplined him.

4. They learned to wait for God's orders, and felt that they had a deep personal relationship with God.

5. His prayers spoke to specific needs. Men trusted him.

Challenge Question:

Peter Marshall had a great love of fun. He cared for both the great and the ordinary, was willing to give time to people, and became upset when things went badly. He showed a great love and concern for his wife and son. As a preacher, he made God real.

The Bell Jar by Sylvia Plath

Multiple Choice:

1. B	6. D	11. C	16. B
2. C	7. B	12. A	17. B
3. C	8. D	13. C	18. B
4. B	9. A	14. A	19. A
5. A	10. D	15. B	20. D

Short Answers:

1. Answers might include: her visit to Lenny's apartment, seeing the falseness of Doreen and Hilda, Marco's attack, the magazine banquet, her date with Constantin.

2. Esther's inner world is the novel's focus. Plath describes Esther's feelings, using flashbacks extensively. For every action, the reader knows Esther's reaction.

3. Her body refuses to allow her to drown. She cries for help after she has taken the overdose. She is able to survive, even without sleep and food. She is able to get back to the asylum after her experience with Irwin.

4. He pretends to be a good, pure person, but he is not. Esther sees Buddy's mother as the kind of prisoner that Esther cannot bear to become.

5. The jar is the reality which closes her in. The image comes from the babies that she sees in the bottle at the medical school. The lifting of the jar represents Esther's returning health. The novel's main question is, "Will the bell jar come down again?"

Challenge Question:

Esther's view of reality is warped by her illness. The reader sees the world through the filter of that illness. Her descriptions of the people in New York, her mother, the hospitals, and the patients are all colored by her intense emotional reactions. She describes feelings attached to various experiences: her attempted drowning, her return to reality after her overdose, her visit to Buddy, the electric shock treatments. As Esther gets better, reality becomes more "real."

As the student answers this challenge question, he or she might consider how the events which Esther narrates might have been seen by Dr. Nolan, Buddy, or Esther's mother.

I Am Third by Gale Sayers with Al Silverman

True or False:

1. F	6. F	11. F	16. F
2. T	7. T	12. T	17. F
3. T	8. F	13. F	18. T
4. F	9. F	14. F	19. F
5. T	10. F	15. T	20. T

Short Answers:

1. Gale became involved in all kinds of sports. He played midget football in grade school. He and his friends practiced sports until late at night instead of becoming involved in drugs or alcohol. He also loved music and spent a lot of time listening to records.

2. Pain for the professional athlete is different from injury. Because he is being paid to perform, the pro must frequently play even if he is hurting. Dr. Fox, the team physician, determined if the professional was really injured in a way that would damage his career. Pain by itself will often be enough to sideline the high school or college player.

3. Sayers and Piccolo were the first black and white roommates in professional football. Brian's happy-go-lucky nature helped open up Gale's quiet reserve. Sayers also learned from Piccolo's courage as Brian faced death.

4. Linda Sayers is the anchor, the steadying influence for Gale. They were married while Gale was a freshman in college. She helped her husband settle down to study so that he could be eligible to play football. She gave him strength as he struggled to recover from his knee injury. Gale usually thought only about the present. Linda helped him to form goals in life and to plan for the future.

5. Gale was first involved while a college student in protesting racial discrimination in housing at the University of Kansas. He works with black children in Chicago in a program for newspaper carriers. Gale Sayers is also involved in helping other blacks by working in Jesse Jackson's "Operation Breadbasket."

Challenge Question:

Sayers gained more self-discipline as he learned to study. His self-confidence improved as he developed a positive self-image which was not dependent only on his football press clippings. After Gale married Linda, he learned how to love and give to another person. His friendship with Brian Piccolo taught Gale the real meaning of courage. Sayers needed this courage himself as he struggled back after his knee injury.

Gale Sayers has found personal satisfaction off the football field both in his work with children and in his new career as a stockbroker. He knows that he can succeed in more than athletics. Gale Sayers was always a talented athlete. His life experiences have made him a complete man.

Beverly: An Autobiography by Beverly Sills
and Lawrence Linderman

Matching:

1. N	5. B	9. I	13. H	17. J
2. G	6. M	10. E	14. A	18. L
3. T	7. K	11. P	15. R	19. Q
4. C	8. S	12. F	16. D	20. O

Short Answers:

1. Beverly Sills's career was influenced by her mother's interest in music, her appearance on various children's shows, her close relationship with her father, the early teaching of Miss Liebling, and listening to Lily Pons.

2. Choices include her early work with Schubert's touring group, her appearance at La Scala, her work with Sarah Caldwell, and her introduction to American audiences through the New York City Opera Company.

3. She was faced with anti-Semitism and was completely ostracized by her husband's friends and family.

4. She decided to retire before her voice wore out and people tired of hearing her. She preferred to give singing all she had for fewer years.

5. Manon, the three queens of Donizetti, Cleopatra in *Julius Caesar*.

Challenge Question:

Her ability to overcome personal difficulties, her work with handicapped children, her ability to work well with other performers, her abilities as a manager and a fundraiser, a personality that reaches out to people, an honest openness about herself.

Madame Sarah by Cornelia Otis Skinner

Matching:

1. K	4. M	7. E	10. J	13. C	16. L	19. Q
2. B	5. A	8. O	11. T	14. D	17. G	20. N
3. P	6. R	9. H	12. F	15. S	18. I	

Short Answers:

1. Sarah was badly neglected by her mother, who preferred to spend time with her gentlemen friends. She was a homely, thin child who did not adapt well to society. Sarah was hungry for love and was easily upset. Her need for attention and affection led to her love affair with her audiences. Her tempestuous disposition provided the raw material for her theatrical brilliance, especially her intensely emotional death scenes.

2. Sarah entertained her audiences by playing on their emotions. People wept again and again for her "Lady of the Camellias." Sarah was an intense patriot, whose spirit appealed to the French love of country. However, Parisian audiences were horrified by Sarah's lack of respect for the traditions of the classic French theater. She refused to play by the rules.

   Paris was shocked by Sarah's outrageous social behavior: her many lovers, her wild parties, and her collection of animals. Rumors about her made audiences around the world wild to attend her performances.

3. Sarah's voice had a golden quality which drew the audiences into whatever role she was playing. The actress had a sense of stage presence so complete that Sarah at sixty could play Joan of Arc at eighteen.

4. Her son Maurice was pampered and spoiled. His spending excesses often came near to bankrupting Sarah, but she continued to give the boy everything he wanted. Her husband, Jacques Damala, was the only man Sarah ever truly fell in love with. A drug addict, he spent her money and abused her until Sarah was forced to get a legal separation.

5. As an old woman, Sarah continued to tour the world. Even after her leg was amputated, she continued to go on stage and to meet her public. Bernhardt refused to recognize the reality of death and aging.

Challenge Question:

Sarah became a romantic legend when she defied society. Bernhardt's acting personified the great passions of love and death. Women fainted at her performances. Romantic young men pulled her carriage through the streets. Her temper tantrums also became legendary. She could throw things one minute and apologize the next. Her violent attacks on her critics were front-page news.

Intensely patriotic, Sarah became the great symbol of France wherever she went. Stories about her strange behavior, such as sleeping in a coffin and living with boa constrictors, were exaggerated to make Bernhardt even more of a legend.

The Gift of Music by Jane Stuart Smith and Betty Carlson

Matching:

1. G	5. L	9. E	13. D	17. C
2. K	6. P	10. J	14. O	18. M
3. B	7. A	11. R	15. F	19. S
4. N	8. T	12. H	16. Q	20. I

Short Answers:

1. "Baroque" literally means "rough or imperfect pearl." This musical style uses contrasting sounds. A full orchestra or chorus will be balanced by a solo voice or instrument. Volume will be balanced by silence. This style was used in the cantatas and oratorios of Bach and Handel. The contrasts were also used in the concertos of Mozart and the symphonies of Haydn. Although many twentieth-century musicians rejected the elaborate form of the Baroque, this music, especially the work of Bach, provided the rules for the moderns to break.

2. Many great composers could not fit into society. Mozart was regarded by many who knew him as a child who never grew up. Wagner was an eccentric, unpleasant man whose violence alienated people everywhere. Chopin and Mendelssohn suffered from severe physical and emotional problems. The darkness of Mahler's life is reflected in his music. Schumann, Tchaikovsky, and Schönberg all had nervous breakdowns.

3. Many great composers drew on the folk melodies of their native lands. Sibelius gave musical form to the spirit of his native Finland. Dvořák expressed the joy of life typical of the Czech people. Bartók collected folk songs in Hungary. Charles Ives's

music contains the strains of many American folk songs. Vaughn Williams drew on the folk melodies of England.

4. Wealthy patrons frequently gave composers the financial freedom to work. Handel went to England under the patronage of George I. Chopin was supported by George Sand. Tchaikovsky received support from Madame von Meck. Composers who lacked such support often died without any recognition for their work. Scott Joplin and Vivaldi are examples of those whose work was recognized long after the death of the creator.

5. Twentieth-century music shocked audiences who were accustomed to traditional sounds. Schönberg's switch to atonal structure made the sound unpleasant. Stravinsky's ballets shocked Parisian audiences when the composer used more natural and less formal sounds. Ives placed clashing melodies in the same composition. The violent sounds of much modern music reflect the increasing chaos of today's world.

Challenge Question:

Being a composer meant sacrificing the ordinary routine of life. Long hours of work were necessary to produce great music. Financial problems continually plagued these musicians. Many, such as Mozart and Scott Joplin, died in terrible poverty. The emotional strain was tremendous. The artistic temperament of men such as Schumann and Mahler drove them to breakdown and suicide.

The wives and families of many composers also suffered. Wagner's obsession with his musical ideal cost him everything. Prokofiev divorced his wife and had her sent to prison so that he could compromise with the Stalinist regime. Some composers, however, were happy in their private lives. At the age of ninety, Sibelius was still giving his wife roses.

All of these composers needed discipline to learn and work. Many of them were lucky in finding teachers from whom they learned the techniques needed to express genius. For all, music had to come first. This priority is always demanded of any creative genius.

The Agony and the Ecstasy by Irving Stone

Matching:

1. M	4. P	7. K	10. Q	13. B	16. S	19. I
2. F	5. D	8. A	11. O	14. T	17. E	20. N
3. R	6. J	9. H	12. L	15. C	18. G	

Short Answers:

1. His father ridiculed his desire to be an artist. None of his brothers brought in any money. The family made constant financial demands throughout his life. He was the only breadwinner.

2. He learned classical poetry and literature, received training in practical politics and debating. In the garden he learned sculpture techniques from the best masters. He

learned what a great man was from Lorenzo, and learned what love was through his relationship with Contessina.

3. He desired to make his statues real, to glorify the human body as God had created it. He took the risk of dissection when the law forbade it so that his statues might come to life.

4. At first, the pope was determined that he paint the ceiling. Michelangelo did not want to. He only wished to return to his sculpture. After he had the vision of the great "Creation" frescoes, the two men constantly fought about the money to fund the project.

5. Michelangelo's statues live and breathe. He painted beautiful frescoes. He knew how to quarry marble. He was an engineer who built defenses for Florence. He was the architect of the dome of St. Peter's.

Challenge Question:

Michelangelo had no family. His art was his legacy to the world. His artistic creations replaced all other relationships. Although he loved Clarissa deeply, he had to abandon her for his work. He lived in constant poverty because he sought excellence in art, rather than settling for second best. He drove himself by working long hours in extremes of heat and cold. His family constantly took advantage of him. His quest for perfection made him a very lonely man.

Oprah by Robert Waldron

True or False:

1. F	4. F	7. F	10. F	13. F	16. F	19. F
2. T	5. T	8. F	11. T	14. T	17. T	20. F
3. T	6. T	9. F	12. F	15. F	18. F	

Short Answers:

1. Her experience with her grandmother made her a survivor. Living with her mother in Milwaukee, she experienced sexual abuse and became a street-wise teenager. She gained stability when she went to live with her father in Nashville.

2. She gained a sense of purpose and became determined to succeed, learned how to do interviews and how to handle people, learned how to deal with failure.

3. Her constant battle with weight, her love of shopping, her willingness to be vulnerable and honest in her interviews are all humanizing aspects of Oprah's character.

4. Walters was the first woman to receive national recognition as a news personality and interviewer.

5. She lived the role of Sophia. These hard experiences had been hers. The role also gave her a chance to be on the inside of the film industry.

Challenge Question:

Audiences respond to her honesty, the way she deals directly with controversial issues. She has a personal appeal as someone that members of the audience would like to talk to in her understanding of how people feel and her willingness to express her own feelings about everything from her weight to her love life. The key to Oprah's success is that the success has not changed her. She is real.

The Picture of Dorian Gray by Oscar Wilde

Multiple Choice:

1. C	4. A	7. A	10. A	13. B	16. C	19. B
2. D	5. B	8. B	11. C	14. C	17. D	20. B
3. D	6. C	9. B	12. C	15. A	18. A	

Short Answers:

1. Basil knows Lord Henry's reputation for immoral living. He is afraid that Lord Henry will corrupt Dorian's beauty and innocence.

2. Lord Henry introduces Dorian to the society in which any behavior which gives pleasure is acceptable. He also sends Dorian a book which becomes Dorian's manual for the pursuit of pleasure.

3. The first change comes as a sign of hypocrisy when Dorian rejects Sibyl. The most drastic transformation is when Dorian sees blood on the hands of the portrait after he murders Basil.

4. Dorian takes the portrait to an unused upstairs room. He covers the portrait with a heavy canvas and places bars across the door so that no one can enter. The room is sealed with a lock to which he has the only key.

5. Dorian's face retains its youthful beauty. His actions become more and more evil. As Dorian Gray destroys others, he also destroys himself. All the evil is registered on the face of the portrait.

Challenge Question:

Dorian Gray makes choices. He decides to reject Sibyl. Although Lord Henry sets up a variety of situations for him, Dorian chooses to participate in these experiences.

Lord Henry believes that he is simply an onlooker to Dorian's actions. The reader, however, sees Lord Henry as the evil genius who destroys others while he himself remains unchanged.

Moral responsibility is affirmed at the end of the novel as Dorian's evil is reflected in his warped and twisted body.

Unit 7
Reflections of the Family

Synopses

A Midwife's Story
by Penny Armstrong

Ballantine Books, New York, 1986.

A *Midwife's Story* is Penny Armstrong's personal recollections of her work as a midwife with the Amish people of Lancaster County, Pennsylvania. An "Englishwoman," as the Amish term outsiders, Penny came to Paradise, Pennsylvania, after training in Glasgow, Scotland, and in Philadelphia. Although opposed by many physicians, Penny received help in establishing her practice from Dr. Stephen Kaufmann.

Penny came to love the Amish way of life. She believed that natural childbirth, when the mother was surrounded by family members, was far superior to the impersonal technology of a hospital. The midwife shared the joys and sorrows of the Amish as they came to trust her. The joyous natural childbirth of Susie and Ephraim was balanced with the tragedy of Leah and Johnny's stillborn daughter.

Penny's professional story is also an account of her personal growth. She matures through her marriage to Richie. She comes to understand pain through her own miscarriage. She finds faith in God and in people as her appreciation increases for the Amish and their ways.

A *Midwife's Story* would be of interest to any student interested in a medical or nursing career.

The Dollmaker
by Harriette Arnow

Macmillan Publishing Company, New York, 1954.

Gertie Nevels, a strong, earthy Kentucky farm woman, has a special skill as a woodcarver. As she watches life in her valley being threatened by the impact of World War II, Gertie's greatest single desire is to own her own land. Her husband Clovis goes to work in a Detroit factory. Gertie's mother insists that her daughter give up the dream of land and join her husband in the city.

"Adjust" is the key to survival. In a wretched housing project, ironically named Merry Hill, Gertie struggles against impossible odds to help her family survive. Reuben, the eldest son, runs away and returns to Kentucky. Things replace meaning. Although she now has a stove and refrigerator, Gertie still dreams of the Kentucky hills. Her solace is a block of mountain wood, from which Gertie intends to carve a figure of Christ. Gertie's strength is almost destroyed when Cassie, the child who cannot adjust, is crushed beneath the wheels of a train.

Gertie's neighbors in the project are also victims of the great machine that gobbles up humanity. Sophronie, who drinks to forget; Mrs. Anderson, who must cope with her husband's ambitions; and Max, who runs away from her brutal husband, are unforgettable characters.

The novel shows the family's gradual destruction. Reuben has run away. Cassie is dead. Clovis, Gertie's husband, knifes a man in a union row. Machines make cheap imitations of Gertie's beautiful carvings. The special block of wood must finally be split to make cheap toys that will help buy groceries.

The Dollmaker pictures a society that crushes the individual. Detroit is a city where dreams die and where good men become killers. The setting complements the powerful characterization. Gertie's family, like her feeble plants, deteriorates in the shadow of the smoking factories. Gertie's remarkable strength against these odds makes her a noble woman.

The Dollmaker can well be compared with Steinbeck's *The Grapes of Wrath* in picturing the struggle for survival of the human spirit.

Père Goriot

by Honoré de Balzac

Modern Library, New York, 1946.

Père Goriot takes a cynical look at fashionable Parisian society, which Balzac called "the Human Comedy." In the boarding house of Madame Vauquer lives Eugène de Rastignac, a law student from the provinces who is determined to find his place in high society. The young man is fascinated by the old pasta maker, Père Goriot, who is visited from time to time by two elegant young women. The old man has sacrificed all his resources so that his daughters, Anastasie and Delphine, might live as aristocrats. Instead of receiving gratitude, the old man is rejected by his daughters and their husbands.

Eugène has a chance to enter society through his cousin, the Viscountess de Beauséant, but the young man needs money for such an adventure. His family bankrupts itself to meet the social climber's needs.

Eugène is both fascinated and repelled by the social whirl he enters. He loves Goriot's daughter, Delphine, but is horrified by her callous treatment of her father. Eugène is tempted by the ex-convict Vautrin to gain his fortune by marrying a wealthy woman, whose brother Vautrin has arranged to have murdered. Because he spends the night in a drunken stupor, Eugène doesn't warn the victim.

As old Goriot lies dying, his indifferent daughters attend a great ball. Only Eugène and the servants are present as Père Goriot is lowered into a pauper's grave.

Balzac's novel is a scathing denouncement of a society where loving sacrifice counts for nothing. Even Eugène, who alone has compassion for Goriot, finally becomes a cog in the social machine. Because Balzac draws his characters with realistic cynicism, *Père Goriot* is a great classic of French literature.

Cold Sassy Tree

by Olive Ann Burns

Ticknor and Fields, New York, 1984.

Cold Sassy Tree recounts the maturing of Will Tweedy, a country boy in Cold Sassy, Georgia. The reader sees through Will's eyes the marriage of his grandfather Rucker to Miss Love Simpson. The town is horrified when the old man remarries a week after his wife's death. Will also comes to terms with the death of his friend and his own developing feelings of love for Lightfoot McLendon, a schoolmate and worker in a nearby cotton mill.

Grandpa and Miss Love horrify the town, especially Will's mother, Mary Willis, and her sister Loma. The couple have their own services on Sunday after Miss Love is ostracized from the local Methodist church. Miss Love is visited by a cowboy, her former boyfriend. Grandpa gets an automobile franchise, which sets the town on its ears.

When Will learns about Miss Love's childhood, the boy understands her need for his grandfather's love. Will, more than anyone else in town, can give Miss Love sympathy.

The last step in Will's maturing takes place when his grandfather dies. Will recognizes the passing of a generation.

Cold Sassy Tree is easy reading. However, students not familiar with southern dialect may have trouble with some of the conversational passages. This book is an excellent example of modern local color literature.

Show Boat

by Edna Ferber

Grosset and Dunlap, New York, 1926.

Show Boat, a tale of life on the Mississippi, is also the story of three women: Kim Ravenal, her mother Magnolia, and her grandmother Parthenia Ann Hawkes. During the 1880's, the showboat was the *Cotton Blossom*, a traveling theater that brought pleasure to the small river towns. The man in Parthenia's life was Captain Andy, who persuaded Parthy to join his traveling life. Magnolia, their daughter, had show business in her blood. Making the mistake of falling in love with charming gambler Gaylord Ravenal, Magnolia had an unstable life, going perpetually from riches to rags, depending on the luck of the cards. When Captain Andy is killed, Parthy becomes the matriarch of the river. Magnolia too returns to showboat life. Only Kim escapes to a different world.

Edna Ferber's local color accounts of showboat life make this book vividly real. Her characters live and breathe for the reader. Any student interested in theater would enjoy *Show Boat*. The novel takes a special look at the actor's life with its joys and difficulties.

Roots

by Alex Haley

Doubleday and Company, New York, 1983.

Roots chronicles Alex Haley's family history. His story becomes the story of all black Americans. The tale begins with Kunta Kinte, a native of Gambia. As he grows to manhood, Kunta is educated in the traditions of his tribe. At the age of eighteen, he is kidnapped by white slavers and brought to America. Although Kunta must learn to adjust to his new situation, he never loses the awareness of his African roots. Kunta's family is started when he marries Bell. The next generation includes Kizzy and her son, Chicken George. George gains fame as a breeder and trainer of fighting gamecocks. Succeeding generations include George's son Tom, Tom's daughter Cynthia, her daughter Beulah, and Beulah's son, who was the author's father.

Roots is a wonderful history of American life from 1767 until the early 1900's. Haley was one of the first writers to tell these events from the black person's viewpoint. Although the Kinte family becomes thoroughly American, the African connection is never lost. Suffering and hardship never quench the spark of life which was Kunta Kinte's greatest gift to his descendants.

Tess of the D'Urbervilles

by Thomas Hardy

Bantam Books, New York, 1971.

Tess of the D'Urbervilles is Hardy's tragic tale of Tess Durbeyfield, a beautiful, sensitive heroine who is victimized both by fate and by the men in her life. When her father becomes convinced that the family belongs to the extinct D'Urberville nobility, Tess goes to be a servant in the home of a supposed relative. Her fresh country beauty attracts Alec D'Urberville, who seduces her. Pregnant, Tess returns to her family.

Attempting to forget her past after her child dies, Tess again leaves home to seek work as a dairy maid. She meets Angel Clare, a rebel clergyman's son. After Angel ardently courts Tess, she agrees to marry him, even though she still struggles with her secrets.

Against her mother's advice, Tess tells Angel on their wedding night about her relationship with D'Urberville. When her husband abandons her, Tess is forced to work as a farm laborer. Even in the hardest circumstances, she still holds out hope for Angel's return.

As she again meets D'Urberville, Tess, despairing of Angel's return, becomes his mistress in exchange for financial help for her family. When Angel does finally come back from South America, he finds Tess at a hotel in a fashionable resort. After seeing Angel again, Tess kills D'Urberville. She and Angel have a few days of happiness before Tess is captured and hanged. Tess ultimately finds nobility and freedom only in death.

Tess of the D'Urbervilles is one of Hardy's most moving fictional portrayals of the final futility of human struggle.

The Portrait of a Lady

by Henry James

New American Library, New

The Portrait of a Lady is the story of Isabel Archer, an unsophisticated girl from Albany, New York. After inheriting a large fortune from her uncle, Isabel seeks to experience life to its fullest. Some significant people in Isabel's life desire to help her. Ralph, her cousin, loves Isabel from a distance. Henrietta Stackpole, an American magazine writer, enjoys Isabel's company while seeing Europe.

Isabel's innocence makes her unsuspecting of the deviousness in others, especially the scheming Madame Merle. Rejecting the marriage proposals of wealthy Lord Warburton and American Caspar Goodwood, Isabel instead marries Gilbert Osmond. The marriage, arranged by Madame Merle, proves to be a stifling disaster for Isabel. Discovering a past relationship between her husband and Madame Merle, Isabel leaves for England to be with Ralph, who is dying. Only for the sake of Osmond's daughter Pansy does Isabel again reject Goodwood and return to her husband.

Henry James pictures beautifully the lifestyle of wealthy Americans in Europe. The author also develops the character of Isabel from a naive innocent to a mature woman who has learned through the hurts she has sustained. *The Portrait of a Lady* shows why Henry James is regarded as one of America's finest social novelists.

The Thornbirds

by Colleen McCullough

Harper and Row, New York, 1977.

The Thornbirds, the story of the Clearys, is a great family saga of Australia. From 1915–1969, the Cleary women experienced struggles and pain, identified closely with the great estate of Drogheda and the thornbird whose song came from its pain. The family experience is seen through the eyes of Feona, the grandmother; Meggie, her daughter; and Meggie's daughter Justine.

As a child of eleven, Meggie Cleary came to Australia with her parents, Fee and Paddy. Mary Carson, Paddy's wealthy sister, hired her brother to manage the great estate. After Mary's death, the Clearys found their destiny united with the vast Australian landscape.

Mary Carson's passion for the young priest Ralph de Bricassart made her leave her fortune to Ralph and her land to the church. Ralph used Mary's money to rise from parish priest to cardinal. Ralph, however, loved Meggie from the time he first saw the child. The priest fought a hard battle between his desire for human love and his commitment to God.

The epic narrates Meggie's disastrous marriage to Luke O'Neill, whom she married instead of the priest she could not have. The generations continue as Dane, Ralph and Meggie's love child, follows his father into the priesthood. Rebellious Justine, Luke's daughter, tries to hide her pain by becoming an actress. For each generation, Drogheda is the well from which strength is drawn.

The Thornbirds gives a vivid description of the Australian landscape: the richness of its plant and animal life, the open spaces, the continuing battle against drought and forest fire. Colleen McCullough has created a vast panorama of twentieth-century Australia.

In recommending this book to students, teachers should note that the narrative contains some sexually explicit scenes which, although very tastefully written, might be troublesome to some students.

Giants in the Earth

by O. E. Rolvaag

Harper Brothers Publishers, New York, 1927.

Giants in the Earth is the story of the Norwegian settlers in the Dakota territory during the 1870's. Per Hansa, his wife Beret, and their children struggle against harsh winters, plagues of locusts, and crop failures to make a living in the new land. Common hardships and joys unite Per Hansa with his neighbors and close friends, Hans Olsa and Tonseten.

Rolvaag paints the pioneer experience with a dark brush. Using powerful similes and metaphors, he pictures the vastness of the empty prairie spaces and the loneliness of winter's isolation. As his farm prospers, Per Hansa must cope with increasing family difficulties. Beret's fears of death and God's wrath threaten to destroy the family. After a traveling minister visits the Spring Creek settlement, Beret's phobias turn to religious fanaticism.

Occupying a special place in the chronicles of western settlement, *Giants in the Earth* is based on the author's personal experiences as an immigrant. The book is dedicated to America's Norwegian community, of which Rolvaag was a part.

A Reckoning

by May Sarton

W. W. Norton, New York, 1978.

A Reckoning is the story of Laura Spelman, who is told by her doctor that she has terminal lung cancer. Fighting for the right to die in her own way, Laura knows that she must make "a reckoning" that will bring into final focus the significant relationships of her life: Sybille, her dominating mother; Jo and Daphne, her sisters; Daisy, Brooks, and Ben, her children.

As Laura's body weakens, her sensitivity becomes keener. While sorting out her own memories, Laura tries to help Harriet Moors, a struggling young novelist. As she and Daphne make a final trip to their childhood home in Maine, Laura tries to find freedom from her mother's domination. She also tries to bring into focus the memories of the special loves in her life: her girlhood friend Ella and her husband, Charles.

May Sarton has written a beautifully sensitive novel about the way in which dying is a part of life. Mature students learning to understand the significant relationships in their own lives will find *A Reckoning* a meaningful reading experience.

East of Eden

by John Steinbeck

Viking Press, New York, 1952.

East of Eden is the saga of the Trask and Hamilton families, founders of dynasties in the Salinas Valley of California. The novel also shows, through intensely poetic description, Steinbeck's strong love for his native state. The story of a love-hate relationship between two pairs of brothers—Adam and Charles Trask, Aron and Caleb Trask—parallels the Cain-Abel story in the biblical book of Genesis.

Bullied by their father, Charles and Adam Trask develop opposite personalities. Because Adam receives the love Charles wants, Charles becomes the aggressor. Adam fulfills his father's wish to join the army; Charles remains at home on the farm. After Adam's return, both brothers are attracted to Cathy Ames, a woman who personifies evil manipulation. Adam finally settles in California, but Cathy abandons him and their twin sons and enjoys a life of prostitution. Samuel Hamilton, the wise father figure, helps restore Adam to life. Lee, the wise Chinese servant, is the steadying force for Adam and his sons.

Steinbeck believes that no individual is programmed by heredity or environment; people shape their lives by their choices. In the years between the Civil War and World War I, Adam's wealth increases and his sons become men. Both boys face the harsh reality of their mother's identity. Aron inherits his mother's looks, Caleb has elements of her personality, but each young man must become his own person. The parallel story of Samuel Hamilton's children shows choice as life's determining factor. Each Hamilton also strives for individuality.

East of Eden is a powerful novel. Steinbeck's descriptive and narrative ability brings scenes and characters to life. Some chapters contain sexually explicit material which may not be suitable for all students. The teacher may use discretion.

Mrs. Miniver

by Jan Struther

Virago Press, London, 1989.

The character of Caroline Miniver, a typical middle-class English lady, was first created to enliven the court page of the *London Times*. As the darkness of World War II approached, Mrs. Miniver became a symbol of British faith and will to survive. Winston Churchill said that *Mrs. Miniver* did more for the nation's will to survive "than a flotilla of battleships." *Mrs. Miniver* was first published in 1939; the newest edition includes letters which contain intimate reflections on the meaning of living in wartime.

An average English couple, Caroline and Clem enjoy life in London and at Starlings, their country estate. Mrs. Miniver solves typical domestic problems: how to hire suitable servants, what guests to invite to a dinner party, how to find appropriate Christmas presents for friends and family members. As World War II approaches, life changes. Mrs. Miniver writes that people "now arrange values instead of chrysanthemums." This small novel in letter form is an affirmation of life's most important values: children, marriage, and faith in God.

The film of *Mrs. Miniver*, starring Greer Garson, differs in content from the book. Both book and film, however, are true to Jan Struther's belief that ordinary good can overcome any evil.

Anna Karenina

by Leo Tolstoy

Bantam Books, New York, 1981.

Anna Karenina is a classic tale of tragic love among the upper classes of Czarist Russia in the middle of the nineteenth century. Beautiful, sensitive Anna is married to Alexey Karenin, a government official twenty years her senior. After helping reconcile her brother Stepan and his wife Dolly, Anna meets Count Vronsky. The two are fatally attracted to each other when they first meet in a train station. Later, at a fashionable embassy ball, Vronsky and Anna begin an affair which will plunge them into catastrophe. Knowing that they are breaking the code of their society, the lovers are unable to rein in their passion.

Anna's husband refuses to give her a divorce; moreover, he forcibly separates Anna from her beloved son, Seryozha. Karenin says that he is willing to take her back but Anna will not end her relationship with Vronsky. After Anna has Vronsky's child, she is rejected by fashionable society.

The lovers are forced to retreat to the country. Vronsky, however, desires a more active life and returns first to Moscow and then to St. Petersburg. Unable to cope with her lover's need for other people and scenes, Anna becomes violently jealous. This jealousy destroys their love and drives Anna first to drug addiction and finally to suicide.

Contrasting the tragedy of Anna and Vronsky is the developing love of Konstantin Levin and Princess Kitty Shtcherbatsky. A country gentleman and free thinker, Levin matures as he finds love and faith in marriage. Kitty also gains beauty and maturity as a wife and mother. Tolstoy's narrative weaves the stories of these two love affairs like contrasting strands in a tapestry.

Anna Karenina is a masterpiece of psychological fiction. Although Tolstoy never gives moral approval to Anna's adultery, he nevertheless helps the reader to sympathize with her sufferings. *Anna Karenina* compares with Hawthorne's *The Scarlet Letter* as a classic study of sin, guilt, and consequences.

The Color Purple

by Alice Walker

Harcourt Brace Jovanovich, New York, 1982.

The Color Purple is a beautiful story of loyalty and giving. Two black sisters, Celie and Nettie, are separated when they are young. Each of the girls must fight for survival and learn the meaning of love. After being raped by her father, Celie is married to a man she does not love. Celie receives the affection she craves from Shug Avery, her husband's mistress. With Shug, Celie moves to Memphis and experiences a new world. Celie learns to appreciate beauty, to notice such simple things as the color purple. A different kind of love is that of Harpo, Celie's stepson, for his wife Sofia.

Nettie, meanwhile, has gone with a missionary couple, Samuel and Corinne, to Africa. These missionaries have also adopted Celie's two children, Olivia and Adam. The villagers in Africa must fight against the white man's attempts to take over their land and destroy their lives. After Corinne's death, Nettie marries Samuel. The couple eventually returns to the United States, where Celie and Nettie are reunited.

The novel has an unusual form. The story of Celie's bitter childhood experience is told in letters that Celie writes to God. Nettie's story comes in her letters to Celie, which Celie's husband refused to deliver. The soft southern dialect of Celie's letters enriches the narrative. Nettie's vivid descriptions make her African experience come alive. Alice Walker has written a beautiful yet profound addition to the literature of the black woman's experience with life. Students should be aware that *The Color Purple* contains sexually explicit scenes and language.

Name_____ Date_____

A Midwife's Story by Penny Armstrong

Place a T before each true statement and an F before each false statement.

_____ 1. When Penny Armstrong wrote this book, she had been a midwife in Amish country for about twenty years.

_____ 2. Penny grew up in a rural farming community.

_____ 3. While training in Scotland, Penny came to respect the English medical community for its care and consideration for the individual patient.

_____ 4. Dr. Kaufmann tried to help Penny get privileges to work in the hospital.

_____ 5. Penny encountered her most hostile opposition from the leaders of the Amish church.

_____ 6. The Amish farmers never use electricity or any kind of modern technology.

_____ 7. Penny believes that mothers should hold and handle their children as soon as possible after the babies are born.

_____ 8. Richie was a young doctor who did his internship in the same hospital where Penny was a nurse.

_____ 9. Richie joined quickly and easily in the work on the Amish farms.

_____ 10. A newly married Amish couple spend the first few months visiting various relatives.

_____ 11. Penny feels that the fathers were generally a problem when she went to deliver their babies.

_____ 12. Amish people did not easily trust outsiders.

_____ 13. Penny had a miscarriage before the birth of her second child.

_____ 14. In Amish homes, young brothers and sisters were generally kept away from the newborns.

_____ 15. Penny believes that surgical intervention in childbirth is never necessary.

_____ 16. Although Penny wanted to build a house in the country, Richie preferred to live in Philadelphia.

_____ 17. Penny records in this book the accounts of several stillborn children.

_____ 18. A "snack" to the Amish means a light lunch of cakes or cookies and coffee.

_____ 19. Penny left her affiliation with Dr. Kaufmann to open her own office.

_____ 20. All Penny's patients were Amish.

© 1991 J. Weston Walch, Publisher

Name_____   Date_____

A *Midwife's Story* by Penny Armstrong

Answer the following questions in two or three complete sentences.

1. How did Penny's opinions of the Amish change as she lived and worked with them?

   _____

   _____

   _____

2. What opposition did Penny encounter from the medical community?

   _____

   _____

   _____

3. How does she contrast the birth procedures in the average hospital with those practiced by a midwife?

   _____

   _____

   _____

4. How did Penny's marriage to Richie help her work?

   _____

   _____

   _____

5. How does the experience of Sam and Helen represent the conflict between the Amish and the outside world?

   _____

   _____

   _____

Challenge Question

Discuss how Penny Armstrong's story shows her to be a dedicated professional who cares deeply for her patients. Explain how her emotional involvement is important in her work.

Name_____ Date_____

The Dollmaker by Harriette Arnow

Match each description in Column A with the correct name in Column B.

Column A	Column B
_____ 1. The vegetable man	A. Gertie's mother
_____ 2. Prejudiced Catholic neighbor	B. Sophronie
_____ 3. Cassie's imaginary friend	C. Callie Lou
_____ 4. The farm Gertie hoped to buy	D. Enoch
_____ 5. Chose factory work over the army	E. Tipton
_____ 6. Cassie's first-grade teacher	F. Mr. Daly
_____ 7. Ran away from home when his dreams were destroyed	G. Mrs. Anderson
_____ 8. Neighbor who moved away because her husband worked for the plant management	H. Miss Huffacre
_____ 9. Literally crushed to death by the machinery of Detroit	I. Gertie
_____ 10. Nevels child who adjusted best to city life	J. Joe
_____ 11. Gertie's brother, who was killed in the war	K. Henley
_____ 12. Gertie's closest friend in the project	L. Clovis
_____ 13. Ran away from home to become a nun	M. Merry Hill
_____ 14. Owner of the factory	N. Reuben
_____ 15. Clovis's friend and accomplice in union activities	O. Clytie
_____ 16. Was determined to have her own piece of land, even in the city project	P. Maggie Daly
_____ 17. Refused to permit Gertie to purchase the land	Q. Flint
_____ 18. Several adjoining alleys in the same slum project	R. Whit
_____ 19. Peddled his mother's dolls on the streets	S. Cassie
_____ 20. Teacher who humiliated Gertie when she visited school	T. Miss Wintle

© 1991 J. Weston Walch, Publisher

Name_____ _____ Date_____

The Dollmaker by Harriette Arnow

Answer the following questions in two or three complete sentences.

1. In the opening chapters of the novel, how does the author show Gertie's strength of character?

   _____

   _____

   _____

2. How is Gertie's mother responsible for the family's destruction?

   _____

   _____

   _____

3. What does the block of wood represent to Gertie?

   _____

   _____

   _____

4. How does Gertie become a source of strength to the others in the alley?

   _____

   _____

   _____

5. Why is Cassie's death the turning point in the novel?

   _____

   _____

   _____

Challenge Question

Write an essay describing the deteriorating effect Detroit has on the Nevels family. How does Gertie fight this destruction? Why does she finally give in?

© 1991 J. Weston Walch, Publisher   *100 More Great Books: Synopses, Quizzes, and Tests*

Name _____   Date_____

Père Goriot by Honoré de Balzac

Select the letter of the word or phrase which correctly completes each sentence.

_____ 1. In the opening pages of *Père Goriot*, Balzac describes in minute detail (A) Eugène's family background (B) the interior of Madame Vauquer's boarding house (C) the salon of the Viscountess de Beauséant (D) the childhood of old Goriot's daughters.

_____ 2. Eugène has come to Paris to (A) work in a large commercial firm (B) study medicine (C) become a lawyer (D) find a rich wife.

_____ 3. When Goriot first arrived at the boarding house, Madame Vauquer (A) hoped to marry him (B) found his appearance disgusting (C) did not know that he had a family (D) made plans to rob him.

_____ 4. Eugène's closest friend was (A) Goriot (B) Vautrin (D) the Count de Trailles (D) Bianchon.

_____ 5. Both of Goriot's daughters have husbands who are (A) foreigners (B) spending their wives' money (C) kind to Goriot (D) members of the French national assembly.

_____ 6. When Eugène tells the Countess de Restaud that he knows her father, she (A) refuses to let him in her house (B) tells Eugène to ask Goriot for money (C) welcomes Eugène as a friend (D) wants to become Eugène's mistress.

_____ 7. Eugène gets money to make his way in society from (A) Goriot (B) his mother and sisters (C) his father (D) Vautrin.

_____ 8. Eugène learns that Vautrin is really (A) Goriot's son (B) a police agent (C) an escaped convict (D) the heir to a large fortune.

_____ 9. Vautrin tempts Eugène to get his fortune by (A) bank robbery (B) becoming a house breaker (C) stealing Anastasie's diamonds (D) marrying Mademoiselle Taillefer.

_____ 10. The Viscountess is abandoned by (A) the Marquis d'Ajuda (B) Eugène (C) the Baron de Nucingen (D) the Count de Restaud.

_____ 11. Vautrin is betrayed to the police by (A) Goriot (B) Madame Vauquer (C) Mademoiselle Michonneau (D) Mademoiselle Taillefer.

(continued)

© 1991 J. Weston Walch, Publisher

100 More Great Books: Synopses, Quizzes, and Tests

Name _____   Date_____

Père Goriot by Honoré de Balzac

_____ 12. In order to see his daughter Delphine, Goriot (A) meets her at the railway station (B) pays the rent on Eugène's apartment (C) follows her to several fashionable parties (D) rents a box at the opera.

_____ 13. Goriot's daughters are all of the following *except* (A) independently wealthy (B) selfish (C) extravagant (D) beautiful.

_____ 14. Goriot's money came from (A) real estate (B) banking (C) jewelry making (D) pasta making.

_____ 15. As Goriot dies, he is cared for by (A) Delphine (B) Bianchon (C) Eugène (D) Madame Vauquer.

_____ 16. Goriot's last act of selflessness is when he pays for (A) Anastasie's dress (B) Eugène's new suit (C) Delphine's carriage (D) his own funeral.

_____ 17. As the old man is dying, Eugène tries to (A) forget about Goriot (B) get the old man to a hospital (C) leave Paris and return home (D) get Goriot's daughters to come to their father's bedside.

_____ 18. When she learns that her father is dying, Delphine (A) comes to care for him (B) goes to the ball anyway (C) leaves for the country (D) spends the night at Eugène's apartment.

_____ 19. As Goriot dies, he (A) curses his daughters (B) tells his daughters that he loves them (C) talks about the past (D) all of the above.

_____ 20. After Goriot's funeral, Eugène (A) goes to see Delphine (B) leaves Paris (C) decides to study medicine (D) commits suicide.

Name _____ Date _____

Père Goriot by Honoré de Balzac

Answer the following questions in two or three complete sentences.

1. How is Eugène affected by his first visit to the Viscountess?

   _____

   _____

   _____

2. What sacrifices has Goriot made for his daughters?

   _____

   _____

   _____

3. How does Eugène take advantage of his mother and sisters?

   _____

   _____

   _____

4. What tempting offer does Vautrin make to Eugène?

   _____

   _____

   _____

5. Why is Goriot's funeral a pathetic event?

   _____

   _____

   _____

Challenge Question

Write an essay describing how Eugène de Rastignac changes from an innocent youth to a man of the world.

© 1991 J. Weston Walch, Publisher

100 More Great Books: Synopses, Quizzes, and Tests

Name_____   Date_____

Cold Sassy Tree by Olive Ann Burns

Place a T before each true statement and an F before each false statement.

_____ 1. The story is told by the grandfather.

_____ 2. The novel begins shortly after Granny Blakeslee's funeral.

_____ 3. Love Simpson came to Cold Sassy to teach school.

_____ 4. Will Tweedy was fourteen when the story took place.

_____ 5. Rucker announced to the town that he was marrying Love so that he could have a son.

_____ 6. Will Tweedy was an only child.

_____ 7. Both Uncle Camp and Will's father worked in Grandfather's store.

_____ 8. Will liked Aunt Loma better than he liked his mother.

_____ 9. In Cold Sassy, everyone knew everyone else's business.

_____ 10. Grandfather looked older after Miss Love trimmed his beard and mustache.

_____ 11. Clayton McAllister was Miss Love's ex-husband.

_____ 12. After her marriage, Miss Love was forbidden to play the piano in the Presbyterian church.

_____ 13. Will's friend, Bluford Jackson, died in a freak accident involving fireworks.

_____ 14. Miss Love immediately insisted that Rucker modernize the house by putting in plumbing and electricity.

_____ 15. Will's father bought the first automobile that Cold Sassy had ever seen.

_____ 16. Will tried to comfort Lightfoot after her father died.

_____ 17. Rucker learned the truth about Miss Love's past from Miss Effie Bell, the neighborhood gossip.

_____ 18. Rucker died of complications resulting from a gunshot wound.

_____ 19. Mary Willis made all the decisions about her father's funeral.

_____ 20. Rucker left all his property to his new wife and his unborn child.

© 1991 J. Weston Walch, Publisher   *100 More Great Books: Synopses, Quizzes, and Tests*

Name _____ Date _____

Cold Sassy Tree by Olive Ann Burns

Answer the following questions in two or three complete sentences.

1. How is Will's reaction to his grandfather's remarriage different from the reaction of the rest of the town?

   _____

   _____

   _____

2. How does Rucker Blakeslee's dominating personality affect the members of his family both positively and negatively?

   _____

   _____

   _____

3. Why is Lightfoot McLendon an impotant part of Will Tweedy's growing-up experience?

   _____

   _____

   _____

4. How did Miss Love's childhood contribute to her desire to marry Rucker?

   _____

   _____

   _____

5. Why is Camp Williams a tragic figure?

   _____

   _____

   _____

Challenge Question

Write an essay discussing how the Cold Sassy tree is a symbol of Rucker Blakeslee.

© 1991 J. Weston Walch, Publisher

100 More Great Books: Synopses, Quizzes, and Tests

Name _____   Date_____

Show Boat by Edna Ferber

Select the letter of the word or phrase which correctly completes each sentence.

_____ 1. Captain Andy was first attracted to Parthy by her (A) free-thinking attitudes (B) good looks (C) fine housekeeping (D) cooking.

_____ 2. Parthy is described as (A) frugal (B) spinsterish (C) puritanical (D) all of the above.

_____ 3. Magnolia learned the songs of the river from (A) her father (B) Queenie and Joe (C) Miss Ellie (D) Julie.

_____ 4. Julie and Steve were forced to leave the *Cotton Blossom* when (A) Captain Andy could no longer afford to pay them (B) Parthy forced them to go (C) the sheriff found out that Julie's mother was black (D) Steve was arrested in a drunken brawl.

_____ 5. Gaylord Ravenal's chief asset was (A) his charm (B) his bankroll (C) his family history (D) his elegant wardrobe.

_____ 6. The most important person in Magnolia's childhood was (A) her mother (B) her father (C) Julie (D) Miss Ellie.

_____ 7. Windy was (A) a gambling buddy of Ravenal's (B) Kim's pet dog (C) a fine river pilot (D) a black kitchen servant.

_____ 8. The members of the *Cotton Blossom* company did all of the following *except* (A) play two shows every day (B) appear in a number of different roles (C) rehearse in the morning (D) make and mend their own costumes.

_____ 9. Magnolia and Ravenal were married (A) on the *Cotton Blossom* (B) at the Palmer House in Chicago (C) by a small-town minister (D) by a justice of the peace.

_____ 10. Magnolia and Ravenal left the *Cotton Blossom* because (A) Captain Andy asked them to go (B) Magnolia did not think that the showboat was a good place for Kim (C) Ravenal was restless (D) the showboat was losing money.

_____ 11. Kim was named for (A) her mother (B) her father's mother (C) the place where she was born (D) Parthy's sister.

(continued)

© 1991 J. Weston Walch, Publisher

Name_____ Date_____

Show Boat by Edna Ferber

_____ 12. Ravenal made most of his money gambling on (A) faro (B) roulette (C) poker (D) horse racing.

_____ 13. Ravenal's financial status could be gauged by (A) his clothes (B) where he ate breakfast (C) where he had dinner (D) his rings and wristwatch.

_____ 14. After Captain Andy's death, Parthy (A) ran the boat herself (B) turned the management over to Ravenal (C) sold the boat (D) came to live with Gay and Magnolia in Chicago.

_____ 15. All of the following articles frequently went to the pawnshop *except* (A) Magnolia's coat (B) the diamond ring (C) Kim's baby bracelet (D) Ravenal's walking stick.

_____ 16. In order to keep Kim in the convent school, Magnolia (A) went back on the stage (B) borrowed money from her mother (C) forced Ravenal to get a steady job (D) joined the Catholic Church.

_____ 17. Ravenal finally (A) made his fortune (B) went into business on the stock exchange (C) died poverty-stricken in San Francisco (D) came back to the showboat.

_____ 18. When Parthy died, she (A) left Magnolia a great deal of money (B) had sold the boat to another company (C) left no will (D) left everything to Kim.

_____ 19. At the end of the novel, (A) Magnolia has returned to the river (B) Kim's husband is managing the showboat (C) the era of showboats is over (D) the showboat has been damaged by hitting a snag in the river.

_____ 20. The strongest character in the novel is (A) Parthy (B) Magnolia (C) Kim (D) Julie.

© 1991 J. Weston Walch, Publisher

Name _____   Date_____

Show Boat by Edna Ferber

Answer the following questions in two or three complete sentences.

1. How does Parthy adapt to life on the *Cotton Blossom?*

   _____

   _____

   _____

2. What people and circumstances influenced Magnolia's childhood?

   _____

   _____

   _____

3. What part does chance play in bringing Gay and Magnolia together?

   _____

   _____

   _____

4. What are the strengths and weaknesses of Gaylord Ravenal's personality?

   _____

   _____

   _____

5. How is Kim different from her mother?

   _____

   _____

   _____

Challenge Question

Describe the influence of Mississippi River life on each of the three women:
Parthenia, Magnolia, and Kim.

© 1991 J. Weston Walch, Publisher   *100 More Great Books: Synopses, Quizzes, and Tests*

Name_____   Date_____

Roots by Alex Haley

Match each name in Column A with the letter of the correct description in Column B.

Column A	Column B
_____ 1. Kizzy	A. A white doctor, Kunta's master
_____ 2. Will Palmer	B. Owner of a lumber mill
_____ 3. Gambia	C. Kunta's African village
_____ 4. Toubob	D. Sold for writing a pass
_____ 5. Massa Lea	E. A gifted blacksmith
_____ 6. Omoro	F. Told Alex the family story
_____ 7. Missy Anne	G. Lost his fortune betting on cockfighting
_____ 8. Fiddler	H. Old black cock trainer
_____ 9. Juffure	I. Kunta's grandmother
_____ 10. Bell	J. The white man
_____ 11. Massa Waller	K. First member of the Kinte family to attend college
_____ 12. Chicken George	L. Country raided by the slave traders
_____ 13. Tom Murray	M. Earned his freedom as a trainer of fighting cocks
_____ 14. Miss Malizy	N. Kunta's wife
_____ 15. Mingo	O. Owner of the family during the Civil War
_____ 16. Yaisa	P. Kunta's father
_____ 17. Bertha	Q. White girl who had a black childhood playmate
_____ 18. Matilda	R. Helped Kizzy after she was raped
_____ 19. Massa Murray	S. George's patient wife
_____ 20. Cousin Georgia	T. Kunta's first friend in the new land

© 1991 J. Weston Walch, Publisher

Name _____ Date_____

Roots by Alex Haley

Answer the following questions in two or three complete sentences.

1. How does the account in *Roots* contradict the common idea that Africans had no civilization before the white man came?

    _____

    _____

    _____

2. How does Kunta survive after he is taken into slavery?

    _____

    _____

    _____

3. How does *Roots* show that not all whites abused their slaves?

    _____

    _____

    _____

4. How do Chicken George and Tom use their talents to provide for their families?

    _____

    _____

    _____

5. How did Alex Haley trace the accuracy of his family history?

    _____

    _____

    _____

Challenge Question

    Write an essay describing how the history of the Kinte family illustrates the capacity of people to adapt and survive.

© 1991 J. Weston Walch, Publisher   *100 More Great Books: Synopses, Quizzes, and Tests*

Name_____ Date_____

Tess of the D'Urbervilles by Thomas Hardy

Select the letter of the word or phrase which correctly completes each sentence.

_____ 1. The person indirectly responsible for the beginning of Tess's tragedy was (A) her father (B) the parson (C) her mother (D) Alec D'Urberville.

_____ 2. Angel Clare first sees Tess (A) on the highway (B) dancing on the village green (C) in the local tavern (D) in the barn at the dairy.

_____ 3. Tess goes to Mrs. Stoke-D'Urberville because (A) her parents talk her into it (B) the family needs the money (C) she finds Alec attractive (D) she is interesting in learning the history of her family.

_____ 4. Alec is finally able to seduce Tess (A) when his mother is gone from the house (B) after a local dance (C) when he deliberately gets them lost in the woods (D) because he has her parents' permission.

_____ 5. After she finds out that she is pregnant, Tess (A) tells D'Urberville of her situation (B) returns home (C) loses the child through a miscarriage (D) decides to give the child up for adoption.

_____ 6. Tess's parents may best be described as (A) uncaring (B) fatalistic (C) abusive (D) polished and cultured.

_____ 7. Tess shows great strength when she (A) resists Angel's proposal of marriage (B) insists on a Christian burial for her child (C) survives after she has been abandoned (D) all of the above.

_____ 8. The character(s) in greatest contrast to Tess is/are (A) her mother (B) Marian and Izzy (C) Mrs. Stoke-D'Urberville (D) Mrs. Crick, the dairyman's wife.

_____ 9. Bad omens occurring on Tess and Angel's wedding day include all of the following *except* (A) a cock crowing during the day (B) a black cat crossing their path (C) Marian's drunkenness (D) Retty's suicide attempt.

_____ 10. Angel's father would not send his son to Cambridge University because Angel (A) refused to become a clergyman (B) had wasted a great deal of money (C) did not agree with his conservative religious opinions (D) refused to marry Mercy Chant.

(continued)

Name_____   Date_____

Tess of the D'Urbervilles by Thomas Hardy

_____ 11. Which of the following does *not* happen on Tess and Angel's wedding day? (A) Angel introduces Tess to his parents. (B) There is a terrible storm. (C) Tess tells Angel the truth about her past. (D) Tess wears the jewels that had belonged to Angel's godmother.

_____ 12. Hardy intends the reader to see Angel's reaction to Tess's confession as (A) indifferent (B) loving (C) cruel (D) hypocritical.

_____ 13. When Tess again meets D'Urberville, he is (A) working on the same farm as she is (B) running for Parliament (C) traveling on the highway (D) preaching to a group of country folk.

_____ 14. Tess's one real friend is (A) Marian (B) Retty (C) her mother (D) Mrs. Crick.

_____ 15. Angel's parents do not help Tess because (A) they are strict and cruel (B) they do not know where she is (C) they disapprove of her relationship with their son (D) they do not know that she and Angel are married.

_____ 16. Tess is pushed back into a relationship with D'Urberville by (A) a renewed attraction for him (B) Angel's absence (C) the death of her father (D) her inability to get work.

_____ 17. When Angel finds Tess, she is (A) happy with D'Urberville (B) very ill (C) working at hard farm labor (D) living a life of high fashion.

_____ 18. Tess kills D'Urberville (A) with a knife (B) with his own gun (C) by poisoning him (D) in the same grove of woods where he seduced her.

_____ 19. Tess and Angel find a brief period of happiness (A) in the home of his parents (B) at Mr. Crick's dairy where they had fallen in love (C) in an empty manor house (D) in the house where they spent their wedding night.

_____ 20. As the story ends, (A) Tess has been exiled to Australia (B) Angel has killed himself (C) Tess is hanged (D) Rev. Clare has disowned his son.

Name_____ Date_____

Tess of the D'Urbervilles by Thomas Hardy

Answer the following questions in two or three complete sentences.

1. Why does Tess have to take the responsibility for her brothers and sisters?

_____

_____

_____

2. How does Tess try to resist D'Urberville's attentions? Why does she finally submit to him?

_____

_____

_____

3. Why does Tess finally decide to tell Angel the truth about herself? How does he react?

_____

_____

_____

4. After Angel abandons her, how does Tess survive?

_____

_____

_____

5. What circumstances make Angel decide to return to his wife? Why is this return too late?

_____

_____

_____

Challenge Question

Write an essay explaining the ways in which Tess Durbeyfield is the victim of fate and circumstances.

© 1991 J. Weston Walch, Publisher   *100 More Great Books: Synopses, Quizzes, and Tests*

Name _____   Date _____

The Portrait of a Lady by Henry James

Select the letter of the word or phrase which correctly completes each sentence.

_____   1. Isabel is persuaded to come to England by (A) Mrs. Touchett (B) Ralph (C) her sister Lillian (D) Caspar Goodwood.

_____   2. Daniel Touchett had made his fortune in (A) shipping (B) farming (C) banking (D) real estate.

_____   3. Isabel receives her first proposal of marriage from (A) Lord Warburton (B) Ralph (C) Gilbert Osmond (D) Chester Goodwood.

_____   4. Isabel refuses Lord Warburton because (A) she is in love with Chester (B) he is too rich (C) she wants to see more of life (D) Ralph is against her marrying him.

_____   5. Isabel's situation changes most drastically when (A) she decides to visit Italy (B) her uncle leaves her a fortune (C) she meets Gilbert Osmond (D) she becomes friends with Madame Merle.

_____   6. Madame Merle is all of the following *except* (A) a sculptor (B) a good liar (C) an accomplished musician (D) a mother.

_____   7. Pansy Osmond (A) is very intelligent (B) rebels against her father's wishes (C) has received a very strict convent education (D) falls in love with Lord Warburton immediately.

_____   8. Gilbert Osmond is (A) deeply sentimental (B) physically abusive of his wife (C) hard and shallow (D) a political radical.

_____   9. The person who loves Isabel most unselfishly is (A) Ralph (B) Pansy (C) Madame Merle (D) Henrietta.

_____   10. Henrietta Stackpole earns her living as (A) a tour guide (B) a paid companion to wealthy women (C) an author (D) an artist.

_____   11. Osmond objects to Edmund Rosier as a husband for Pansy because (A) he is an American (B) he is not wealthy enough (C) he is an old friend of Isabel's (D) Madame Merle did not like him.

(continued)

© 1991 J. Weston Walch, Publisher   *100 More Great Books: Synopses, Quizzes, and Tests*

Name_____ Date_____

The Portrait of a Lady by Henry James

_____ 12. After their marriage, Gilbert and Isabel Osmond live in (A) Florence (B) Rome (C) Paris (D) England.

_____ 13. Osmond's personality is best reflected in (A) his art collection (B) his library (C) his clothing (D) his circle of friends.

_____ 14. Isabel learns who Pansy's mother was from (A) Madame Merle (B) the Countess Gemini (C) Mrs. Touchett (D) Gilbert himself.

_____ 15. To get Pansy away from Rosier, her father sends his daughter (A) to England (B) to New York (C) back to the convent (D) to live with her aunt.

_____ 16. Isabel leaves Rome to (A) get Pansy away from her father (B) secretly meet Goodwood (C) avoid Madame Merle (D) be with Ralph, who is dying.

_____ 17. Isabel learns all of the following *except* (A) the Countess Gemini is really Pansy's mother (B) Madame Merle arranged her marriage to Osmond (C) Ralph had been responsible for her inheriting a fortune (D) her husband was capable of great cruelty.

_____ 18. Henrietta Stackpole finally decides to (A) give up her writing career (B) live in England permanently (C) not marry anyone (D) stop giving people advice they don't ask for.

_____ 19. At the end of the novel, Isabel has decided to (A) return to America (B) remain in England (C) return to her responsibilities (D) elope with Goodwood.

_____ 20. Isabel Archer may be described as all of the following *except* (A) attractive (B) intellectually curious (C) devious and scheming (D) honest and ethical.

Name _____   Date_____

The Portrait of a Lady by Henry James

Answer the following questions in two or three complete sentences.

1. What part did fate play in Isabel's going to Europe with her aunt?

   _____

   _____

   _____

2. Why did Isabel reject Lord Warburton's offer of marriage?

   _____

   _____

   _____

3. In what ways was Isabel's marriage to Gilbert Osmond a terrible failure?

   _____

   _____

   _____

4. How does the Countess show that she is a true friend to Isabel?

   _____

   _____

   _____

5. In what ways is Madame Merle the villain of the novel?

   _____

   _____

   _____

Challenge Question

Write an essay discussing the character development of Isabel Archer. What circumstances shape her into a mature woman?

Name_____   Date_____

The Thornbirds by Colleen McCullough

Match each description in Column A with the correct name in Column B.

Column A   **Column B**

_____ 1. Received a life sentence for killing a man with his bare hands   A. Paddy

_____ 2. Italian cardinal who made it possible for Ralph to advance in   B. Feona
          the Church
                                                                                 C. Sister Agatha
_____ 3. Died when he was trapped in a fire on the plains
                                                                                 D. Luke
_____ 4. Left the wealth of Drogheda to Ralph and the Church
                                                                                 E. Ralph
_____ 5. Drowned off the coast of Greece while attempting to rescue
          other swimmers   F. Hal

_____ 6. Loved the masculine work involved in cutting sugarcane   G. Frank

_____ 7. Sheltered and protected Meggie after she was abandoned by   H. Dane
          her husband
                                                                                  I. Stuart
_____ 8. German soldier who took shelter in St. Peter's Cathedral
                                                                                 J. Contini-Verchese
_____ 9. Assumed the management of Drogheda after his father was killed
                                                                                 K. Bob
_____ 10. Loved her sons but ignored the needs of her daughter
                                                                                 L. Patsy
_____ 11. Became an actress to avoid admitting how much she needed her
           mother's love   M. Mary Carson

_____ 12. Island where Ralph and Meggie consummated their love   N. Justine

_____ 13. His protection of a child grew into his love for a woman   O. Drogheda

_____ 14. The Cleary twin who was severely wounded in World War II   P. Anne Mueller

_____ 15. Faithful housekeeper who cared for and taught the children   Q. Matlock

_____ 16. Meggie's cruel and abusive schoolteacher   R. Mrs. Smith

_____ 17. Killed by a wild boar while trying to rescue his father   S. Meggie

_____ 18. Cleary son who died in infancy   T. Rainer Hartheim

_____ 19. Came to Rome to ask the Cardinal to reclaim the body of her son

_____ 20. Great estate which frames all the action of *The Thornbirds*

© 1991 J. Weston Walch, Publisher   *100 More Great Books: Synopses, Quizzes, and Tests*

Name _____   Date_____

The Thornbirds by Colleen McCullough

Answer the following questions in two or three complete sentences.

1. How did the Clearys' life change when they moved to Drogheda from New Zealand?

   _____

   _____

   _____

2. What problems did inheriting Mary Carson's wealth cause for Father Ralph?

   _____

   _____

   _____

3. Why was Luke O'Neill such a terrible husband?

   _____

   _____

   _____

4. How does Dane's death finally unite Ralph and Meggie?

   _____

   _____

   _____

5. How does the setting influence the action in *The Thornbirds*?

   _____

   _____

   _____

Challenge Question

Write an essay describing how the title, *The Thornbirds*, represents the personalities of Meggie, Feona, and Justine Cleary.

Name_____   Date_____

Giants in the Earth by O. E. Rolvaag

Select the letter of the word or phrase which correctly completes each sentence.

_____   1. In Norway, Per Hansa had been a (A) hunter (B) farmer (C) fisherman (D) merchant.

_____   2. The eldest child in the family was (A) Ole (B) Store-Hans (C) And-Ogden (D) Pedermond.

_____   3. During the first year of their settlement on the land, Per Hansa did all of the following *except* (A) build a large frame house (B) clear land for crops (C) plant trees (D) build a house and barn together.

_____   4. Per Hansa's closest friend was (A) Henry Solum (B) Hans Olsa (C) Tonseten (D) Sam.

_____   5. Beret was different from other women in the community because of her (A) sewing ability (B) musical talent (C) fear (D) inability to have children.

_____   6. Per Hansa broke the law when he (A) traded with the Indians (B) killed game out of season (C) refused to have his children baptized (D) moved the markers he found on his land.

_____   7. The pony, Injun, was (A) brought with the settlers from Minnesota (B) received as payment for medical services (C) presented to Per Hansa when his son was born (D) used to haul lumber from Sioux Creek.

_____   8. The greatest destruction to the crops was caused by (A) blizzards (B) hailstones (C) locusts (D) high winds.

_____   9. The closest non-Norwegian neighbors were (A) Irish (B) English (C) Spanish (D) French.

_____   10. The wives in the Norwegian community included all of the following *except* (A) Bridget (B) Beret (C) Sorine (D) Kjersti.

_____   11. Per Hansa received his first significant cash payments for (A) potatoes (B) wheat (C) lumber (D) furs.

(continued)

© 1991 J. Weston Walch, Publisher

Name_____   Date_____

Giants in the Earth by O. E. Rolvaag

_____ 12. Most of Beret's fears were caused by (A) guilt (B) isolation (C) feelings of inadequacy (D) hatred for her husband.

_____ 13. The choice for justice of the peace for the small community was (A) Per Hansa (B) Tonseten (C) Hans Olsa (D) Henry Solum.

_____ 14. In an attempt to please his wife, Per Hansa (A) bought new furniture (B) built a large addition onto his house (C) had the walls of his sod home painted white (D) ordered new clothes for her from Chicago.

_____ 15. The pioneer woman Kari (A) provided a good companion for Beret (B) had gone mad looking for her child's grave (C) brought Beret news of her family in Norway (D) tried to kidnap Store-Hans.

_____ 16. When the minister came, the church services were held (A) in an open field (B) at Hans Olsa's (C) in the schoolhouse (D) in Per Hansa's home.

_____ 17. During the plague of locusts, Beret (A) tried to hide in the large chest (B) worked with her husband to drive the insects away (C) ran madly onto the prairie (D) attempted suicide.

_____ 18. Hans Olsa caught pneumonia when he (A) attempted to save his cattle (B) went to town for supplies (C) fell through the ice into the river (D) tried to rescue a stranded child.

_____ 19. Beret persuaded her husband to go through the snow for (A) medicine (B) the doctor (C) food supplies (D) the minister.

_____ 20. At the end of the novel, Per Hansa (A) remarries (B) loses his farm (C) freezes to death (D) is elected to the newly formed state legislature.

© 1991 J. Weston Walch, Publisher   *100 More Great Books: Synopses, Quizzes, and Tests*

Name_____   Date_____

Giants in the Earth by O. E. Rolvaag

Answer the following questions in two or three complete sentences.

1. After they decide to settle at Spring Creek, what steps do Per Hansa and his neighbors take to cultivate the wild prairie?

    _____

    _____

    _____

2. In what ways is Beret different from the other pioneer women?

    _____

    _____

    _____

3. What aspects of Per Hansa's success can be attributed to good luck?

    _____

    _____

    _____

4. Why is the minister's arrival significant to the community?

    _____

    _____

    _____

5. Why is religion both a positive and a negative influence in the lives of the Spring Creek settlers?

    _____

    _____

    _____

Challenge Question

Many books and television shows, such as *Little House on the Prairie*, glorify the American pioneer experience. Write an essay discussing Rolvaag's view of people's battle to win the land. How does his book differ from such a typical romantic approach?

Name_____ Date_____

A *Reckoning* by May Sarton

Select the letter of the word or phrase which correctly completes each sentence.

_____ 1. Most of the novel is set in (A) New York (B) Boston (C) Maine (D) Switzerland.

_____ 2. Laura's age is approximately (A) 50 (B) 75 (C) 45 (D) 60.

_____ 3. The dominating influence of Laura's childhood was (A) her mother (B) her father (C) Cousin Hope (D) Ella.

_____ 4. Laura's mother was always (A) very wealthy (B) nagging and complaining (C) acting (D) urging Laura to get married.

_____ 5. Laura insists that Dr. Goodwin (A) give her cobalt treatments (B) allow her to die at home (C) not tell her children (D) call in another specialist.

_____ 6. Laura finds great pleasure in (A) music (B) poetry (C) the company of her pets (D) all of the above.

_____ 7. The first person Laura tells that she is dying is (A) Ella (B) Aunt Minna (C) Harriet Moors (D) Mary O'Brien.

_____ 8. Laura wants to help Harriet because (A) she needs some work to occupy her mind (B) she needs to relate to someone younger (C) she relates to Harriet's family problems (D) she needs the money she gets from working with Harriet.

_____ 9. Laura's husband had been (A) an editor (B) a lawyer (C) a career diplomat (D) a doctor.

_____ 10. When Sybille cared for Laura when she was ill, Laura felt (A) trapped (B) angry (C) safe and protected (D) lonely.

_____ 11. Her relationship with Ella had made Laura feel (A) free (B) inadequate (C) complete (D) unfeminine.

_____ 12. The last family function that Laura was able to attend was (A) Brooks and Ann's wedding (B) Jo's graduation (C) her mother's funeral (D) Laurie's birthday party.

(continued)

© 1991 J. Weston Walch, Publisher *100 More Great Books: Synopses, Quizzes, and Tests*

Name _____   Date _____

A *Reckoning* by May Sarton

_____ 13. The starkest contrast in the novel concerns (A) Laura's health (B) Sybille's helpless condition (C) Daisy's reaction to her mother's illness (D) Ben's conversations with Laura.

_____ 14. Harriet Moors's greatest problem is (A) poor writing style (B) lack of money (C) fear and insecurity (D) no support for her work from her family.

_____ 15. As Laura becomes more seriously ill, she finds her greatest comfort in her relationship with (A) Daisy (B) Mary (C) Jo (D) Daphne.

_____ 16. During her stay in the hospital, Laura feels (A) depersonalized (B) lonely (C) comfortable (D) in great pain.

_____ 17. Laura experiences all the following physical symptoms *except* (A) hair loss (B) nausea (C) sleeplessness (D) physical weakness.

_____ 18. Dr. Goodwin tells Laura that he can promise her (A) a remission (B) another six months (C) spring (D) no additional time.

_____ 19. Which of the following people is least able to deal with the fact of Laura's death? (A) Jo (B) Ben (C) Daisy (D) Ann

_____ 20. Laura is ready to die (A) after Ben comes (B) when she can no longer eat (C) after she talks with Ella again (D) after she and Daphne visit their childhood house in Maine.

Name_____ _____ Date_____

A *Reckoning* by May Sarton

Answer the following questions in two or three complete sentences.

1. Explain what Laura means when she says that she must make a "reckoning" based on real connections.

   _____

   _____

   _____

2. Why had Laura's relationship with Daisy been so difficult?

   _____

   _____

   _____

3. How had Ella and Charles saved Laura from Sybille's domination?

   _____

   _____

   _____

4. Why does Laura decide to give her lapis lazuli necklace to her granddaughter?

   _____

   _____

   _____

5. As Laura's health wanes, why does she value Mary O'Brien more and more?

   _____

   _____

   _____

Challenge Question

Discuss the new understanding of life which Laura Spelman gains as she faces death.

© 1991 J. Weston Walch, Publisher

Name_____   Date_____

East of Eden by John Steinbeck

Select the letter of the word or phrase which correctly completes each sentence.

_____ 1. Cyrus Trask gained his fame (A) as an inventor (B) as a writer (C) as a soldier and patriot (D) selling automobiles.

_____ 2. Cyrus's favorite gift from his son was (A) a pup (B) a knife (C) a sword (D) a watch.

_____ 3. Charles Trask's face was scarred in (A) battle (B) a fight with Adam (C) a barroom brawl (D) an accident on the farm.

_____ 4. Cathy Ames was able to trick all of the following *except* (A) Lee (B) Adam (C) Mr. Edwards (D) Joe.

_____ 5. According to Steinbeck, Cathy was a monster because (A) she was born with no hands (B) she did evil things (C) she killed her parents (D) she had no sense of right and wrong.

_____ 6. Lee's one great ambition was to (A) go back to China (B) get married (C) learn how to cook (D) open a bookstore.

_____ 7. The woman in the novel who is in most complete contrast to Cathy is (A) Abra (B) Liza Hamilton (C) Alice (D) Faye.

_____ 8. Samuel Hamilton failed financially because (A) he had poor land (B) he was too generous (C) people stole his valuable inventions (D) all of the above.

_____ 9. Charles and Caleb are alike in that (A) both drink a lot (B) both served in the army (C) both tried to win their father's love (D) both have scars on their faces.

_____ 10. The most consistently steady character in the novel is (A) Tom Hamilton (B) Mr. Edwards (C) Lee (D) Abra.

_____ 11. Cathy's major weakness is (A) liquor (B) money (C) morphine (D) apples.

_____ 12. Adam's greatest financial failure involved (A) beans (B) lettuce (C) automobiles (D) cattle.

(continued)

© 1991 J. Weston Walch, Publisher

100 More Great Books: Synopses, Quizzes, and Tests

Name_____   Date_____

East of Eden by John Steinbeck

_____ 13. Adam decided to move to Salinas (A) because Samuel advised him to (B) so that his sons would have better schools (C) because his wife was there (D) because the farm had gone bankrupt.

_____ 14. Steinbeck was related to (A) Adam Trask (B) Kate (C) Olive Hamilton (D) Joe Valery.

_____ 15. Kate left all her money to (A) Charles (B) Caleb (C) Aron (D) Adam.

_____ 16. The word "timshel" refers to (A) wisdom (B) farming (C) choice (D) greeting.

_____ 17. Lee returns from San Francisco because (A) he couldn't find a store to buy (B) no one would hire a Chinese man (C) he had been robbed (D) he was lonely.

_____ 18. When Aron learns who his mother is, he (A) kills her (B) kills himself (C) joins the army (D) becomes a priest.

_____ 19. The most prosperous member of the Hamilton family at the end of the novel is (A) Tom (B) Will (C) Dressie (D) Samuel.

_____ 20. The money Cal earned for his father is (A) given to Adam as a Christmas present (B) lost on the stock market (C) invested (D) burned.

© 1991 J. Weston Walch, Publisher

Name _____ Date _____

East of Eden by John Steinbeck

Answer the following questions in two or three complete sentences.

1. How were Charles and Caleb Trask alike in their relationships with their fathers?

   _____

   _____

   _____

2. Why does Lee speak at first with a Chinese accent? Why does he later change?

   _____

   _____

   _____

3. Discuss how Samuel Hamilton represents the power of goodness.

   _____

   _____

   _____

4. List some of the lives that were ruined by Cathy (Kate's) destructiveness.

   _____

   _____

   _____

5. How does the Salinas Valley become a character in this novel?

   _____

   _____

   _____

Challenge Question

Write an essay discussing how the Trask and Hamilton families were different. How did the personality of the father influence the children in each family?

Name_____ _____ Date_____

Mrs. Miniver by Jan Struther

Place a T before each true statement and an F before each false statement.

_____ 1. Starlings was the Minivers' townhouse in London.

_____ 2. All of the Miniver family enjoyed fireworks on holidays.

_____ 3. Mrs. Miniver generally did not save her lists of social engagements from one year to the next.

_____ 4. Vin was the Minivers' eldest son.

_____ 5. Clem Miniver was a lawyer.

_____ 6. Mrs. Adie, the housekeeper, was always afraid the worst would happen.

_____ 7. Toby and Judy Miniver were sent to the country for protection when the bombing of London began.

_____ 8. Mrs. Miniver did not enjoy weekend visits to the country houses of Clem's friends.

_____ 9. Mrs. Miniver refused to have herself or her children fitted for gas masks.

_____ 10. Although Mrs. Adie was a very poor cook, the Minivers kept her because they could not get any other help.

_____ 11. The whole Miniver family enjoyed hop picking in the fall.

_____ 12. Judy Miniver had great difficulty choosing a doll on her birthday.

_____ 13. For Mrs. Miniver, the rain-swollen river became a symbol of the tide of evil that threatened to engulf the world.

_____ 14. Mrs. Miniver never made any Christmas lists until after her children were born.

_____ 15. When the Minivers traveled to Scotland, Clem did all the driving.

_____ 16. The Lane-Pontifexes were people the Minivers invited to dinner because they felt they had to.

_____ 17. Vin always enjoyed most the last day of his summer vacation.

_____ 18. Mrs. Miniver brought children who had been displaced by the war to live at Starlings.

_____ 19. Mrs. Miniver had never traveled to the European continent.

_____ 20. Mrs. Miniver believed that the best hope for world peace lay with the children.

© 1991 J. Weston Walch, Publisher

Name_____ Date_____

Mrs. Miniver by Jan Struther

Answer the following questions in two or three complete sentences.

1. How does Mrs. Miniver show her love of nature?

   _____

   _____

   _____

2. Why is Starlings such a special place to all the members of the Miniver family?

   _____

   _____

   _____

3. Why is having herself and the children fitted for gas masks such a crisis experience in Mrs. Miniver's life?

   _____

   _____

   _____

4. How does Mrs. Miniver try to "do a mole" and revisit her own childhood?

   _____

   _____

   _____

5. How does her visit to the European continent just before the outbreak of war affect Mrs. Miniver's viewpoint?

   _____

   _____

   _____

Challenge Question

Write an essay describing why Caroline Miniver became a symbol of hope for an English nation under siege.

© 1991 J. Weston Walch, Publisher

100 More Great Books: Synopses, Quizzes, and Tests

Name_____ Date_____

Anna Karenina by Leo Tolstoy

Select the letter of the word or phrase which correctly completes each sentence.

_____ 1. Anna travels from St. Petersburg to Moscow so that she may (A) do some shopping (B) enjoy the pleasures of fashionable society (C) help reconcile her brother and his wife (D) be a traveling companion for Vronsky's mother.

_____ 2. All of the following are true of Vronsky *except* (A) he was dominated by his father (B) he is a nobleman (C) he is a military officer (D) women find him attractive.

_____ 3. Kitty refuses Levin's first offer of love because (A) she finds Levin too rustic and disgusting (B) her father does not approve of Levin (C) Kitty thinks that she is in love with Vronsky (D) Levin is not a Christian.

_____ 4. Anna and Vronsky begin their affair while they are (A) in the train station (B) dancing a mazurka (C) visiting Stepan and Dolly (D) attending the opera.

_____ 5. Before his marriage, Levin's greatest interest is in (A) experimental farming (B) science (C) local politics (D) writing poetry.

_____ 6. Alexey Karenin is all of the following *except* (A) considerably older than Anna (B) gentle and sensitive (C) politically prominent (D) concerned about keeping his reputation intact.

_____ 7. Anna almost dies when (A) Vronsky deserts her (B) Alexey refuses to let her see their son (C) Vronsky's daughter is born (D) she is thrown from a horse.

_____ 8. Levin first realizes the gentle beauty of his wife when (A) she cares for his dying brother (B) their son is born (C) he first visits her home in Moscow (D) he compares her personality with those of her sisters.

_____ 9. Vronsky is injured when (A) Anna's husband challenges him to a duel (B) a gun goes off by accident (C) a carriage in which he is riding turns over (D) Levin tries to shoot him.

_____ 10. Levin's greatest character weakness is (A) greed (B) religious doubt (C) jealousy (D) poor financial judgment.

(continued)

© 1991 J. Weston Walch, Publisher   *100 More Great Books: Synopses, Quizzes, and Tests*

Name_____   Date_____

Anna Karenina by Leo Tolstoy

_____ 11. The greatest obstacle to Anna's gaining a divorce from her husband is (A) her need of money (B) Karenin's jealousy of Vronsky (C) Anna's love for her son (D) the danger to Anna's social position.

_____ 12. The only friend who is willing to visit Anna and Vronsky while they are exiled in the country is (A) Kitty (B) Princess Betsy (C) Countess Lilova (D) Dolly.

_____ 13. Levin is strongly attracted to Anna when (A) he sees her portrait (B) he visits Vronsky's country estate (C) he takes tea with her (D) all of the above.

_____ 14. Levin's land reform plans would permit (A) the workers to have a share in the profits (B) a communistic form of government (C) no more private ownership (D) men of Levin's social class to make more money.

_____ 15. When she is afraid that Vronsky's love for her is dying, Anna (A) again becomes pregnant (B) makes plans to return to her husband (C) begins taking morphine and opium (D) appeals to Dolly for help.

_____ 16. Anna's husband, in finally refusing a divorce, is influenced by (A) his love for his son (B) a psychic (C) the leaders of his political party (D) his brother.

_____ 17. Vronsky's love for Anna begins to dwindle because (A) he is having an affair with somebody else (B) Anna is beginning to lose her beauty (C) Vronsky craves the companionship of other people (D) Vronsky knows that his relationship with Anna is against the law.

_____ 18. Levin's greatest emotional crisis comes (A) when Kitty rejects him (B) when he is married (C) when his crops fail (D) when his son is born.

_____ 19. Anna dies when (A) she is struck by a train (B) she overdoses with morphine (C) Vronsky shoots her (D) she tries to bear Vronsky another child.

_____ 20. Levin finally finds God through (A) his conversations with a priest (B) his love for Kitty and his child (C) a supernatural revelation (D) reading the Bible.

© 1991 J. Weston Walch, Publisher

100 More Great Books: Synopses, Quizzes, and Tests

Name_____ Date_____

Anna Karenina by Leo Tolstoy

Answer the following questions in two or three complete sentences.

1. Why are Anna and Vronsky attracted to each other?

_____

_____

_____

2. What role does Stepan, Anna's brother, play in the novel?

_____

_____

_____

3. What does Levin learn about Kitty when his wife goes with him to visit his dying brother?

_____

_____

_____

4. How does Anna's love for her son conflict with her love for Vronsky?

_____

_____

_____

5. What weaknesses in Russian society does Tolstoy picture in *Anna Karenina*?

_____

_____

_____

Challenge Question

Write an essay contrasting the relationship of Anna and Vronsky with the developing marriage of Kitty and Levin. What does Tolstoy seem to be saying about the nature of love as he pictures these characters for his readers?

© 1991 J. Weston Walch, Publisher   *100 More Great Books: Synopses, Quizzes, and Tests*

Name_____ Date_____

The Color Purple by Alice Walker

Select the letter of the word or phrase which correctly completes each sentence.

_____ 1. Celie is most troubled by (A) the fact that her father raped her (B) her physical ugliness (C) the family's poverty (D) her inability to read.

_____ 2. Mr. _____ marries Celie because (A) she has borne his child (B) he can't have Nettie (C) his children are fond of Celie (D) her father threatens him with a gun.

_____ 3. All of the following are true of Celie *except* (A) she sings well (B) she tries to be a good housekeeper (C) she works hard in the field (D) she tries to take care of her husband's children.

_____ 4. Shug Avery comes to stay at Celie's home because (A) she couldn't find a hotel room (B) Mr. _____ wants to marry her (C) Shug is very sick (D) Shug wants Celie to make her costumes for her.

_____ 5. Mr. _____ tells Nettie to leave because (A) she can read (B) she is causing trouble among his children (C) he wants her to go to work (D) she will not let him make love to her.

_____ 6. Celie never gets Nettie's letters because (A) Mr. _____ hides them (B) the ship that carried them went down at sea (C) Samuel refused to let Nettie write to her sister (D) Shug burned all the letters.

_____ 7. As she matures, Celie learns what love means from her relationship with (A) Nettie (B) Olivia (C) Shug (D) Sofia.

_____ 8. When Celie tells Harpo to beat up Sofia, (A) Harpo leaves home (B) Mr. _____ beats up Celie (C) Sofia gives Harpo two black eyes (D) Harpo refuses.

_____ 9. After Sofia leaves him, Harpo (A) tries to kill himself (B) turns their home into a juke joint (C) runs away to Memphis (D) goes after her to bring her back.

_____ 10. Sofia is sent to prison for (A) attacking the mayor's wife (B) robbery (C) beating her husband (D) sitting in the white section of the bus.

(continued)

© 1991 J. Weston Walch, Publisher

Name _____ Date_____

The Color Purple by Alice Walker

_____ 11. Nettie goes with Samuel and Corinne to Africa (A) to teach the natives the Bible (B) to take care of the children (C) to help with the farming project (D) because Corinne is ill.

_____ 12. Nettie's attitude toward the African natives may be best described as (A) contempt (B) pity (C) deep respect (D) resentment and prejudice.

_____ 13. The natives of Olinka most value (A) gold (B) rubber (C) oil (D) roofleaf.

_____ 14. Corinne comes to hate Nettie because she thinks that (A) Samuel loves Nettie (B) Nettie is taking her place with the natives (C) Nettie is the mother of Adam and Olivia (D) Nettie is attempting to steal her husband.

_____ 15. Celie finds a special form of self-expression through (A) painting (B) pottery (C) sewing (D) singing.

_____ 16. Celie is most devastated when (A) she thinks that Nettie is dead (B) Shug leaves her (C) she is raped by her father (D) she is forced to marry Mr. _____ .

_____ 17. The natives of Olinka are destroyed by (A) disease (B) famine (C) the white man's greed (D) war with a neighboring tribe.

_____ 18. After Sofia leaves him, Harpo lives with (A) Shug (B) Celie (C) Mary Agnes (D) Odessa.

_____ 19. Celie learns from Nettie that (A) Olivia is not really her child (B) the man who raped her was not her father (C) Shug has committed murder (D) Samuel is dead.

_____ 20. Adam, Celie's son, shows his love for Talia by (A) going to live with her in the jungle (B) refusing to come to America (C) marking his face like hers (D) renouncing his family and joining her tribe.

© 1991 J. Weston Walch, Publisher

Name _____ Date_____

The Color Purple by Alice Walker

Answer the following questions in two or three complete sentences.

1. What difficulties does Celie face after she marries Mr. _____ ?

_____

_____

_____

2. How does the letter form of the novel bring the characters to life?

_____

_____

_____

3. How does her relationship with Shug Avery change Celie's life?

_____

_____

_____

4. What strengths does Celie admire in Sofia?

_____

_____

_____

5. How does Nettie find the strength to cope with the difficulties of her situation?

_____

_____

_____

Challenge Question

Write an essay to compare and contrast the personalities of Celie and Nettie. How are the sisters alike? How are they different?

Answer Keys

A Midwife's Story by Penny Armstrong

True or False:

1. F	4. T	7. T	10. T	13. F	16. F	19. T
2. T	5. F	8. F	11. F	14. F	17. F	20. F
3. F	6. F	9. T	12. T	15. F	18. F	

Short Answers:

1. At first she thought them cold and without feeling. She found that they were people who cared deeply and who accepted her after they learned to trust her. She found their way of life to be deep and rich. She developed her own faith by what she learned from them.

2. The doctors in the hospital campaigned against her as a midwife and as a woman. Midwives, in the opinion of these men, could be equated with witch doctors who practiced dangerous medicine.

3. Natural childbirth encourages the mother to help herself with as little medical intervention as possible. The child is given to the mother immediately after it is born. Hospitals are cold and impersonal. The mother is often drugged and surgical techniques are commonplace. Mother and baby are separated. Penny feels that natural childbirth is healthier for both mother and child.

4. Richie fitted in with the Amish community. His participation in farming helped the Amish accept both him and Penny. He also gave Penny the moral support she needed. Richie put up with interrupted sleep and sometimes even went along to help insecure fathers.

5. Sam's loving Helen would have taken him away from his family and from all the traditions in which he had been brought up. Helen would never fit into the Amish ways and did not want to give up her nursing career.

Challenge Question:

Penny was well trained and careful in her medical techniques. She went to the women whenever calls came in. She also learned from their ways. Katie, whose baby was the first Penny delivered, taught her the ease of nature. Penny learned family unity from Katie and Ike, whose mentally handicapped daughter Emma was a witness to birth. She grieved with Reuben and Rebecca, whose son Benjamin had a brain tumor. The death of Johnny and Leah's daughter drove her to question the meaning of life.

Penny's deep feeling for the Amish people made her one with them. She was able to care. She found peace for herself and oneness with the land, even through seeing Sarah, the mentally handicapped vegetable seller. The reader feels that Penny Armstrong will probably have a long, successful career as a midwife. The book also reinforces the importance of caring as part of any medical career.

The Dollmaker by Harriette Arnow

Matching:

1. J	6. H	11. K	16. I
2. F	7. N	12. B	17. A
3. C	8. G	13. P	18. M
4. E	9. S	14. Q	19. D
5. L	10. O	15. R	20. T

Short Answers:

1. She stops the car. She performs the operation that saves Amos's life. She manages the farm herself. She teaches her children and has her own strong religious faith.

2. Her mother refuses to allow Old John to sell Gertie the land. She insists that Gertie take the children to Detroit.

3. The block of wood is her link with home, the outlet for her creativity, a source of comfort when she is hurt. Working with the wood is the mark of Gertie's individuality. It's what makes her special.

4. She comforts Sophronie. She takes care of children and irons Mr. Anderson's shirts. Her determination to make the place beautiful inspires others. The gifts of her carved objects bring beauty into their drab lives. Max especially receives comfort from Gertie's words and actions.

5. Hers is the death of innocence which is crushed by all that is horrible and ugly. Gertie's spirit is almost broken by this as she blames herself for the child's death.

Challenge Question:

The family loses its link with the land. This loss is symbolized by shabby surroundings and the poor quality of city food. Reuben rebels against the city and runs away. Cassie is crushed beneath the wheels of a train. Clytie and Enoch become more and more city children. Clovis changes from a gentle man who tinkers with machines into a man who kills those who attack him.

Gertie fights this by trying to keep human contact with her neighbors. She tries to raise plants and to grow flowers. She continues to hold her dream of bringing the Christ figure from the wood. She is defeated when she knows that her husband has killed a man. She must also give up the wood to make cheap, imitation dolls so that the family can survive.

Père Goriot by Honoré de Balzac

Multiple Choice:

1. B	4. D	7. B	10. A	13. A	16. A	19. D
2. C	5. B	8. C	11. C	14. D	17. D	20. A
3. A	6. A	9. D	12. B	15. B	18. B	

Short Answers:

1. When he visits his cousin, Eugène is dazzled by the social world to which he wants to belong. As he dines there, he contrasts the elegance of his cousin's house with the shabbiness of Madame Vauquer's. This visit begins Eugène's determination to enter society.

2. Goriot has given his fortune to his daughters. The father lives in poverty so that his children may live in elegance. As he dies, Goriot gives the money that could have made him more comfortable so that his daughter may have a beautiful dress.

3. Eugène takes all the money that his mother and sisters can send him. He uses this gift to buy gloves and to rent a carriage so that he can enter society.

4. Vautrin will have young Taillefer murdered to give Victorine a legitimate claim to her father's fortune. Eugène will then marry Victorine and claim the money. In return, Vautrin will receive enough money for a plantation in America.

5. Goriot is buried in a pauper's grave. His daughters do not attend the funeral. Only their empty carriages are there. For the father who has given everything, the burial represents the perfect indifference of his children.

Challenge Question:

Eugène has come to Paris from the provinces. As the story moves along, Eugène is torn between his growing affection for Goriot and his attraction to Delphine and the social status that she represents. When he sees the elegance of his cousin's home, Eugène is like a small child outside a toy shop. He wants to be inside the world of fashion.

As his infatuation for Delphine grows, Eugène becomes more accepting of the sacrifices that her father has made. Eugène also expects sacrifices from his family so that he can pursue his selfish ambitions.

Eugène is a good man who is helpless against the cruel tide of society's indifference. He is horrified by Vautrin's schemes, but is too drunk to prevent the murder. He tries to make Goriot's daughters understand their father's pathetic situation, but he cannot change them.

In Balzac's world, wealth is the only real power and virtue. For all his good intentions, Eugène does not escape its trap. At the end of the novel, knowing exactly what Delphine is, Eugène by choice returns to her world.

Cold Sassy Tree by Olive Ann Burns

True or False:

1. F	6. F	11. F	16. T
2. T	7. T	12. F	17. F
3. F	8. F	13. T	18. F
4. T	9. T	14. F	19. F
5. F	10. F	15. T	20. F

Short Answers:

1. The family is shocked. The town regards this as a hot bit of gossip and enjoys the scandal. Will is more accepting. He likes Miss Love. He wants to see them both happy.

2. Will's strength of character comes from Rucker. The old man dominates by choosing Will's career and keeping his sons-in-law financially dependent. Camp's suicide resulted in part from Rucker's constant put-downs.

3. She represents his first adolescent sexual awareness through the kiss on the train track, his holding her in the cemetery, and his dismay when she marries someone else.

4. Miss Love was raped by her father when she was twelve and rejected by McAllister. Rucker represents the only security that Love has ever known.

5. He desires to please both his wife and his father-in-law, but is never able to satisfy either of them. After constant brow-beating, suicide becomes the only way out.

Challenge Question:

The tree is one of a kind. It stands out with bright scarlet leaves, and has very strong roots. Rucker is a flashy, dominating man with a strong personality. His generation had the kind of roots that gave the community its identity.

The tree was cut down after Rucker died. This represented both the old ways passing and the death of a generation.

Show Boat by Edna Ferber

Multiple Choice:

1. D	6. B	11. C	16. A
2. D	7. C	12. A	17. C
3. B	8. A	13. B	18. A
4. C	9. C	14. A	19. A
5. A	10. C	15. C	20. A

Short Answers:

1. Parthy takes over the management of the boat. She manages the physical details of the boat. She insists on high moral standards for the actors. Secretly she loves the excitement and would not want to be left home. Parthy can manage everybody except Windy and Captain Andy.

2. Her father is the love of Magnolia's childhood. She inherits his vitality and his love of the river. Doc, a member of the company, tells her all the stories of the river. Queenie and Joe teach her their songs. Julie is the friend from whom Magnolia learns about love.

3. He arrives after Julie and Steve have left. Schultz also leaves to find Miss Ellie. These openings leave a place in the company for a man of Ravenal's talents. Also his luck is down and he needs a job. Magnolia at the time is an impressionable teenager who is captivated by Ravenal's charms.

4. Ravenal's strengths are his depth of feeling, his charm, and his genuine love for Magnolia and his daughter. His weaknesses are his instability and his dependence on luck. Ravenal is not an evil man, he is a weak one.

5. Magnolia is easily influenced. She is very passive until Ravenal's failure forces her to act. In the end she returns to the life she has always known. Kim is the child of the city rather than the river. Kim takes care of her mother. The daughter has the strong strain of Parthy's personality. She knows what she wants and she goes after it.

Challenge Question:

The determination in Parthy's personality remains strong as she adapts to river life. The businesswoman comes out in her when she makes a success of the boat after Andy's death. Rather than changing Parthy, the river brings out the traits that are already there.

Magnolia is the child of the river. The Mississippi runs through her dreams. Memories of the river help her survive the ups and downs of her life with Ravenal. The river songs form the spiritual base of her personality.

Kim is a combination of her grandmother and her mother. She has Parthy's energy and determination. Kim also has the strength to survive her unstable childhood. Even though Kim does not return to the river, her showboat background strongly influences her life as an actress.

Roots by Alex Haley

Matching:

1. D	4. J	7. Q	10. N	13. E	16. I	19. O
2. B	5. G	8. T	11. A	14. R	17. K	20. F
3. L	6. P	9. C	12. M	15. H	18. S	

Short Answers:

1. Haley describes the customs and rituals of Kinte's tribe. Each person has his place in a structured society. The people are devout Muslims. Children become adults as functions and traditions are passed from one generation to another.

2. At first, Kinte survives by his anger—his determination to be free. After he is bought by Waller, Kunta finds his place through the friendship of Fiddler and the love of Bell. Although Kinte adapts to survive, he never loses the sense of his African heritage.

3. Waller is very humane. He sells the slaves only if they break his rules. Lea is much more brutal. Even he is seen as a human being who is a victim of his own weakness. Murray allows Tom and his family a great deal of liberty. The whites are seen as victims

of their own system. When the "massas" are afraid, they take this fear out on the blacks.

4. George uses his money from the cockfight to buy gifts for his family. Tom's skills as a blacksmith make life much better, and are eventually used to support the family when freedom comes.

5. Haley went to Africa to check the tribal roots. He checked the shipping records and the government census reports to verify all of the family stories.

Challenge Question:

Kunta survives his sea voyage. Even after his foot is cut off, he rises to the position of the master's driver. Kizzy survives after the birth of her son. George and Tom make profits by their special skills. The women (Matilda, Irene, and Cynthia) lend support to their men. The Kinte family are seen in this book as people whose spirit and intelligence will help them to survive all difficulties.

Tess of the D'Urbervilles by Thomas Hardy

Multiple Choice:

1. B	6. B	11. A	16. C
2. B	7. D	12. D	17. D
3. A	8. B	13. D	18. A
4. C	9. B	14. A	19. C
5. B	10. C	15. B	20. C

Short Answers:

1. Tess's parents are weak people who live on drink and dreams. Tess must look after the younger children. She is sent to the D'Urbervilles to fulfill her father's ambitions. Her mother does not care enough to help Tess when her child dies. After John's death, Tess must again sell herself to Alec so that the family can survive.

2. Tess whips the horses so that Alec can't kiss her in the carriage. She will walk rather than ride with him. She avoids him as he chases her on his mother's estate. She finally submits to him when Alec deliberately leads her into the deep woods, where Tess has no defense or protection.

3. She decides to tell him the truth after she hears of Retty's suicide attempt. Tess is an honest person who does not want to live with deception. Angel's confession of his own affair also leads her to be truthful. Angel rejects her. He says that she is not the woman he thought she was. In this scene the reader sees Angel Clare as a hypocrite.

4. She does all sorts of hard farm work. She is at the mercy of the climate and the hard men that she must work for. After her father's death, she goes back to D'Urberville so that he will help her family. She is convinced by then that Angel has abandoned her.

5. Angel receives two letters: one from Tess herself and one from Marian and Izzy. He also remembers that Izzy had told him that Tess would die for him. He arrives too late and finds Tess as D'Urberville's mistress. To be reunited even briefly with Angel, Tess must kill the man she hates.

Challenge Question:

Tess is a victim of D'Urberville's passions and Angel Clare's weakness. Fate conspires against her when the parson happens to tell her father of their link with the noble family. No kindly fates protect her from D'Urberville. She happens to be at the same dairy with Angel. After he abandons her, she again runs into D'Urberville by chance. When John dies and the family is evicted, fate forces Tess to accept D'Urberville. When Tess tries to contact Angel's parents, circumstances result in failure. Tess's only act of independent nobility is the murder of her tormentor. For this act, Tess pays with her life.

The Portrait of a Lady by Henry James

Multiple Choice:

1. A	5. B	9. A	13. A	17. A
2. C	6. A	10. C	14. B	18. B
3. D	7. C	11. B	15. C	19. C
4. C	8. C	12. B	16. D	20. C

Short Answers:

1. Isabel's aunt arrived in Albany before Mr. Goodwood did. Mrs. Touchett's stories about Europe excited Isabel's imagination and made her reject Goodwood.

2. When Warburton first proposed, Isabel still wanted to see more of life. Her curiosity would not let her settle into the comfortable life that he offered.

3. She was completely stifled. Osmond wanted to shape her and to leave her no mind of her own. Isabel was forced to maintain a pretense of happiness where none existed. Only her cousin Ralph saw through this pretense.

4. The Countess tells Isabel the truth about the relationship between Osmond and Madame Merle. She also tells Isabel who Pansy's mother is.

5. Madame Merle is a scheming manipulator who desires to control others. She sets Isabel up for an unhappy marriage with Osmond. She poses as Isabel's friend when in fact she is deceitful and dangerous. Isabel is free only when she unmasks Madame Merle.

Challenge Question:

At the beginning of the novel, Isabel is naive, but curious about the outside world. She accepts her aunt's patronage and seems to have little strength of her own. After her uncle leaves her a fortune, Isabel becomes more independent, but is still unsuspecting of the evil in others. When Ralph tries to warn her about Osmond's real nature, Isabel will not listen.

After realizing that her husband is not genuine, Isabel gains strength as she is forced to fight for her individuality. She will not allow herself to be manipulated. She tries to save Pansy from the same manipulation, but fails.

Isabel rejects Goodwood's offer of an easy escape from an intolerable marriage. She shows at the end of the novel the strength that she has gained when she returns to her husband and her responsibilities.

The Thornbirds by Colleen McCullough

Matching:

1. G	4. M	7. P	10. B	13. E	16. C	19. S
2. J	5. H	8. T	11. N	14. L	17. I	20. O
3. A	6. D	9. K	12. Q	15. R	18. F	

Short Answers:

1. In New Zealand, the Clearys were poor. Coming to Drogheda gave them financial security. The sons in the family liked working on the land and easily found a place. Fee and Meggie had the hardest time coping with the isolation and the hard work. Australia also gave Meggie Father Ralph. Meeting him when she was a child changed her life forever.

2. Ralph could not destroy Mary's will and turn down the opportunity for advancement her money offered. Taking this wealth meant leaving Meggie and Drogheda. The wealth also made it more difficult for Ralph to find God, to be the priest he should be.

3. Luke was completely selfish. He had no consideration for Meggie's feelings or her physical comfort. He left her alone when Justine was born because he preferred to be with his male friends. Luke used Meggie because he needed her money to further his own desires. He had no regard for her as a person.

4. Meggie tells Ralph that Dane is his son. Finally all pretense between them is dropped, and Ralph finds in her arms relief for the grief and pain he has carried for so long.

5. Drogheda is the background for all the action. The passions of the characters are symbolized by the fires; the droughts are the loneliness and separation. Australia is the source of energy for all the Clearys. Even those who, like Justine, find their destiny elsewhere draw strength from the land.

Challenge Question:

Like the thornbird, whose song comes from its pain, each of the women's greatest love relationships are bought with pain. Feona, Meggie, and Justine all find grief in the process of loving. Feona first loved Frank's father. She finds out too late that she loved Paddy. Meggie's love for Ralph is mingled with the painful knowledge that she must always give him up to the Church.

After Meggie's love is transferred to Dane, she loses him also, first to the Church and then to death. Justine must experience great pain in the loss of her brother before she can accept Rain's love.

Giants in the Earth by O. E. Rolvaag

Multiple Choice:

1. C	4. B	7. B	10. A	13. B	16. D	19. D
2. A	5. C	8. C	11. D	14. C	17. A	20. C
3. A	6. D	9. A	12. A	15. B	18. A	

Short Answers:

1. At first the settlers live in their wagons. Then they build sod houses thatched with branches. The land must be dragged and the grass rooted out so that crops can be planted. While doing this dragging, Per Hansa removes the markers that the Irish have placed as claim to his land. Then the actual crops can be planted. Their first harvest does not come until a year and a half after their arrival.

2. The other women live with the same difficulties, but they are emotionally able to cope. Beret is obsessed with fear and darkness. She constantly urges her husband to leave the land, which she fears is turning men into monsters. A psychic of sorts, Beret constantly sees visions of death. Her seeming "normality" after the minister comes is fear changed to religious fanaticism. Her behavior with Hans Olsa shows that Beret is still obsessed with death.

3. The wheat he plants too early still grows; thus, Per Hansa has the earliest crop. He happens to be left behind when the Indians arrive. After treating the sick brave, he receives a pony. While the neighbors' crops are attacked by the locusts, Per Hansa's are spared. Ironically, he is destroyed, not by the rigors of the land, but by his wife's obsessions.

4. The minister's preaching provides a needed outlet for the entire community. His Norwegian minister's garb is a link with the traditions of their homeland. Baptizing their children and solemnizing marriages gives the people a right feeling about their new community.

5. Religion is positive for most of the people as it puts familiar beliefs back in the center of their daily lives. Talking with the minister and receiving communion relieves guilt feelings for many. For Beret, however, religion becomes an obsession with sin and guilt. That obsession forces Per Hansa into the snowstorm and ultimately to his death.

Challenge Question:

In romantic versions of pioneer life, the hard-working farmer wins. *Giants in the Earth* shows people who work hard against the elements, but lose through forces beyond their control. The "giants" are finally the elements, which destroy those who fight them. Per Hansa, who has succeeded in every other attempt and is a prosperous farmer, dies in the snow. Hans Olsa, the community leader, dies as a result of trying to save his cattle.

Rolvaag is a naturalist, a philosopher who sees humanity as the victim of an indifferent nature. His God seems perfectly indifferent to human suffering. People may strive and find nobility in that striving, but puny human effort will be defeated in the end.

A Reckoning by May Sarton

Multiple Choice:

1. B	4. C	7. B	10. A	13. B	16. A	19. A
2. D	5. B	8. C	11. C	14. C	17. A	20. C
3. A	6. D	9. B	12. D	15. B	18. C	

Short Answers:

1. A "reckoning" means an understanding of the significant events and people in her past. The "real connections" are putting into proper perspective those things which are most significant. Before her life ends, Laura feels that she must reach the core of its meaning.

2. Daisy was always a rebel, never doing what was asked or expected. Daisy felt that her mother was constantly criticizing her. Laura had felt the same criticism from Sybille. Daisy and Laura only come to understand each other as Laura becomes more ill. Finally, Laura must lean on Daisy as the mother becomes the child.

3. Ella came to visit Laura and kept her alive emotionally and mentally in spite of Sybille's attempts to stifle Laura. Her marriage to Charles provided an escape for Laura from Sybille's control.

4. Sybille had given Laura the necklace when Laura turned twenty-one. Laura gave her grandchild the necklace as a symbol of the continuity of generations.

5. Mary kept Laura's family at a distance and protected Laura in her illness from too much of her children's and sisters' love. She also took care of Laura gently and tactfully. Mary recognized both Laura's physical and emotional needs and helped Laura prepare to die.

Challenge Question:

Going toward death for Laura is a "meaningful journey." As she comes to terms with her past, she is able to face the unknown future. The trip to Maine with Daphne places her childhood in proper perspective. Through Harriet Moors's experience, Laura finds new depth in her relationship with Ella. Laura experiences close bonding with her son Ben and becomes closer to her daughter Daisy. As she resolves one by one these complex relationships, especially her feelings for her dominating mother, Laura Spelman is finally ready to let go of life.

East of Eden by John Steinbeck

Multiple Choice:

1. C	5. D	9. C	13. B	17. D
2. A	6. D	10. C	14. C	18. C
3. D	7. B	11. B	15. C	19. B
4. A	8. D	12. B	16. C	20. C

Short Answers:

1. Both boys try to gain their fathers' affection and fail. Both give gifts which are rejected. Each boy takes his revenge by hurting the brother whom the father loves.

2. People expect the Chinese to speak broken English. Lee later reveals his philosophical nature to people whom he trusts—first to Samuel, then to Adam and his sons.

3. Samuel is the life-giving figure. He assists at birth. Even though his land will not produce, Samuel helps to make others rich. His goodness may be attacked by evil, but not destroyed by it. Samuel gives this rich heritage to his sons and daughters.

4. Cathy kills her parents. She attacks Mr. Edwards. She tries to destroy Adam. She kills Faye slowly. She drives Aron into battle, where he is killed.

5. Steinbeck begins each section of his novel with a description. The characters are joined to the landscapes in which they live. Ironically, Adam fails even though his land is rich; Samuel succeeds even though his is poor.

Challenge Question:

The Hamiltons were an open family. The relationship between husband and wife was close. Liza, the mother, was a strong force in shaping her family. Samuel was close to his children. The Hamilton children became individuals because their father and mother gave them strength. The Trask boys were weakened by their parents' failures.

Adam Trask was distant to his sons. Cathy, the mother, was an evil influence. Knowing her identity almost destroyed both boys. Lies resulted in destruction, especially of Aron, the idealist.

Mrs. Miniver by Jan Struther

True or False:

1. F	4. T	7. F	10. F	13. T	16. T	19. F
2. T	5. F	8. T	11. T	14. F	17. F	20. T
3. F	6. T	9. F	12. T	15. F	18. T	

Short Answers:

1. Her love of nature is shown in her appreciation of the sights and sounds of spring, enjoyment of picnics, love of gardening and outdoor life at Starlings, and in activities such as tree trimming and hop picking.

2. Starlings gets them out of London. They spend holidays and vacations there away from the crowds. The Minivers remodeled much of the house themselves. The place reflects the closeness of their family.

3. The gas masks make the ugliness of the war something that comes close. War is no longer a faraway reality. The deaths of Mrs. Miniver's children now become a real possibility.

4. She returns to the home where she had lived as a child and looks to find a coin she had hidden. She only finds the memory.

5. She realizes that people of all nations have the same needs. War becomes something invented by the politicians. Differences in languages make barriers between people. Mrs. Miniver feels that differences could be solved if people, especially children, learned to communicate on a basic level.

Challenge Question:

Caroline Miniver stands for basic family values. She loves and protects her own family. She is not blind to the suffering of others. The fate of Germany's Jews concerns her. She has compassion for a child who is almost injured. She has a sense of humor. She can laugh at her own minor crises, such as the difficulties of choosing an engagement book. She learns to cope when her husband is away. She is a preserver of the past. Her Christmas lists are a wonderful symbol of the values that matter.

Anna Karenina by Leo Tolstoy

Multiple Choice:

1. C	6. B	11. C	16. B
2. A	7. C	12. D	17. C
3. C	8. A	13. D	18. D
4. B	9. B	14. A	19. A
5. A	10. C	15. C	20. B

Short Answers:

1. Anna finds the younger, more virile Vronsky attractive as she contrasts him with her older husband. The passion that is missing in Anna's relationship with Karenin is the main ingredient in her relationship with Vronsky. He loves Anna because her beauty fulfills his fantasy of the ideal woman. First at the ball and later in St. Petersburg, the two allow their feelings free rein. Each time one of them considers breaking the relationship, passion again dominates over common sense.

2. Stepan is a weak man who cannot manage his own marriage. He is also not strong enough to help his sister's. Prince Stepan seems to move through the world in a lighthearted manner. Neither his own difficulties nor Anna's tragic death seems to affect him very much. Stepan is a shallow playboy, both at the beginning and at the end of the novel.

3. Levin had seen Kitty as a fragile woman who needed protection from all unpleasantness. He is amazed when Kitty is able to nurse Nicholai and to cope with death in a way that Levin himself cannot. During their courtship, Levin saw Kitty as a kind of china doll. As his wife nurses the dying man, Levin learns how strong Kitty is. This scene also provides an important link in the story. As Nicholai dies, Kitty learns that she is expecting Levin's child.

4. Anna loves her son Seryozha, even though she feels little for the boy's father. Her secret visit to Seryozha on his birthday tears her apart inside. However, Anna's love for Vronsky is too strong for her to end the affair, even for the sake of her child. In the end, Anna's choice costs her both her son and Vronsky. The ultimate realization of this wrong choice drives Anna to suicide.

5. Tolstoy, through the character of Levin, criticizes a farming system in which those who do the work reap none of the benefits. The Russian aristocracy in the novel is pictured, for the most part, as a group of weaklings. The political comedy of the elections which Levin attends shows what fools the nobles are. Even Levin is at first drawn into this. Attempts at social reforms, such as Vronsky's hospital and Levin's profit-sharing plan, are too minor to have any real impact. Tolstoy, writing fifty years before the Russian revolution, explains clearly the social problems which eventually led to the communist revolution.

Challenge Question:

Levin's marriage to Kitty is within the framework of society and follows the moral law. The young couple mature as individuals and grow to love each other through shared difficulties. From love such as theirs, the family structure will gain strength. Levin's jealousy and his momentary infatuation with Anna are almost comic when compared to the pain he experiences while Kitty suffers in childbirth. In the storm scene in the last section of the novel, Levin and Kitty reaffirm their love. These two will be the survivors.

Anna and Vronsky love outside the law. In giving vent to their passion, these two think only of themselves. Levin and Kitty, in contrast, are always linked with others. Passionate love is like a destructive forest fire. Anna and Vronsky lose everything that gives their lives meaning. Vronsky is forced to resign from his regiment. Anna is separated from her son. Identity is gone. The child of this union has no name.

Anna and Vronsky are finally destroyed because passionate love alone is not enough to make a life. Tolstoy sees his characters as moral, social beings. Without that social and moral structure, Anna and Vronsky are so lost that suicide is the only escape. Anna is the character who bears the greatest moral burden and is forever outcast. After her death, Vronsky can again be acceptable to polite society.

The Color Purple by Alice Walker

Multiple Choice:

1. B	6. A	11. B	16. B
2. B	7. C	12. C	17. C
3. A	8. C	13. D	18. C
4. C	9. B	14. C	19. B
5. D	10. A	15. C	20. C

Short Answers:

1. She had to cope with his physical brutality and refusal to work, the difficulty in taking care of his children, poverty and hardship, her separation from Nettie.

2. The letters offer honest descriptions of life as the two women see it. They use the language of ordinary black speech. Nettie's vivid first-hand descriptions of her African experience are particularly gripping.

3. Shug gives Celie love. She teaches Celie to find pleasure in her own body and in the world around her. Shug believes that each person is good because each one carries God within. Shug also gets Nettie's letter so that Celie can know that her sister is alive.

4. Sofia is strong. She will not let Harpo abuse her. She can fight for herself and stand up to anyone in the world. Sofia, who survives even prison, becomes Celie's model for the person who can make it through anything.

5. Nettie has a deep faith in God. She loves Adam and Olivia and they love her. She also has a deep respect for the African people and a belief in their ways of life. Nettie also gains strength in her love for Samuel after Corinne's death.

Challenge Question:

Both women are survivors who overcome the brutality of their early lives. Celie finds meaning as a person in her relationship with Shug. Nettie's reality is in caring for Olivia and Adam and later in her love for Samuel. Both are deeply bonded to the people they care for. Nettie can strike out on her own in a way that Celie cannot. The author shows that the two women face the same problems, but in different worlds.

Index of Titles

The letter designation beside each title indicates the type of literature.

F—Fiction   NF—Nonfiction   B—Biography